# ESSENTIALS for design

## ADOBE® INDESIGN® CS

level two

### Robin B. McAllister

**Prentice Hall**
Upper Saddle River, New Jersey 07458

**Publisher and Vice President:** Natalie E. Anderson
**Executive Editor:** Jodi McPherson
**Acquisitions Editor:** Melissa Sabella
**Editorial Assistant:** Alana Meyers
**Senior Media Project Manager:** Cathleen Profitko
**Senior Marketing Manager:** Emily Knight
**Marketing Assistant:** Nicole Beaudry
**Senior Managing Editor:** Gail Steier de Acevedo
**Project Manager, Production:** Vanessa Nuttry
**Manufacturing Buyer:** Vanessa Nuttry
**Interior Design:** Thistle Hill Publishing Services, LLC
**Cover Design:** Blair Brown
**Cover Printer:** Coral Graphics
**Printer/Binder:** Von Hoffman Press

Credits and acknowledgments borrowed from other sources and reproduced, with permission, in this textbook appear on the appropriate page within the text.

The fonts utilized in these training materials are the property of Against The Clock, Inc., and are supplied to the legitimate buyers of the Against The Clock training materials solely for use with the exercises and projects provided in the body of the materials. They may not be used for any other purpose, and under no circumstances may they be transferred to another individual, nor copied or distributed by any means whatsoever.

A portion of the images supplied in this book are copyright © PhotoDisc, Inc., 201 Fourth Ave., Seattle, WA 98121, or copyright ©PhotoSpin, 4030 Palos Verdes Dr. N., Suite 200, Rollings Hills Estates, CA. These images are the sole property of PhotoDisc or PhotoSpin and are used by Against The Clock with the permission of the owners. They may not be distributed, copied, transferred, or reproduced by any means whatsoever, other than for the completion of the exercises and projects contained in this book.

Against The Clock and the Against The Clock logo are trademarks of Against The Clock, Inc., registered in the United States and elsewhere. References to and instructional materials provided for any particular application program, operating system, hardware platform, or other commercially available product or products do not represent an endorsement of such product or products by Against The Clock, Inc.

Photoshop, PageMaker, Acrobat, Adobe Type Manager, GoLive, Illustrator, InDesign, Premiere, and PostScript are trademarks of Adobe Systems Incorporated. Macromedia Flash, Generator, FreeHand, Dreamweaver, Fireworks, and Director are registered trademarks of Macromedia, Inc. QuarkXPress is a registered trademark of Quark, Inc. Macintosh is a trademark of Apple Computer, Inc. CorelDRAW!, procreate Painter, and WordPerfect are trademarks of Corel Corporation. Access, FrontPage, Publisher, PowerPoint, Word, Excel, Office, Microsoft, MS-DOS, and Windows are either registered trademarks or trademarks of Microsoft Corporation.

Other product and company names mentioned herein may be the trademarks of their respective owners.

Copyright © 2005 by Prentice Hall, Inc., Upper Saddle River, New Jersey, 07458. All rights reserved. Printed in the United States of America. This publication is protected by copyright and permission should be obtained from the publisher prior to any prohibited reproduction, storage in a retrieval system, or transmission in any form or by any means, electronic, mechanical, photocopying, recording, or likewise. For information regarding permission(s), write to: Rights and Permissions Department.

10 9 8 7 6 5 4 3 2 1

ISBN 0-13-146649-6

## ABOUT THE SERIES EDITOR

**Ellenn Behoriam** is president and founder of Against The Clock, Inc. (ATC), one of the nation's leading content providers. Ellenn and her staff have successfully produced many of the graphic arts industry's most popular and well-received books and related series. These works include the *Electronic Cookbook*, *Workflow Reengineering*, *Teams and the Graphic Arts*, *Adobe Photoshop Creative Techniques*, *Adobe Illustrator Creative Techniques*, and *QuarkXPress 6: Creating Digital Documents*, the foundation for the QuarkXPress Trainer certification programs. The Against The Clock series, published in concert with Prentice Hall/Pearson Education, includes more than 26 titles that focus on applications for the graphic and computer arts industries.

Against The Clock also worked with Pearson to develop the *Companion for the Digital Artist* series. These titles focus on specific and fundamental creative concepts, including design, Web site development, photography, typography, color theory, and copywriting. The concise and compact works provide core concepts and skills that supplement any application-specific education, regardless of which textbooks are being used to teach program skills.

Under Ellenn's leadership and direction, ATC is currently developing more than 20 titles for the new *Essentials for Design* series. Her staff and long-established network of professional educators, printers, prepress experts, workflow engineers, and business leaders add significantly to ATC's ability to provide current, meaningful, and effective books, online tutorials, and business-to-business performance and workflow-enhancement programs.

## ABOUT THE AUTHOR

**Robin McAllister** has been speaking and writing about creating effective pages since before desktop publishing was invented, and has been involved in the printing and publishing industry since the late 1960s. In the process of teaching others, he has written various "how to" guides and training manuals for general distribution and to solve company-specific issues. Rob is the author of a series of eight books for Delmar Publishers on a variety of desktop-publishing topics.

Rob is a team leader within America Online's Computing Community. He is also a technical editor for *Electronic Publishing* and has been writing and editing for Against The Clock for over five years.

## ACKNOWLEDGMENTS

We would like to thank the professional writers, artists, editors, and educators who have worked long and hard on the *Essentials for Design* series.

And thanks to the dedicated teaching professionals: Dan Workman of Akron University and Cuyahoga Community College; Janet C. Frick of Training Resources LLC; Jill Mudge of Souhegan High School; and Sherri Brown of Trident Technical College. Your insightful comments and expertise have certainly contributed to the success of the *Essentials for Design* series.

Thanks to Debbie Davidson for her help in managing the workflow, and to Dean Bagley for his work on the illustrations.

Thank you to Angelina Kendra, copy editor and final link in the chain of production, for her help in making sure that we all said what we meant to say.

And a very special thank you to Erika Kendra, production designer, technical consultant, partner in crime, and friend.

And to Melissa Sabella, Anne Garcia, Jodi McPherson, and Vanessa Nuttry.

# CONTENTS AT A GLANCE

| | | |
|---|---|---|
| | Introduction | xviii |
| PROJECT 1 | Expanding Document Layout Skills | 1 |
| PROJECT 2 | Building and Managing Long Documents | 53 |
| PROJECT 3 | Applying Advanced Typesetting Functions | 103 |
| PROJECT 4 | Working with Tables | 139 |
| PROJECT 5 | Working with Color | 175 |
| PROJECT 6 | Controlling and Editing Documents | 209 |
| PROJECT 7 | Managing Output | 245 |
| PROJECT 8 | Creating HTML and XML Documents | 291 |
| | Integrating Project | 323 |
| | Task Guide | 341 |
| | Glossary | 353 |
| | Index | 363 |

# TABLE OF CONTENTS

| | | |
|---|---|---|
| **INTRODUCTION** | | XVIII |
| **PROJECT 1** | **EXPANDING DOCUMENT LAYOUT SKILLS** | **1** |
| Lesson 1 | Controlling Pages | 6 |
| Lesson 2 | Controlling Text Flow | 15 |
| Lesson 3 | Using Templates to Manage Documents | 17 |
| Lesson 4 | Using Grids to Facilitate Production | 23 |
| Lesson 5 | Using Guides for Effective Layout | 27 |
| Lesson 6 | Using Layers for Diversity | 29 |
| Lesson 7 | Automating Layout Adjustment | 32 |
| Lesson 8 | Creating Documents That Fold | 35 |
| Lesson 9 | Automating Production with Presets | 39 |
| | *Checking Concepts and Terms* | 42 |
| | *Skill Drill* | 43 |
| | *Challenge* | 47 |
| | *Portfolio Builder* | 52 |
| **PROJECT 2** | **BUILDING AND MANAGING LONG DOCUMENTS** | **53** |
| Lesson 1 | Creating Document Sections and Custom Numbering | 59 |
| Lesson 2 | Extracting and Placing Notes | 61 |
| Lesson 3 | Creating Jumps | 62 |
| Lesson 4 | Building Libraries | 64 |
| Lesson 5 | Building Lists | 69 |
| Lesson 6 | Building Indexes | 73 |
| Lesson 7 | Creating a Master Book Document | 79 |
| Lesson 8 | Merging Multiple Files into a Book | 83 |
| Lesson 9 | Printing and Exporting Books | 89 |
| | *Careers in Design* | 91 |
| | *Checking Concepts and Terms* | 92 |
| | *Skill Drill* | 93 |
| | *Challenge* | 96 |
| | *Portfolio Builder* | 101 |
| **PROJECT 3** | **APPLYING ADVANCED TYPESETTING FUNCTIONS** | **103** |
| Lesson 1 | Mastering Text Frame Options | 109 |
| Lesson 2 | Applying Hyphenation Parameters | 112 |
| Lesson 3 | Justifying Text | 114 |
| Lesson 4 | Aligning Margins Optically | 115 |
| Lesson 5 | Copying Text Attributes | 117 |
| Lesson 6 | Creating Custom Glyph Sets | 119 |
| Lesson 7 | Nesting Styles for Productivity | 121 |
| Lesson 8 | Setting Type on a Path | 122 |
| | *Checking Concepts and Terms* | 128 |
| | *Skill Drill* | 130 |
| | *Challenge* | 134 |
| | *Portfolio Builder* | 138 |

### PROJECT 4 — WORKING WITH TABLES .......................139

| | | |
|---|---|---|
| **Lesson 1** | Creating Tables | 143 |
| **Lesson 2** | Importing Tables from Other Programs | 145 |
| **Lesson 3** | Modifying Tables and Text | 148 |
| **Lesson 4** | Formatting Tables and Cells | 149 |
| **Lesson 5** | Working with Rows and Columns | 152 |
| **Lesson 6** | Merging and Splitting Cells | 154 |
| **Lesson 7** | Working with Strokes and Fills | 156 |
| **Lesson 8** | Managing Cell Contents | 157 |
| **Lesson 9** | Inserting Graphics and Nested Tables | 159 |
| | *Careers in Design* | 162 |
| | *Checking Concepts and Terms* | 163 |
| | *Skill Drill* | 165 |
| | *Challenge* | 169 |
| | *Portfolio Builder* | 173 |

### PROJECT 5 — WORKING WITH COLOR .......................175

| | | |
|---|---|---|
| **Lesson 1** | Building RGB Colors | 180 |
| **Lesson 2** | Building CMYK Colors | 182 |
| **Lesson 3** | Building Tints from Spot Colors | 184 |
| **Lesson 4** | Creating Mixed Inks | 186 |
| **Lesson 5** | Creating Transparency | 188 |
| **Lesson 6** | Creating Realistic Drop Shadows | 190 |
| **Lesson 7** | Feathering Objects | 191 |
| **Lesson 8** | Flattening Transparent Objects for Printing | 193 |
| **Lesson 9** | Managing Color | 195 |
| | *Checking Concepts and Terms* | 201 |
| | *Skill Drill* | 203 |
| | *Challenge* | 205 |
| | *Portfolio Builder* | 208 |

### PROJECT 6 — CONTROLLING AND EDITING DOCUMENTS ..........209

| | | |
|---|---|---|
| **Lesson 1** | Converting Text to Outlines | 213 |
| **Lesson 2** | Making and Releasing Compound Paths | 215 |
| **Lesson 3** | Using the Pathfinder | 216 |
| **Lesson 4** | Grouping and Ungrouping Objects | 217 |
| **Lesson 5** | Aligning and Distributing Objects | 219 |
| **Lesson 6** | Creating Nested and Inline Elements | 220 |
| **Lesson 7** | Importing and Creating Clipping Paths | 223 |
| **Lesson 8** | Creating Text Wraps | 227 |
| | *Careers in Design* | 233 |
| | *Checking Concepts and Terms* | 234 |
| | *Skill Drill* | 235 |
| | *Challenge* | 239 |
| | *Portfolio Builder* | 243 |

## PROJECT 7 — MANAGING OUTPUT ...245

- Lesson 1  Trapping Images ...251
- Lesson 2  Setting Up Bleeds and Slugs ...253
- Lesson 3  Printing Your Document ...256
- Lesson 4  Exporting EPS Files ...261
- Lesson 5  Using the Separations Preview Palette ...264
- Lesson 6  Preflighting Documents ...267
- Lesson 7  Exporting Files to a GASP ...270
- Lesson 8  Using Advanced PDF Features ...272
  - *Checking Concepts and Terms* ...280
  - *Skill Drill* ...282
  - *Challenge* ...287
  - *Portfolio Builder* ...290

## PROJECT 8 — CREATING HTML AND XML DOCUMENTS ...291

- Lesson 1  Creating Hyperlinks ...295
- Lesson 2  Packaging for GoLive ...297
- Lesson 3  Exporting to SVG ...299
- Lesson 4  Exporting JPEG ...301
- Lesson 5  Tagging XML Document Content ...302
- Lesson 6  Assigning Structure in an XML Document ...305
- Lesson 7  Exporting XML ...307
- Lesson 8  Importing XML ...310
  - *Careers in Design* ...313
  - *Checking Concepts and Terms* ...314
  - *Skill Drill* ...315
  - *Challenge* ...318
  - *Portfolio Builder* ...322

**INTEGRATING PROJECT** ...323

**TASK GUIDE** ...341

**GLOSSARY** ...353

**INDEX** ...363

## HOW TO USE THIS BOOK

*Essentials* courseware from Prentice Hall is anchored in the practical and professional needs of all types of students. The *Essentials* series presents a learning-by-doing approach that encourages you to grasp application-related concepts as you expand your skills through hands-on tutorials. As such, it consists of modular lessons that are built around a series of numbered step-by-step procedures that are clear, concise, and easy to review.

*Essentials* books are divided into projects. A project covers one area (or a few closely related areas) of application functionality. Each project consists of several lessons that are related to that topic. Each lesson presents a specific task or closely related set of tasks in a manageable chunk that is easy to assimilate and retain.

Each element in the *Essentials* book is designed to maximize your learning experience. A list of the *Essentials* project elements, and a description of how each element can help you, begins on the next page. To find out more about the rationale behind each book element and how to use each to your maximum benefit, take the following walk-through.

# WALK-THROUGH

**Project Objectives.** Starting with an objective gives you short-term, attainable goals. Each project begins with a list of objectives that closely match the titles of the step-by-step tutorials. ▶

**OBJECTIVES**

*In this project, you learn how to*

- Build colors using the CMYK model
- Create tints from spot colors
- Mix spot and process inks
- Apply transparency to objects
- Create realistic drop shadows
- Feather objects
- Flatten transparent objects for printing
- Import color from other documents
- Manage color for printing

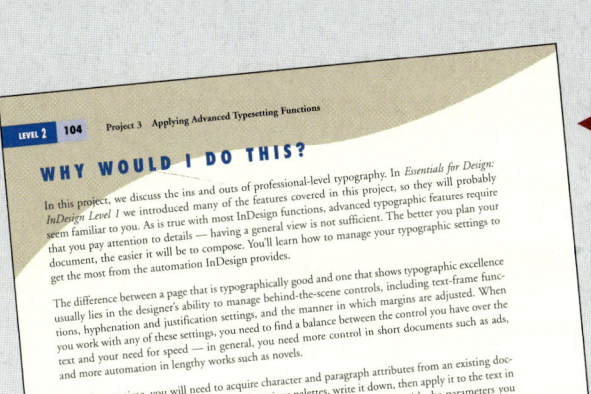

LEVEL 2 104 Project 3 Applying Advanced Typesetting Functions

WHY WOULD I DO THIS?

In this project, we discuss the ins and outs of professional-level typography. In *Essentials for Design: InDesign Level 1* we introduced many of the features covered in this project, so they will probably seem familiar to you. As is true with most InDesign functions, advanced typographic features require that you pay attention to details — having a general view is not sufficient. The better you plan your document, the easier it will be to compose. You'll learn how to manage your typographic settings to get the most from the automation InDesign provides.

The difference between a page that is typographically good and one that shows typographic excellence usually lies in the designer's ability to manage behind-the-scene controls, including text-frame functions, hyphenation and justification settings, and the manner in which margins are adjusted. When you work with any of these settings, you need to find a balance between the control you have over the text and your need for speed — in general, you need more control in short documents such as ads, and more automation in lengthy works such as novels.

From time to time, you will need to acquire character and paragraph attributes from an existing document. You could check the information in various palettes, write it down, then apply it to the text in your working document. With InDesign, though, you can click the type with the parameters you wish to copy, then highlight the text to which you wish to apply them. You can copy attributes within a single document, or between different ones.

Of course, the ability to copy attributes is not a substitute for good style sheet practices. You will learn in this project how to "nest" character styles within paragraph styles. This extends the value of the paragraph style, because you can define the action to affect only specific words or letters. You might, for example, want to have run-in text that would put the first four words in small caps.

LEVEL 2 148 Project 4 Working with Tables

LESSON 3 Modifying Tables and Text

InDesign allows you to either convert text to a table format or convert an existing table to text. InDesign only imports Excel files and Word tables into InDesign tables, so if you import plain, delimited text files from other sources, you need to convert that text into a table. You can use this function to convert any tabular data (not just imported data) into a table.

When converting text to a table, InDesign begins a new row when it encounters a return character, and a new column when it encounters a tab character. You must make sure text is properly formatted with tabs between fields and returns separating records (lines) before converting to a table.

Conversely, when you convert a table to text, InDesign removes the gridlines, sets tabs at each column, and ends each row with a return. You might want to convert an InDesign table to text if, for example, you need a client (or anyone who doesn't use InDesign) to edit the text. Having the versatility to work with either text or tables is very useful.

Convert Text to a Table

1 **Open the document (table_practice.indd) that you created in the previous exercise.**

The cursor should be one line below the table you imported.

2 **Place the file renwear.txt; uncheck the Show Import Options and Replace Selected Item boxes.**

The text imports as a tab-delimited document, containing more information (including the columns you didn't place previously) than that shown in Figure 4.12.

FIGURE 4.13

3 **With the cursor immediately in front of the text you just placed, press the Enter key to force the type to the next frame, then create a second page, and link the text to the second page.**

◀ **Why Would I Do This?** Introductory material at the beginning of each project provides an overview of why these tasks and procedures are important.

**Visual Summary.** A series of illustrations introduces the new tools, dialog boxes, and windows you will explore in each project. ▼

VISUAL SUMMARY

When you create tables in InDesign, you use the Table menu and the Table palette. Many of the options are similar to those in word-processing programs such as Microsoft Word. When you create a new table, you define the number of rows (horizontal) and columns (vertical). Text in the table defaults to the typeface in use when you create the text frame into which the table is placed.

FIGURE 4.1

Number of horizontal rows of cells in the body portion of the table. Header and footer rows are defined separately

Number of vertical columns of cells in the table.

Header rows and footer rows repeat if a table flows onto another frame or page.

FIGURE 4.2

In addition to typing data directly into a table, you can import tables from other programs, such as FileMaker, Microsoft Word, or Microsoft Excel. Imported tables are placed into InDesign in the same way as text and graphics are — with the File>Place command (or its shortcut, Command/Control-D). When importing files from programs such as Excel, you can specify which worksheet to place, and even the cell range.

You have several options when importing a spreadsheet. If you import an unformatted table, then InDesign's default formatting is applied to the text. If you import a formatted table, then the formatting defined in the spreadsheet program is applied; you can, however, specify a cell alignment of your choice after you import a formatted table. Importing a table as unformatted tabbed text results in

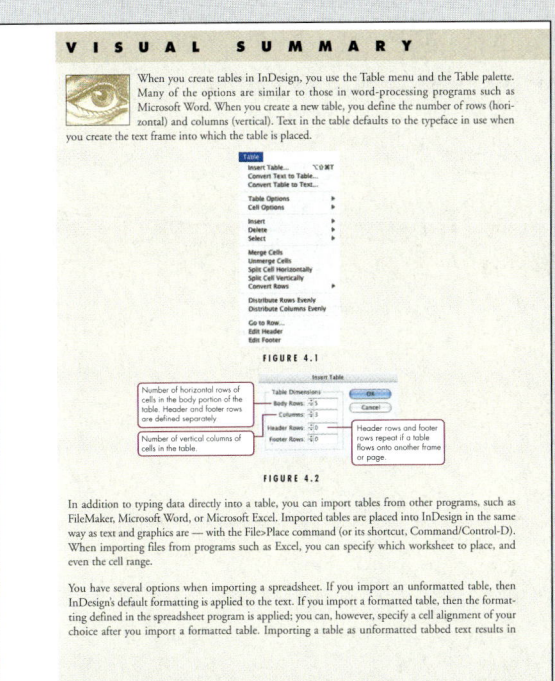

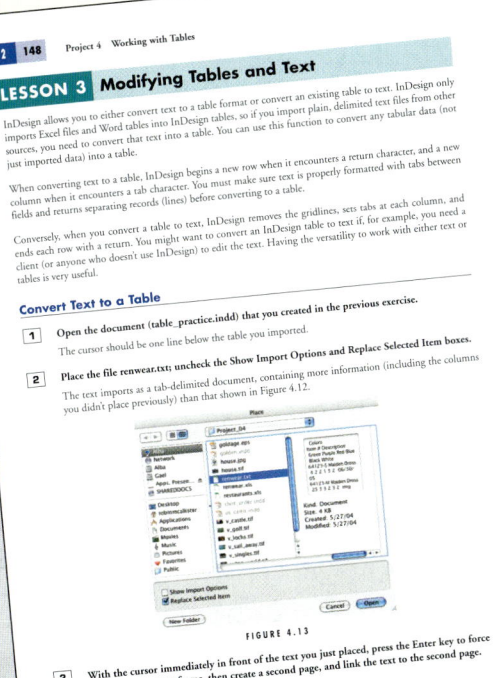

◀ **Step-by-Step Tutorials.** Hands-on tutorials let you learn by doing and include numbered, bold, step-by-step instructions.

**If You Have Problems.** These short troubleshooting notes help you anticipate or solve common problems quickly and effectively.

*To Expand Your Knowledge...*

TIPS FOR CONSTRUCTING A MASTER DOCUMENT

- The page size, margins, columns, and gutters are irrelevant unless you intend to use it as a layout template for other documents.
- You should include any proprietary fonts and colors in the master document.
- If a client prefers a particular font for the majority of jobs, you should change the Normal paragraph style to use that font.
- If the client prefers a specific style of hyphenation and justification, you should define an appropriate H&J routine in the master document.
- You should create common styles for tables of contents that can be imported into any project.
- If you import paragraph or character styles from the master document, the fonts used in those styles must be installed on your computer. If they are not, InDesign displays a missing-font warning when you try to import them.
- Once imported, master-document items become part of the document you are working with. There is no link to the master document, so imported items can be modified within the new document without affecting the master. Similarly, changes to the master document aren't automatically updated in the new document.

**To Extend Your Knowledge.** These provide extra tips, shortcuts, alternative ways to complete a process, and special hints about using the software.

**Careers in Design.** These features offer advice, tips, and resources that will help you on your path to a successful career.

CAREERS IN DESIGN

PRODUCING DOCUMENTS

Producing lengthy documents involves skills beyond those needed for what many of us think of as "standard" work. Designing and producing ads and brochures requires meticulous attention to detail — including doing the math so the folds fall in the right place — but the detail work needed for book production is of a different nature.

Book designers must know who their target audience is and take their needs into consideration when designing both the layout and the styles of the publication. This book, for example, was designed to fulfill a number of specific needs of the reader. It lies flat, so you can use it easily at a computer workstation. It provides many visual aids, because graphic artists often learn best when graphics confirm what they have done. The type is large and well-leaded, so it can be easily read while operating a computer.

As your skills evolve, you should learn to take advantage of all the tools that apply to your jobs. Style sheets, for example, are one of the most underutilized tools in every publishing program. Even for producing ads, style sheets are valuable.

When you build longer documents, you will have to decide whether to break a single document into sections or to merge several smaller documents into a single large one. The final decision often depends on the total length of the document. For instance, you could create a year-end compilation of all the magazines in a volume, which would require using the book function retroactively.

Throughout your graphics career, you will likely use some of these features more than others. Many graphic artists never use the Table of Contents feature — they don't produce long documents, or they pass off the production of front and back matter to specialists in those functions. Very few create indexes, because indexing is a specialty in itself, and appeals more to extreme "left brain" thinkers than to creative artists.

As you design and produce longer documents, you will find that planning, more than anything else, is the key to efficiency. Never skimp on the preparatory work, unless you don't mind spending considerably more time than necessary figuring things out as you go along.

**End-of-Project Exercises.** Extensive end-of-project exercises emphasize hands-on skill development. You'll find three levels of reinforcement: Skill Drill, Challenge, and Portfolio Builder.

Project 4 Working with Tables 165 LEVEL 2

SKILL DRILL

Skill Drills reinforce project skills. Each skill reinforced is the same, or nearly the same, as a skill presented in the lessons. Detailed instructions are provided in a step-by-step format. You must perform Skill Drills 1 and 2 sequentially. Drills 3 and 4 should also be completed sequentially.

**1. Create a Calendar**

You have just been assigned the job of creating a desktop calendar. In this exercise you will create the basis — the grid and the dates — for a calendar that a specialty company will sell. The calendars will be glued onto a base that will have the client's information foil stamped. There will not be much room on the calendar for clients to make notes.

1. Create a new one-column document, 5.5 in. × 3.5 in. with 0.25-in. margins. It should not have a master text page. Save it as "calendar_2006.indd".
2. Choose Adobe Caslon Pro as your typeface and create a text frame that fully fills the space within the margins.
3. Type the word "January" at the top of the page and style it Adobe Caslon Semibold, 18 pt., centered. Press the Return/Enter key.
4. Insert a table with 7 rows and 7 columns.
5. Highlight the bottom 6 rows and change their height to exactly 0.417 in.
6. Highlight the top row and assign its cells Adobe Caslon Pro Semibold, 9 pt., centered. Type the days of the week in these cells.
7. When you have typed "Saturday" press the Tab key to advance to the next line. Interestingly, 2006 begins on a Sunday. Type "1".
8. Advancing through the calendar by pressing the Tab key, type the date in each cell, accepting default size and placement.
9. Add 3 pt. below the name of the month.
10. Save the document and leave it open for the next Skill Drill.

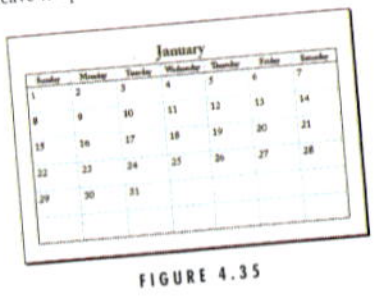

FIGURE 4.35

LEVEL 2 134 Project 3 Applying Advanced Typesetting Functions

CHALLENGE

Challenge exercises expand on, or are somewhat related to, skills presented in the lessons. Each exercise provides a brief introduction, followed by instructions presented in a numbered-step format that are not as detailed as those in the Skill Drill exercises. You should perform the first two and the last two of these exercises in the order in which they appear.

**1. Create Custom Glyphs**

You are the designer for a bookstore that is creating a series of bookmarks. They want a "touch of class" and have selected the Adobe Caslon Pro family of type. They want to use ornaments in the corners and a dingbat at the end of the verses on the bookmarks. The easiest way to accomplish this is to create a set of custom glyphs that can sit on the desktop and be applied at will.

1. Change the font to Adobe Caslon Pro Italic.
2. Open the Glyphs palette, show Ornaments, and choose New Glyph Set from the Options menu. Name the glyph set "Caslon Ornaments".
3. Click the acorn dingbat to select it and choose Add to Glyph Set>Caslon Ornaments. You may want to change the size of the display in the Glyphs palette by clicking the sizing icon in the lower right.
4. Add two sets of corner dingbats to the Caslon Ornaments palette, so your bookmarks will have some variety.
5. Add the right-pointing hand to your palette.
6. Choose Entire Font and scroll down until you see the alternate swash characters.
7. Add the "Th" ligature and all swash capital letters, since you may be using drop caps for your bookmarks.
8. Choose Options>View Glyph Set>Caslon Ornaments to view your new Glyphs palette.
9. Leave the palette open for the next Challenge.

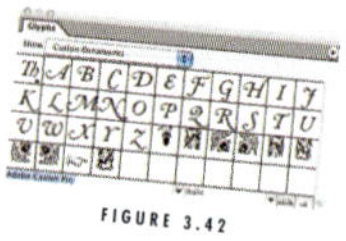

FIGURE 3.42

**Portfolio Builder.** At the end of every project, these exercises require creative solutions to problems that reinforce the topic of the project. ▶

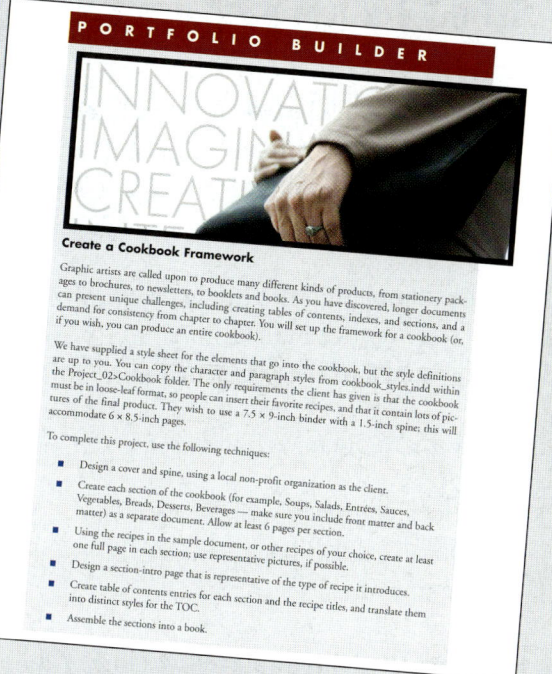

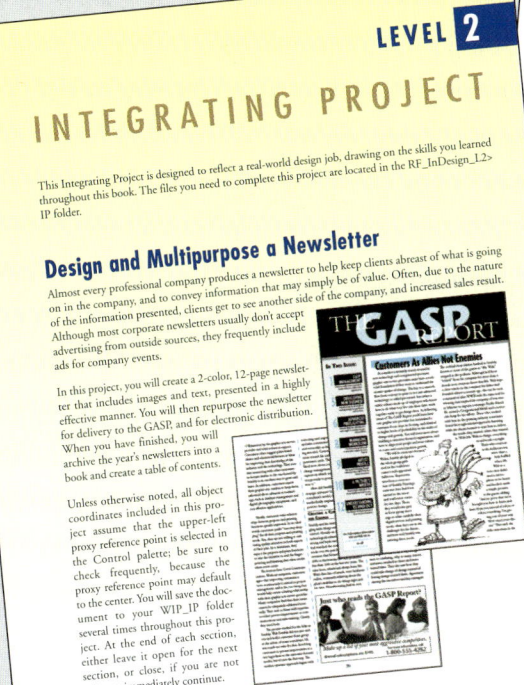

**Integrating Projects.** Integrating projects are designed to reflect real-world graphic-design jobs, drawing on the skills you have learned throughout this book. ◀

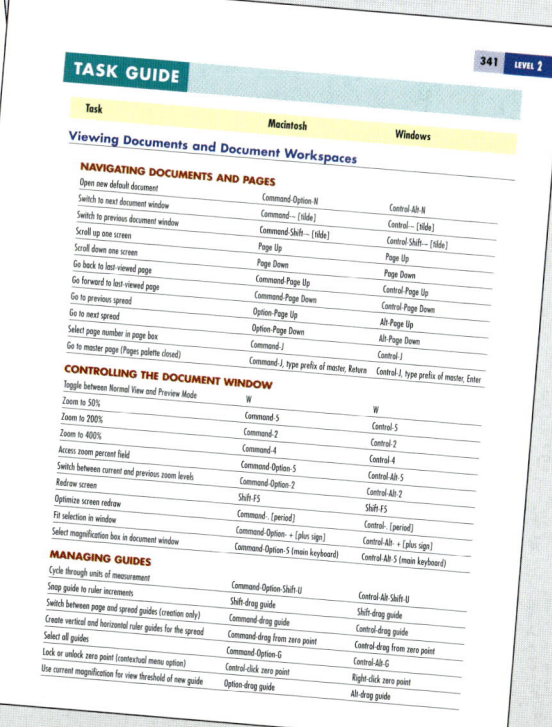

**Task Guides.** These charts, found at the end of each book, list alternative ways to complete common procedures and provide a handy reference tool. ▶

## STUDENT INFORMATION AND RESOURCES

**Companion Web Site (www.prenhall.com/essentials).** This text-specific Web site provides students with additional information and exercises to reinforce their learning. Features include: additional end-of-project reinforcement material, online Study Guide, easy access to *all* resource files, and much, much more!

Before completing the projects within this text, you need to download the Resource Files from the Prentice Hall Companion Web site. Check with your instructor for the best way to gain access to these files or simply follow these instructions:

1. From an open Web browser, go to http://www.prenhall.com/essentials.

2. Select your textbook or series to access the Companion Web site. We suggest you bookmark this page, as it has links to additional Prentice Hall resources that you may use in class.

3. Click the Student Resources link. All files in the Student Resources area are provided as .sea files for Macintosh users and .exe files for those using the Windows operating system. These files do not require any additional software to open.

4. Click the Start Here link for the platform you are using (Macintosh or Windows).

5. Once you have downloaded the proper file, double-click that file to begin the self-extraction process. You will be prompted to select a folder location specific for your book; you may extract the file to your hard drive or to a removable disk/drive.

    The Start Here file contains three folders:

    - **Fonts.**
    - **RF_InDesign_L2.** You can place this folder on your hard drive, or on a removable disk/drive.
    - **Work_In_Progress.** You can place this folder on your hard drive, or on a removable disk/drive.

6. Locate the project files you need from the list of available resources and click the active link to download. There is a separate file for each project in this book (e.g., Project_01, Project_02, etc.).

7. Once you have downloaded the proper file, double-click that file to begin the self-extraction process. You will be prompted to select a folder location specific to your book; you should extract the project-specific folders into the RF_InDesign_L2 folder that was extracted from the Start Here file.

**Resource CD.** If you are using a Resource CD, all the fonts and files you need are provided on the CD. Resource files are organized in project-specific folders (e.g., Project_01, Project_02, etc.), which are contained in the RF_InDesign_L2 folder. You can either work directly from the CD, or copy the files onto your hard drive before beginning the exercises.

Before you begin working on the projects or lessons in this book, you should copy the Work_In_Progress folder from the Resource CD onto your hard drive or a removable disk/drive.

**Fonts.** You must install the ATC fonts to ensure that your exercises and projects will work as described in the book. Specific instructions for installing fonts are provided in the documentation that came with your computer.

If you have an older version (pre-2004) of the ATC fonts installed, replace them with the fonts in this folder.

**Resource Files.** Resource files are organized in project-specific folders, and are named to facilitate cross-platform compatibility. Words are separated by an underscore, and all file names include a lowercase three-letter extension. For example, if you are directed to open the file "graphics.eps" in Project 2, the file can be found in the RF_InDesign_L2> Project_02 folder. We repeat these directions frequently in the early projects.

**The Work In Progress Folder.** This folder contains individual folders for each project in the book (e.g., WIP_01, WIP_02, etc.). When an exercise directs you to save a file, you should save it to the appropriate folder for the project in which you are working.

The exercises in this book frequently build upon work that you have already completed. At the end of each exercise, you will be directed to save your work and either close the file or continue to the next exercise. If you are directed to continue but your time is limited, you can stop at a logical point, save the file, and later return to the point at which you stopped. In this case, you will need to open the file from the appropriate WIP folder and continue working on the same file.

**Typeface Conventions.** Computer programming code appears in a monospace font that `looks like this`. In many cases, you only need to change or enter specific pieces of code; in these instances, the code you need to type or change appears in a second color and `looks like this`.

# INSTRUCTOR'S RESOURCES

**Customize Your Book (www.prenhall.com/customphit).** The Prentice Hall Information Technology Custom PHIT Program gives professors the power to control and customize their books to suit their course needs. The best part is that it is done completely online using a simple interface.

Professors choose exactly what projects they need in the *Essentials for Design* series, and in what order they appear. The program also enables professors to add their own material anywhere in the text's presentation, and the final product will arrive at each professor's bookstore as a professionally formatted text.

To learn more about this new system for creating the perfect textbook, go to www.prenhall.com/customphit, where the online walk-through demonstrates how to create a book.

**Instructor's Resource Center.** This CD-ROM includes the entire Instructor's Manual for each application in Microsoft Word format. Student data files and completed solutions files are also on this CD-ROM. The Instructor's Manual contains a reference guide of these files for the instructor's convenience. PowerPoint slides with more information about each project are also available for classroom use.

**Companion Web site (www.prenhall.com/essentials).** Instructors will find all of the resources available on the Instructor's Resource CD-ROM available for download from the Companion Web site.

**TestGen Software.** TestGen is a test generator program that lets you view and easily edit test bank questions, transfer them to tests, and print the tests in a variety of formats suitable to your teaching situation. The program also offers many options for organizing and displaying test banks and tests. A built-in random number and text generator makes it ideal for creating multiple versions of tests. Powerful search and sort functions let you easily locate questions and arrange them in the order you prefer.

QuizMaster, also included in this package, enables students to take tests created with TestGen on a local area network. The QuizMaster utility built into TestGen lets instructors view student records and print a variety of reports. Building tests is easy with TestGen, and exams can be easily uploaded into WebCT, Blackboard, and CourseCompass.

Prentice Hall has formed close alliances with each of the leading online platform providers: WebCT, Blackboard, and our own Pearson CourseCompass.

**OneKey.** OneKey lets you in to the best teaching and learning resources all in one place. OneKey for *Essentials for Design* is all your students need for out-of-class work conveniently organized by chapter to reinforce and apply what they've learned in class and from the text. OneKey is all you need to plan and administer your course. All your instructor resources are in one place to maximize your effectiveness and minimize your time and effort. OneKey for convenience, simplicity, and success.

**WebCT and Blackboard.** Each of these custom-built distance-learning courses features exercises, sample quizzes, and tests in a course management system that provides class administration tools as well as the ability to customize this material at the instructor's discretion.

**CourseCompass.** CourseCompass is a dynamic, interactive online course management tool powered by Blackboard. It lets professors create their own courses in 15 minutes or less with preloaded quality content that can include quizzes, tests, lecture materials, and interactive exercises.

**Performance-Based Training and Assessment: Train & Assess IT.** Prentice Hall offers performance-based training and assessment in one product — Train & Assess IT.

The Training component offers computer-based instruction that a student can use to preview, learn, and review graphic design application skills. Delivered via Web or CD-ROM, Train IT offers interactive multimedia, and computer-based training to augment classroom learning. Built-in prescriptive testing suggests a study path based not only on student test results but also on the specific textbook chosen for the course.

The Assessment component offers computer-based testing that shares the same user interface as Train IT and is used to evaluate a student's knowledge about specific topics in software including Photoshop, InDesign, Illustrator, Flash, and Dreamweaver. It does this in a task-oriented, performance-based environment to demonstrate students' proficiency and comprehension of the topics. More extensive than the testing in Train IT, Assess IT offers more administrative features for the instructor and additional questions for the student. Assess IT also enables professors to test students out of a course, place students in appropriate courses, and evaluate skill sets.

# INTRODUCTION

Introduced in 2000, Adobe InDesign is a powerful, design-oriented publishing tool. As its name indicates, this page-layout program focuses on giving you the tools to create powerful, effective documents. It allows you to bring together text and graphics — prepared in the program itself or imported from other sources — and to produce documents that may be printed to a local or networked printer, taken to a printer or other graphic arts service provider (GASP), published to the World Wide Web, or distributed as interactive electronic documents.

Now that you've completed our introductory book, *Essentials for Design: InDesign Level 1*, you're ready to create more complex and exciting documents. Becoming an expert is hard work, but it should also be fun and fulfilling. Although some of the more advanced topics and features require careful reading and study to master the concepts, the projects and exercises you'll produce as you progress through the book are examples of real-world creative jobs.

This book is designed to expand your knowledge of InDesign and to help you produce exciting and effective documents efficiently. You will discover that you can accomplish tasks more easily using the advanced tool sets and skill sets than you could before. You will also take your skills beyond InDesign, to interact with other programs and disciplines beyond print production.

We encourage you to look at the big picture — what you're actually creating — and make design and production decisions based on the end products, rather than establish blanket rules. The skills you learn can be applied to virtually any document, from a business card to a 208-page catalog, and can be expanded to include interactive electronic documents. As you progress, you will find that careful planning will make producing your documents easier and more enjoyable.

As you work through this course, pay attention not only to the details — the step-by-step tasks associated with lessons within the projects — but also to the principles behind them. Most lessons and Skill Drills demand absolute attention to detail, but many of the Challenges and Portfolio Builders give you opportunities to express yourself creatively. In addition, we encourage you to go beyond the projects and experiment on your own, rather than limit yourself solely to ideas presented in the book.

This course is focused on design and print production techniques, for the most part. The latter chapters expand your creative vision to include creating interactive and extensible documents. We also recognize that just because a program allows you to perform a given function, that may not be the best way to attain your goal — and we include those cautions; we point out limitations to features.

InDesign is a young and evolving, but very powerful, product with enormous potential. We believe you will enjoy working and experimenting with it as you master its features.

# PROJECT 1

## LEVEL 2

# Expanding Document Layout Skills

## OBJECTIVES

*In this project, you learn how to*

- Control documents using multiple masters
- Control documents with multiple-page spreads
- Control the flow of text
- Use templates effectively
- Control documents using grids

- Use guides for effective layout
- Set up and use layers
- Adjust layouts automatically for multi-purposing
- Create documents that fold (for several applications)
- Use presets to automate production

**Project 1  Expanding Document Layout Skills**

# WHY WOULD I DO THIS?

Throughout your career in graphic design, you will likely produce many types of documents. In addition to simple one-page documents such as flyers and posters, you may also work on small items such as business cards and postcards, brochures with straightforward or complex folding requirementss, longer publications such as books and annual reports, or documents such as directories or catalogs that have repeated elements. Although every type of project has a unique set of requirements, proper production always begins with a carefully constructed file. InDesign's advanced page-layout functions simplify the tasks associated with creating useful, professional documents.

Every year, an enormous amount of time and money is wasted due to production errors when documents created with an application such as InDesign are sent to commercial printers. In this project, you will learn how to create layouts that don't require extra manipulation.

InDesign provides a great deal of control over the final pagination of a document. You can use masters and templates to create a standard design and layout for a new document, then easily add, delete, and move pages; you can also create multi-page spreads and fold-outs. Text flow options and automatic layout adjustment give you even more control.

InDesign's ability to use layers allows you to create multiple versions of a document within the same file, using the same graphics. Similar to the stacking order of elements with which you are already familiar, layers are much more powerful tools for creating multiple versions of documents.

When the layout of a document changes — whether the document is being repurposed, or clients simply changed their minds — it is important to maintain the relative positions of all elements on the page. InDesign's Layout Adjustment feature (though imperfect) can save immeasurable time during this process. It works best with layouts that depend heavily on ruler guides, margins, and page columns, and where objects are aligned with guides.

When documents are folded, you must account for the imperfections of the mechanical folding devices, and for the thickness of the paper itself. You also need to allow space for registration and trim marks. Always work with your service provider when determining proper folding and bleed allowances. The issues presented here have little to do with design, per se. Layout and page geometry are governed by specific variables, including mechanical limitations in the production process. As a result, the topics covered in this project's lessons should be regarded as rules, not simply suggestions. It doesn't matter how good your design looks in principle if it's cut off the edge of the page.

Project 1    Expanding Document Layout Skills    3    LEVEL 2

# VISUAL SUMMARY

Whether you use one master in a document or many, the process of creating and applying them to pages is the same. Masters are simply tools that will speed your work — they automate the repetitive, mundane tasks of adding elements such as running heads and feet or graphic elements that appear on several pages.

Masters are listed in the top section of the Pages palette; you can apply them to document pages by dragging them on top of page icons, or by assigning them when the page is created. Although a pair of left and right masters is usually created, they can be mixed in a spread.

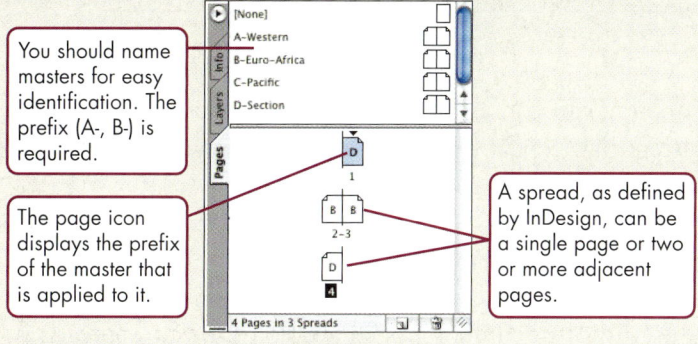

FIGURE 1.1

You can allow pages to shuffle (that is, to become either right- or left-hand pages following normal numbering sequences) or you can lock them in their relative positions. You can define pages to remain together as spreads, regardless of how many pages are inserted. This procedure is often used when building books with foldout pages.

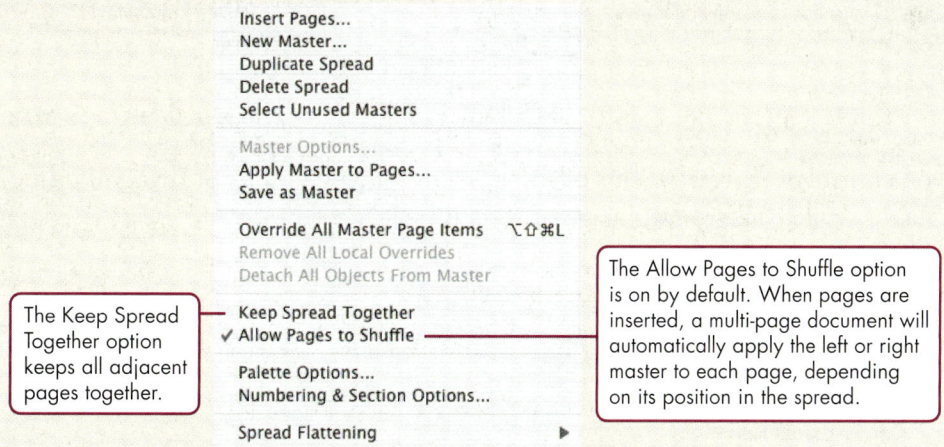

FIGURE 1.2

You can flow text into documents manually, semi-automatically, or automatically. When flowing text manually, text loaded in the cursor fills only a single frame at a time; you must click the out port of that text frame to reload the cursor to continue flowing text. Semi-autoflow also fills one frame at a time, but the cursor is automatically reloaded after each frame is filled; this process continues until all the text is flowed into frames. Autoflow, which gives you the least control over the process, adds pages and frames until all text is flowed into the document.

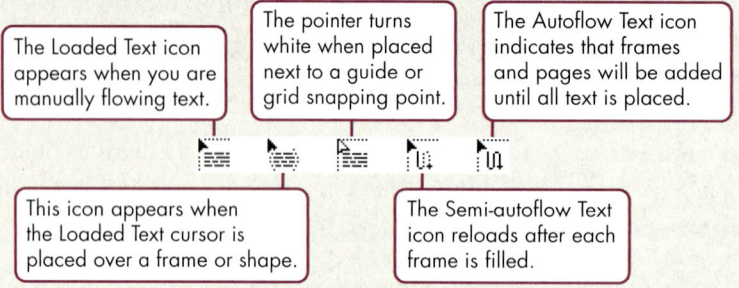

**FIGURE 1.3**

Templates are documents that can contain styles, colors, and master pages. They are useful with documents such as newsletters that repeat on a regular basis. Anything that you can save in a regular document can be included in a template.

Grids and guides make laying out a well-designed page much easier. They provide "snap to" points for objects and for text, resulting in reasonably precise positioning. The baseline crid is used for positioning type; it's especially useful for documents that have columns and spreads in which type needs to align vertically.

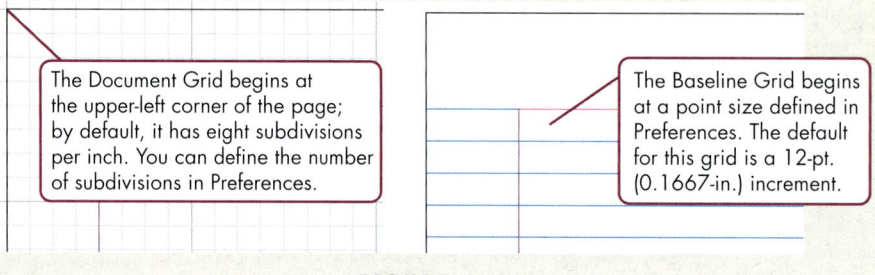

**FIGURE 1.4**

Layers give you control over the elements of a document that are visible, or that will print. You could, for example, use a single background image or several images, or you could create a separate layer for text in different languages.

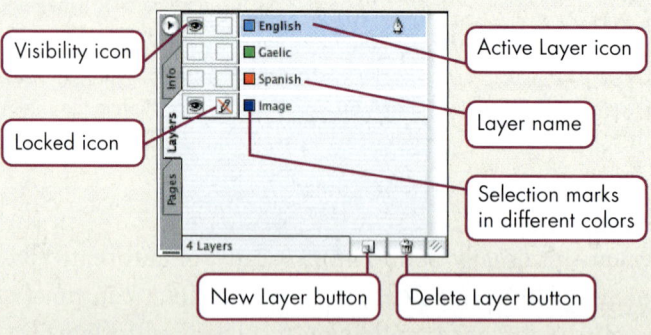

**FIGURE 1.5**

When you change a layout, regardless of whether you resize it proportionally, InDesign gives you the tools to reformat — to a reasonable degree — the necessary elements using the document's underlying structure as the basis. It is your decision how much of the job to allocate to InDesign and how much you want to exercise direct control over.

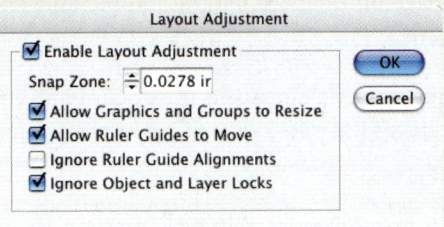

FIGURE 1.6

Folding and trimming pages to their final size is called *finishing*. If the document is a bound book, the groups of folded pages (called *signatures*) are assembled then given a final trim. It is at this point that a project lives or dies; if the document has been incorrectly constructed, words could be trimmed off, or pages could be improperly formatted.

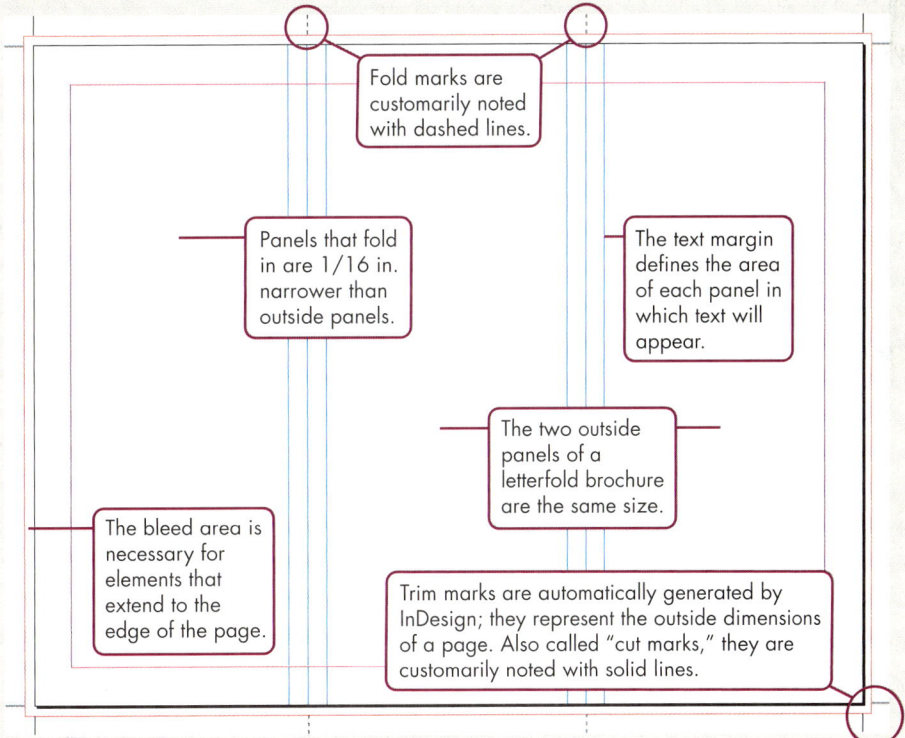

FIGURE 1.7

# LESSON 1  Controlling Pages

As you should remember from *Essentials for Design: InDesign Level 1*, a master is a non-printing document page on which you can place repeating elements. Those elements can include frames for text and graphics, running heads and feet, guides, automatic page numbers, standard graphic and text elements, and any other element that repeats throughout the document.

If you need to, you can delete or alter master elements in the document. For example, you may wish to remove a running foot if a photograph bleeds off the page, or you might want to change the color of the page number so it will show against the photo.

An InDesign document can contain many masters. Multiple masters are often used in longer documents that require several formats. You can assign different masters to different pages, or change a page's existing master.

InDesign's page-control features allow you to alter pages from standard numbering (beginning with Arabic number 1) and right/left page arrangement; you can even add additional pages to a spread. Documents created with facing pages maintain a relative right/left page arrangement by default.

## Apply the First Master

**1**  **Open the document atwt_travel.indd from the RF_InDesign_L2>Project_1 folder.**

If the warning about broken links appears, click the Fix Links Automatically button. As was the case with the first book in this series, *Essentials for Design: InDesign Level 1*, resource files are located in the appropriate Project folder within the RF_InDesign_L2 folder.

**2**  **Resize the Pages palette so you can see all the master pages. Drag the horizontal separator downward, if necessary.**

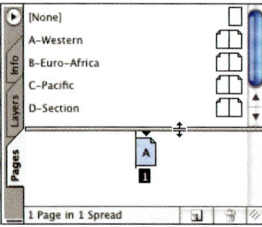

FIGURE 1.8

**3**  **From the Pages palette, drag the D-Section master onto the first (and only) document page icon.**

The outline of the document page's icon in the panel turns black as you drag the master icon over it.

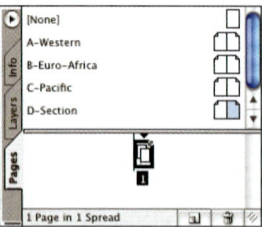

FIGURE 1.9

**4** **Command/Control-Shift-click all four frames (individually) on the document page to unlock them. Click the large background frame last.**

If you click the background frame before clicking other frames, it will be brought forward in the stacking order and you will be unable to click the frames below.

**5** **Click anywhere on the pasteboard to deselect the frames, then click the large background frame to activate it.**

**6** **Place the file Europe_section.jpg, then choose Object>Arrange>Send to Back to send the frame to the back of the stacking order.**

The image fills the frame, which moves to the back of the stacking order. You can also send an element to the back of the stacking order by pressing Command/Control-Shift-[.

**7** **Click the small square frame in the upper right. Place the file euro_Africa.eps.**

The imported image is far too large for the frame.

**8** **Choose Object>Fitting>Fit Content Proportionally.**

The image resizes and fills the frame edge to edge.

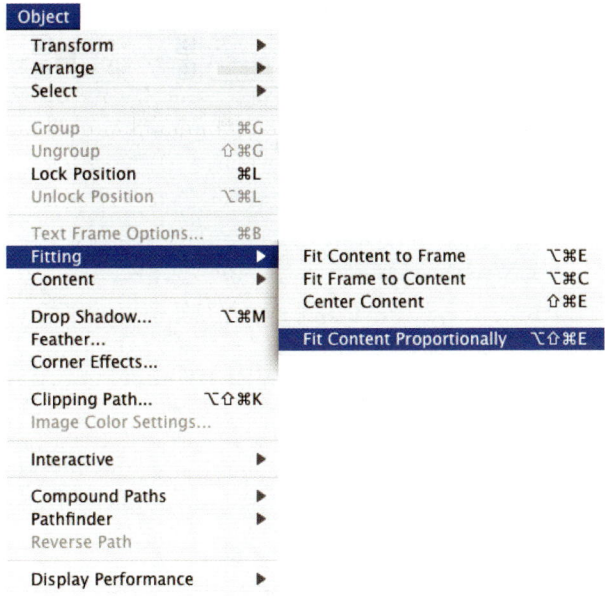

FIGURE 1.10

**9** **Select the smaller of the two remaining frames. Place the file Europe_head.eps. Click inside the frame with the Direct Selection tool, and position the headline wherever you think it looks best.**

10. **Select the remaining frame and place the file Europe_1.doc. Click in the frame with the Type tool and select all the text. From the Paragraph Styles palette, assign the VITW style.**

    The text imported as black text, which wouldn't stand out against the very dark background. The VITW style is identical to the VIT style, except that the text is white instead of black.

11. **Click the first paragraph and reassign it the VITW1 style.**

    The paragraph loses its indent, and the first letter becomes a two-line drop cap. If you wish, you may create a gold color swatch to color the drop cap. The formula for gold used in the headline is C:0, M:25, Y:100, K:0.

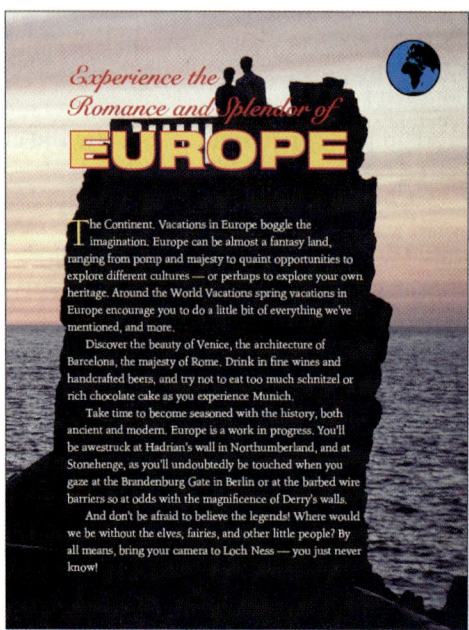

FIGURE 1.11

12. **Save the document to the Work_In_Progress>WIP_01 folder and leave it open to continue working on it.**

    As in *Essentials for Design: InDesign Level 1*, you should save your files in the appropriate WIP folder within the Work_In_Progress folder, unless instructed to do otherwise.

## Apply Additional Masters

**1** Open the Insert Pages dialog box from the Pages palette Options menu, and insert two pages after Page 1, based on the B-Euro-Africa master.

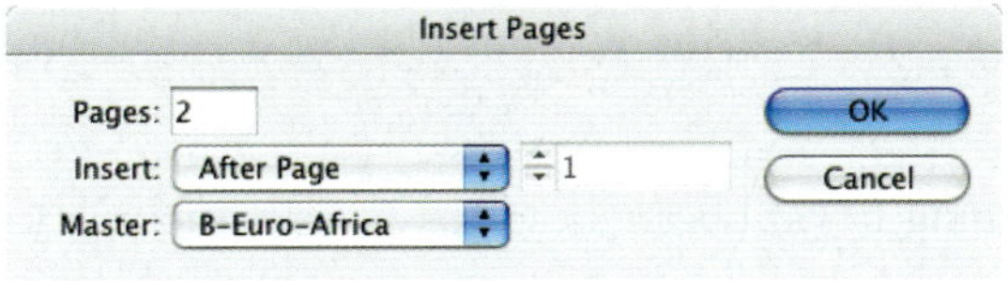

FIGURE 1.12

**2** With the Selection tool, Command/Control-Shift-click each of the pages in this spread to unlock them.

The bounding box appears for each page, and the in and out ports become visible.

**3** Click the out port on Page 2, then position the cursor over Page 3.

The cursor turns into a Thread icon.

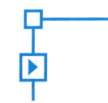

FIGURE 1.13

**4** Click to link these two pages.

The in port on the text frame on Page 3 acquires a triangle, indicating that this frame is linked to another so text can thread between them.

FIGURE 1.14

**5** Place the file europe_2.rtf into the frame on Page 2. The styles have been applied in Microsoft Word.

**6** Save your work.

**7** Insert one page after Page 3 based on the D-Section master.

**8** With the Selection tool, Command/Control-Shift-click each frame on this page to unlock them.

9. Place the following files into the frames and perform actions as indicated:

| Frame | File | Action |
| --- | --- | --- |
| Large background frame | caribbean_section.jpg | Send frame to back. |
| Small square frame at upper left | western.eps | Fit content to frame proportionally. |
| Smaller of two remaining frames | caribbean_head.eps | Position pleasingly in frame with Direct Selection tool. |
| Remaining frame | caribbean_1.rtf | Adjust inset spacing, vertical justification, and frame size to achieve a pleasing fit. |

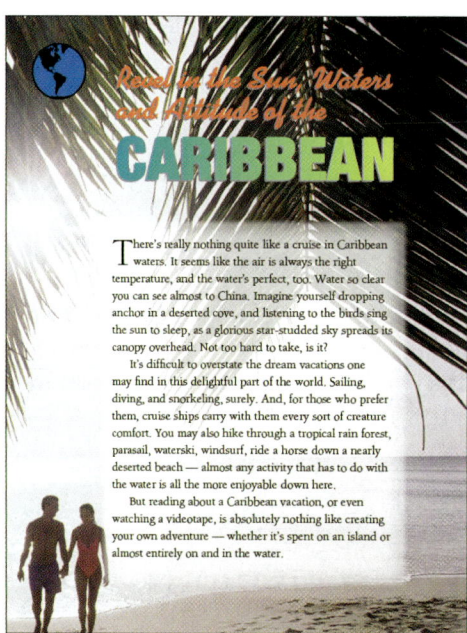

**FIGURE 1.15**

10. **Save and close the file.**

A travel brochure like this one could continue for many pages, but this exercise has adequately demonstrated the principle of using multiple masters to speed the production process.

## Create a Fold-Out

**1** Open the document page_control.indd.

**2** From the Pages palette Options menu, choose Allow Pages to Shuffle, unchecking the option.

The checkmark next to the menu option disappears, indicating that this feature has been deactivated.

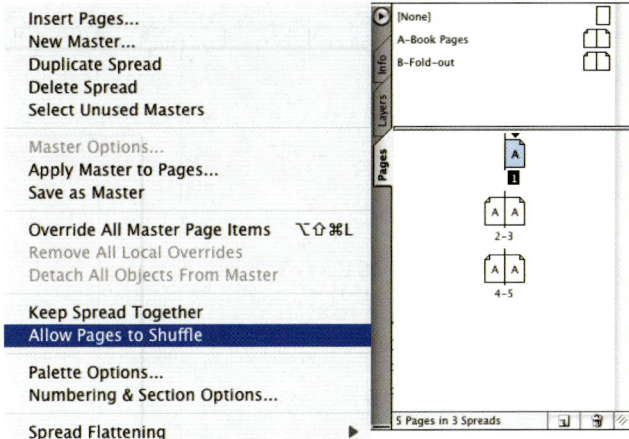

**FIGURE 1.16**

**3** Click the page numbers of Spread 4–5 and apply the B-Fold-out master to these pages by dragging the master to the spread.

Be sure to drag the master to the spread numbers, not the spread's pages. The spread's icon displays a black outline when you've moved the master over the page numbers.

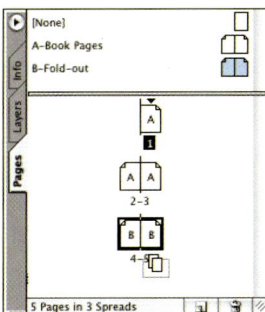

**FIGURE 1.17**

**4** Deselect the B-Fold-out master by clicking anywhere in the Master area of the Pages palette.

**5** **Drag a right page from the B-Fold-out master to the right of Page 5.**

A second page is added to the right of the spine. You can tell you're inserting a page (rather than simply applying a master to a page) because the cursor changes to a double-arrow insertion icon, and a heavy bar indicating a new page appears to the right of the spread.

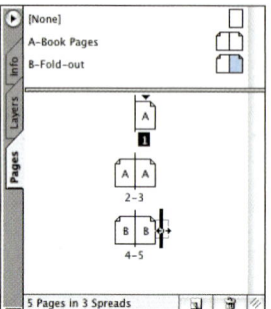

**FIGURE 1.18**

The Pages palette now looks like Figure 1.19:

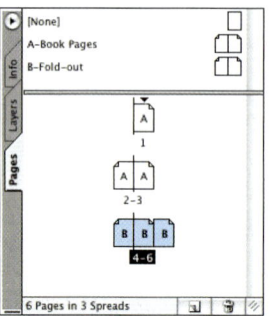

**FIGURE 1.19**

**6** **Insert another spread based on the A-Book Pages master after the three-page spread you just created.**

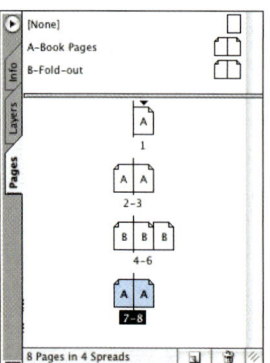

**FIGURE 1.20**

**7** Apply the B-Fold-out master to Spread 7–8, then insert another left page based on the B-Fold-out master before Page 7. Choose Keep Spread Together from the Pages palette Options menu.

This creates the back of the Spread 4–6 foldout.

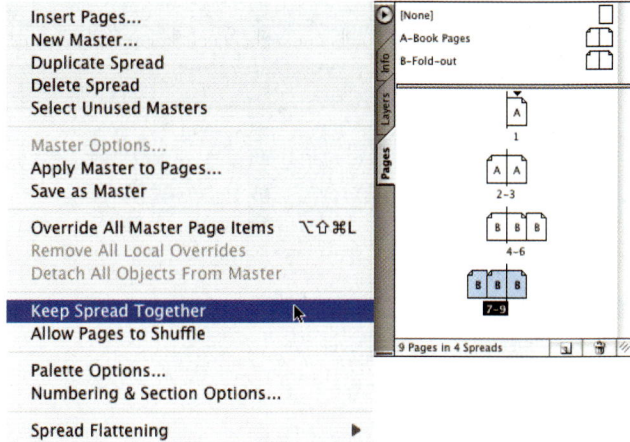

FIGURE 1.21

**8** Choose Insert Pages from the Pages palette Options menu and insert two pages based on the A-Book Pages master after Page 9.

The new pages are appended to Spread 7–9 rather than inserted as a new spread.

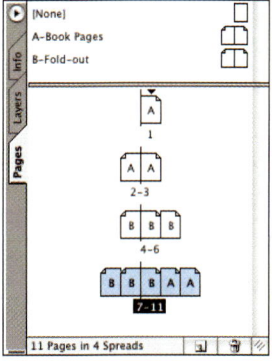

FIGURE 1.22

**9** Leave the document open for the next exercise.

## Control Page Numbering

Pages are not arbitrarily numbered. When you create a foldout, as you did in the previous exercise, the additional pages are considered as extensions of the base pages of the document. In a typical publication, right-hand (*recto*) pages are odd-numbered and left-hand (*verso*) pages are even-numbered.

**1** In the Pages palette of the open document, page_control.indd, click the first page of Spread 7–11.

**2** From the Pages palette Options menu, choose Numbering & Section Options.

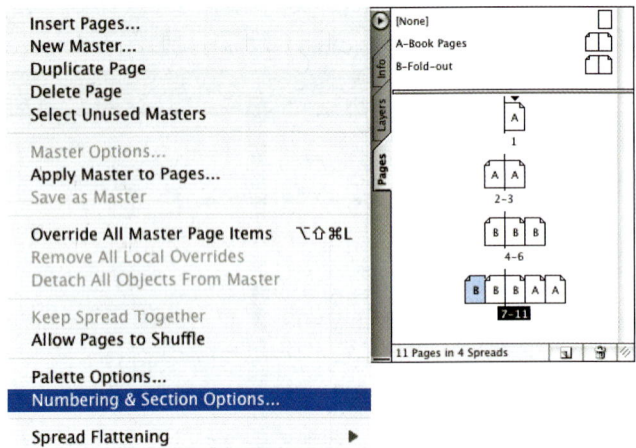

**FIGURE 1.23**

**3** Click the Start Section box if it is not already selected. Click the Start Page Numbering at button and enter "6" in the text field.

This overrides the automatic page numbering and begins numbering the spread as it should be numbered.

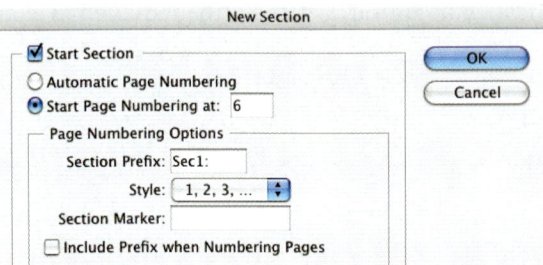

**FIGURE 1.24**

If you had another spread in the document, you would create another new section, beginning the numbering at 8.

**4** Close the file without saving.

## To Extend Your Knowledge...

### CONTROLLING PAGINATION

If your document is set up with facing pages, as the document in the previous exercise was, the Allow Pages to Shuffle option maintains left/right page arrangements when you add or delete pages, keeping left pages even numbered and right pages odd numbered. This option is activated by default, and you should generally leave it on. If you turn it off, spreads are not maintained, and you can end up with single-page spreads. If you set up a document without facing pages, or turn facing pages off in the Document Setup dialog box, then the Allow Pages to Shuffle option has no effect.

# LESSON 2  Controlling Text Flow

In *Essentials for Design: InDesign Level 1*, you manually flowed text into short documents such as ads. Manually flowing text is generally the best solution for short documents with limited space, when you need very tight control over the flow of text. When you manually or semi-automatically place and flow text, InDesign flows the text only into the frame (or linked frames) that you select. In some cases, though, you might want to break a thread between frames or add a new frame to a thread. When paginating lengthy documents such as books, you can use automatic text flow to create as many pages and frames as a placed story needs.

## Autoflow Placed Text

**1**    **Open the file autoflow.indd.**

**2**    **Choose File>Place to place the text file dead_souls.txt, but don't click in the document with the Loaded Text icon yet.**

You can also press Command/Control-D to place a file.

**3**    **Move the cursor to the upper-left corner of the page, where the margins intersect.**

**4**    **Hold the Option/Alt key down.**

The cursor changes to a Semi-autoflow icon.

**FIGURE 1.25**

**5**    **Click once.**

The page is filled with text and the pointer is reloaded with text.

**6**    **Drag a master from the Master section of the Pages palette into the Pages section, creating Page 2.**

**7**    **Position the cursor over the new page and hold down the Shift key.**

The cursor changes to the Autoflow icon.

**FIGURE 1.26**

**8**    **Click once.**

The entire story is autoflowed; new pages are created to accommodate the length of the story, and new text frames are created based on the page margin settings.

**9**    **Save the file and keep it open for the next exercise.**

## Add a Frame to a Thread

**1** With the file autoflow.indd still open, choose View>Show Text Threads.

You can also make text threads visible by pressing Command-Option-Y/Control-Alt-Y.

**2** Adjust the top of the text frame so the frame fills the lower half of Page 3.

**3** Select the Rectangle Frame tool, and draw a new frame in the area above the frame you just resized.

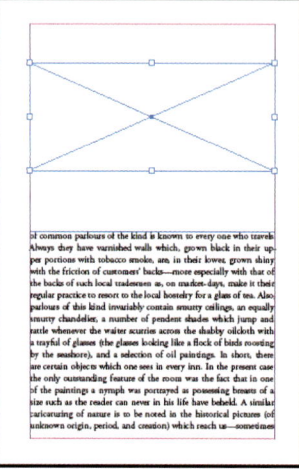

FIGURE 1.27

**4** To rethread the text through this new frame, click the out port of the frame on Page 2.

The cursor appears as a Thread icon, indicating that text is going to be relinked.

**5** Move the Loaded Text icon over the new frame and click.

The text reflows through the new frame, then continues to the next frame on the page.

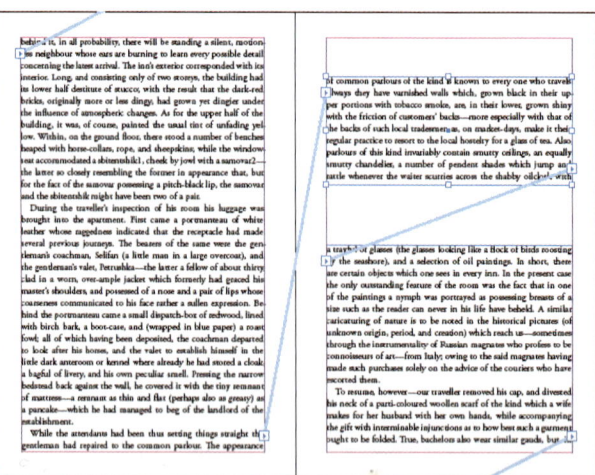

FIGURE 1.28

**6** Select the upper frame on Page 3 with the Selection tool, and press the Delete/Backspace key.

The text in the deleted frame flows into the frame below once again.

**7** Save and close the file.

## To Extend Your Knowledge...

### MANAGING TEXT IN FRAMES

You can separate a threaded text frame from the rest of the thread so the included text is no longer linked to another text stream. As you just learned, if you delete a threaded frame, the text simply rethreads to the next frame in the thread. To "disconnect" a frame and remove its text from the thread, you need to copy the frame and paste it where needed. If you copy and paste more than one threaded frame simultaneously, the copies remain threaded together.

## LESSON 3  Using Templates to Manage Documents

A template is a special type of InDesign document that is intended for repeated use. For example, a newsletter usually uses the same layout designs, fonts, masthead graphics, and styles. Instead of opening a past issue and clearing out all the content, you can make a template that is essentially an empty document waiting for content.

When you open a template, you actually open an untitled copy of the template ready for content. If you want to modify a template, you can choose File>Open, locate the template, then click the Open Original button in the Open a File dialog box.

A template contains not only document geometry — page sizes and margins — but also all masters used in the document, the color palette used, style sheets, and standard graphic elements. It is worth the time to set up a template for documents that will be printed several times with different but similar content.

### Set The Base Template

**1** Create a new 8.25 × 10.5-in document with portrait orientation, facing pages, a master text frame, 3 columns, and a 0.1667-in gutter. Define 0.5-in. top and outside margins, and 0.75-in. bottom and inside margins. Allow a 0.125-in. bleed on all four edges. If bleed options are not visible, click the More Options button.

**2** Double-click the A-Master and, from the Pages palette Options menu, choose Master Options for "A-Master".

In the Master Options dialog box that appears, you can rename the master.

**3** **Rename the page "Basic" and click OK.**

This will become the master for your standard magazine page.

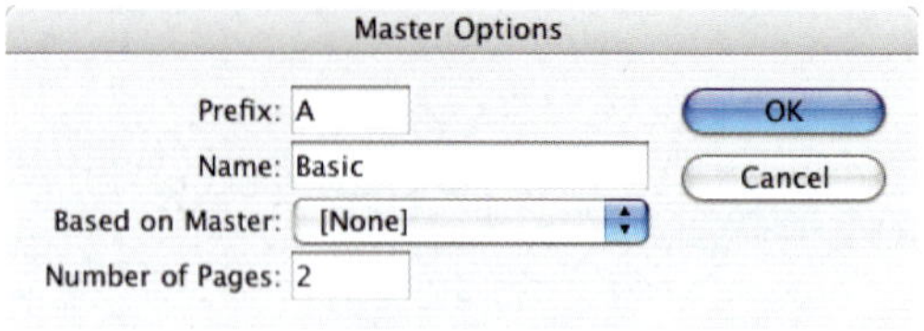

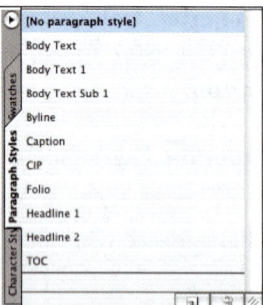

FIGURE 1.29

**4** **Create a text frame on the left-hand master with the following dimensions:**

X: 0.5 in.    W: 7.0 in.
Y: 9.8 in.    H: 0.4 in.

This is the frame for the running foot, or *folio*.

**5** **With the Type tool active, choose Type>Insert Special Character, then choose Automatic Page Number. Then choose Type>Insert Special Character>Right Indent Tab. Following the tab, type "July 2005".**

This creates the running foot. For each issue, you will change the month in this frame.

Instead of using the menu, you can type Command-Option-Shift-N/Control-Alt-Shift-N to add an automatic page number, and Shift-Tab to add a right-indent tab.

FIGURE 1.30

**6** **Create an identical frame on the right master and type "Gulf Coast Life", then add a right-indent tab and an automatic page number.**

**7** **From the Paragraph Styles palette Options menu, choose Load All Styles. Navigate to your Project_01 folder, select mag_styles.indd, and click Open.**

The styles from this document are added to the palette. You can add styles from any existing document or template, or completely populate your styles palettes with pre-existing styles.

FIGURE 1.31

Project 1   Expanding Document Layout Skills

**8** Apply the Folio style to the text you entered on both masters.

**9** Highlight Gulf Coast Life and change it to Adobe Garamond Pro Italic.

Your Basic master is completed.

**10** Save the file as a template (in the Format/Save as Type menu) named "gulf_coast_life.indt" in your WIP_01 folder and leave it open for the next exercise.

InDesign automatically assigns the .indt extension.

## Add Additional Masters

**1** If the document gulf_coast_life.indt is not open, select File>Open. Click the Open Original radio button, and choose the document from your WIP_01 folder.

Choosing Open Original allows you to edit an existing template rather than creating a new document based on that template.

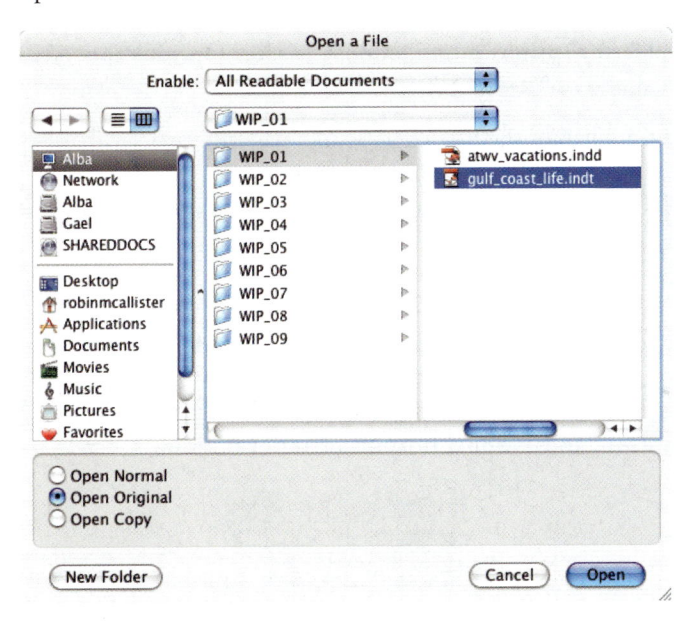

FIGURE 1.32

**2** From the Preferences menu, choose Composition and click the Text Wrap Only Affects Text Beneath button.

**3** Click the A-Basic master, and select Duplicate Master Spread "A-Basic" from the Pages palette Options menu.

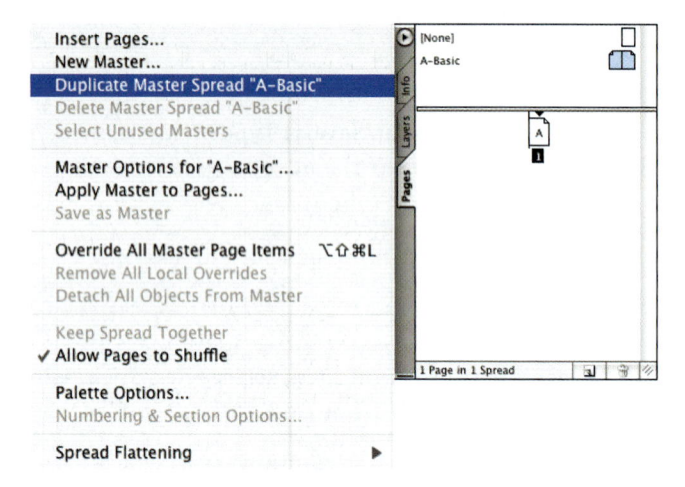

**FIGURE 1.33**

**4** From the Pages palette Options menu, choose Master Options for "A-Basic copy" and change the master page's name to "Recto-1".

This master will be applied to the first page of any magazine articles that begin on a right-hand page.

**5** With the upper-left proxy reference point selected, create a frame with the following dimensions:

X: 8.25 in.  W: 8.375 in.
Y: –0.125 in.  H: 5.375 in.

The main picture for the article will be inserted in this frame.

**6** With the frame selected, choose Window>Type & Tables>Text Wrap. Choose the Wrap Around Bounding Box option, and assign a bottom offset of 0.25 in.

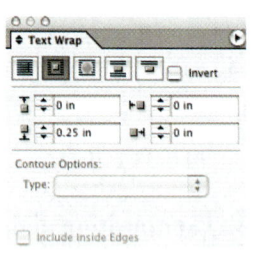

**FIGURE 1.34**

**7** Duplicate the Recto-1 master and rename it "Verso-1".

This master will be applied to the first page of any magazine articles that begin on a left-hand page.

**8** Modify the graphic frame dimensions as follows:

    X: –0.125 in.    W: 11.3472 in.
    Y: –0.125 in.    H: 5.375 in.

The image will cross the gutter, tying the two pages together.

**9** Save the template file and close it.

You could have created a number of additional page types, such as the publisher's page, table of contents, and others. This abbreviated example, however, illustrates the concept sufficiently.

## Work with Your Template

**1** Open the template gulf_coast_life.indt from your WIP_01 folder. Be sure the Open Normal button is checked.

The template opens as an untitled document.

**2** Click the first page of the document, then select Layout>Numbering & Section Options.

**3** Click the Start Page Numbering at button and enter "18" in the text field. Click OK.

The page becomes a left-hand page, and the new page number is reflected in the Pages palette.

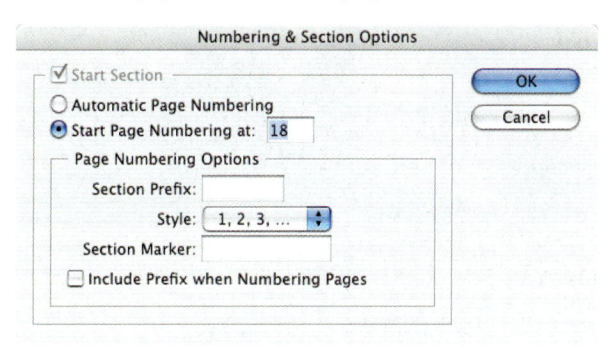

FIGURE 1.35

**4** In the Pages palette, drag a new C-Verso-1 page to the right of the spine.

The graphic frame appears on both pages of the layout.

**5** Command/Control-Shift-click the graphic frame and place the image evening_cookout.tif.

The image spans both pages.

**6** Command/Control-Shift-click the text frame on Page 18 to unlock it. Place the text file glitz.doc in the frame.

The type flows into the frame.

**7** Create a new text frame the width of the three columns on the first page, covering part of the picture.

Here's an opportunity for you to use your design skills.

**8** Unlock the right-hand page and link the text to that page.

**9** Click the out port of the frame you just created, then link it to the main text frame.

**10** Adjust the format of the headline text ("It's Not All Glitz and Glamour…") to 60/60 Adobe Garamond Pro Semibold Italic, aligned left. Assign a color of Paper to the byline, and set an appropriate space above the paragraph. Position the type attractively over the photo; with the headline selected, click with the Eyedropper tool to pick up a color from the fire.

**11** If necessary, insert a frame break from the Type>Insert Break Character menu to force the first paragraph to the main text frame.

Alternately, press Shift-Enter (on the numeric keypad).

**FIGURE 1.36**

**12** Save your document as "gclife_0705.indd" and close it.

# LESSON 4  Using Grids to Facilitate Production

Most successful documents are based on a carefully built structure called a *grid*, the basis of which includes document setup and margins. InDesign offers two distinct types of layout tools: grids are fixed in place and can't be moved, and layout guides can be moved and deleted as necessary.

The document grid is designed for aligning objects. When working in inches, it is practical to accept the default of 8 subdivisions per one-inch grid; if you work in picas, 12 subdivisions are more logical. Objects will snap to the document grid based on the snap zone specified in the Guides & Pasteboard preferences. You can supplement the document grid by assigning layout guides for aligning specific objects.

The baseline grid, unlike the document grid, is used exclusively for aligning text. To use it well requires careful planning. The grid should match or be an increment of the text leading, and should allow for any necessary space above or below the paragraph. Baseline grids are especially useful when used in conjunction with pictures.

## Set a Document Grid

**1**   Open atwt_travel.indd from your WIP_01 folder. Update links if necessary, then open the Grids pane of the Preferences dialog box.

Preferences are found under the InDesign menu on the Macintosh and under the Edit menu on Windows.

**2**   In the Document Grid section, choose a color from the pop-up menu to use as the grid color.

**3**   Set the horizontal gridline every 6p0 with 12 subdivisions.

**4**   Set the vertical gridline every 72 pt with 12 subdivisions. Be sure the Grids in Back box is checked. Click OK.

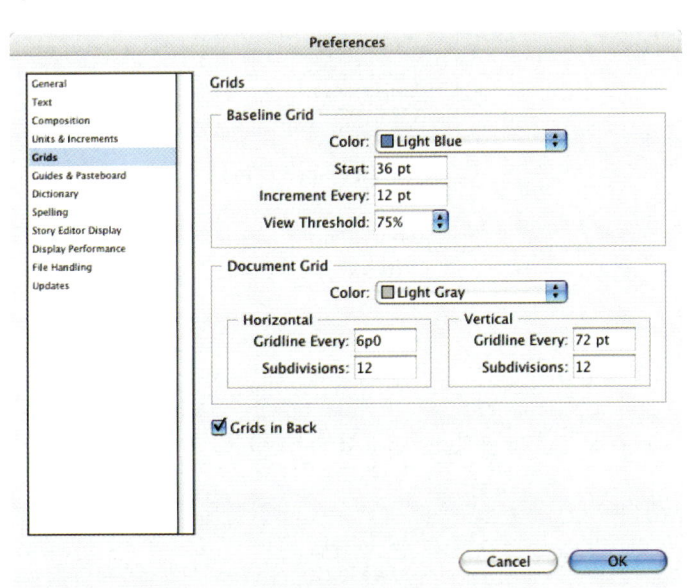

**FIGURE 1.37**

**5** Choose View>Show Document Grid. If your view magnification is set below 100% you see only 6 subdivisions, even though you specified 12. With the view at 100% or higher, all 12 subdivisions are visible.

**6** Choose View>Snap to Document Grid.

**7** Create a rectangular frame and move it slowly with the Selection tool. Notice how it snaps to each of the 12 subdivisions.

**8** Delete the frame.

**9** Choose View>Hide Document Grid to turn off the snap feature.

**10** Save the file and leave it open.

## Set and Use Baseline Grids

**1** Return to or open atwt_travel.indd from your WIP_01 folder; choose View>Show Baseline Grid and navigate to Page 2.

**2** To show the kind of results that can occur when the baseline grid is used improperly, click in the first paragraph of the second column on the page (the one starting with "Italy is not just…"). Click the Align to Baseline Grid button in the Paragraph Control palette.

The baseline of each line of text snaps to the next highest grid. Because the leading is 15 pt. and the default baseline grid is set to 12-pt. increments, each line of text is reassigned a leading of 24 pt. This is unacceptable.

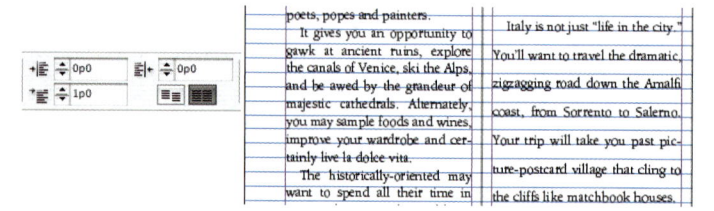

**FIGURE 1.38**

**3** In the Grids preferences, set the baseline grid to start at 45.5 pts. with increments every 15 pts. Click OK.

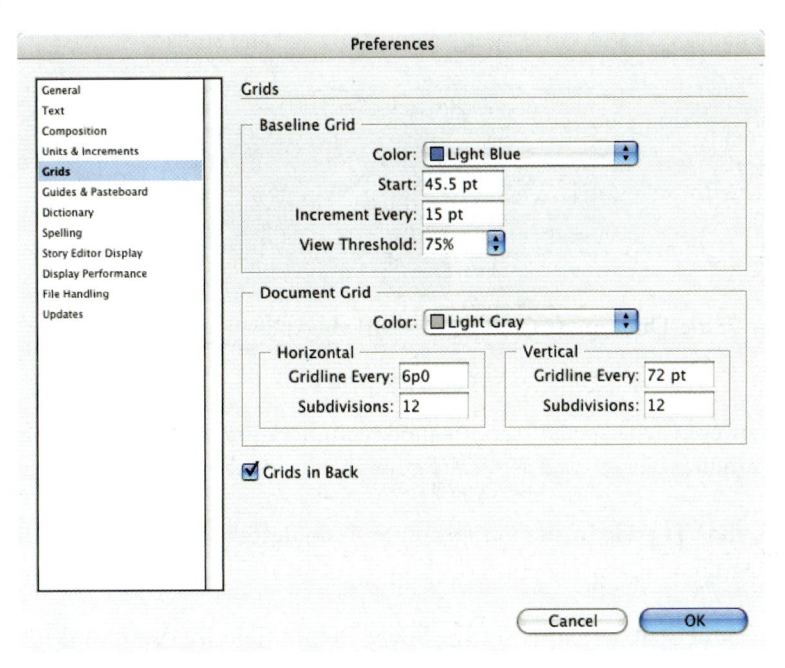

FIGURE 1.39

**4** Select all the text in the story and set it to align to the baseline grid.

The text aligns and the columns balance.

**5** Before dealing with more complex specifications, add a picture. Create a frame in the upper-right corner of Page 2 — it doesn't matter how large it is. From the Text Wrap palette, select Wrap Around Bounding Box and set the left offset to 0p9. Leave the other offsets at 0.

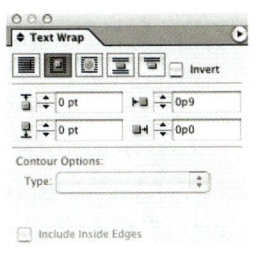

FIGURE 1.40

**6** **Place biking.jpg in the frame. Select Object>Fitting>Fit Frame to Content and position the frame along the right margin of the page.**

The text automatically aligns horizontally across the page and spread.

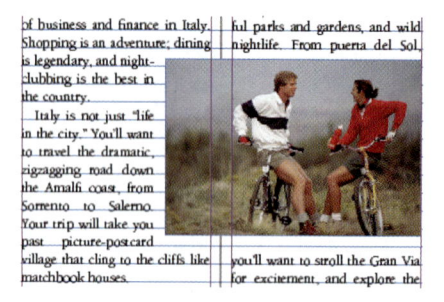

**FIGURE 1.41**

Sometimes, however, type specification is more complex; subheads, for example, may have different leading than running text, as well as specifications for space above and below paragraphs.

**7** **Double-click the VH style in the Paragraph Styles palette to access the Modify Paragraph Style Options dialog box.**

**8** **In the Indents and Spacing pane, set the Space Before field to 10 pt. and the Space After field to 3 pt. Click OK to close the dialog box.**

You see very erratic spacing, which you need to fix.

**9** **In the Grids preferences, change the increment of the baseline grid to 5 pt. and click OK.**

The 3-pt. space after the paragraph is overridden by the grid increment.

**10** **Change the space after the VH style to 0 pt.**

The space under the paragraph disappears. Note that the 10-pt. space before each paragraph is preserved and, because 10 pt. is divisible by 5 (the increment of the baseline grid), the paragraphs align to the baseline without any extra space between paragraphs.

**11** **Save and close the document.**

The first column is still not justified because of the 10-pt. space above the VH paragraph style. The Italian Adventure headline is at the top of the column, so it does not have the compensating space above to achieve proper alignment. You could simply eliminate all the space before and after paragraphs in the entire story to balance the columns, or you could experiment with the space before and after settings of all the styles to determine spacing that matches that of the baseline grid.

## To Extend Your Knowledge...

### ABOUT VERTICAL JUSTIFICATION

Because it can be difficult to obtain perfect alignment across a page, many designers choose not to align the bottoms of columns, preferring to maintain a good interaction between headlines and text.

## LESSON 5  Using Guides for Effective Layout

You can drag layout guides to a page or spread from the horizontal and vertical document rulers. Some designers love guides and use them for all their work; others use them as seldom as possible. To use guides well, they must be positioned accurately, and they should not clutter the screen.

Guides may be placed on masters to ensure consistent positioning of elements on each page. Sometimes this is done when a page is laid out in columns and rows. More often, however, guides are positioned interactively to aid placement on a single page.

Guides dragged from the horizontal and vertical rulers may be positioned with the cursor directly over a page or outside the page. Guides dragged over the page, called *page guides*, affect that page only. *Spread guides* are dragged over the pasteboard and affect the entire spread.

To delete guides, you can simply select them with either the Selection tool or the Direct Selection tool and press Delete. Guides created on a master may be deleted from a document page by pressing Command/Control-Shift when selecting the guide, then pressing Delete. Guides created on one layer affect all other layers, but can only be deleted or moved when the layer on which they were created is active.

### Work with Guides

1. Create a new, letter-size, one-page document with facing pages; accept the default margins and columns.

2. Select the A-Master spread in the Pages palette and drag a new spread below Page 1.

3. With the cursor over the pasteboard (not over the page), drag a guide from the horizontal ruler to 0.375 in.

   Use the Control palette to position the guide if necessary — guides can be difficult to position in smaller page views. If you work at 100%, you will be able to place the guide by simply dragging. Note that the guide crosses the whole spread.

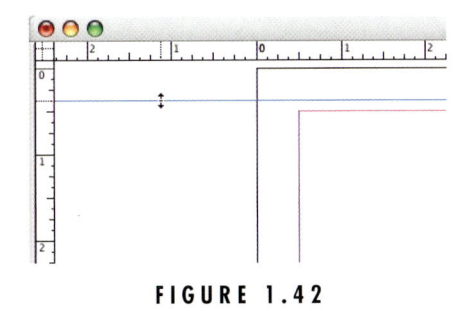

**FIGURE 1.42**

**4** Now position a horizontal and vertical guide simultaneously. Press Command/Control and drag from the ruler intersection (zero point) to X: 1 in, Y: 1 in.

Note that these are spread guides. You can reposition each guide individually in the Control palette.

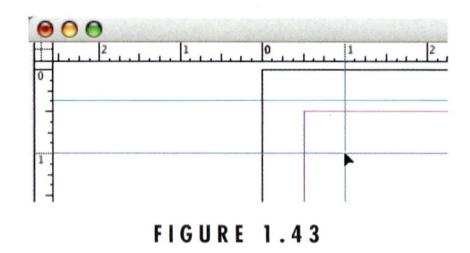

**FIGURE 1.43**

It's pretty easy to create guides interactively, but it becomes tedious when you want to position numerous guides "by the numbers." InDesign's Create Guides dialog box is very useful for setting up equally sized columns or rows, such as those you'd use to create a six-panel brochure (just remember to adjust the appropriate guides to allow for the short panel). This feature doesn't, however, allow you to specify exact positioning of guides.

**5** Create another two-page spread below Spread 2–3.

InDesign will position those pages centered on your monitor.

**6** Choose Layout>Create Guides. Set 3 rows, 2 columns, and 0.333-in. gutters. Click the Fit Guides to Page button. Click OK.

The new guides appear on both pages of the spread. The Create Guides function operates across an entire spread, not just the current page.

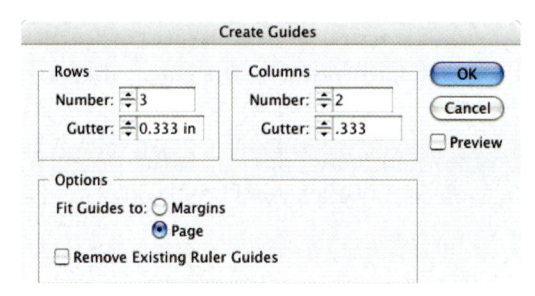

**FIGURE 1.44**

**7** Save the document as "guide_layer.indd" and keep it open for the next exercise.

## To Extend Your Knowledge...

### USING GUIDES EFFECTIVELY

Fitting the guides to the page is absolutely accurate. If you use the Fit Guides to Margin option, they may not exactly match the folds and trim of your document.

When using guides extensively for layout, it is a good idea to lock them (View>Lock Guides) if they weren't created on the master. As you may discover, it is very easy to accidentally click and move a guide, throwing your entire layout off.

Project 1    Expanding Document Layout Skills         **LEVEL 2**

## LESSON 6    Using Layers for Diversity

You should be familiar with the stacking arrangement of objects in InDesign documents. The item most recently created is placed in front, and the stacking order can be changed by moving items backward and forward in the stack with the Object>Arrange commands. Layers add further structure to the stacking order. Each layer can have stacked elements within it; like stacked elements, layers may be rearranged, and can be either hidden or shown. Items on hidden layers do not print, simplifying the production of versioned documents.

Unlike individual elements, however, layers function independently of one another. You can lock an entire layer so elements placed on it can't be accidentally moved or altered. You can lock a layer's guides independently of its content. Using the Paste Remembers Layers option on the Layers palette menu, items pasted from one page to another are pasted automatically to the layer on which they originated. You can hide layers from view; it is quite easy to move selected objects from one layer to another unlocked, visible layer.

To place objects on a layer, you select the desired layer in the Layers palette to make it active, then create or paste an object on that layer. As long as the layer remains active, all objects you create are placed on that layer. To place objects on a different layer, you need to select the appropriate layer before creating the objects.

In the Layer Options dialog box (accessed from the palette's Options menu), you can rename a layer and turn various options on or off. You can change the lock and visibility settings of an individual layer's guides without affecting all the guides in the document.

The color selected in the Layer Options dialog box determines how object bounding boxes display in that layer. Guides appear in the same color while they're being dragged into position. Once a guide is placed, however, it is displayed in the color you chose in the Ruler Guides Preferences dialog box.

### Build the Basic Layout

**1**  **Continue with the open guide_layer.indd file. Activate the Layers palette, which by default resides in the same palette bay as the Pages palette.**

**2**  **Choose Layout>Create Guides, click the Remove Existing Ruler Guides button, then click OK.**

This is a quick way to delete all guides.

**3**  **On Page 1 of the document, place clogs.tif at X: –0.125 in., Y: –0.125 in., with the upper-left proxy reference point active.**

This allows the image to bleed off the page.

**4**  **Resize the image proportionally with the Selection tool by holding Command/Control-Shift while dragging the lower-right corner of the bounding box. Stop when the right edge of the image is bleeding off the edge of the page about 0.125 in. (or W: 8.75 in.).**

**5** Place windmill.tif at X: –0.125 in., Y: 5.667 in. and drag the bottom edge of the frame up to crop the bottom of the image.

The height should be approximately 5.4375 in., just enough for a bleed at the bottom of the page. Note that the top of this image overlaps the clogs.

**FIGURE 1.45**

**6** Send the windmill image to the back to hide the overlap.

**7** Save the document and leave it open for the next exercise.

## Set the Language Layers

**1** Continue in the open document, guide_layer.indd. In the Layers palette, choose Layer Options for Layer 1, and rename the layer "English".

**2** Create three new layers named "Spanish", "French", and "Italian".

You can either click the New Layer button at the bottom of the palette, or choose New Layer from the palette Options menu. The latter lets you choose a name and color in the same step.

**3** Click the English layer, select the Type tool, and drag a new text frame to fill the open area at the lower right. Type "When visiting Holland, please bring your own shoes." Set the type as Caflisch Script Pro, 60 pt., auto-leading, centered. Resize the frame as needed to fit the copy.

**4** Change to the Selection tool and copy the text frame. Click the Spanish layer to select it and paste the frame using Edit>Paste in Place, which pastes the frame in the same position as the original item. Click the Eyeball icon of the English layer to hide it. Select all the text with the Type tool and replace it with "Al visitar Holanda, traiga por favor sus propios zapatos."

When you click the Eyeball icon to hide the English layer, the images disappear along with the English type. You'll fix this later.

**5** Hide the Spanish layer and switch to the French layer. Paste the frame in place again. Type "En visitant la Hollande, apportez svp vos propres chaussures."

It's very common for copy to get longer when translated from English. You can resize the frame or the type's point size to make it fit.

**6** Hide the French layer and repeat the process for the Italian layer, replacing the copy with "Nel visitare l'Olanda, proti prego i vostri propri pattini."

**7** Save the document and leave it open for the next exercise.

## Adjust and Print a Layered Document

**1** Continue in the open document. Hide the Italian layer and make a new layer named "Images".

You need to move the images to their own layer if they are to print with any language besides English.

**2** Shift-click both images on the English layer, then use the Selection tool to drag the colored dot on the right side of the layer list (which indicates the layer on which selected objects appear) to the Images layer.

The images move to the new layer. Dragging the colored dot is an easy way to move selected objects to any other visible, unlocked layer.

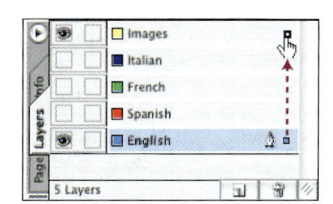

**FIGURE 1.46**

**3** Lock the Images layer by clicking the Lock icon in the Layers palette.

The red slash through the pen and the Lock icon indicate that the layer is locked.

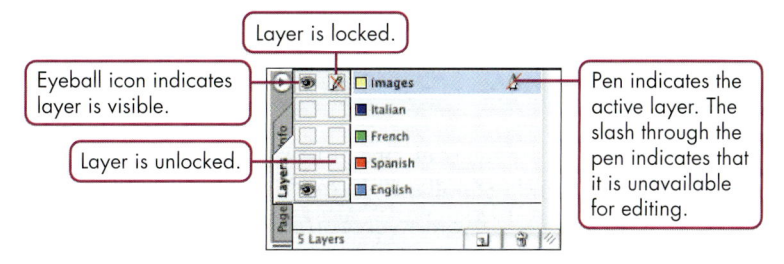

**FIGURE 1.47**

**4** Move the Images layer to the bottom of the layer stack by dragging its name to the bottom of the palette.

The images now form the base layer for the entire document. This doesn't affect the results, but it gives the document organization; if type overlaps images, it's critical to move the images to the back.

**5** **Turn off the English layer by clicking its Eyeball icon. Turn on any of the other language layers to see how they work.**

You can see how creating a document with special needs, such as multiple languages, can be greatly simplified by using layers.

**6** **Print one of the language layers.**

Hidden layers do not print.

**7** **Save the document as "Holland_flyer.indd" and keep it open.**

## To Extend Your Knowledge...

### MORE ABOUT MANAGING LAYERS

The Paste Remembers Layers option on the Layers palette Options menu allows you to copy or cut from one page to the same layer on any other page. If you cut or copy objects to a document that doesn't have the same layers already present, the necessary layers are created. If you turn this option off, objects from different layers are pasted to the active layer, even if you paste to another document.

To move objects to a locked or hidden layer, hold the Command/Control key as you drag the selection indicator. To copy rather than move selected objects, hold Option/Alt as you drag the indicator. Use Command-Option or Control-Alt to copy objects to locked or hidden layers.

To duplicate a layer, select its name in the Layers palette and either choose Duplicate Layer from the Options menu or drag it to the New Layer button at the bottom of the palette. To delete one or more layers, you can drag their names to the Delete button (with the trashcan icon) at the bottom of the palette.

To consolidate layers, you can merge them. To do so, first click the target layer to select it, then Shift-click to select the layers you wish to merge into the target layer. To complete the merge, choose Merge Layers from the Options menu.

## LESSON 7 Automating Layout Adjustment

InDesign offers a Layout Adjustment feature that can save quite a bit of time when you need to change a document's page size, orientation, margins, and columns. Although it's not perfect, this feature can perform some of the more basic adjustments needed to get a layout to conform to a change. Layout Adjustment is turned off by default; to enable it, you can simply choose Layout>Layout Adjustment and check the Enable Layout Adjustment box.

Layout Adjustment maintains relative proportions and placement of all elements on a page. Depending on the choices you make in the Layout Adjustment dialog box, it can:

- reposition margin guides while maintaining margin widths.
- add or remove column guides if a new layout specifies a different number of columns.
- keep objects that are aligned to guides in the same relative positions, even if the guides are moved during layout adjustment.
- resize objects that are aligned to parallel margin, column, or ruler guides, or to ruler guides on three sides, so objects stay aligned to the guides.
- move objects to maintain the same relative positions on a page, if the page size or orientation changes.

Layout adjustment works best with layouts that depend heavily on ruler guides, margins, and page columns, and where objects are aligned with guides. It works less well on loosely designed pages that don't use guides, margins, or page columns.

## Adjusting a Layout

1. With the document Holland_flyer.indd open, select the Images layer, unlock it, and drag ruler guides to the left edge of the images and the top of the clogs image.

2. Select the French layer, click its Eyeball icon to make it visible, and drag page or spread guides to the left and top of the text frame.

3. Make sure the windmill image is set behind that of the clogs. Lock the Images layer.

**FIGURE 1.48**

**Project 1** Expanding Document Layout Skills

**4.** Choose Layout>Layout Adjustment and check the Enable Layout Adjustment box. Leave the other settings at their defaults and click OK.

**5.** Choose File>Document Setup and change the orientation from Portrait (tall) to Landscape (wide).

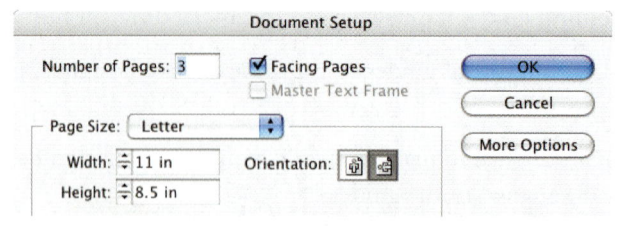

**FIGURE 1.49**

**6.** Click OK to see the results of the layout adjustment.

While not perfect, the new layout maintains the image bleeds, the relative position and width of the text frame, and the relative position of the windmill image. To finish the job, you would need to resize images and text, and possibly crop an image to achieve a design similar to the original.

**FIGURE 1.50**

**7** Undo the adjustment, delete the guides on all layers, and change the document orientation back to Landscape.

Without the guides as a basis for adjustment, the result can be messy. Here, you'd also need to resize the text frame to clean up the design.

**FIGURE 1.51**

**8** Close the file without saving.

## LESSON 8 Creating Documents That Fold

The physical structure of a document's pages is sometimes referred to as ***page geometry***, which refers to not only the width and height of a document and the page imposition, but also how the document folds, how images bleed, and press and post-press requirements.

When working with folding documents, many people mistakenly assume that the trim size of a job is the size it appears after folding. In fact, the trim size of a folded document is actually the size of the sheet after it has been folded and the excess cut away. There are two basic principles to remember when dealing with documents that fold:

- Paper has thickness. The thicker the paper, the more allowance you need to plan for the fold.
- Folding machines are mechanical devices. These machines operate at high speed and are accurate to about 0.0125 in. Paper sometimes shifts as it flows through a machine's paper path, just as it can do in a laser printer or photocopier.

It's always a good idea to create folding grids on a master layout, so you can easily apply the same set of guides to any page in the document. This is far quicker than manually placing the guides on individual pages. Master pages are used in the exercise in this lesson.

Once you have created a folding grid, it is also a good idea to save the document as a template so you can apply the same guides to any similar document. Every time you want to create a letterfold brochure, for example, you can open the template and begin with an empty file that contains only the correct guides and marks.

## Create a Six-Panel Brochure

There are many names for this type of document. It is most commonly referred to as a "trifold" brochure, even though there are only two folds. The brochure consists of two outside panels at full size, with a panel 1/16 in. narrower that folds inside.

**1** Create a new letter-size (11 × 8.5 in.), two-page, one-column document with facing pages, landscape orientation, with 0.25-in. margins on all four sides and a 0.125-in. bleed on all four sides.

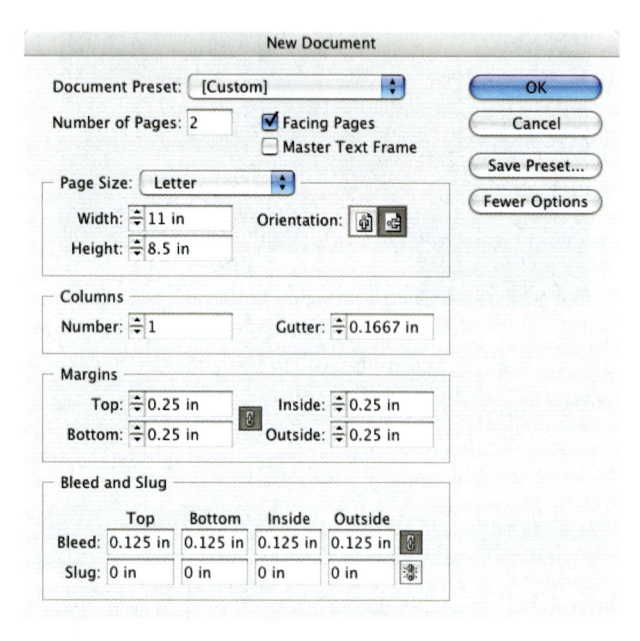

FIGURE 1.52

**2** Set the Ruler Units Origin to Page in the Units and Increments preferences.

**3** Click the icon of the first page in the Pages palette, then choose Layout>Numbering & Section Options. Change the Start Page Numbering value to 2.

This forces the first page to the left side of the spread, and allows you to view both pages at once.

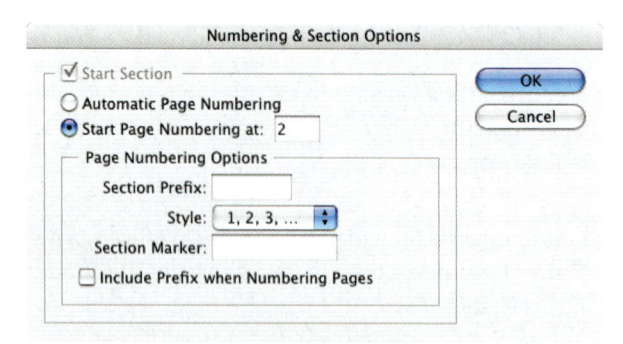

FIGURE 1.53

**4** Double-click the A-Master in the Pages palette. Choose Master Options from the palette menu and rename this master "Six-panel Brochure", then click OK.

FIGURE 1.54

**5** On the master layout, drag vertical guides for folds to the following settings; use the X field in the Control palette to set the final guide positions:

| Left Master | Right Master |
|---|---|
| 3.6875 in. | 3.625 in. |
| 7.375 in. | 7.3125 in. |

These guides are positioned where the brochure is designed to fold. If the brochure were set up incorrectly using three equal panels — or worse, three separate pages per side — there would be only two possible solutions: you could simply slice off the extra 1/16 in. from the third panel and hope nothing important was lost, or you could rebuild the entire file correctly.

**6** To delineate the live copy area, drag guides –0.25 in. (to the left) and +0.25 in. (to the right) of the folding guides.

These guides create the margins inside the brochure. The outside margins were created when you originally defined the page size. You can easily define the positions of the guides in the Control palette by entering the position of the folding guide, then typing –0.25 or +0.25. When in doubt, let the computer do the math. The inside panels are narrower, to allow for the fold.

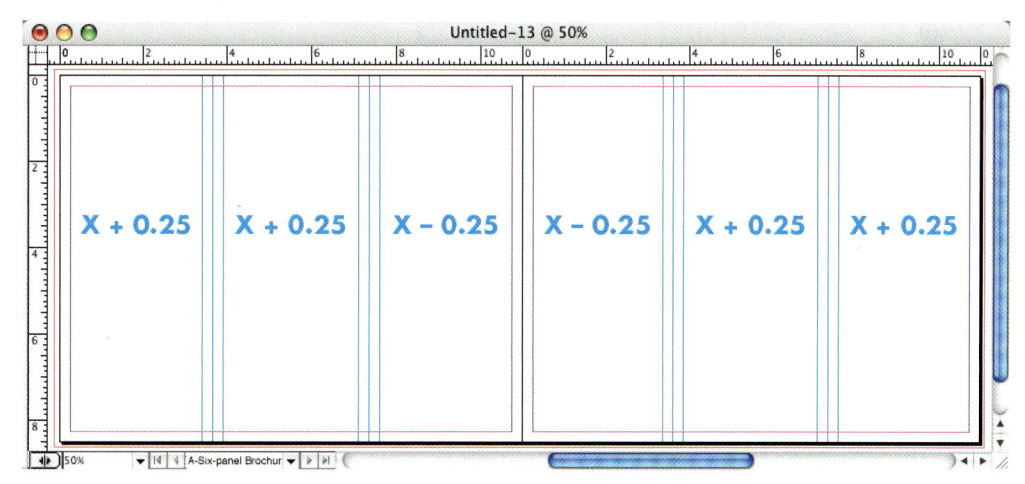

FIGURE 1.55

**7** Draw a 0.25-in vertical line with a weight of 0.5 pt. Use the Stroke palette to make it a dotted line. On the left-facing page, position it at X: 3.6875 in., Y: –0.25 in. with the upper-middle proxy reference point selected.

**8** Use the Step-and-Repeat command (Edit>Step and Repeat) to duplicate the rule you just created with a horizontal offset of 3.6875 in.

You can also press Command/Control-Shift-V to access the Step-and-Repeat command.

**9** Select both of these rules, and use the Step-and-Repeat command to duplicate both rules with a vertical offset of 8.75 in. and a horizontal offset of 0.

**10** Draw a rectangular frame 0.375 in. high and 4 in. wide, with a stroke of None and a fill of Paper. Position the frame at X: 3.5 in, Y: –0.125 in. using the upper-left proxy reference point.

This method of covering up elements on a page is referred to, tongue in cheek, as "electronic white-out." It is being used because it is necessary to have the fold marks touch the page if they are to print.

**11** Copy and paste the frame, positioning it at X: 3.5 in, Y: 8.25 in.

**12** Copy all four folding marks plus the "white-out" and paste it on the right-hand page at X: 3.441 in., Y: –0.25 in.

**13** Choose Edit>Select All, then choose Object>Lock Position.

Every element on the page (including the guides) is locked into position, so you can't accidentally move them.

**14** Save the document as a template named "six_panel.indt".

Setting up folding templates can be tedious, but it certainly saves you time in the future.

## LESSON 9  Automating Production with Presets

InDesign has three distinct sets of presets — all of which can help you speed production. If you worked through *Essentials for Design: InDesign Level 1*, you used the PDF export presets to produce proofs for the monitor and for printing to a desktop printer. We'll discuss the PDF export presets and the printing presets later in this book. In this chapter, you will become acquainted with document presets.

You might want to think of a document preset as a mini-template. They can be used as starting points for templates, or as the basis for jobs that have the same orientation, margins, columns, and bleed. You've already used some of InDesign's standard presets when you started a new document and accepted the defaults.

Some jobs that would reasonably use custom presets include theater posters, postcards, envelopes, and ads for publications that use set sizes. The preset gets you through the setup phase quickly, and into the process of creating the document.

### Create and Use a Postcard Preset

**1**  Choose File>Document Presets>Define.

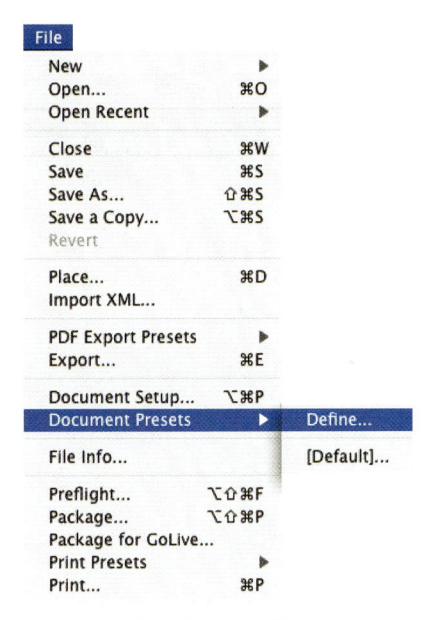

FIGURE 1.56

**2**  In the Document Presets dialog box, click New.

**3**  In the New Document Preset dialog box, name the preset "Postcard 6 x 4".

You may have a number of "Postcard" presets. This will allow you to quickly access the one you want by including its size in the preset name.

**4** Fill in the rest of the postcard settings as follows:

    Number of Pages:   2
    Page Width:   6 in.
    Page Height:   4 in.
    Column Number:   1
    Margins:   0.25 in. (all sides)
    Bleed:   0.125 in. (all sides)

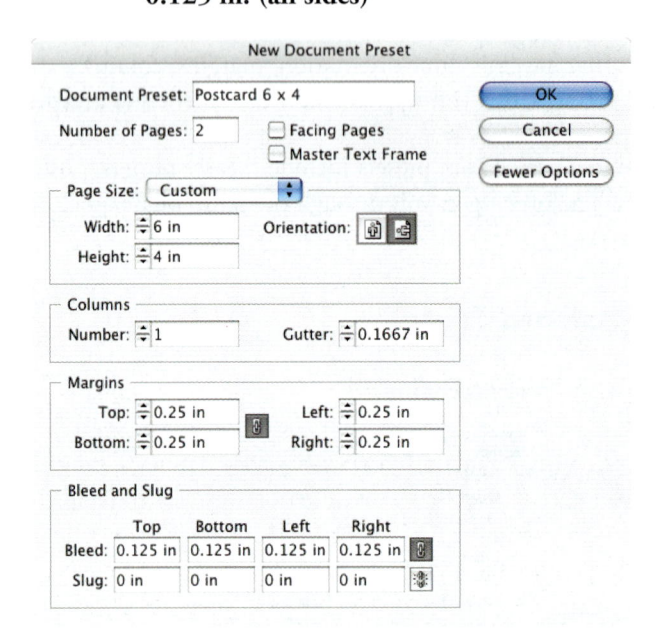

**FIGURE 1.57**

**5** Click OK to accept these document presets.

The preset is created and stored.

**6** Create a new file and choose the Postcard 6 × 4 preset from the Document Preset menu.

A two-page document with margins and bleeds already in position appears.

**7** On the first page, place the file rose_hill.tif.

The height fits exactly; position the width to taste.

**8** On the second page, place the file rose_hill_promo.eps in the upper-left corner of the page.

The text takes up the left-hand third of the postcard, leaving you adequate room for your address information.

**9** Save the document as "rose_hill_postcard.indd".

Because you used the preset, you were able to complete the entire job in about the same time it would have taken to fill in the document information.

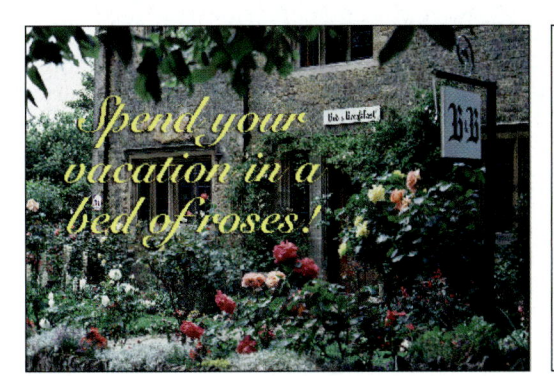

**FIGURE 1.58**

# SUMMARY

In this project, you learned many important tools for making the document-layout process more efficient. You created and used a number of masters to speed the production process. You added fold-outs to spreads — and learned that a spread with three pages must be backed up with another of the same size. You managed page numbering and page positioning (right and left) by adding sections to your documents. You learned the proper technique for creating a document that will fold. You created document templates for instances when you will re-use elements within documents, and you created and used document presets. You used layers to add depth and diversity to a document, and you used the automatic layout adjustment feature to simplify the repurposing process.

# KEY TERMS

| | | |
|---|---|---|
| autoflow | master | stacking order |
| baseline grid | page geometry | template |
| document grid | preset | thread |
| fold-out | recto | trim |
| folio | repurpose | verso |
| grid | section | visibility icon |
| guide | shuffle | |
| layer | spread | |

# CHECKING CONCEPTS AND TERMS

## MULTIPLE CHOICE

**Check the letter of the correct answer for each of the following:**

1. What constitutes a spread in an InDesign document?
   a. A single page, or two or more adjacent pages
   b. Pages that are connected by a graphic
   c. Three pages that make a fold-out
   d. The front and back pages of a document

2. When are pages termed verso and recto?
   a. When they are output as negative film, right-reading
   b. When they contain politically correct verses
   c. When they are upside down
   d. When they are left and right

3. Which settings can be defined in document presets?
   a. All elements in a document
   b. Margins, columns, and guides
   c. Page size, orientation, margins, and columns
   d. Number of pages and style sheets

4. When creating a six-panel brochure, which of the following is true?
   a. All panels should be equal.
   b. The front panel should be narrower than the back.
   c. The back panel should be the same size as the panel that folds in.
   d. The panel that folds in should be narrower than the other two.

5. When using layers in a document…
   a. You cannot include stacking within a layer.
   b. Common elements should be on their own layer.
   c. Opacity of layers will not let lower layers show through.
   d. Common elements should be on the uppermost layer.

6. Which of the following is true of masters?
   a. Left and right masters can be mixed in a document.
   b. The first page in the document must contain the A-Master.
   c. Masters can contain only columns and guides.
   d. Masters can be included in documents, but not in templates.

7. If pages are allowed to shuffle…
   a. They will become left- and right-hand pages following normal numbering sequences.
   b. The page numbers will become jumbled, making for difficult pagination.
   c. Pages can only be single-sided.
   d. Any linked text will flow to the next page in sequence.

8. When placing text from a file…
   a. The Loaded Text icon allows you to flow text manually.
   b. The Autoflow Text icon adds frames and pages until all text is placed.
   c. The Semi-autoflow Text icon stops flowing text at the end of each page or frame.
   d. All of the above.

9. Which is true of the baseline grid?
   a. It forms a checkerboard on the document for easy placement.
   b. It can be modified only through Preferences.
   c. Its default color of gray cannot be modified.
   d. It always begins at the top margin.

10. Which is true of layout adjustment?
    a. Relative positions of objects are retained.
    b. Image position is retained, but bleeds are not.
    c. Images retain their absolute size.
    d. Stacking order is not maintained.

## DISCUSSION QUESTIONS

1. Most of the features discussed in this project have to do with automating document production. What are the relative values of masters, presets, and templates? When would you use one or the other of these features?

2. Explain the differences and similarities between using document layers and working with the stacking order. Are there instances in which working with layers could introduce unwanted complexity in documents? How would you overcome this?

# SKILL DRILL

Skill Drills reinforce project skills. Each skill reinforced is the same, or nearly the same, as a skill presented in the lessons. Detailed instructions are provided in a step-by-step format. You must perform the Skill Drills in order.

## 1. Create a Newsletter Master

A medical organization regularly produces a two-color newsletter that is printed by a commercial printer. Some months it is six pages, and some months it is four. You have been assigned to set up the master for the newsletter, which was previously produced using styles.

1. Create a new, two-page, letter-size document, with portrait orientation; facing pages; a master text frame; three columns with 0.1667-in. gutters; 0.5-in. inside, outside, and bottom margins; a 0.75-in. top margin; and no bleeds.

2. In the Composition preferences, click the Text Wrap Only Affects Text Beneath button.

3. From the Pages palette Options menu, turn the Allow Pages to Shuffle option off.

4. Drag one A-Master spread to the right of Page 1 and one spread to the left of Page 4.

    This gives you the option of using a six-page document — at least it will after you apply some modifications.

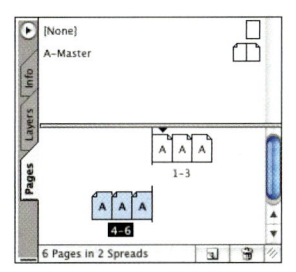

    **FIGURE 1.59**

5. From the Paragraph Styles Options menu, choose Load All Styles. Navigate to yh_old.indd and click Open.

6. In the Swatches palette, delete all colors except None, Paper, Registration, and Black. Select Load Swatches, and again navigate to yh_old.indd and click Open.

   You now have all the styles and colors you need for your two-color document.

7. On the left A-Master, create a text frame as follows:

   | X: 0.5 in.   | W: 7.5 in.   |
   |--------------|--------------|
   | Y: 0.375 in. | H: 0.375 in. |

8. Type "Your Health", then insert an em space followed by an automatic page number. This page number will merely serve as a placeholder. You will need to manually enter page numbers on the pages to which the A-Master is applied. Apply the Running Head paragraph style.

9. Click the frame and use the Step-and-Repeat command once with an 8.5-in. horizontal offset.

   The pages next to the spine will fold in. They need to be 1/16 inch narrower than the outside pages.

10. Select document Page 1. Draw a solid half-point vertical line 0.5 in. long and position it at X: 0.6225 in., Y: –0.4 in.

11. Step and repeat the line with a vertical offset of 11.4 in.

    Because the line is drawn as a solid line, it is understood as a cut line.

12. Apply electronic white-out to cover the part of the lines that touch the page. Be sure the center of the white frame is aligned with the center of the vertical rule.

13. Step and repeat both lines and their white-out horizontally 8.4375 in. From the Stroke palette, change the solid stroke to a dotted line.

14. Step and repeat the dotted lines and whiteout 8.5 inches horizontally.

15. Apply the fold and trim marks in reverse order on the second spread.

16. Save the document as a template named "your_health_6.indt" and leave it open.

## 2. Adjust the Pages

Now that you have all the marks in place, you need to adjust the document's margins and pagination information.

1. Continue in the open document. Navigate to Page 1 of the first spread and choose Layout>Margins and Columns. Make the inside (left) margin 0.5625 in.

2. Select the header frame and the text frame on this page (Command/Control-Shift-click), and adjust it to X: 0.5625 in., W: 7.4375 in.

3. Go to Page 6 on the second spread and choose Layout>Margins and Columns. Make the inside (right) margin 0.625 in.

4. Select the header frame and the text frame on this page (Command/Control-Shift-click), and adjust it to X: 0.5 in., W: 7.4375 in.

5. Command/Control-Shift-click each of the header frames on Pages 1–3. Change the automatic page numbers on Pages 1 and 2 to "5" and "6", respectively. Delete the header on Page 3, which will become Page 1 of the newsletter.

6. Command/Control-Shift-click each of the header frames on Pages 4–6. Change the automatic page numbers on Pages 4, 5, and 6 to "2", "3", and "4", respectively.

7. Create a second master page as a two-column page, and name it "2-Column".

8. Drag the master on top of Page 2 (the first page in the second group of pages).

9. Save the template and leave it open.

## 3. Add Common Items

In addition to repeating elements, there are common items to each newsletter you will publish. You will place those common items in this Skill Drill.

1. In the open document, go to Page 1 (the third page in the first group of pages) and place the file yh_nameplate.indd at X: 0.5 in., Y: 0.375 in.

2. Create a new text frame with the following dimensions:

    X: 0.82 in.     W: 6.9 in.
    Y: 2.3 in.      H: 0.25 in.

3. Access the Text Frame Options dialog box, and set the vertical justification to Center.

4. Type "Spring 2005" as a placeholder into this text frame and format it as 12-pt. ATC Oak Normal. Center it in the frame.

**FIGURE 1.60**

5. Create a text frame the width of the live area, beginning at Y: 2.875 in., 0.75 in. in height.

6. Command/Control-Shift-click the main text frame on this page to release it. Drag the top of the frame to 3.625 in. Link the frame you created in Step 5 to this frame.

7. Go to Page 2 and place the file yh_masthead.indd at X:0.5 in., Y: 8.2 in.

8. On Page 2, create a text frame filling the width of the first column, with a height of 1.3 in. Immediately below it, create a new text frame as follows:

    X: 0.5 in.      W: 3.667 in.
    Y: 2.125 in.    H: 6.0 in.

9. In the upper left and upper right of the column respectively, place the images "muire.tif" and "land.tif".

10. In between the pictures, type the words, "It's About Your Health" with each word on its own line. Format the type as ATC Laurel Medium 24/24, centered.

**FIGURE 1.61**

11. Save the document and close it.

## 4. Use the Template

When you use a template, it opens an untitled document to which you must assign a name. This protects the template against being overwritten.

1. Open the document your_health_6.indt from your WIP_01 folder.

   Notice that it is an untitled document.

2. Save the file as "your_health_ini.indd", where "ini" is your initials.

3. Go to Page 1, click in the narrow, three-column text frame you created, and place the file yh_grant.txt.

4. Create a graphic frame extending across the two right columns at Y: 4.825 in., with a height of 5.05 in.

   The space beneath the photo would normally hold a caption.

5. Assign a 0.0625-in. text wrap around the bounding box.

6. Place the photo researcher.tif in the frame you created in Step 4.

7. Click the out port to load the overset text.

8. Go to Page 3 (the middle page in the second group of pages) and link the overset text.

**FIGURE 1.62**

9. Save the file and close it.

With the template already created, it would be an easy matter to add several stories and pictures to this newsletter.

# CHALLENGE

Challenge exercises expand on, or are somewhat related to, skills presented in the lessons. Each exercise provides a brief introduction, followed by instructions presented in a numbered-step format that are not as detailed as those in the Skill Drill exercises. The first two exercises should be performed sequentially.

## 1. Create a Greeting Card Preset

You have been commissioned to create a set of greeting cards for an Irish gift shop. The first card will be for Christmas, and you will create subsequent cards on various themes, including weddings. All cards in the line will be the same size, so they will be able to use the same size envelope to realize cost savings.

1. Open the New Document Preset dialog box.
2. Name the preset "Irish Greetings".
3. Make the preset two non-facing pages, with no master text frame.
4. The width is 12.5 in. and the height is 6.25 in.
5. Assign the document two columns with a 0.25 in. gutter.

You aren't really going to use two columns, but this will virtually eliminate the need to measure.

6. Make all the margins 0.125 in.

7. Assign a standard bleed of 0.125 in.

    You don't need a bleed for all of these cards, but some may require one.

8. Click OK twice to accept the preset.

## 2. Create a Greeting Card in Two Languages

The gift shop's owner has discovered that items containing the Gaelic language are good sellers, even if most of the customers can't read or speak the language. You're going to create this card in both Gaelic and English.

1. Create a new document using the Irish Greetings preset.

2. Set up four layers named "Base", "English", "Gaelic", and "Generic". Position the Base layer at the bottom.

3. Place the front cover artwork, card_art.ai, on the Base layer, in the right-hand column of Page 1.

4. Place the logo art, irish_greetings.ai, centered and aligned to the bottom margin of the back cover.

5. Centered on the right-hand panel of the second page, type the greeting in a festive typeface of your choosing:

    "Season's Greetings
    Beannachtai na Nollag
    With our good wishes
    For a Joyous Christmas
    and a
    Happy New Year"

    We chose Adobe Caslon Pro, and used some of the alternate capital letters to give the greeting a festive look.

6. Switch to the English layer and type, in a size and style that you deem appropriate:

    "Merry
    Christmas
    to You"

7. Turn off the English layer and, in the same size and style, type the Gaelic greeting on its layer:

    "Nollaig
    Shona
    Dhuit"

8. Turn off the Gaelic layer and type the generic greeting on the Generic layer:

    "Season's
    Greetings"

9. Print the Base layer and any one of the other layers.

10. Save the document as "layered_card.indd" and close the file.

## 3. Manage a Document with Grids

Aligning text across a document is an art — especially if you want text in columns to align. You have learned that the baseline grid can be useful in doing this, but you must use a well thought-out plan for creating your layout. There are some elements that will simply not align properly, and you can exclude them from the cross-column alignment. In the following exercises, the layout for the article promoting the state of New Hampshire was reasonably well planned, but there are some challenges associated with effectively aligning the columns of text.

1. Open the document nh_promo.indd.
2. The headlines seem very spacey. Make the baseline grid visible to see what is happening.
3. The columns on the first page on the left align properly, so you can ignore them; however, the second and third columns are in alignment with one another, but not with the first.
4. Apply the H2 paragraph style to the headlines and turn on Baseline Grid Alignment.

    The headlines now align, but the text still doesn't.

5. Turn on the baseline alignment for the T style. Some serious spacing problems are evident.
6. Examine the H2 paragraph style. It is currently set up with 12-pt. leading, with 10 pt. above and 2 pt. below. Can the issue be resolved using the baseline alignment guides?
7. Turn off the baseline alignment for the H2 style.

    That fixes the problem by forcing the first lines of the two non-complying columns to align to the baseline, while allowing the H2 style (the sum of the space above plus space below equals 12 pt.) to function normally.

8. Go to Page 3. The bulleted text and the italic text in the second column have serious spacing problems as well.
9. Click in the bulleted text and turn the baseline alignment off. Since the italic text was based on the bulleted text style, the problem is solved for both.
10. Save the file.

## 4. Design Two Eight-Panel Brochures

Unlike the typical six-panel brochure, the eight-panel brochure can be set up in two different ways: the double-parallel fold and the barrel-fold (or roll-fold) brochure. The double-parallel folds in half (+1/16 in. for the outside panel), then in half again. The barrel-fold folds each panel inside one another with the two outside panels being of equal size. At issue when choosing which folding style to use is how you want to guide your readers along as they unfold the brochure. Both brochures begin with a standard 14 × 8.5-in. (legal-size) sheet of paper.

1. Create a new two-page, legal-size, landscape document with 0.25-in. margins and a 0.125-in. bleed.
2. To create a double-parallel fold brochure, begin by determining the size of each panel.
   The formula is $(x+1/32) + (x+1/32) + (x-1/32) + (x-1/32) = 14$ in., or $4x = 14$ in., so $x = 3.5$ in. ($1/32 = 0.03125$).
3. Set up fold marks for the first side. The two left panels are the wide panels; the right panels are the narrow ones. Remember, you can let the computer do the math.

4. Set up margins 0.25 in. to the left and right of each fold.

**FIGURE 1.63**

(x+1/32) 3.5313"   (x+1/32) 3.5313"   (x–1/32) 3.46875"   (x–1/32) 3.46875"

5. Set up the second page as a mirror image of the first one.
6. Save the document as "8_panel_parallel.indt" and close it.
7. Repeat Step 1 to begin creating a template for a barrel-fold brochure.
8. Determine the size of each panel. The two outside panels are full-size, and each successive panel must be 1/32 in. narrower than the previous one. The formula (which gets a bit ridiculous) is $(x+3/128) + (x+3/128) + ((x+3/128)-1/32) + (((x+3/128)-1/32)-1/32) = 14$ in. $(3/128=0.0234375)$ As before, $x=3.5$ in.
9. Set up fold marks for the first side. The two left panels are wide panels, the third panel is narrower, and the fourth panel is the narrowest.
10. Set up margins 0.25 in. to the left and right of each fold.

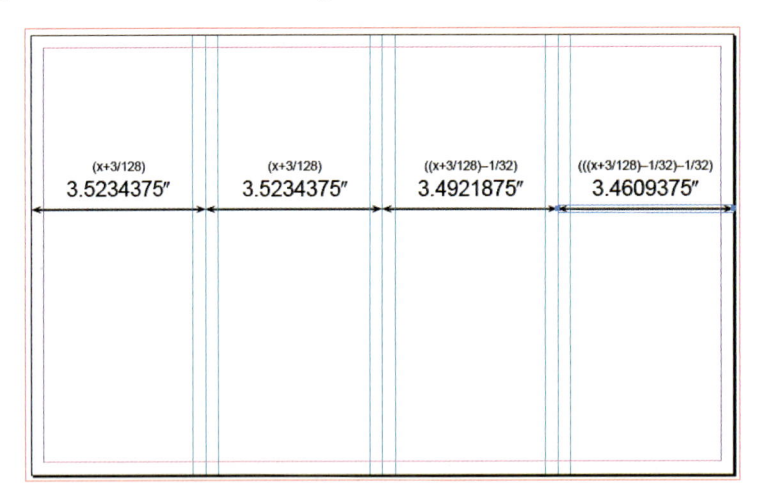

**FIGURE 1.64**

(x+3/128) 3.5234375"   (x+3/128) 3.5234375"   ((x+3/128)–1/32) 3.4921875"   (((x+3/128)–1/32)–1/32) 3.4609375"

11. Set up the second page as a mirror image of the first one.
12. Save the document as "8-panel_barrel.indt" and close it.

## 5. Repurpose a Document Layout

In the exercise within the project, you radically restructured a document from portrait to landscape orientation. That occurs most often when you repurpose a print page for the Web. It is more common, though, to have to change a document to fit a different-size printed page. A common example, which we present in this exercise, is to change an ad from a "standard" magazine-layout size to a smaller layout that would fit into a program booklet.

1. Open the document ohara.indd. This ad fits comfortably in a standard magazine page.

2. Drag ruler guides to the top and left of all frames

3. Enable the Layout Adjustment option.

4. Change the size of the document to 5 in. × 7.5 in., the size of a full-page ad in a program book.

   The document restructures itself. As you see, the process is far from perfect. The images are correct, but the type will have to be resized.

5. Resize the type, moving it as needed.

6. Save the file as "ohara_modified.indd" and close it.

**FIGURE 1.65**

# PORTFOLIO BUILDER

## CREATE A PRESENTATION FOLDER

As a graphic designer, you always want to offer a professional and visually appealing presentation when you submit your work for review by a potential employer or client. To accomplish that goal, you will design and produce a folder to contain your résumé and samples of your work.

A printer has provided die-cut templates for you to use when designing the layout. This file — folder.indt — is in the Project_01 folder. The templates show how the job will fold; solid lines indicate cuts, and dotted lines indicate folds.

To complete this project, use the following techniques:

- Create a document large enough to contain the entire template images.
- Design each side of the folder on a separate page of the layout.
- Place the template files on a separate layer, and create your design within the boundaries of the template.
- Include your name and contact information at least once on the inside of the folder and once on the outside of the folder.

PROJECT **2**

LEVEL **2**

# Building and Managing Long Documents

## OBJECTIVES

*In this project, you learn how to*

- Build documents in collaboration with others
- Create meaningful document sections
- Apply custom page-numbering systems
- Create jumps to continue content to non-contiguous frames
- Build libraries of common elements
- Build tables of contents and similar lists
- Build indexes
- Create a master document
- Merge multiple files into a book
- Print and export books

# WHY WOULD I DO THIS?

Building books, magazines, directories, and other long documents is a time-consuming process. In most cases, you will not be the only person working on the project, unless you have a very long lead time — and in the graphic arts industry that seldom happens. As we discussed in *Essentials for Design: InDesign Level 1*, illustrators, designers, editors, and compositors are vital whether documents are long or short. The project addresses the additional challenges associated with producing long documents — documents that may run into the hundreds of pages.

InDesign can, in theory, support a document with 9,999 pages. In practice, you would have to be crazy to attempt to produce such a tome; there are simply too many glitches that can happen when working on a computer. Imagine getting to page 8,000, then discovering that the file became corrupt! With the techniques described in this project, you can create documents with up to 99,999 pages. You will also learn how to create sections within documents. You will then learn how to link several files together into a common **book** document.

You will also learn how to use a **library** — these provide a consistent point of reference for often-used linked files, such as company logos or specific passages of text. Using libraries makes it easy for a group of designers to work together on a project or series of projects for a particular job. You will learn to coordinate text styles, masters, hyphenation and justification routines, and treatment of widows and orphans.

A number of tasks associated with longer documents are not particularly difficult to do, but they require attention to detail. You will learn to extract **notes** from running text and place them as footnotes. You will also learn to create **jumps** ("continued on" or "continued from" references) when you place text that is not contiguous in a layout.

InDesign allows you to create several types of **lists**. The most common list is a **table of contents**, but you could also create a list of advertisers, a list of categories such as you might find in a Chamber of Commerce directory, or any other type of list that you could define using a style. In addition to lists, you will create an **index**, which allows readers to reference important topics in your documents.

You have already worked with a number of InDesign features that are essential when creating and working with long documents, such as styles, masters, and templates. In this project, you will take what you have learned one large step farther.

# VISUAL SUMMARY

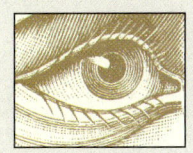

Building long documents allows you to work with several of InDesign's advanced features. While some never work with a document longer than 32 or 64 pages, others will regularly manage books containing several chapters of that length — books in excess of 1,000 pages are certainly not rare.

One of the tools you will find most valuable is InDesign's New Section dialog box. This Pages palette option allows you to start documents on even or odd pages and even combine several numbering schemes within a document.

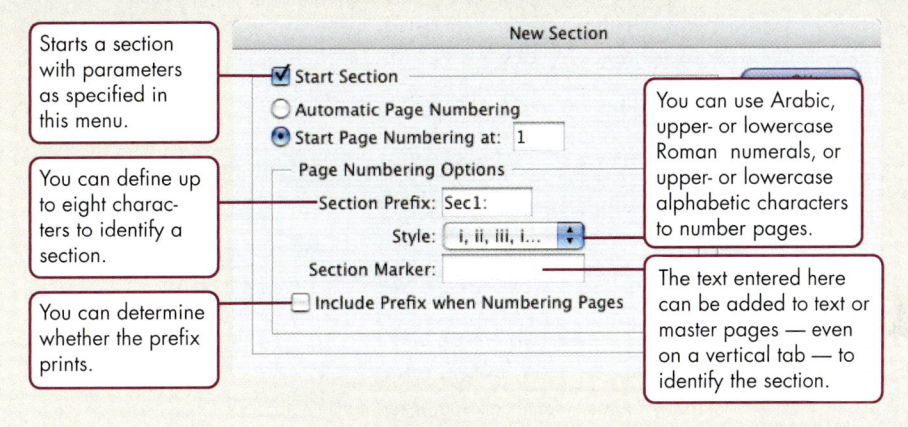

Starts a section with parameters as specified in this menu.

You can define up to eight characters to identify a section.

You can determine whether the prefix prints.

You can use Arabic, upper- or lowercase Roman numerals, or upper- or lowercase alphabetic characters to number pages.

The text entered here can be added to text or master pages — even on a vertical tab — to identify the section.

**FIGURE 2.1**

When you produce documents containing several articles, you will frequently want to continue an article several pages after it begins in the publication. Although most readers don't like being shuffled around, it may be necessary because of design considerations — perhaps there is not enough of the article to fill a full page, and the next article requires a full-page graphic, or perhaps advertising space was sold that requires specific placement.

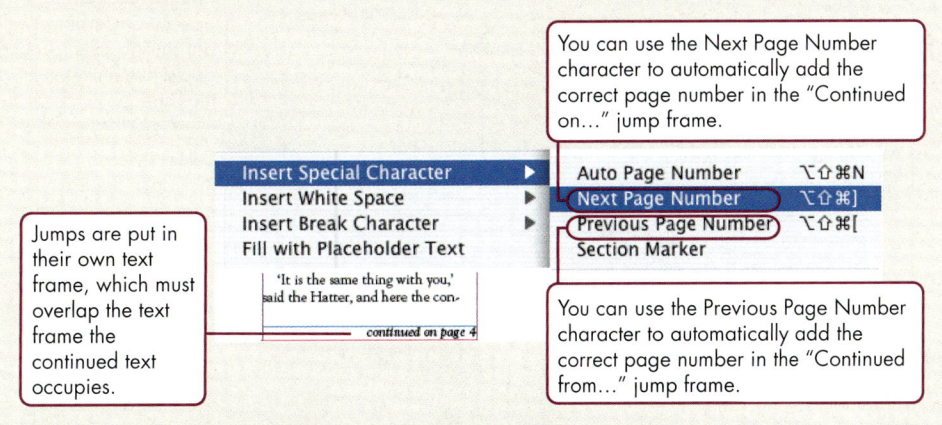

You can use the Next Page Number character to automatically add the correct page number in the "Continued on…" jump frame.

Jumps are put in their own text frame, which must overlap the text frame the continued text occupies.

You can use the Previous Page Number character to automatically add the correct page number in the "Continued from…" jump frame.

**FIGURE 2.2**

Libraries contain links to often-used artwork and text. They can be identified simply by file name, or they can also contain metadata — descriptions or keywords that will help you identify the image more easily than simply viewing the thumbnail.

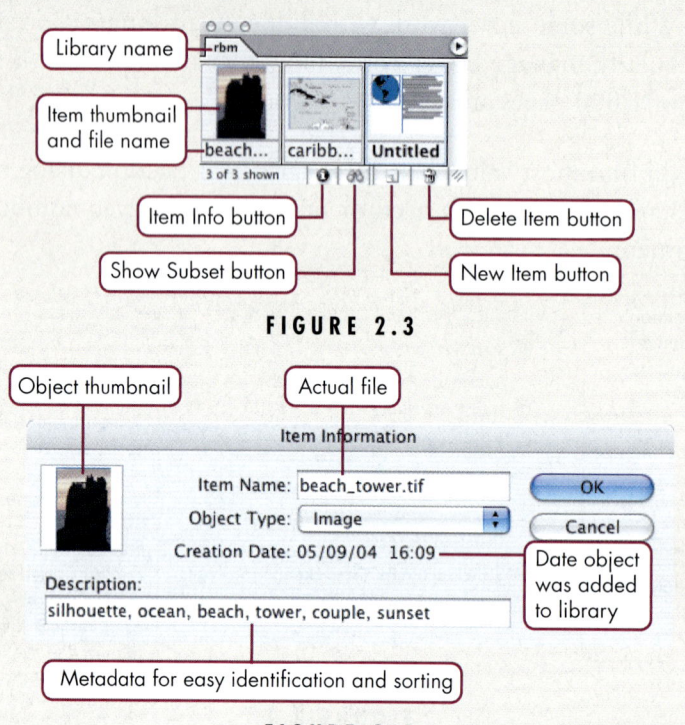

**FIGURE 2.3**

*Callouts:* Library name; Item thumbnail and file name; Item Info button; Show Subset button; Delete Item button; New Item button

**FIGURE 2.4**

*Callouts:* Object thumbnail; Actual file; Date object was added to library; Metadata for easy identification and sorting

The Table of Contents dialog box is the control center for the creation of all lists — not just tables of contents (TOCs). You select the document paragraph styles you want to include in the list, then choose formatting options such as the application of different paragraph and character styles to the list entry and page number.

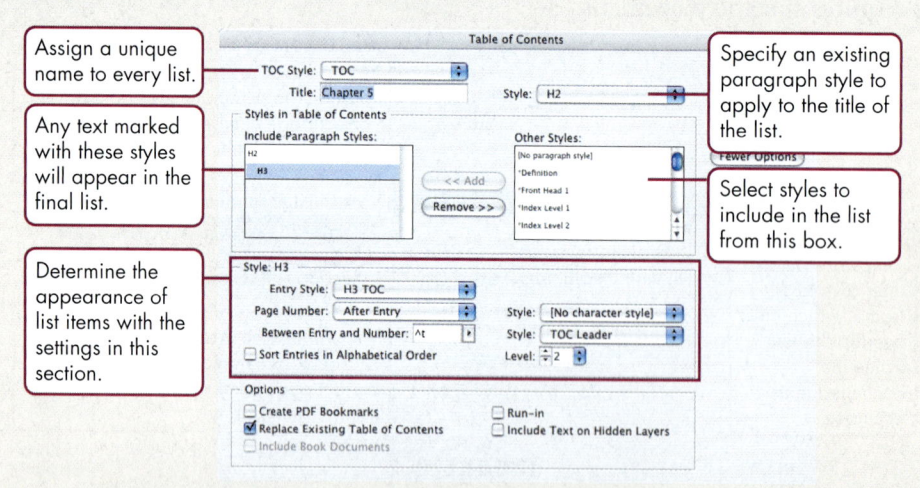

**FIGURE 2.5**

*Callouts:* Assign a unique name to every list. Any text marked with these styles will appear in the final list. Determine the appearance of list items with the settings in this section. Specify an existing paragraph style to apply to the title of the list. Select styles to include in the list from this box.

Indexes help readers find specific items of interest. For example, if your document deals with publishing programs, you might have references to database publishing, which could include references to XML and to various database programs; by looking up the subject in the index, readers can go directly to the topics that interest them.

The Index palette has two modes: topic and reference. In topic mode, only the indexed subjects are listed. In reference mode, indexed subjects and the pages on which they appear are listed. You can add new page references and other management functions, such as cross-referencing, to the index using the Options menu.

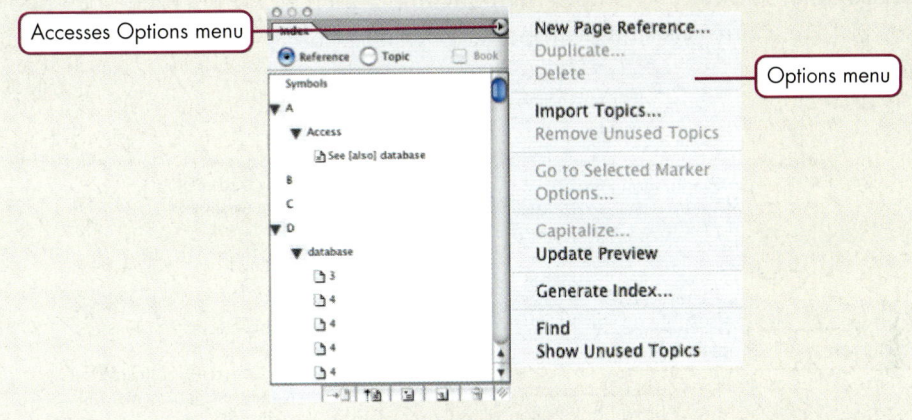

**FIGURE 2.6**

After all the topics are included in the index, you select Generate Index from the Index palette Options menu. Although the Generate Index dialog box is large and intimidating, it is very straightforward when you dissect it.

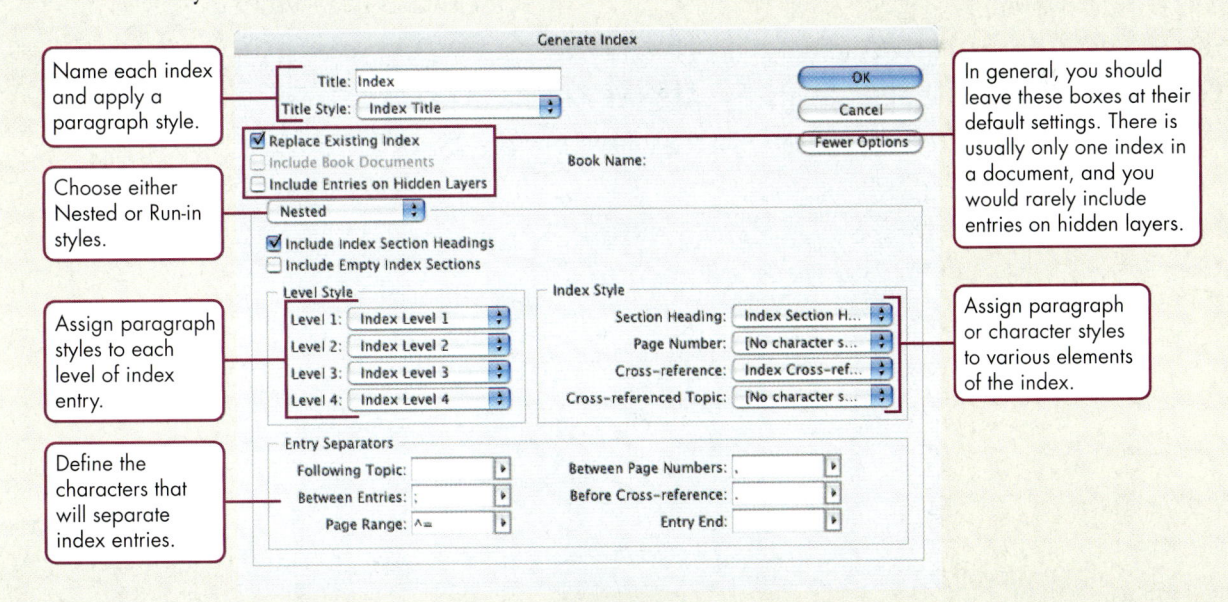

**FIGURE 2.7**

You can create master documents that hold all the needed styles and colors for documents for specific clients. These can be saved as templates — if you need the page geometry — or simply as documents from which you can import the styles and fonts. You will often populate these master documents by loading styles and colors from other documents.

When you combine multiple documents into a single document using InDesign's Book feature, all style and color elements are controlled by a master document. After you create a new book, the Book palette appears. Initially, the palette is empty; you need to add the chapter files that make up the entire book. By default, the first chapter you add to the book becomes the master document, but you can change this at any time. You can have more than one book open at a time; each open book has its own tab in the Book palette. Only one book can be active at any time.

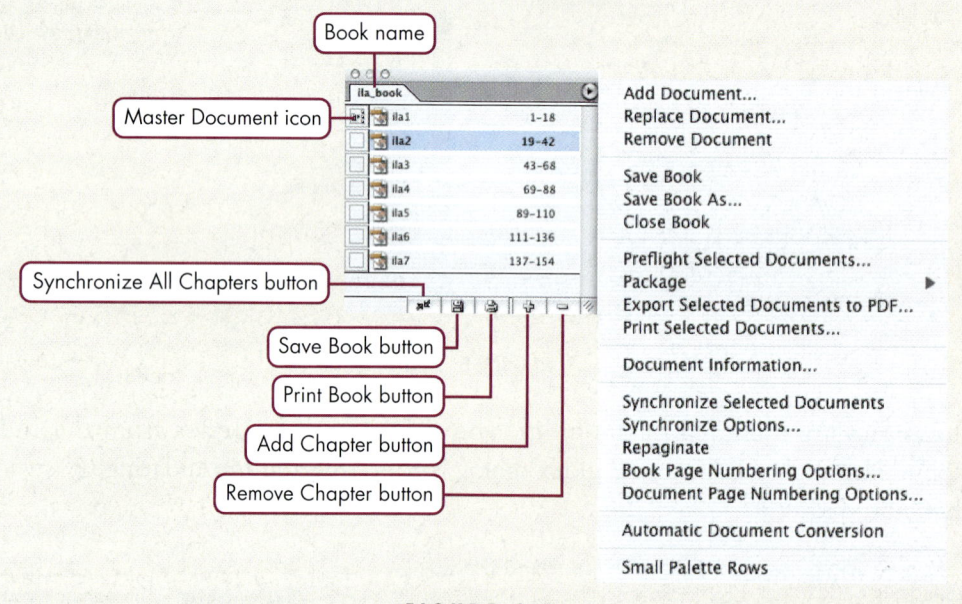

**FIGURE 2.8**

# LESSON 1  Creating Document Sections and Custom Numbering

Within a single file, discrete parts of documents may be defined as sections. Designers often create separate sections for a book's front matter (such as copyright and Library of Congress data, acknowledgments, table of contents, preface, and introduction), body (the main part of the book), and back matter (including appendices, index, and references). These three basic sections sometimes have independent numbering systems; for example, it's common to set page numbers for front matter in lowercase Roman numerals (i, ii, iii); page numbers for back matter, especially appendices, often have alphabetic prefixes (such as A-1, B-6).

To ensure that everyone is literally on the same page, you should set your Page Numbering preference (the View menu in General preferences) to Section Numbering. This view shows how each section in a document is numbered (for example, i, ii, iii, iv or 33, 34, 35, 36). A section may begin on any page, and continue numbering from that page number rather than numbering the pages from 1 through the last page.

## Create Document Sections and Numbering

**1**  **Open lwi_cookbook.indd.**

This is a 64-page document; there are different masters for the distinct divisions in the document, and there are numerous paragraph styles.

**2**  **Update links if prompted. Go to the Pages 2–3 spread.**

Pages 3 and 4 have blank space on which the table of contents will be placed.

**3**  **Set up the sections. Click the Page 3 icon in the Pages palette. From the Pages palette Options menu, select Numbering & Section Options.**

**4**  **Check the Start Section box, set the style to lowercase Roman numerals (i, ii, iii), start the page numbering at 1, then click OK.**

Be sure to leave the default section prefix. This allows you to have two sections that have the "same" number without introducing confusion. The prefix will not print unless you check the Include Prefix when Numbering Pages box.

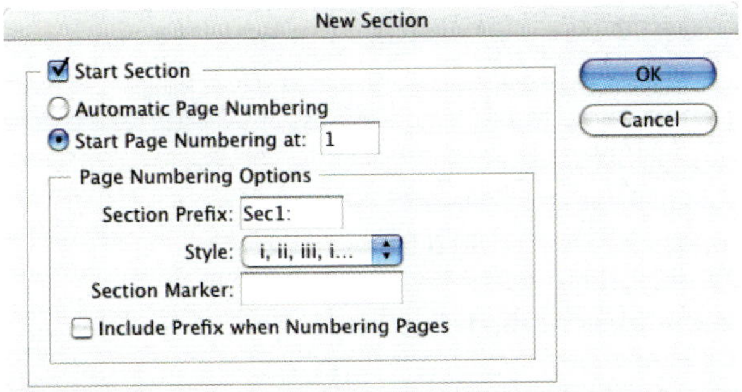

FIGURE 2.9

5. Highlight the Page v icon in the Pages palette. From Numbering & Section Options, start a new section using Arabic numerals (1, 2, 3), and start the page numbering at 1. Click OK.

**FIGURE 2.10**

6. Highlight the Page 53 icon in the Pages palette. Use the New Section dialog box to start a new section with the page numbering beginning at 1. In the Section Prefix text field, type "I – ". Click the Include Prefix when Numbering Pages box. In the Section Marker box, type the word "Index".

The index will be placed on these pages.

**FIGURE 2.11**

7. Navigate to the I-Master layout, and place the cursor in the text box in the bottom-right corner of the left page.

8. From the Type menu, select Insert Special Character>Section Marker.

The word Section appears in the text frame.

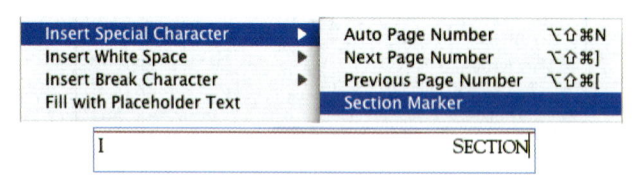

**FIGURE 2.12**

9. Insert another section marker to the left of the mirrored text box on the right page.

10. Navigate to Spread 2–3 in the "I" (index) section.

The word "Section" has been replaced by the word you typed as the Section Marker, "Index".

11. Save the document to your WIP_02 folder and close it.

## LESSON 2 Extracting and Placing Notes

*The Journal of Mind and Behavior* is an interdisciplinary publication published quarterly; it is heavily noted and referenced. Generally speaking, notes can be ***footnotes*** (at the "foot" or bottom of a page) or ***endnotes*** (at the end of a chapter or even at the end of the entire book). Footnotes, when created in text, are usually placed immediately following the text they reference.

When you work with notes, your first task is to locate the notes, then copy and paste them to their appropriate positions in the document. While endnotes can be placed in the normal text stream, footnotes should always be placed in their own text frame (otherwise they will flow incorrectly if text is added to or deleted from a page). Footnotes should be placed on the same two-page spread as the text that references them if that is at all possible. Sometimes extensive footnotes have to flow to the next page in the spread, or even to a following spread. Unless it is impossible to locate them differently, footnotes should never appear on the page preceding the text that references them. Because Adobe InDesign does not provide an automatic method for producing footnotes, it is important for you to learn how to place them onto the text page.

### Extract and Place Notes

**1** Open the document journal.indd. If it does not open to Page 1, go to Page 1.

*The Journal of Mind and Behavior* is a collection of articles with a number of references in the text. These references need to be placed at the bottom of each page so the reader doesn't have to flip to the end of the chapter to check them.

**2** With the Selection tool, double-click the N paragraph style. Notice the 9-pt. leading and 6-pt. space before paragraphs. Click Cancel to close the Paragraph Style Options dialog box.

**3** There are 11 lines of note text, requiring a 110-pt. space. Create a text frame 4.333 in. wide and 110 points high. Position it at X: 0.7083 in., Y: 6.2917 in. and select Text Wrap Around Bounding Box. Assign a top offset of 0.1528 in.

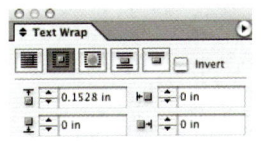

**FIGURE 2.13**

**4** Open the Text Frame Options dialog box (Object>Text Frame Options). Set the First Baseline Offset menu to Leading, and set the Top Inset Spacing field to 0.1528 in.

You can also open the Text Frame Options dialog box by pressing Command/Control-B.

**5** Cut and paste each paragraph of note text (with the paragraph style N — the type is considerably smaller) into the new text frame in the order they appear on the page.

**6** **In front of each footnote, type the reference number and a period ("3.", "4.") followed by an en space.**

Footnoting begins with 1, but this example begins in the middle of an article — footnotes 1 and 2 fell on earlier pages.

**7** **Apply the Note Number character style to each number you enter.**

This charactr style overrides the paragraph style (whic formats numbers in the text as Oldstyle numbers ), so the footnote numbers appear as standard "lining" figures.

**8** **Assign the N1 paragraph style to the first footnote paragraph.**

A horizontal rule is placed above the paragraph.

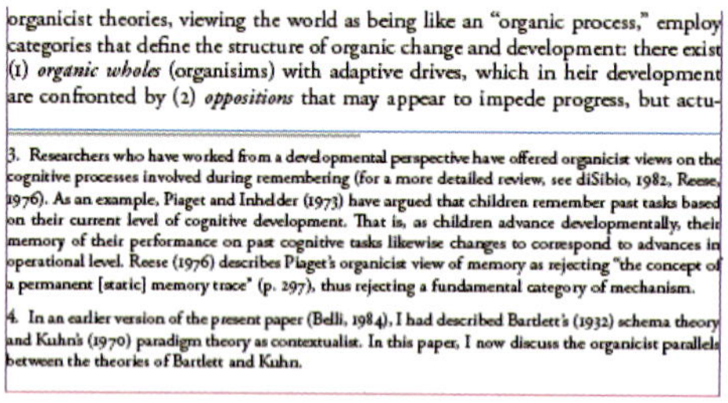

organicist theories, viewing the world as being like an "organic process," employ categories that define the structure of organic change and development: there exist (1) *organic wholes* (organisims) with adaptive drives, which in heir development are confronted by (2) *oppositions* that may appear to impede progress, but actu-

3. Researchers who have worked from a developmental perspective have offered organicist views on the cognitive processes involved during remembering (for a more detailed review, see diSibio, 1982, Reese, 1976). As an example, Piaget and Inhelder (1973) have argued that children remember past tasks based on their current level of cognitive development. That is, as children advance developmentally, their memory of their performance on past cognitive tasks likewise changes to correspond to advances in operational level. Reese (1976) describes Piaget's organicist view of memory as rejecting "the concept of a permanent [static] memory trace" (p. 297), thus rejecting a fundamental category of mechanism.

4. In an earlier version of the present paper (Belli, 1984), I had described Bartlett's (1932) schema theory and Kuhn's (1970) paradigm theory as contextualist. In this paper, I now discuss the organicist parallels between the theories of Bartlett and Kuhn.

**FIGURE 2.14**

**9** **Save the document and close it.**

## LESSON 3 Creating Jumps

When you are working with documents such as newspapers, newsletters, and magazines, it's often necessary to carry an article one or more pages ahead. If the article continues on the next page, no notation is necessary; when the article jumps ahead several pages, however, a ***jump*** or "continued on" line is placed where the article leaves off and a "continued from" line is placed where the article picks up again. With InDesign, you can insert jump lines semi-automatically; InDesign also automatically updates them if pages or stories are moved.

An InDesign jump line consists of a small text frame that touches a frame containing a story that is continued on or from another page. The jump line (or more properly, the jump frame) can include any text, but it must include a special character referring to the next or previous page number. You can insert these characters with either the Type>Insert Special Character>Next Page Number/Previous Page Number menu commands, or from the contextual menu that appears by Control/right-clicking when the Type tool is active in the jump frame.

If pages are inserted or deleted, or if a continued story is moved elsewhere, the jump to/from page number updates automatically, as long as the entire story remains threaded.

## Create Jumps

**1** **Open daily_monsoon.indd.**

The text in this document is already threaded; all you need to do is add the jumps.

**2** **At the bottom of the third column, create a text frame the width of the column at X: 5.6389 in., Y: 10.111 in., with a height of 0.1389 in.**

**3** **If the Text Wrap palette is not already visible, choose Window>Type & Tables>Text Wrap to activate it. Assign a Text Wrap Around Bounding Box with a 13-pt. top offset.**

You can also press Command-Option-W (Macintosh) or Control-Alt-W (Windows) to open the Text Wrap palette.

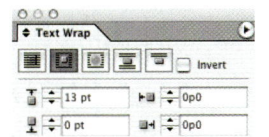

FIGURE 2.15

**4** **Click the Type tool in the frame and select the Jump To paragraph style. Type "continued on page [space]".**

**5** **Control/right-click with the mouse to bring up the contextual menu.**

**6** **Choose Insert Special Character>Next Page Number.**

InDesign inserts the number "4", the page onto which the text has been flowed.

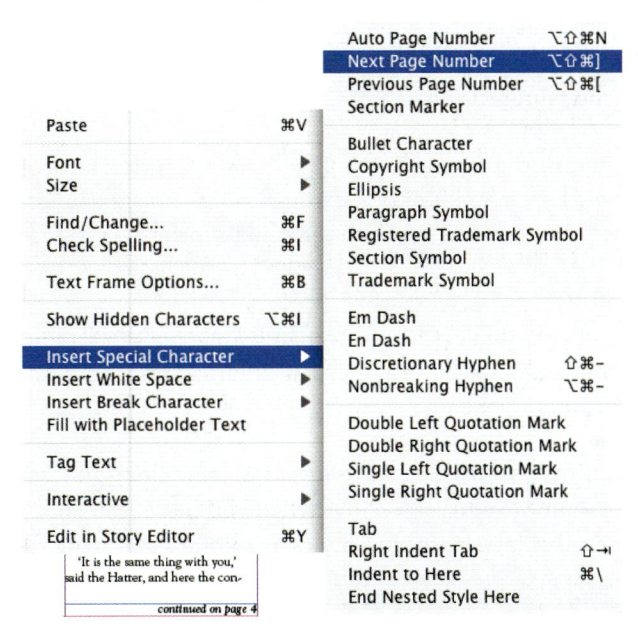

FIGURE 2.16

**7** Go to Page 4. At the top of the upper-left column create a text frame the width of the column, with a height of 10 pt.

**8** Assign a Text Wrap Around Bounding Box with a 16-pt. bottom offset.

**9** Click the Type tool in the frame and apply the Jump From paragraph style. Type "continued from page [space]".

**10** Control/right-click to bring up the contextual menu. Select Insert Special Character>Previous Page Number.

InDesign inserts the number "1", the page from which the text has been flowed.

**11** From the Pages palette, add two pages before Page 4.

**12** Return to Page 1 and scroll to the bottom right to view the updated numbering.

InDesign has updated the jump line to reflect that the text now continues on Page 6.

**13** Save the document and close it.

## LESSON 4 Building Libraries

InDesign library files act as containers for placed page elements, such as text, images, PDF and EPS art, grouped objects, and artwork created in InDesign, as well as for structural elements such as ruler and column guides. Libraries can help with multiple-file projects that share common elements and structural items — any item in a library can be placed into any open document with its link intact. If an image referenced in a library is ever updated, then the library is updated the next time it is opened, just like a regular InDesign document. Large images aren't stored in the library file, but text and smaller items are copied and stored within the library file, rather than linked from the source document.

Although you can replicate some of the functionality of a library by storing images and other objects in a regular document that acts as a holding tank, a library lets you add descriptions or keywords (referred to as ***metadata*** — data about data) to objects. You can organize the Library palette to display or hide objects that meet a set of search criteria.

Libraries are opened with the standard File>Open command. You can open multiple libraries simultaneously; the Library palette displays a separate tab for each. Open libraries can be shown or hidden by choosing the name of the library from the Windows menu.

Items added to a library retain their formatting attributes; for example, if you scale an image to 50% before adding it to the library, then the image remains at 50% when you place it in another document. Library items also retain text formatting, as well as layer positions. Styles in a library that have the same names as styles in the open target document are not copied, but styles with unique names are added to the target document's appropriate style palettes.

## Create and Populate a Library

**1** Open the document library.indt.

**2** Choose File>New>Library and save it as [your initials].

You are immediately prompted to save the library. InDesign automatically adds the file extension ".indl".

You will add four items to the library using a different method for each.

**3** Drag the tower image to the open Library palette.

That's all you need to do to place a link to the towers image in the library. A small thumbnail and the file name appear in the Library palette.

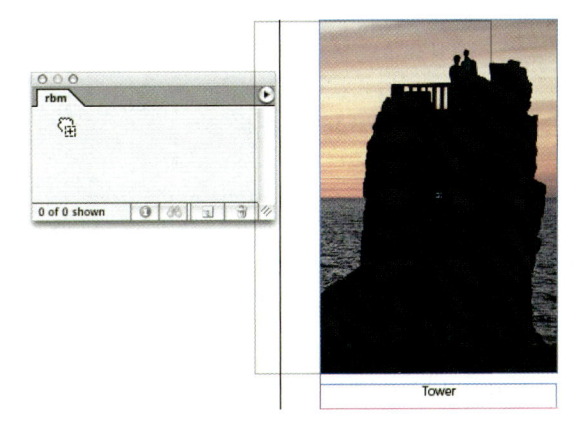

FIGURE 2.17

**4** Delete the tower image by clicking the Delete Item button (with the trashcan icon) at the bottom of the palette; answer Yes when asked for confirmation.

**5** Repeat Step 3, except hold the Option/Alt key while dragging the image.

This adds the tower image to the library, and also opens the Item Information dialog box, where you can add metadata.

**6** Type "silhouette, ocean, beach, tower, couple, sunset" in the Description field, then click OK.

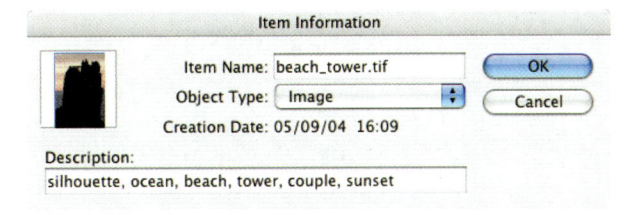

FIGURE 2.18

**7** Select the Caribbean image and click the New Item button at the bottom of the Library palette to add it.

If you press the Option/Alt key as you click the New Item button, the Item Information dialog box opens.

**8** Scale the western.eps graphic to 150%. Select it, then Shift-click the typography article. Choose Add Item from the Library palette Options menu.

Both items are added to the library as a single, ungrouped, untitled object. Pressing the Option/Alt key while making the menu selection opens the Item Information dialog box.

**9** Close the file without saving.

The library remains open.

## Place Library Items

**1** Create a new document using the default settings.

**2** Drag an item out of the library onto the document page.

**3** Select the western.eps graphic and the typography article group in the library; Shift-click to select the second item. Drag them both onto the document page.

Items from the library are placed on the document page and a link is established to the original object. The graphic retains its scaling and the two objects retain their relative positions when they are placed on the target page.

**4** Delete the items you just placed, then place them again using the Place Item(s) command in the Library palette Options menu.

**5** Leave the document open for the next exercise.

## Set Library Options

**1** Open the library file libopts.indl. Choose Thumbnails or List View, whichever you prefer, from the Library palette menu.

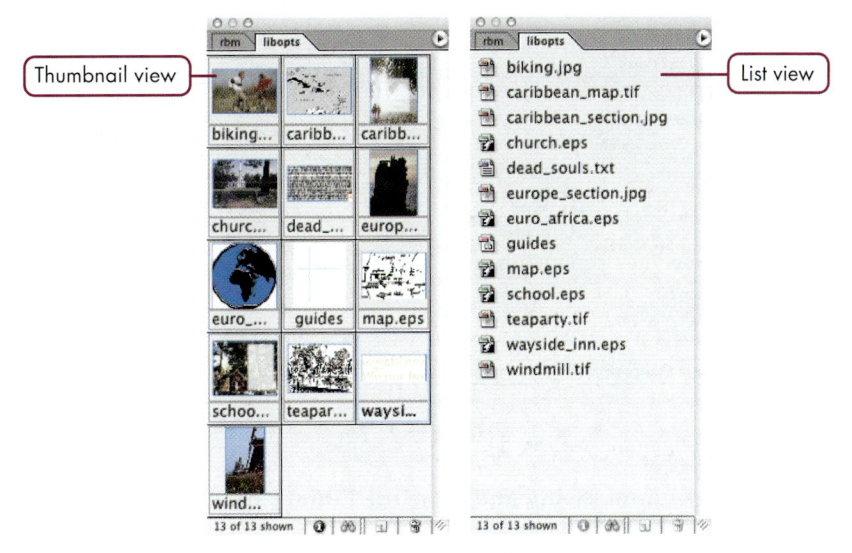

**FIGURE 2.19**

**2** Click the Show Subset button at the bottom of the palette, or choose Show Subset from the Options menu.

**3** Choose Object Type, Equal, and EPS from the appropriate Parameters menus, then click OK.

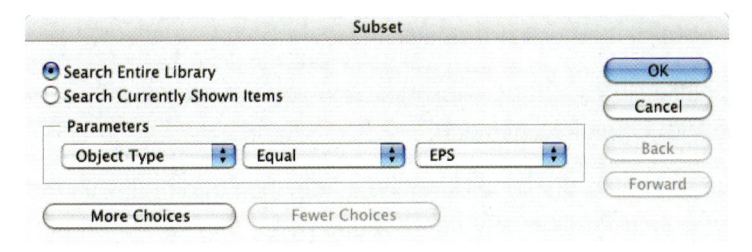

**FIGURE 2.20**

This subset shows only EPS files.

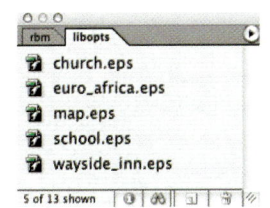

**FIGURE 2.21**

**4** Choose Show All from the palette's Options menu, then click the Show Subset button again. Click the More Choices button twice.

Clicking this button doesn't give you different options, but it does give you the ability to conduct more focused searches, which is useful for large InDesign libraries. Experiment with these extra search parameters.

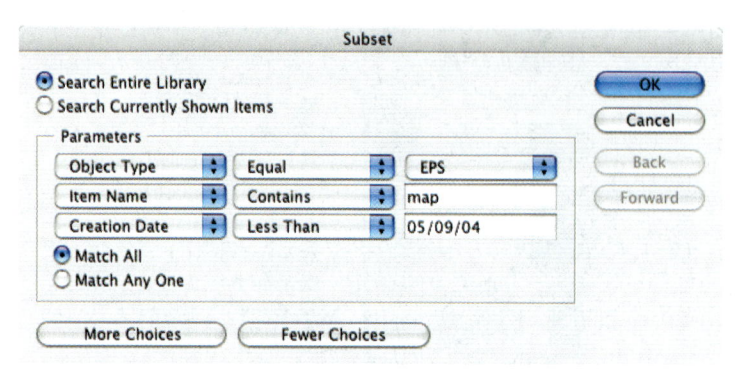

**FIGURE 2.22**

**5** Close the document without saving and close the Library palette to close the library.

## To Extend Your Knowledge...

### MORE ABOUT LIBRARIES

You can search through an already selected subset by clicking the Search Currently Shown Items button. The Match All option shows only items that meet all the parameters; the Match Any One option shows any item that meets at least one parameter.

Closing the Library palette closes all open libraries. You can open a recently closed library by choosing its name from the File>Open Recent menu.

You can add ruler guides to a library by clicking the guide, then adding it with the New Item button. To add multiple guides, they must be the only items on the page; they are added to the library using the Add All Items On Page option.

## LESSON 5  Building Lists

Professional page-layout programs have largely automated the process of document production. Before these tools became available, tables of contents, indexes, and other types of lists were manually (and laboriously) created from page proofs by examining each page and writing down the appropriate list entries and page numbers. The lists were assembled, typeset, and merged with the rest of the document. The process was extremely time-consuming, required precise attention to detail (as does the process today), and was prone to error — especially if the book was ever revised.

InDesign's tools automate the process of creating various lists, including tables of contents. A table of contents (TOC) is essentially a list of items based on paragraph styles and referenced by page numbers. The items can be subject headings, names, captions, or any other text marked with a particular paragraph style. For example, you could create a table of illustrations based on the Caption paragraph style. As another example, you might create a table of contents based on several levels of subject headings.

You can create special styles for formatting lists. If you plan your project carefully, you can predefine the appearance of different lists of document items. For example, you can define a style named "TOC1" that specifies the formatting of all TOC entries based on the Heading 1 style.

An InDesign list is created in an unthreaded, separate text frame. Although a list frame can be threaded to another to create a long list, it should never be threaded with any main document frames. The contents of a list frame are deleted when you regenerate the list, so if you thread the list frame to a document frame, it would be easy to accidentally delete the contents of the entire document.

You should not make changes to a generated list, because the process is completely automated and any changes will be lost when the list is regenerated. Instead, you should edit the original document paragraphs that are marked with the styles included in the list, then regenerate the list. The same applies to formatting — it's better to create and edit any special list styles you want to use instead of manually formatting the contents of the list.

### Create a Table of Contents

**1**  **Open aia5.indd.**

This is a chapter from Against The Clock's *Adobe Illustrator: Advanced Digital Illustration*; the images have been removed to speed performance.

**2**  **Insert two pages before Page 89, based on the L-Front Matter master.**

The first new page will hold the new TOC. The second will remain blank, but it could be used, for example, to hold a list of illustrations.

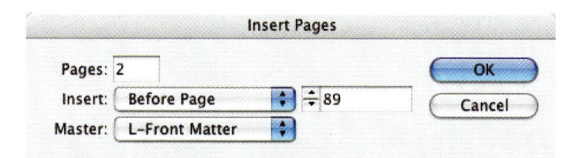

**FIGURE 2.23**

**3** In the Paragraph Styles palette, select the H2 style and choose Duplicate Style from the Options menu. Rename the style "H2 TOC". In the Basic Character Formats pane, change the type size to 12 pt. with 14-pt. leading. In the Tabs pane, set a right tab at 7.1389 in. with a Period-Space leader, and then click OK.

These new paragraph styles are intended for use only to format the elements of the final TOC.

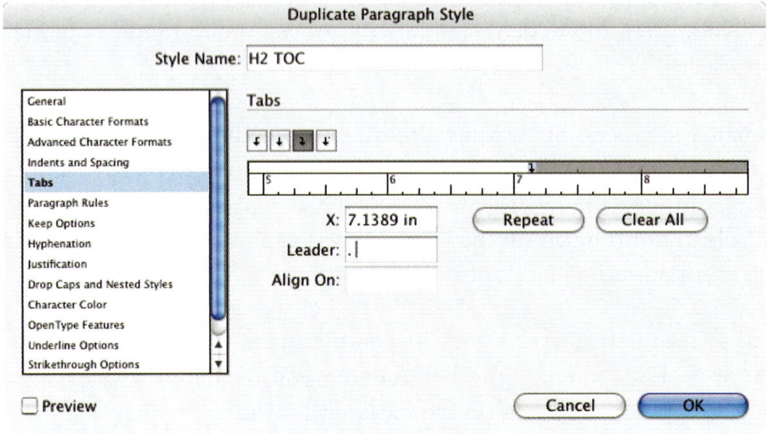

**FIGURE 2.24**

**4** Duplicate the H3 style, rename it "H3 TOC" and change the type style to ATC Oak Normal. Apply the same right-tab settings as in H2 TOC, then click OK.

**5** Create a character style named "TOC Leader" defined as 10/14 ATC Oak Normal.

**6** Open the TOC dialog box by choosing Layout>Table of Contents. Click the More Options button.

**7** Highlight the H2 style (not the H2 TOC style) in the Other Styles list, and click Add. Do the same for H3.

**8** Highlight the H2 style in the Include Paragraph Styles list. In the Style H2 area, select H2 TOC in the Entry Style menu. Select TOC Leader in the Between Entry and Number Style menu. Accept the default setting of 1 in the Level menu.

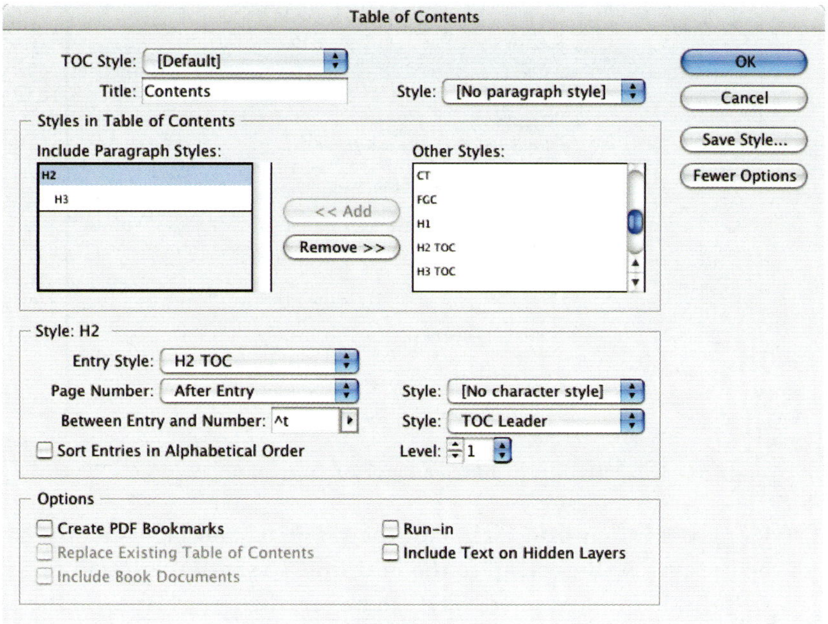

**FIGURE 2.25**

**9** Highlight H3 in the Include Paragraph Styles list; select H3 TOC as its entry style, and assign the TOC Leader style with a level of 2.

**10** In the Title field, type "Chapter 5" and assign it the H2 style.

**11** Click the Save Style button, name the TOC style "TOC", then click OK.

**FIGURE 2.26**

**12** Click OK in the TOC dialog box to generate the list.

The Loaded Text icon is now ready to be placed.

**13** If you aren't already on Page 1, go there. Make sure guides and frame edges are visible. The L-Front Matter master has a text frame on it, so click the Loaded Text icon within that frame on Page 1 to place the new TOC.

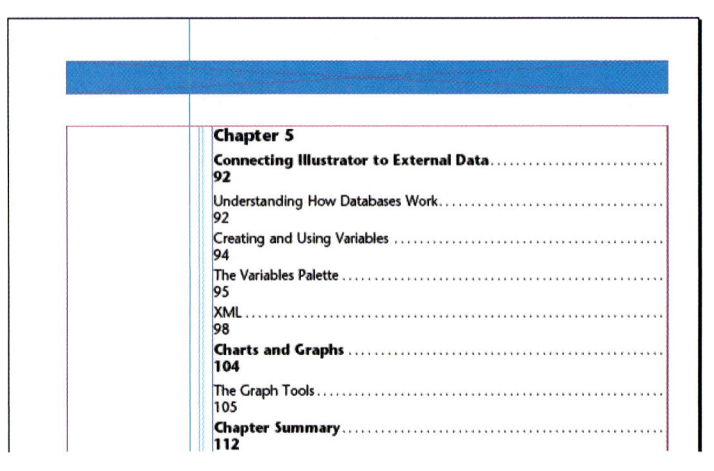

**FIGURE 2.27**

**14** The TOC styles need a little work. First, edit the H2 TOC and H3 TOC styles to adjust the right tab so the list entries don't wrap to the next line. Reset the right tab to 5.375 in. for both styles. Add a 0.25-in. left indent to H3 TOC to better distinguish it from the H2 TOC heading.

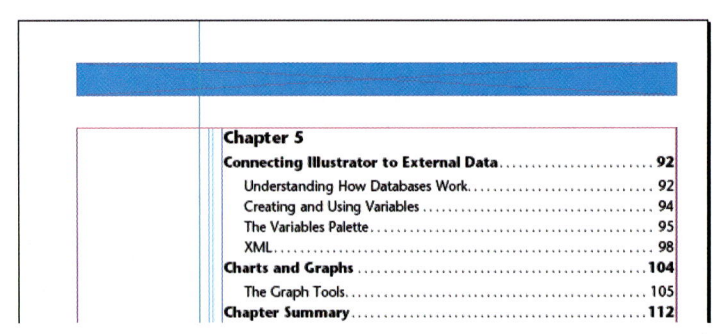

**FIGURE 2.28**

**15** Save the document to your WIP_02 folder, keeping the same name; you'll use it again later.

## *To Extend Your Knowledge...*

### EDITING TOC STYLES

You can save TOC styles from within the TOC dialog box. To manage or further edit TOC styles, you can simply choose Layout>Table of Contents Styles. Each style's settings are summarized below the list of available TOC styles. You can create a new TOC style or make any needed changes. You can also import TOC styles from other InDesign documents.

If you want the page numbers to have a different style than the rest of the TOC entry, you can create a character style and select it in the Page Number Style menu.

## LESSON 6  Building Indexes

Before sophisticated page-layout software became available, indexes were usually created by adding the appropriate page numbers to a list of words written on index cards, which could then be shuffled into alphabetic order. Creating indexes with InDesign, however, involves assigning special markers to words or terms throughout the electronic document with the Index palette. This is still a laborious process, but it's much better than the old way.

Regardless of the method you use, there is always a *topic*, typically one or more words, and a *reference*, which is usually the page number on which the topic is found. There can also be *cross-references* to other topics.

Index entries can appear once, or they can appear many times in a document; no matter how often a term appears, you can choose to add every occurrence to the index automatically. InDesign tracks the position of each entry as pages are added, deleted, or moved. You can create a single index that includes reference terms from all the linked documents in a book project.

### Create a Simple Index

1. If it is not already open, open aia5.indd.

2. Go to Page 92, where the main text begins.

3. Your client has given you a list of topics that she wants included in the index: database, record, fields, variable, XML, SVG, ODBC, data set, HTML, fileref, Access, Excel, FileMaker

4. Locate the word "XML" in the first sidebar of the page. Using the Type tool, double-click the word to select it.

5. Open the Index palette (Window>Type & Tables>Index); then choose New Page Reference from the palette's Options menu to open the New Page Reference dialog box. When it appears, click the Add All button on the right. This locates every occurrence of the word "XML" within the document. Scroll through the list at the bottom of the dialog box to "X", where the new reference appears. Click Done.

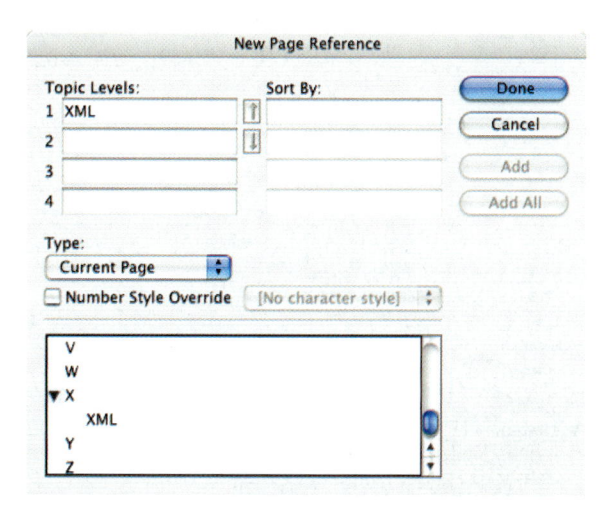

FIGURE 2.29

**6** In the Index palette, scroll down to view all the page numbers that are included in the XML reference.

The word "XML" is added to the list, along with placeholders for the entire alphabet. The page numbers here are not necessarily in order, but they will be properly ordered in the final index; page numbers will not be duplicated.

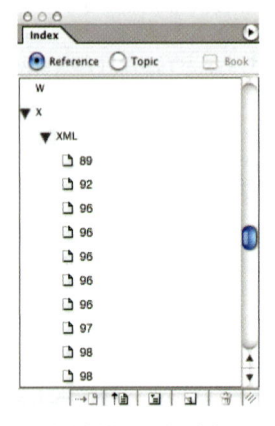

FIGURE 2.30

**7** Use the Edit>Find/Change command to locate the rest of the topics that your client identified. In each case, use the Add All option when creating a new page reference.

**8** After you have added all the topics, save the document. Go to the last page, and add another page based on the I-Index Opener master.

**9** Click the Generate Index button at the bottom of the Index palette. Click the More Options button, if necessary.

The large, somewhat intimidating Generate Index dialog box appears.

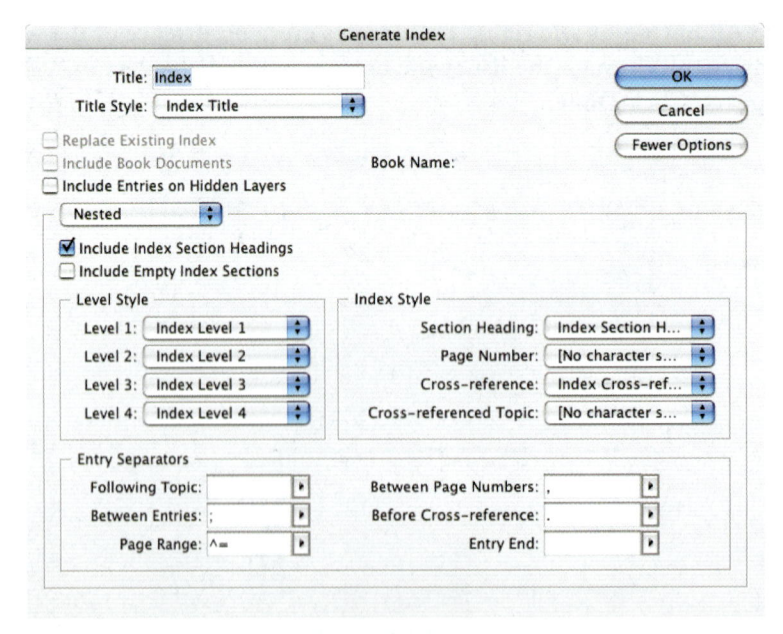

FIGURE 2.31

**10** Click OK to generate the index.

For now, you will leave all of the options at their default settings.

**11** Click the Loaded Text icon in the first column of the page you just created to place the index.

**Index**

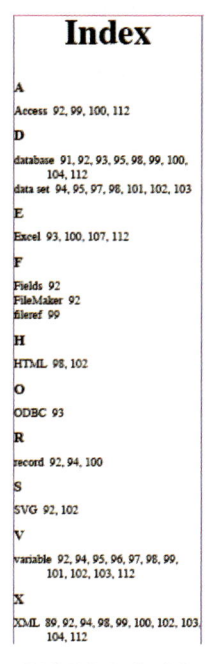

A
Access 92, 99, 100, 112
D
database 91, 92, 93, 95, 98, 99, 100, 104, 112
data set 94, 95, 97, 98, 101, 102, 103
E
Excel 93, 100, 107, 112
F
Fields 92
FileMaker 92
fileref 99
H
HTML 98, 102
O
ODBC 93
R
record 92, 94, 100
S
SVG 92, 102
V
variable 92, 94, 95, 96, 97, 98, 99, 101, 102, 103, 112
X
XML 89, 92, 94, 98, 99, 100, 102, 103, 104, 112

**FIGURE 2.32**

**12** Save the file and leave it open for the next exercise.

## Edit the Index

Although InDesign's default settings create a perfectly usable index, you can customize the appearance of the final index by adjusting settings such as the format of the page number references and the order in which the index terms are sorted. Index entries can refer to ranges of pages instead of one or more individual pages (for example, "XML 5–8" instead of "XML 5, 6, 7, 8").

**1** In the open aia5.indd file, scroll down to the "X" entries in the Index palette.

You're going to edit the XML entry.

**2** Highlight the Page 98 icon and choose Page Reference Options from the Index palette Options menu.

Alternately, you could double-click the Page 98 icon.

**Project 2** Building and Managing Long Documents

**3** In the Type menu, select For Next # of Pages and enter "7" in the Number field. Click OK and scroll down to the XML entry.

A range entry for Pages 98–104 has been added.

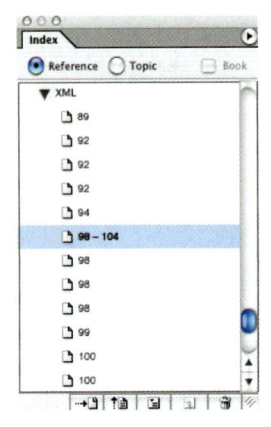

FIGURE 2.33

**4** Re-generate the index.

Individual pages in this range have been replaced by the page range 98–104.

**5** Return to the Index palette and delete the topics Access, Excel, and FileMaker by choosing Delete Topics from the Options menu.

**6** Using the Type tool, select any word in the layout text. From the Index palette Options menu, select New Page Reference; in the Symbols window at the bottom, select the word "database" as the first-level entry.

**7** Type "Access" in the Topic Level 2 field, then click the Add button.

Access is added as a second-level entry under the primary entry "database".

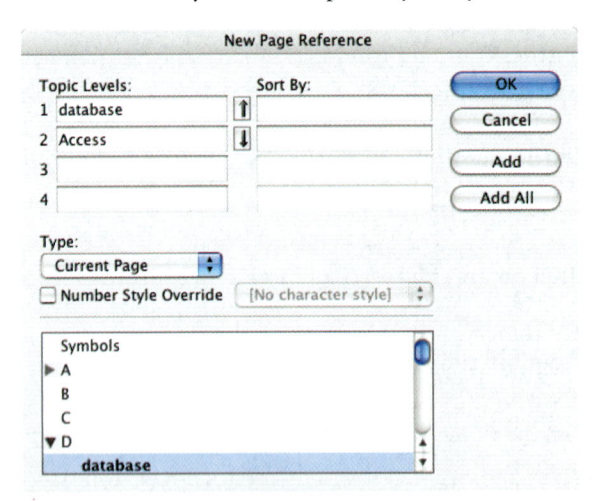

FIGURE 2.34

**8** Repeat Step 7 for the words "Excel" and "FileMaker".

**9** Generate the index.

All the database programs now show up as secondary to the main topic "database".

**Index**

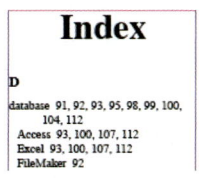

D
database 91, 92, 93, 95, 98, 99, 100, 104, 112
   Access 93, 100, 107, 112
   Excel 93, 100, 107, 112
   FileMaker 92

**FIGURE 2.35**

**10** Save the file and leave it open.

## To Extend Your Knowledge...

### RANGES OF INDEX ENTRIES

InDesign offers a number of range selectors:

**To Next Style Change** continues the range until a new paragraph style is encountered.

**To Next Use of Style** continues the range until the next use of the current style is encountered.

**To End of Story** continues the range until the end of the current text thread.

**To End of Document** continues the range until the last page of the document.

**To End of Section** continues the range until a new section begins.

**For Next # of Paragraphs** and **For Next # of Pages** allows you to specify the number of paragraphs or pages for which the range extends.

**Suppress Page Range** turns off the range feature.

### SORT ORDER AND REFERENCE ORDER

When indexing terms such as acronyms and expressions that begin with articles, you can double-click the term in the Index palette, then type the sort word in the Topic Options dialog box Sort By field. You might, for example, want to sort XML under "extensible" since it is an acronym for "Extensible Markup Language."

You can also change the reference order, as is often done with proper names — you would want "Mark Twain" to be sorted as "Twain, Mark." To do this, in the Index palette, select Topic, then double-click a topic to edit. Edit the topic as desired, then click OK.

## Create Cross-references

**1** Continue in the open document.

You're going to add cross-references that will make it easier for readers to find specific information.

**2** In the Index palette, click the Reference button and choose New Cross-reference from the Options menu.

**3** Type the word "Access" in the first Topic Level field, then type "database" in the Referenced field. Make sure See [also] is selected in the Type menu.

The options available are See, See [also], See herein, See also herein, and [Custom Cross Reference], which allows you to create your own cross-reference term. When See [also] is selected, entries with page number or subentities are assigned "See also" and those without page numbers or subentities appear as "See."

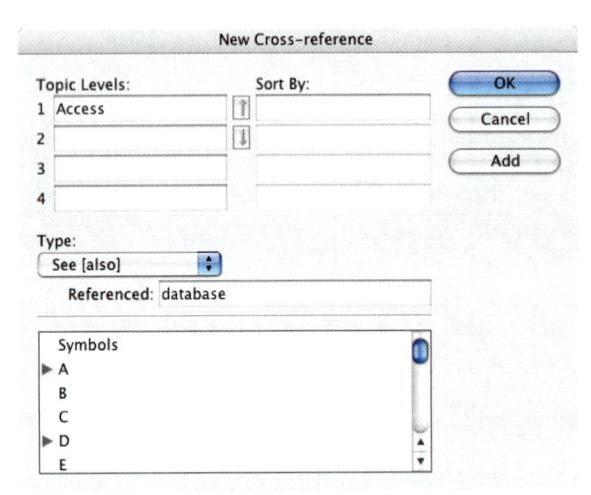

**FIGURE 2.36**

**4** Click the Add button, and leave the window open.

Access is added as a first-level topic that is cross-referenced to the database topic.

**5** In the first Topic Level field, type "Excel" and click Add, then type "FileMaker" and click Add.

Both topics are added and cross-referenced to the database topic.

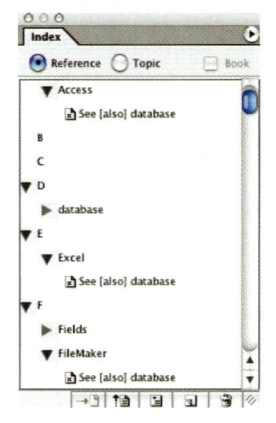

FIGURE 2.37

**6** Generate the index again.

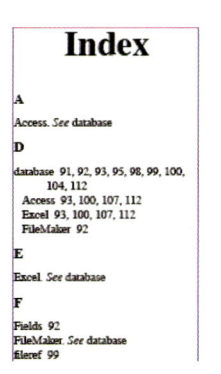

FIGURE 2.38

**7** Save and close the file.

## LESSON 7  Creating a Master Book Document

You have already applied the principles of building a master document, both in Project 1 and earlier in this project. Master documents are useful when you wish to maintain consistency from document to document. If you want to create documents that share the same layout, then you should develop a template that includes fonts, colors, styles, and page geometry. If you simply need to maintain consistency in styles, colors, and fonts, however, then you can create a master document instead.

Master documents provide consistency when you are working with long, multiple-file publications (such as a book with many chapters), or groups of documents that must adhere to a common set of specifications (such as a series of newsletters for the same client). A master document isn't a special kind of file; it's a plain InDesign document or template.

## Import Styles

**1** Create a new document using any page settings you like.

The InDesign defaults are fine. Unlike templates, master documents aren't used to define page geometry settings.

**2** From the Paragraph Styles palette Options menu, choose Load Paragraph Styles.

**FIGURE 2.39**

**3** From your WIP_02 folder, select the aia5.indd document you worked on earlier in this project, then click Open.

All the paragraph styles in the aia5.indd file are imported into the new, untitled document.

**4** Choose Edit>Undo, and repeat Step 2, only this time choose Load All Styles.

Both paragraph and character styles are loaded into the current document. This function works the same way from the Character Styles palette.

**5** Save the document as "master.indd" in your WIP_02 folder and leave it open for the next exercise.

## *To Extend Your Knowledge...*

### SELECTING STYLES TO IMPORT

You can't pick and choose which styles you will import (short of importing only paragraph or only character styles). All styles in the selected document are imported into the current, open document. You can delete unwanted or unused styles as you wish after importing.

## Import Swatches

Importing color and gradient swatches involves a different technique than importing styles. You can import swatches from other InDesign documents, Adobe Illustrator 8 documents, and EPS files created in Adobe Illustrator 8.

**1** In the open document, master.indd, choose Select All Unused from the Swatches palette Options menu, then delete the selected swatches.

**2** Choose New Color Swatch from the Options menu. In the dialog box that appears, choose Other Library from the Color Mode menu.

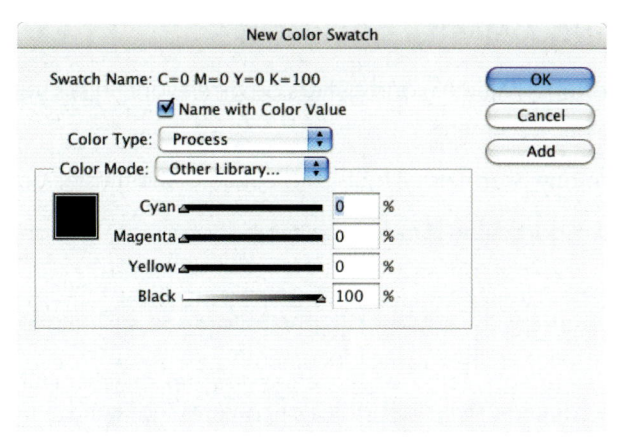

**FIGURE 2.40**

**3** In the new dialog box that appears, select bugswatch.indd and click Open.

All available color swatches from the bugswatch file are listed in the New Color Swatch dialog box.

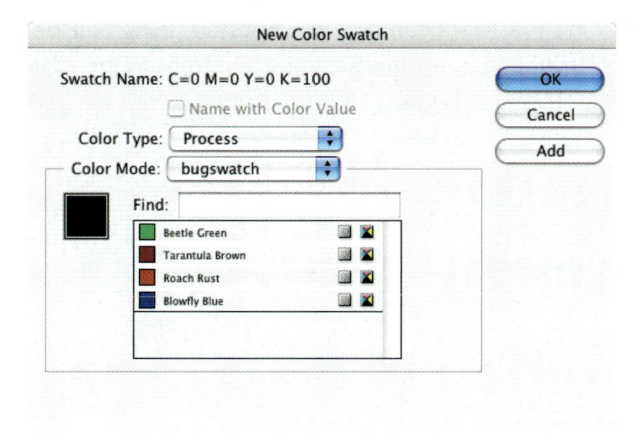

**FIGURE 2.41**

**4** Highlight any swatch in the dialog box (pick your favorite bug) and click OK.

The swatch loads into the current document's Swatches palette. You can only select one swatch at a time using this method. You can't replace a swatch in the current document with an imported one if the swatches have the same name.

**5** Select Load Swatches from the Swatches palette Options menu.

**6** Choose faireisles.indd, then click Open.

All colors in the document are added to the current document's Swatches palette. You can choose this option when you want to add all swatches to your master document.

**7** Save and close the file.

## *To Expand Your Knowledge...*

**TIPS FOR CONSTRUCTING A MASTER DOCUMENT**

- The page size, margins, columns, and gutters are irrelevant unless you intend to use it as a layout template for other documents.
- You should include any proprietary fonts and colors in the master document.
- If a client prefers a particular font for the majority of jobs, you should change the Normal paragraph style to use that font.
- If the client prefers a specific style of hyphenation and justification, you should define an appropriate H&J routine in the master document.
- You should create common styles for tables of contents that can be imported into any project.
- If you import paragraph or character styles from the master document, the fonts used in those styles must be installed on your computer. If they are not, InDesign displays a missing-font warning when you try to import them.
- Once imported, master-document items become part of the document you are working with. There is no link to the master document, so imported items can be modified within the new document without affecting the master. Similarly, changes to the master document aren't automatically updated in the new document.

# LESSON 8  Merging Multiple Files into a Book

Long documents are frequently split into multiple files during the design and production process, then combined at the end of the process to create the final product. There are four primary reasons for doing so:

- Files with fewer pages are easier to control and navigate.
- When documents are broken into separate files, several compositors can work on different parts of the project without running the risk of ruining another person's work.
- The final document can be produced faster because several people can work on the project simultaneously.
- If a long document is split into multiple chapters, you don't lose the entire project if a single file becomes corrupt or is deleted accidentally.

InDesign's Book feature makes the process of building large jobs extremely easy; it automates many of the tasks that previously required careful comparison of page proofs for every page in the document. This doesn't mean you don't need to pay attention to detail, but it does relieve you of much manual toil.

When a single project is composed of several files, referred to as ***chapters***, it becomes very important to maintain consistency from one document to the next. An InDesign book file is essentially a container that tracks links to each file that represents a book chapter. The book file allows you to track each part of the whole job so the group of chapter files can be treated as a single unit. This offers several benefits:

- You can define a master document for the book. The master document serves as the source of all styles and colors in the book.
- You can synchronize the styles and color swatches of all chapters to the master document in the book. Updates made in the master document will affect all other chapters.
- You can easily generate a table of contents and an index that's comprehensive for the entire book.
- You control the page and section numbering of each file in the job, and in the entire book, without having to change the section options in individual chapter files.
- You can change the order of chapters within the book layout, and automatically renumber pages according to the chapter order. You can add, delete, and replace chapters.
- You can preflight, package, export, and print the entire book at once regardless of the number of chapters.

The chapters used in the following exercises are a snapshot of an in-progress ATC book, and are intended to demonstrate a real-world project that uses a large number of linked images, fonts, and styles. These are not the final, edited files. The styles in Chapter 5 have been changed to use some ATC reader fonts and the OpenType fonts that are included with InDesign. In this exercise, you synchronize the entire book to replace the original styles with those from Chapter 5, which are updated to use the fonts available to you.

## Create a Book

**1** **Locate the RF_EID2>Project_2>ila_book_files folder. Copy the folder into your WIP_02 folder.**

Inside are seven InDesign documents and seven folders containing the images used in these documents; the eighth 00_ila folder contains artwork common to the seven chapters.

**2** **Choose File>New>Book. Name the book file "ila_book.indb" and save it in your WIP_02 folder.**

**3** **From the Book palette Options menu, open the Book Page Numbering Options dialog box. Turn off the Automatic Pagination feature.**

This speeds up the process of adding chapters to the book.

**4** **Click the Add Chapter button (with the "+" icon) at the bottom of the Book palette. In the Add Documents dialog box that appears, highlight all seven numbered files (from ila1.indd to ila7.indd) and click Open to add them to the book.**

You can hold the Shift key and select several chapter files all at once from the Add Documents dialog box. After adding the chapters, it can take a few minutes for InDesign to temporarily open and inspect each document. These files cannot be added directly from a CD; they must reside on your hard drive or a network drive.

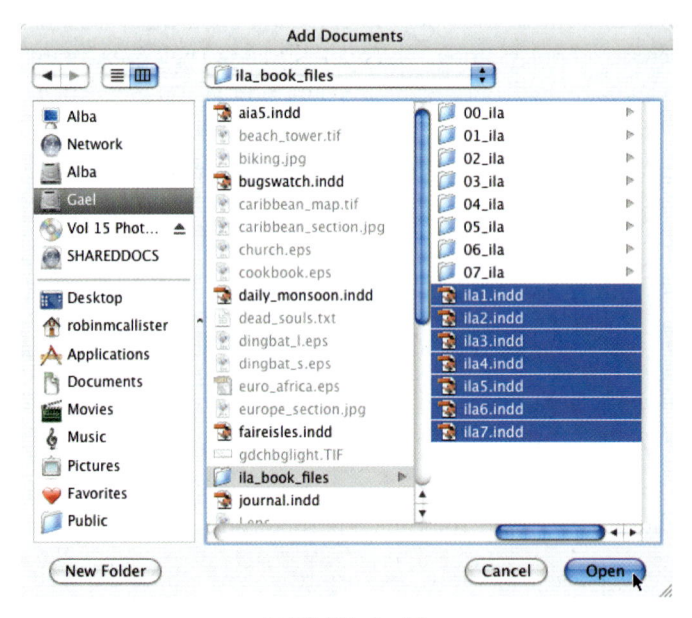

**FIGURE 2.42**

**5** When you've added all seven chapters, verify that they appear in the correct order in the Book palette. (If you Shift-clicked to select multiple chapter files, they may appear out of order; to rearrange chapters, drag each one to the correct position.)

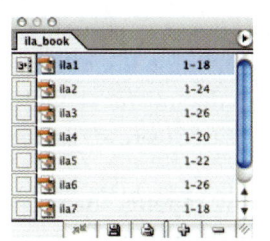

**FEATURE 2.43**

**6** Designate ila5.indd as the master document (style source) by clicking the open square to the left of the chapter's entry in the Book palette list.

Any changes you make to shared elements in this chapter, such as styles and color definitions, will be carried over to the other chapters.

**7** Choose Repaginate from the Book palette Options menu.

This prompts InDesign to examine the numbers of the pages in all the chapters and ensure that each chapter starts on the correct page number. If you receive any messages about missing fonts, dismiss them. After a few minutes of processing, your Book palette should look like Figure 2.44.

**FIGURE 2.44**

**8** Save the book (use the Book palette Options menu) and leave it open.

## Fix Image Links

**1** Open each chapter file from the ila_book_files folder and fix any broken image links. Ignore any missing-font warnings.

Image links can't be fixed from the Book palette. Each chapter has images in its corresponding folder inside the ila_book_files folder, and also the common images found in the 00_ila folder.

**2** Check the Links palette in each chapter and make sure there aren't any red or yellow icons, which indicate missing images or links that need to be updated. Save and close each chapter file after relinking.

## Synchronize the Book

When a book is synchronized, the styles and colors in each chapter are matched to those in the master document; any styles and colors that appear in the master document will also appear in all chapters, even if they were not previously used in those chapters. If the same element already exists in the other chapters, the definition from the master document overrides the definition in the other files. The synchronization process does not affect any elements that are not in the master document — but in a well-planned and executed project, there shouldn't be any elements in chapter files that aren't already in the master document.

**1** Deselect all the chapters in the Book palette, then either click the Synchronize Book button at the bottom of the Book palette, or choose Synchronize Book from the palette menu. You may (but should not) see the warning shown below. Click OK to dismiss it.

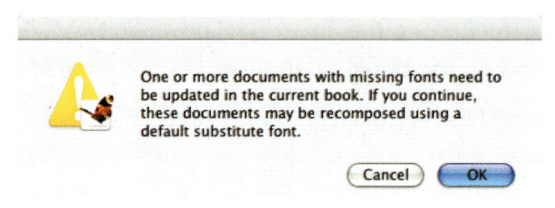

FIGURE 2.45

**2** During the synchronization process, you may (but should not) see the warning below for several chapters. Click OK to dismiss it and continue.

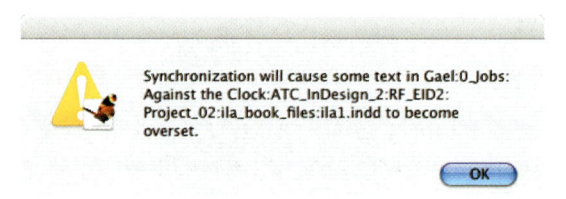

FIGURE 2.46

A progress box tells you what's going on during the synchronization process.

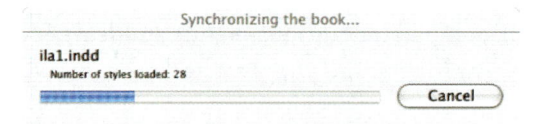

FIGURE 2.47

Once the process finishes, a completion notice appears.

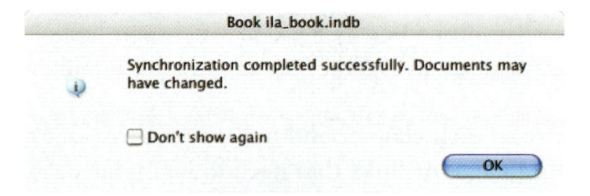

FIGURE 2.48

The message that "Documents may have changed" is expected, because you replaced all of the styles in each chapter with those from the master document.

**3** Open ila1.indd by double-clicking its entry in the Book palette. Check each spread for overset text, and adjust text frames to make the text fit.

Most instances of overset text are in the sidebar text frames, which are sized tightly to their contents. Overset text is common when chapters that use missing fonts are synchronized to adopt the fonts defined in a master document's styles.

**4** Save and close ila1.indd, then repeat the overset-text repair process in the files ila2.indd, ila3.indd, and ila4.indd; save and close each file as you fix it.

The rest of the chapters should not have any overset text.

## Create a Table of Contents

You can easily create a table of contents or another type of list that covers every chapter in a book, if the style names you want to include in the TOC are consistently used and applied throughout every chapter. Creating an index for a book works the same way as creating a TOC. Both require a separate document to be added to the open Book palette.

**1** Open the ila_book.indb file if necessary. Open a copy (not the original) of ila1.indd. In the Pages palette, select Pages 2–18 by clicking the icon for Page 2, then Shift-clicking the Page 18 icon. Choose Delete Spreads from the Pages palette menu and confirm that you want to do this.

**2** The remaining page has the B-Chapter Opener master applied to it. Select everything on the page, then delete it all. Drag the L-Front Matter master to Page 1 to apply it. Add another page based on the "L" master.

**3** Select Page 1 and choose Numbering & Section Options from the Pages palette Options menu. Change the page-numbering style to lowercase Roman numerals (i, ii, iii).

**4** Save this file as "ila_toc.indd".

**5** Add ila_toc.indd to the book. Move it to the top if necessary.

**6** From the Layout menu, choose Table of Contents Styles and click the Load button. In the Open a File dialog box, locate and open the aia5.indd file you saved to your WIP_02 folder earlier in this project.

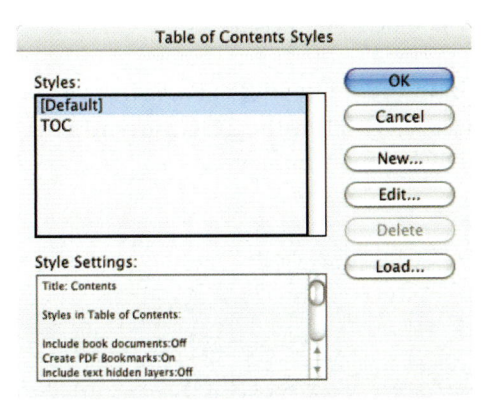

**FIGURE 2.49**

**7** Click the TOC style, then click OK.

**8** Choose Repaginate from the Book palette menu to make sure the page counts are all updated.

**9** Choose Layout>Table of Contents.

InDesign scans all the book files to check style names, then it shows the TOC dialog box.

**10** In the Title field type "Contents" and choose the H1 style. At the bottom of the dialog box, check the Include Book Documents box. Leave the other options as they are.

Everything else is picked up from the TOC style you created earlier. Note that the TOC Style menu changes from TOC to TOC [Custom] because of the minor changes you just made.

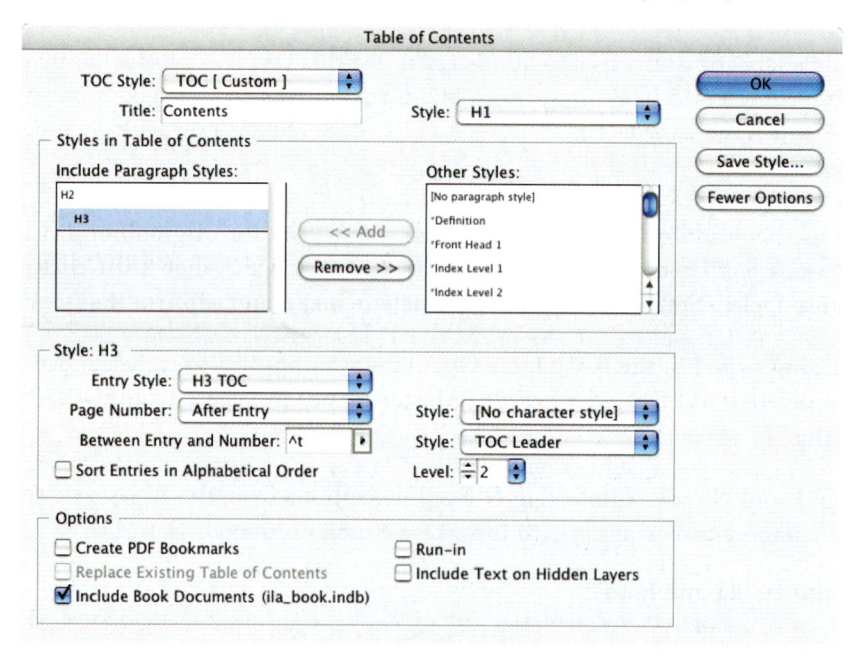

**FIGURE 2.50**

**11** Click OK to generate the TOC.

If you receive a warning about including items in overset text, click Yes to continue. you should not have any overset text in any book chapter because you checked for this in the last exercise.

**12** Click the Loaded Text icon in the frame on Page i, using the guide on the left as a margin (make guides visible, if necessary). Flow the TOC story to Page ii. Delete all lines that lack a topic, and those that read "Chapter Summary."

Your TOC should look similar to Figure 2.51.

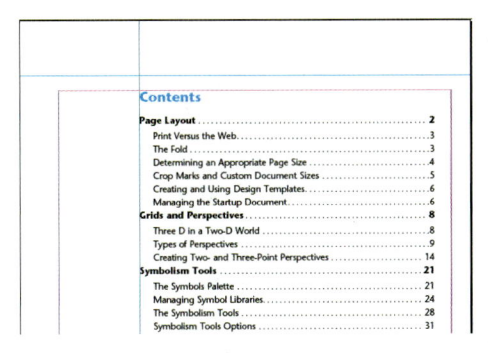

**FIGURE 2.51**

**13** Save and close ila_toc.indd. Leave the book file open.

## LESSON 9  Printing and Exporting Books

With InDesign's Book feature, you can easily print and export any or all documents in a book. In either case, you choose to print or export from the Book palette Options menu. If no chapters are selected, the entire book will be printed or exported; if specific chapters are selected, they alone will be printed or exported.

The only export options that make sense for a large document are PDF, HTML, and XML; exporting a book as EPS or SVG creates a separate file for every page in the book. We discuss HTML, XML, SVG, and advanced EPS and PDF export later in this book.

### Export the Book

**1** With none of the chapters selected, choose Export Book to PDF from the Book palette Options menu.

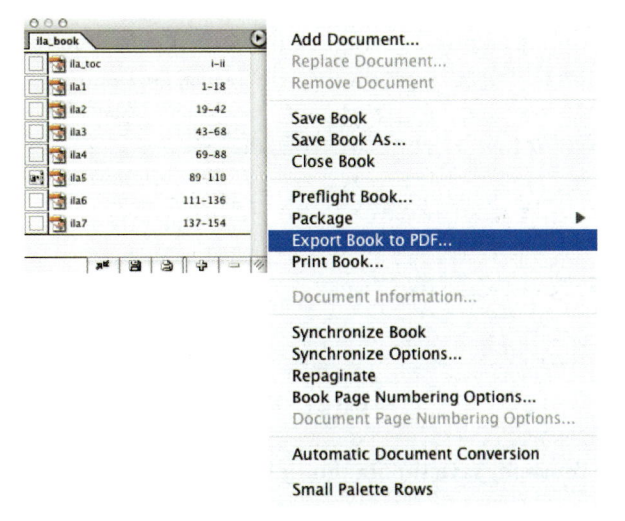

**FIGURE 2.52**

**2** Save the exported PDF file, accepting the default file name "ila_book.pdf".

**3** In the Export PDF dialog box, choose [Screen] from the Preset menu, and click Export.

**FIGURE 2.53**

Go get a cup of coffee, because this will take awhile. A progress box appears while InDesign generates the PDF.

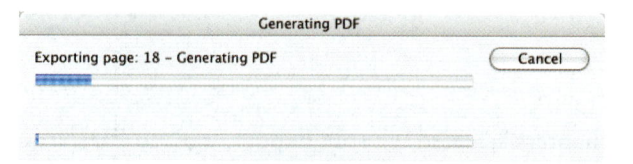

**FIGURE 2.54**

When exporting or printing a book, InDesign temporarily opens each file in the book. The open book icon next to each chapter's page range indicates which files are open.

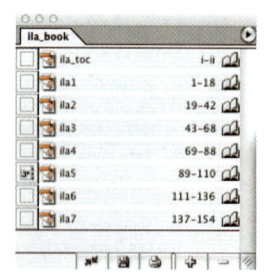

**FIGURE 2.55**

**4** When the export is finished, save the ila_book.indb file and close InDesign.

**5** Locate the exported PDF file, ila_book.pdf, and open it in Acrobat Reader to look at the finished product.

Project 2  Building and Managing Long Documents    **91**    LEVEL 2

# SUMMARY

In the production of lengthy documents, particularly those that cross several linked files, consistency is important. Dividing a document into logical sections can be helpful for keeping track of your files. Knowing how to create story jumps is an important technique for helping your readers follow the flow of your document. Efficiently creating and managing lists such as tables of contents and indexes is another valuable skill that improves the readability of long documents.

InDesign makes it easy for you to create and share styles, master pages, templates, and master documents. InDesign libraries offer another useful tool for staying organized. Many of the tasks associated with managing multiple chapters in a book-length publication were previously extremely tedious. InDesign's Book utility automates those tasks and even makes it easy to create a comprehensive table of contents for a book.

# CAREERS IN DESIGN

### PRODUCING DOCUMENTS

Producing lengthy documents involves skills beyond those needed for what many of us think of as "standard" work. Designing and producing ads and brochures requires meticulous attention to detail — including doing the math so the folds fall in the right place — but the detail work needed for book production is of a different nature.

Book designers must know who their target audience is and take their needs into consideration when designing both the layout and the styles of the publication. This book, for example, was designed to fulfill a number of specific needs of the reader. It lies flat, so you can use it easily at a computer workstation. It provides many visual aids, because graphic artists often learn best when graphics confirm what they have done. The type is large and well-leaded, so it can be easily read while operating a computer.

As your skills evolve, you should learn to take advantage of all the tools that apply to your jobs. Style sheets, for example, are one of the most underutilized tools in every publishing program. Even for producing ads, style sheets are valuable.

When you build longer documents, you will have to decide whether to break a single document into sections or to merge several smaller documents into a single large one. The final decision often depends on the total length of the document. For instance, you could create a year-end compilation of all the magazines in a volume, which would require using the book function retroactively.

Throughout your graphics career, you will likely use some of these features more than others. Many graphic artists never use the Table of Contents feature — they don't produce long documents, or they pass off the production of front and back matter to specialists in those functions. Very few create indexes, because indexing is a specialty in itself, and appeals more to extreme "left brain" thinkers than to creative artists.

As you design and produce longer documents, you will find that planning, more than anything else, is the key to efficiency. Never skimp on the preparatory work, unless you don't mind spending considerably more time than necessary figuring things out as you go along.

# KEY TERMS

| | | |
|---|---|---|
| book | library | section |
| continued from | list | synchronize |
| continued on | master document | table of contents |
| cross-reference | metadata | TOC |
| index | note | topic |
| jump | reference | |

# CHECKING CONCEPTS AND TERMS

## MULTIPLE CHOICE

**Check the letter of the correct answer for each of the following:**

1. Which of InDesign's features will help you organize text and graphics files for use in multiple documents?
   a. Document presets
   b. Book palette
   c. Library
   d. File Manager

2. When creating a "jump" or "continued on" element, it is important to:
   a. Know which page the text is going to jump to.
   b. Be sure the jump frames touch the frames containing the text stream.
   c. Use a discrete paragraph style for the jump.
   d. Double-check to be sure all links are up-to-date.

3. How do you create footnotes or endnotes in InDesign?
   a. Use the Notes dialog box.
   b. Cut and paste from text and manually move the notes to their own text frame.
   c. Keep the notes in the main text stream.
   d. Use specific Notes styles.

4. What do you use to create lists in InDesign?
   a. The Table of Contents dialog box
   b. Special characters and character styles
   c. The Book palette
   d. None of the above

5. How are indexes created?
   a. Using the Topic mode of the Index palette
   b. Using the Reference mode of the Index palette
   c. Using the Cross-reference mode of the Index palette
   d. All of the above

6. If you want to start a document on Page 22, you must use
   a. Book palette
   b. Numbering & Section Options
   c. Master pages
   d. Layout adjustment

7. Which of the following can you accomplish using the Table of Contents utility?
   a. Insert leader characters
   b. Create a list of advertisers
   c. Apply a style sheet
   d. All of the above

8. What does a master document contain?
   a. Page geometry for the document
   b. TOC and index, if applicable
   c. All common images used in the document
   d. All styles and colors used in the document

9. Where is metadata typically found?
   a. Library palette
   b. Book palette
   c. Index palette
   d. TOC palette

10. What happens when a book is synchronized?
    a. All chapters take on the master pages of the first chapter.
    b. A spell-check is automatically performed.
    c. All chapters take on the master document's shared features.
    d. The document is pre-flighted to ensure there are no inconsistencies.

## DISCUSSION QUESTIONS

1. When building a multi-chapter book, why would you — or why would you not — prefer to break the book into separate chapters? In what circumstances would breaking the book up become almost mandatory? When would you want to keep the book together as a single unit?

2. Explore the idea of using libraries. How do you envision using libraries most effectively? Create a number of scenarios where using a library would be most effective.

# SKILL DRILL

Skill Drills reinforce project skills. Each skill reinforced is the same, or nearly the same, as a skill presented in the lessons. Detailed instructions are provided in a step-by-step format. You must perform the first two Skill Drills in order; Skill Drills 3 and 4 can be performed in any order.

## 1. Build the TravelAmerica Library

You have been assigned to create a quarterly promotional piece for TravelAmerica, a group that specializes in travel plans in the United States and Canada. Their catalog is divided into the basic categories of air travel, travel by train, and driving vacations. Each vacation type has its own icon. The agency uses a number of other icons in the publication. In this drill, you will set up the basic images for use in the catalog.

1. Open the document ta_images.indd.

2. Create a new library and save it to your WIP_02 folder as "ta_lib.indl".

3. Add the first row of five stars to the library by dragging it into the Library palette.

   The stars images in the upper-left corner of the page were all created in InDesign. They constitute the rating system the agency uses for their vacations. You will have to add in each row of stars individually.

4. Double-click the stars to assign them a name and metadata. Name the image "5-star" and in the description field, type "Rating, Best, 5-Star".

5. Option/Alt-drag the rest of the star images, assigning them appropriate names and metadata.

6. Resize all the "mode of travel" images proportionally to a width of 1 in. Add them to the library, including "mode", along with other descriptive words, in their metadata, so they can be sorted by subgroup.

7. Resize all the "destination" images proportionally to a height of 2 in. Add them to the library, including "destination", along with other descriptive words, in their metadata.

8. Add the TravelAmerica logo using the New Library Item button.

9. Close the document ta_images.indd without saving. Leave the library open.

## 2. Create the Base TravelAmerica Catalog

In addition to needing a library, the document must be divided into sections for each mode of travel. In this drill, you apply what you learned about creating sections, and add standard elements from the library to each section. You will also add a section to hold the table of contents, using a secondary numbering format.

1. With ta_lib.indl still open, open the document ta_spring.indd. You will see that it has 36 text pages and 4 pages set aside for the front and back covers.

2. Double-click the Auto Tours master to activate it.

3. Drag the car.eps image from the library to the left and right masters, and position it at X: 0.35, Y: 0.5 and X: 7.15, Y:0.5, respectively.

4. Drag the train.eps and plane.eps images to the same positions on their respective masters.

5. Click Page 1 and choose Numbering & Section Options. Ensure that the Start Section box is checked; click the Start Page Numbering at button and enter "1" in the field, then click OK.

6. Start a new section on Page 3 and be sure the Automatic Page Numbering button is active. Apply the Auto Tours master to Pages 3–16 by selecting the pages and pressing the Option/Alt key when selecting the master.

7. Start a new section on Page 17 and apply the Rail master to Pages 17–28. Start a new section on Page 29 and apply the Air master to Pages 29–36.

8. Insert two pages at the start of the document, based on the TOC master.

9. From Numbering & Sections Options, assign lowercase Roman numerals as the page-numbering style.

10. Save and close the document.

## 3. Extract Notes from Text

Whether you're publishing a book, journal, magazine, or newsletter — or even a catalog or specification sheet — you may need to extract notes from the text. As you noted in the exercises for this project, extracting notes requires diligence, but it is not particularly difficult. In this Skill Drill and the following one, you'll be putting the finishing touches on GraphiCom's newsletter, *Focus On Communication*.

1. Open the document focus.indd. This six-page newsletter is almost ready to be printed. There are just a couple of tweaks that remain.

2. Go to Page 4. You'll see some indications of overset text, but that's not the immediate concern.

3. Locate the notes text. It is sans-serif text, smaller than the standard text, in the first column. It is tagged with the Note style.

4. Create a text frame with the following dimensions:

   X: 3.0833 in.   W: 4.9167 in.
   Y: 9.75 in.     H: 0.4167 in.

   Assign a text wrap around the bounding box with no offset.

5. In the Text Frame Options dialog box, define a 0.1667-in. minimum first baseline offset.

6. Cut the Note text from the running text and paste it into the text frame you just created; since it is the first (and only) note in the frame, assign the Note 1 paragraph style.

   The overset problems are resolved.

7. Save the document and leave it open for the next Skill Drill.

## 4. Wrap Text around Images

It's great when writers are able to write to available space. Sometimes that just isn't possible — and sometimes an image is added that takes up unanticipated space. You may have noticed when you opened the newsletter that there was overset text on the first page. The text overset consists of a number of paragraphs that will have to be continued.

1. If it is not already open, open the document focus.indd and go to Page 1.

2. Create a new text frame at Y: 9.9593 in. the width of the third column, with a height of approximately 0.333 in. Select Text Wrap Around Bounding Box.

3. Type the words "Continued on page [space]" and assign the Jump style.

4. Control/right-click to activate the contextual menu, and select Insert Special Character>Next Page Number.

5. With the Selection tool, click the overset symbol (the "+") in the out port of the large text frame.

6. Go to Page 5 and, with the loaded cursor, drag a new text frame in the first column. Allow the text to fill the frame. You will adjust its size later.

7. Create a text frame:

   X: 0.5 in.    W: 2.333 in.
   Y: 1.25 in.   H: 0.4167 in.

   Select Text Wrap Around Bounding Box.

8. Assign the Jump style and type the following exactly:

   "Project Management
   continued from page [space]"

   Restyle the first line ATC Pine Bold 10/11.

9. Control/right-click to activate the contextual menu and select Insert Special Character>Previous Page Number.

10. Adjust the height of the text frame below the jump to 4.5 in.

11. Save the document and close it.

# CHALLENGE

Challenge exercises expand on, or are somewhat related to, skills presented in the lessons. Each exercise provides a brief introduction, followed by instructions presented in a numbered-step format that are not as detailed as those in the Skill Drill exercises. You must perform these exercises in the order in which they appear.

As the lead designer for the Body Solution account, you are coordinating the efforts of two designers. Each of your designers has created one chapter of a booklet that will be sent to health-care providers around the country as a free handout for patients. As the project coordinator, it is your job to make sure that each chapter of the document is consistent with the others, and to create the front and back matter.

## 1. Create a Book

Both designers are familiar with the concepts of creating publications, and both have worked from the same template, so there should be few surprises in store for you. In this exercise you will create the book file that will serve as the container for the entire book.

1. Copy the files fitness2.indd, fitness_front.indd, and fitness_back.indd to your WIP_02 folder.

2. Begin by creating a new book. Save it as "fitness_book.indb".

3. Add the document fitness1.indd. Note that the file is added as the master document.

4. Add the files fitness2.indd, fitness_front.indd, and fitness_back.indd.

5. Click the fitness_front item in the Book palette and drag it up until a dark line appears above the file name. This moves the fitness_front file before the fitness1 file, without changing the master document of the book.

6. Leave the book open for the next exercise.

## 2. Synchronize the Book and Set Sections

Now that you have the basic parts of the book assembled, you need to ensure they are in synch with one another, and that their sections are logically aligned.

1. With the book file fitness_book.indb active, double-click fitness1 in the Book palette to open the file.

2. Double-click fitness2 in the Book palette to open the file.

3. Arrange the two documents on your screen so you can see the chapter titles in each.

4. Click in the empty area of the Book palette so no document is highlighted.

5. Choose Synchronize Options from the Book palette Options menu.

6. Make sure All Styles is checked and click Synchronize. When the process is complete, you see a message that documents may have changed. Click OK. Both chapter titles should appear in blue.

7. Save the fitness1 file and leave it open. Save the fitness2 file and close it.

8. Go to the first page (document Page 5) of the fitness1 document and restart the numbering as Page 1. Notice that the fitness_front and fitness1 documents both begin on Page 1.

9. Save the fitness1 document and close it.

10. Open the fitness_front document. Change the numbering style to lowercase Roman numerals (i, ii, iii, iv).

11. Save the document and leave it open.

12. Choose Save Book from the Book palette Options menu.

## 3. Build the Table of Contents

Since this booklet is designed as a reference source, and is not for light reading, it should have a table of contents (TOC). You're going to use the Table of Contents feature, and place the TOC in the first section of the book.

1. With fitness_front open, choose Layout>Table of Contents Styles.

2. Click New in the Table of Contents Styles dialog box.

3. In the TOC Style field, type "Contents Style" and delete any text from the Title field. Click the More Options button, if necessary, to expand the dialog box.

4. Highlight Chapter Title in the Other Styles window and click Add to move that style into the Include Paragraph Styles window.

5. With Chapter Title highlighted in the Include Paragraph Styles window, choose TOC1 from the Entry Style menu (under Style: Chapter Title). Make sure the Page Number menu is set to After Entry and the Level menu is set to 1.

6. Highlight Subhead in the Other Styles window and click Add to move that style into the Include Paragraph Styles window. With Subhead highlighted, choose TOC2 from the Entry Style menu. Make sure After Entry is selected in the Page Number menu and the Level menu is set to 2.

7. Make sure the Include Book Documents check box is selected in the New Table of Contents Style dialog box and click OK. The Contents style now appears in the Table of Contents Styles dialog box. Click OK.

8. Navigate to Page iii of the open document.

9. Choose Layout>Table of Contents. Make sure Contents Style is selected in the TOC Style menu, and the Title field is empty. Click OK.

10. When the Table of Contents dialog box disappears, the cursor is loaded with the table of contents text.

11. Click the text frame on Page iii to place the table of contents.

12. Save the file and close it.

## 4. Tag Index Terms in the First File

When you build an index, the hardest part is determining which words will be referenced. InDesign makes the actual indexing relatively easy. In this exercise and the next one you will identify the index terms for InDesign to reference.

1. Double-click fitness1 in the Book palette to open the file.

2. Select Window>Type & Tables>Index to show the Index palette. Make sure the Book check box is selected.

3. Highlight the word "diet" in the third paragraph after the subhead and click the Create a New Index Entry button in the Index palette. Review the default values in the New Page Reference dialog box. The highlighted word appears in the first Topic Levels field, and the Type menu is set to Current Page. Click Add All, then click Done.

4. Highlight the words "binge eater" in the second line of the same paragraph and click the Create a New Index Entry button in the Index palette. In the New Page Reference dialog box, change the text in the Topic field to "binge eating". Click Add, then click Done.

5. Highlight "exercise program" in the next paragraph and add this new index entry. Add all instances of the word.

6. Navigate to Page 2 of the document. From the first paragraph after the What to Expect subhead, add all instances of "weight loss".

7. From the next paragraph add all references to "weight reduction", "baseline strength", and "injuries" to the index.

8. Highlight "back" halfway through the second paragraph on the page and create a new index entry. In the New Page Reference dialog box, click the button with the down-arrow icon to move "back" into the Topic Level 2 field. Scroll through the alphabetical list and expand the "I" list. Place the insertion point in the Topic Level 1 field and double-click "injuries" in the list of terms. Click Add All, then Done to add the second-level term to the index.

9. Highlight "knee" in the same paragraph. Using the same technique as in Step 8, add "knee" as a second-level entry under "injuries."

10. Continue adding first-level terms. Find each item in the text and add all instances of the item to the index.

| | | |
|---|---|---|
| pain | alternate exercises | measurements |
| results | weight training | metabolism |
| eating habits | strength | routines |
| aerobics | body fat | interval training |
| treadmill | stationary bike | stairclimber |
| calories | weighted cardio | workout |
| maximum aerobic power training | | |

11. Navigate to Page 3 of the open document. In the first paragraph, highlight the word "benefits" and add it as a Topic Level 2 under the "exercise program" Level 1 entry.

12. At the bottom of Page 3, highlight "Daniel Mercer". Press Command/Control-Shift-F8 to reverse the text and add it as a page reference.

13. In the Index palette, expand the list of references for the term "interval training". Highlight the second Page 4 reference and click the Go To Selected Marker button in the Index palette. Click the Delete button in the Index palette and click Yes to dismiss the warning.

14. In the text (at the location of the index marker you just deleted), highlight "interval training" and create a new index entry. In the New Page Reference dialog box, choose See also from the Type menu.

15. Expand the "M" list in the bottom window. Drag "maximum aerobic power training" into the Referenced text field below the Type menu. Click Add, then click Done to add a cross-reference.

16. Save the file and close it.

## 5. Tag Index Terms in the Second File

1. Double-click fitness2 in the Book palette to open the file.

2. Highlight the word "Stretch" in the chapter heading and add it as a new entry.

3. In the New Page Reference dialog box, change the Topic Level 1 field to "stretching". Choose To End of Document from the Type menu. Click Add, then click Done.

4. Navigate to Page 13 of the document. Highlight "Calf" in the first subhead and add it as a new index item. Make this entry a Level 2 entry under the Level 1 topic "stretching."

5. Choose To Next Use of Style from the Type list and choose Subhead from the Style menu. Add the item to the list.

6. Highlight "Glute" in the next subhead and add it as a second-level term under the first-level term "stretching." Assign it the same type and style as you did the word "Calf."

7. Repeat this process to add the topics of each subhead to the index as second-level terms under the first-level term "stretching." The topics begin on Page 13 and end on Page 17.

8. Locate in the text and add Current Page references as first-level index items for the following terms:

    | fitness | weight training | aerobics |
    | flexibility | muscle tension | muscle strains |
    | circulation | heart rate | body temperature |
    | clothing | muscle | posture |
    | spine | ligaments | |

9. Save the file and close it.

## 6. Build the Index

1. Double-click fitness_back in the Book palette to open the file. Show the Paragraph Styles palette.

2. Choose New Style from the Options menu. Define new paragraph styles as follows:

   | | |
   |---|---|
   | Name: | Index Head |
   | Font: | ATC Maple Medium |
   | Size: | 10 pt. |
   | Space Before: | 0.111 in. |
   | | |
   | Name: | Index Level 1 |
   | Font: | ATC Laurel Book |
   | Size: | 10 pt. |
   | Space Before: | 0.028 in. |
   | | |
   | Name: | Index Level 2 |
   | Font: | ATC Laurel Book |
   | Size: | 10 pt. |
   | Left Indent: | 0.2 in. |
   | Space Before: | 0.028 in. |

3. Define a new character style:

   | | |
   |---|---|
   | Name: | Cross Reference |
   | Font: | ATC Laurel Book Italic |
   | Size: | 10 pt. |

4. Check the Book box in the Index palette.

5. Click the Generate Index button.

6. In the Generate Index dialog box, delete the text from the Title field. Click More Options, if necessary.

7. Check the Include Book Documents box.

8. Make sure the Include Index Section Headings box is checked, and choose Index Head from the Section Heading Style menu.

9. Choose Cross Reference from the Cross-reference Style and Cross-reference Topic Style menus.

10. Make sure the Level 1 Style menu is set to Index Level 1, and the Level 2 Style menu is set to Index Level 2.

11. Click OK to build the index. A warning appears, asking if you want to save. Click Yes.

12. When the Generate Index dialog box disappears, the cursor is loaded with the index text.

13. Hold down the Option/Alt-Shift keys and click at the top of the first column on the page to place the index.

14. Drag the center-bottom handle of the left text column upward so it ends after the "F" index entries. Close up the second column to end after the "R" entries.

15. Save the file and close it. Close the book file.

# PORTFOLIO BUILDER

## Create a Cookbook Framework

Graphic artists are called upon to produce many different kinds of products, from stationery packages to brochures, to newsletters, to booklets and books. As you have discovered, longer documents can present unique challenges, including creating tables of contents, indexes, and sections, and a demand for consistency from chapter to chapter. You will set up the framework for a cookbook (or, if you wish, you can produce an entire cookbook).

We have supplied a style sheet for the elements that go into the cookbook, but the style definitions are up to you. You can copy the character and paragraph styles from cookbook_styles.indd within the Project_02>Cookbook folder. The only requirements the client has given is that the cookbook must be in loose-leaf format, so people can insert their favorite recipes, and that it contain lots of pictures of the final product. They wish to use a 7.5 × 9-inch binder with a 1.5-inch spine; this will accommodate 6 × 8.5-inch pages.

To complete this project, use the following techniques:

- Design a cover and spine, using a local non-profit organization as the client.
- Create each section of the cookbook (for example, Soups, Salads, Entrées, Sauces, Vegetables, Breads, Desserts, Beverages — make sure you include front matter and back matter) as a separate document. Allow at least 6 pages per section.
- Using the recipes in the sample document, or other recipes of your choice, create at least one full page in each section; use representative pictures, if possible.
- Design a section-intro page that is representative of the type of recipe it introduces.
- Create table of contents entries for each section and the recipe titles, and translate them into distinct styles for the TOC.
- Assemble the sections into a book.

PROJECT 3

LEVEL 2

# Applying Advanced Typesetting Functions

## OBJECTIVES

*In this project, you learn how to*

- Work more effectively with text frames
- Align margins of text optically
- Copy text attributes
- Apply hyphenation and justification
- Balance lines of ragged text
- Create custom glyph sets
- Nest one style inside another
- Work with the baseline grid more effectively
- Set type on a path

# WHY WOULD I DO THIS?

In this project, we discuss the ins and outs of professional-level typography. In *Essentials for Design: InDesign Level 1* we introduced many of the features covered in this project, so they will probably seem familiar to you. As is true with most InDesign functions, advanced typographic features require that you pay attention to details — having a general view is not sufficient. The better you plan your document, the easier it will be to compose. You'll learn how to manage your typographic settings to get the most from the automation InDesign provides.

The difference between a page that is typographically good and one that shows typographic excellence usually lies in the designer's ability to manage behind-the-scene controls, including text-frame functions, hyphenation and justification settings, and the manner in which margins are adjusted. When you work with any of these settings, you need to find a balance between the control you have over the text and your need for speed — in general, you need more control in short documents such as ads, and more automation in lengthy works such as novels.

From time to time, you will need to acquire character and paragraph attributes from an existing document. You could check the information in various palettes, write it down, then apply it to the text in your working document. With InDesign, though, you can click the type with the parameters you wish to copy, then highlight the text to which you wish to apply them. You can copy attributes within a single document, or between different ones.

Of course, the ability to copy attributes is not a substitute for good style sheet practices. You will learn in this project how to "nest" character styles within paragraph styles. This extends the value of the paragraph style, because you can define the action to affect only specific words or letters. You might, for example, want to have run-in text that would put the first four words in small caps.

Many designers repeatedly use certain characters from several different fonts — such as Adobe Caslon, or a pi font such as Zapf Dingbats or Universal Math. In such a case, you may want to build a custom glyph set, which can include any combination of special characters from different fonts. If you choose to build a glyph set, you may want to include links to the original fonts to ensure that you will access the correct character.

You may occasionally want to set headline text on a path. You could use an illustration program to bind the headline to an image. While this may be the preferred method, the fact is that production crunches may get in the way of "elegance." InDesign makes it quick and easy to set type on a path (and even to apply some special effects, which we discuss in Project 5).

Project 3   Applying Advanced Typesetting Functions    **105**   LEVEL 2

# VISUAL SUMMARY

Many people think of "editing text" as direct intervention with copy content; InDesign, however, has many features that allow you to interact indirectly with text. You can define many of these settings in the Text Frame Options, Hyphenation, and Justification dialog boxes. Using the Adobe Single-Line Composer gives you tight control over your document; using the Adobe Paragraph Composer allows you to automate production. With the Optical Margin Alignment utility, you can "hang" punctuation outside the text frame.

All text is placed inside a frame — by default, the text fills the frame completely, with the first baseline positioned so that a typeface's ascender brushes the top of the frame. Because of design considerations, this is not always the best solution. You can adjust the default frame settings in the Text Frame Options dialog box.

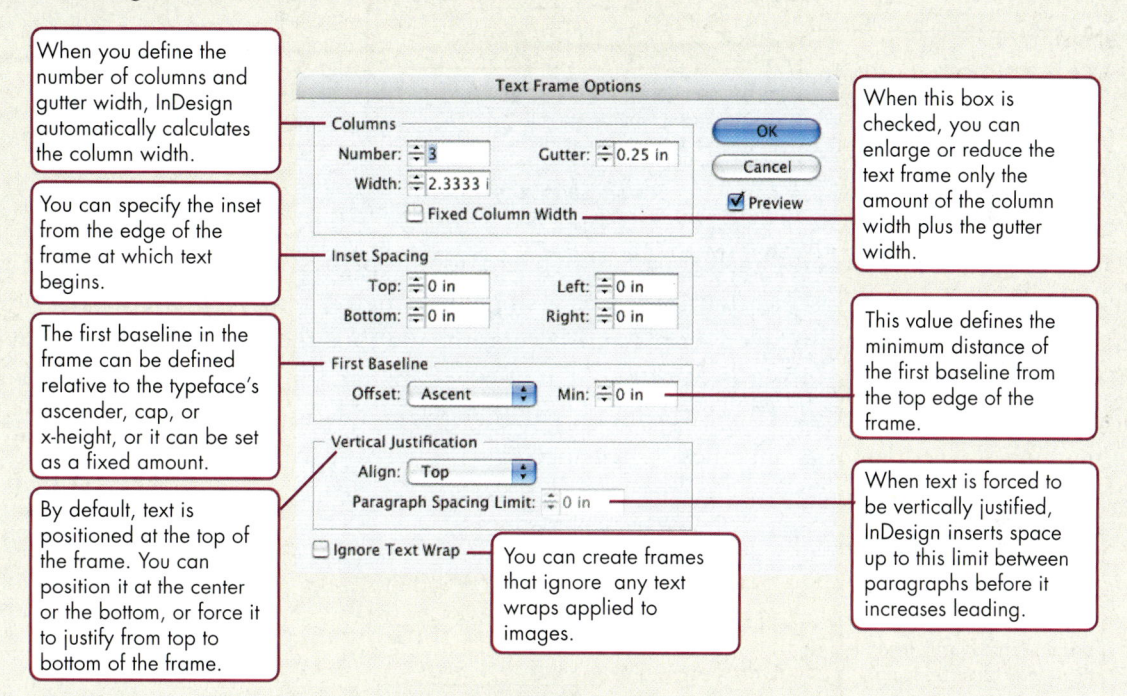

When you define the number of columns and gutter width, InDesign automatically calculates the column width.

You can specify the inset from the edge of the frame at which text begins.

The first baseline in the frame can be defined relative to the typeface's ascender, cap, or x-height, or it can be set as a fixed amount.

By default, text is positioned at the top of the frame. You can position it at the center or the bottom, or force it to justify from top to bottom of the frame.

When this box is checked, you can enlarge or reduce the text frame only the amount of the column width plus the gutter width.

This value defines the minimum distance of the first baseline from the top edge of the frame.

When text is forced to be vertically justified, InDesign inserts space up to this limit between paragraphs before it increases leading.

You can create frames that ignore any text wraps applied to images.

**FIGURE 3.1**

When a document includes hyphenation, several factors must be taken into consideration. First, while it is acceptable to hyphenate after the first two letters of a word, it is generally unacceptable to hyphenate before the last two letters, so "ac-ceptably" is OK, but "acceptab-ly" is not. A limit of three hyphens in a row is generally acceptable in books, but for advertising the limit is lower — often just a single hyphen is tolerable. Capitalized proper nouns should not be hyphenated, but the first word of a sentence may be.

**Hyphenation Settings**

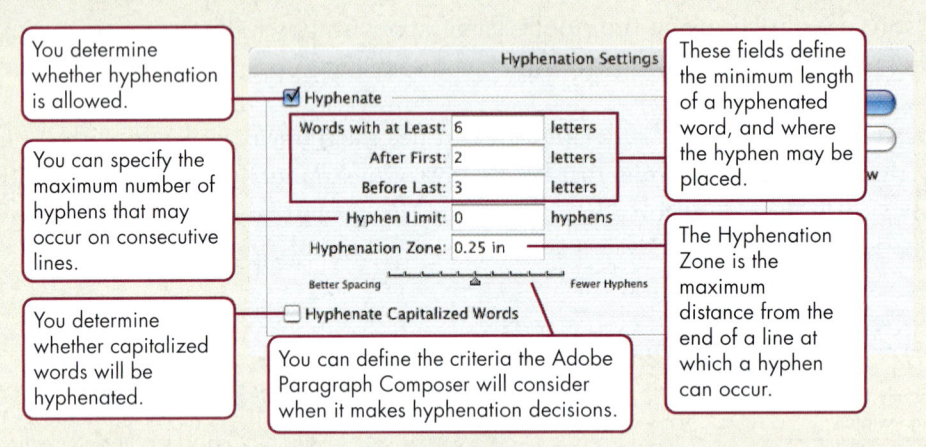

- You determine whether hyphenation is allowed.
- Hyphenate ☑
- Words with at Least: 6 letters
- After First: 2 letters
- Before Last: 3 letters
- Hyphen Limit: 0 hyphens
- Hyphenation Zone: 0.25 in
- Better Spacing ——— Fewer Hyphens
- ☐ Hyphenate Capitalized Words

- You can specify the maximum number of hyphens that may occur on consecutive lines.
- You determine whether capitalized words will be hyphenated.
- You can define the criteria the Adobe Paragraph Composer will consider when it makes hyphenation decisions.
- These fields define the minimum length of a hyphenated word, and where the hyphen may be placed.
- The Hyphenation Zone is the maximum distance from the end of a line at which a hyphen can occur.

**FIGURE 3.2**

The justification parameters are closely linked to hyphenation properties, so much so that we usually refer to hyphenation and justification (H&J) as a single parameter. These parameters define the amount of spacing allowed between words and letters, the amount that glyphs will be scaled to achieve justification; the justification and hyphenation parameters function in concert with one another. The Minimum, Desired, and Maximum parameters are only used when text is justified to both margins. Ragged text uses only the Desired spacing.

**Justification**

|                | Minimum | Desired | Maximum |
|----------------|---------|---------|---------|
| Word Spacing:  | 80%     | 100%    | 133%    |
| Letter Spacing:| 0%      | 0%      | 0%      |
| Glyph Scaling: | 100%    | 100%    | 100%    |

- Auto Leading: 120%
- Single Word Justification: Align Left
- Composer: Adobe Paragraph Composer

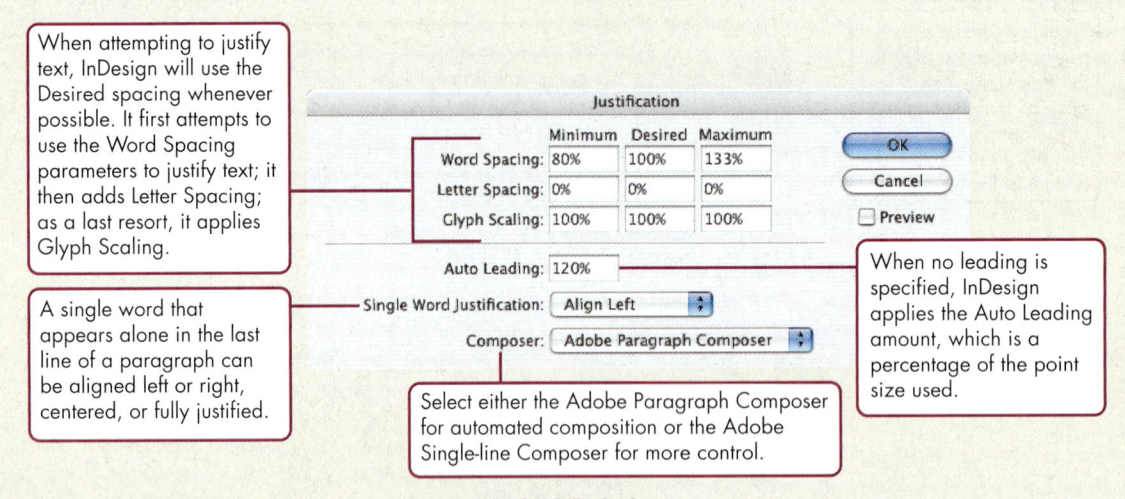

- When attempting to justify text, InDesign will use the Desired spacing whenever possible. It first attempts to use the Word Spacing parameters to justify text; it then adds Letter Spacing; as a last resort, it applies Glyph Scaling.
- A single word that appears alone in the last line of a paragraph can be aligned left or right, centered, or fully justified.
- Select either the Adobe Paragraph Composer for automated composition or the Adobe Single-line Composer for more control.
- When no leading is specified, InDesign applies the Auto Leading amount, which is a percentage of the point size used.

**FIGURE 3.3**

InDesign employs two features in addition to the Adobe Paragraph Composer that directly (and very easily) aid in making your pages look much better. The first is Optical Margin Alignment, which "hangs" punctuation — and some parts of letters — outside the margin. The second feature balances lines of ragged type, particularly effective for headlines or call-outs. It relieves the compositor of the necessity of repeatedly adjusting line breaks every time the text is edited or the font size is changed.

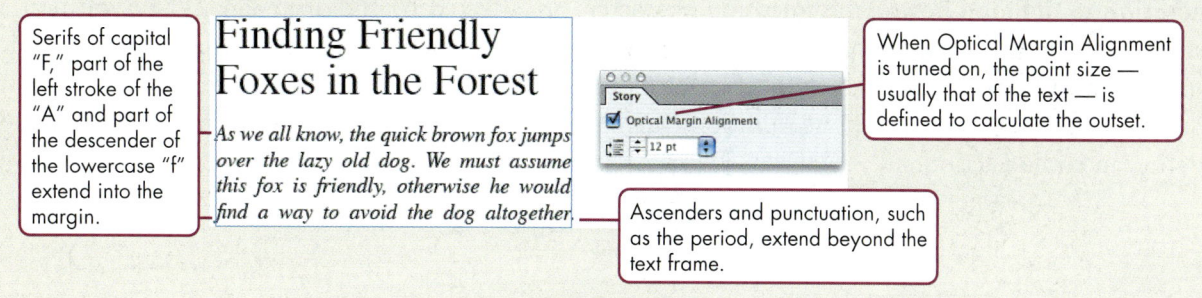

- Serifs of capital "F," part of the left stroke of the "A" and part of the descender of the lowercase "f" extend into the margin.
- When Optical Margin Alignment is turned on, the point size — usually that of the text — is defined to calculate the outset.
- Ascenders and punctuation, such as the period, extend beyond the text frame.

**FIGURE 3.4**

The Eyedropper tool can be used to copy character and paragraph formats from one selection of type to another, or to apply a color from a graphic to the type. When applying either formats or colors, the object the formatting is applied from can be either in the same or in a different document. This can be particularly handy when you need to copy a style from a document in which style sheets were not used.

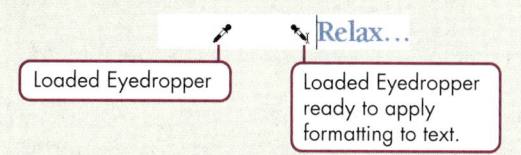

- Loaded Eyedropper
- Loaded Eyedropper ready to apply formatting to text.

**FIGURE 3.5**

Not every font contains all the glyphs you will use regularly — and some characters that are in most fonts are not always easy to access. InDesign allows you to create a set of custom glyphs that can remain open while you compose your documents. The glyphs you add to the set can be linked to the font from which they originate, or they can be selected from the font set with which you are composing the document.

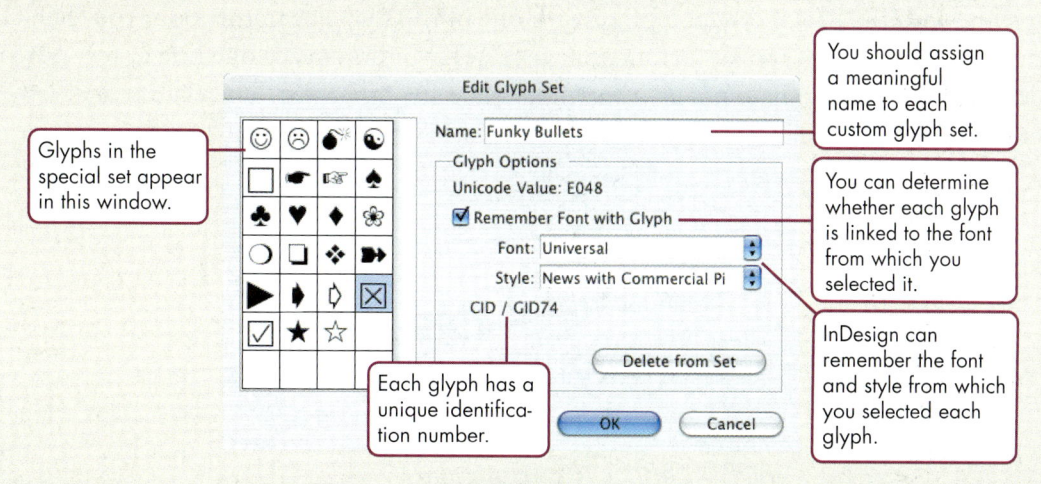

- Glyphs in the special set appear in this window.
- Each glyph has a unique identification number.
- You should assign a meaningful name to each custom glyph set.
- You can determine whether each glyph is linked to the font from which you selected it.
- InDesign can remember the font and style from which you selected each glyph.

**FIGURE 3.6**

In some cases, you might want to apply more than one style to a paragraph. You could manually apply paragraph and character styles — but this can be time-consuming, and it leaves room for inconsistency. When you worked with drop caps before, you learned that you can embed a character style in addition to defining how many lines and characters are affected by the drop cap. When you nest a style, you can apply a style to a given number or words or characters, or apply the style to a specific instance in the paragraph, such as an en space or another character. To define a nested style, you must create a character style, specify its duration (such as number of sentences, words, or characters), and define an ending action.

**FIGURE 3.7**

You can add motion to documents by setting type on a path. To do so, you first define the path by drawing a line with the Pencil or Pen tool, or with one of the shape or frame tools; you then click the line with the Text on a Path tool and enter your text. You can only place one line of text onto a path. Once text is placed, you can manipulate it very much like any other text. There are several "effect" and alignment options available.

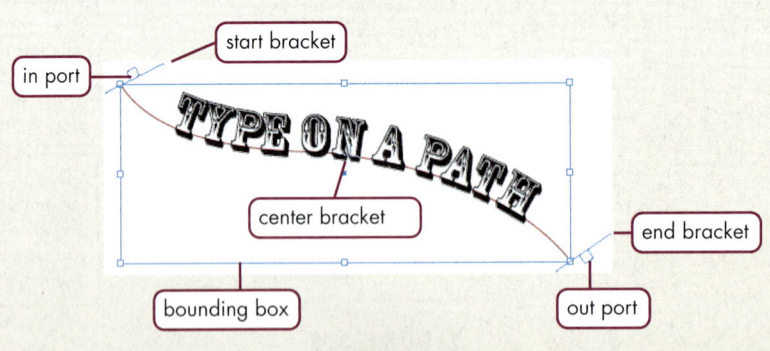

**FIGURE 3.8**

Project 3    Applying Advanced Typesetting Functions    109    LEVEL 2

## LESSON 1  Mastering Text Frame Options

You have previously learned to place text in frames, and to adjust text-frame insets to hold text away from bordered frames. You have learned that you can edit many of the text frame's properties using the Text Frame Options dialog box that you access from the Object menu or the contextual menu that appears when you Control/right-click.

When you define a fixed column width, your text frame will enlarge or reduce in only full-column widths; the columns do not resize proportionally. Text is reflowed through the new columns.

You have already worked with inset spacing — the amount of space between the edge of a text frame and the actual text area — many times. The First Baseline setting is closely related to inset spacing — it defines the position of the first baseline of text relative to the text-inset value. Adjusting the first baseline can be especially valuable when you are attempting to align columns of text that have first lines of different font sizes.

In this lesson, you will learn how to align top and bottom margins when leading specifications are fighting you. You will be able to make minor adjustments that can mean the difference between a page that looks good and one that looks great.

### Control Text Using Frame Options

**1**   **Open the document solutions.indd from the Project_03 folder. Be certain frame edges are visible.**

The first page of this document has been constructed with several text frames. You will first adjust the two-column frame.

**2**   **Activate the frame by clicking it with the Selection tool. Control/right-click, then choose Text Frame Options from the contextual menu.**

You can also press Command/Control-B to open this dialog box.

**3**   **Check the Preview box, and set the Vertical Justification Align menu to Justify.**

Notice that the right column now looks very spacey. You can tighten that up by *carding*, inserting extra space between paragraphs, or *feathering*, inserting space between lines.

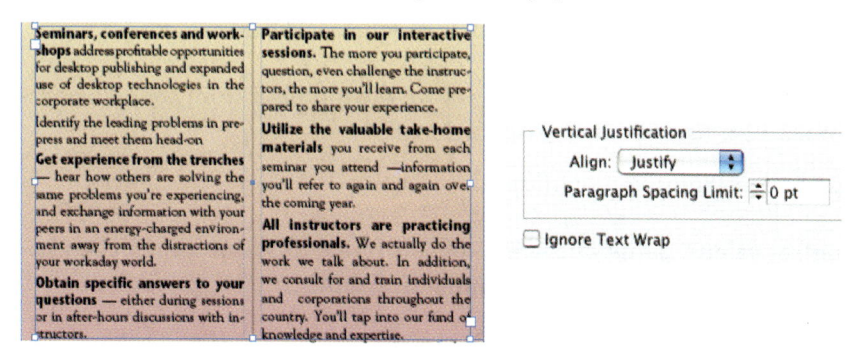

FIGURE 3.9

Project 3  Applying Advanced Typesetting Functions

4. **Change the Paragraph Spacing Limit field to 7 pt. — half a line space. Click OK.**

   Because of the structure of the information, that's a pretty good solution for this material.

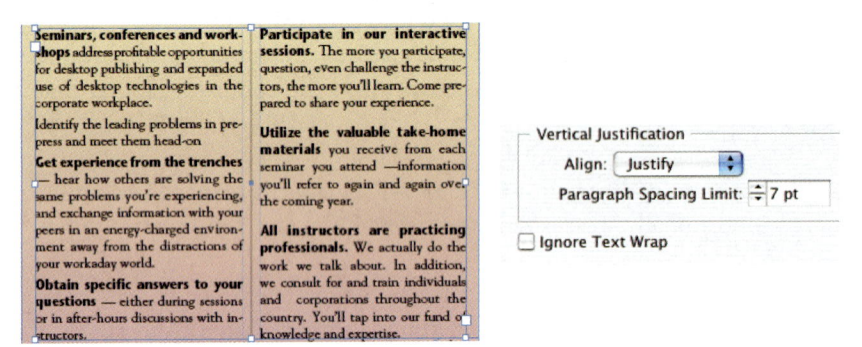

   **FIGURE 3.10**

5. **Double-click Page 2 to activate it.**

   The inset frames containing photos at the top of the page are fine — you can't apply vertical justification to frames that contain graphics, anyway. There is a problem with the larger boxed frame (with the headline "About Your Instructors"), however.

6. **Click the "About Your Instructors" frame with the Selection tool and open the Text Frame Options dialog box. Assign an inset spacing of 12 pt. for the top, and 1p0 for the left and right. Click OK.**

   **FIGURE 3.11**

   The large text frame in the middle of the page needs no insets — it has no border, and it's the same color as the background. You can still make it look better, though.

7. **In the Text Frame Options dialog box, remove the top inset from the "The Schedule" text. Assign a minimum first baseline offset of 31 pt.**

   This makes both columns start on the same baseline.

8. **In the Control palette, adjust the height of this frame to 312 pt., then click in one of the paragraphs with the Type tool to determine the leading.**

**9** In the Text Frame Options dialog box, check the Preview box and set the Vertical Justification menu to Justify. Set the Paragraph Spacing Limit field to half the leading and click OK.

Because there is text on both sides of them (as opposed to the bullets in the first column), the bulleted items in the second column look too far apart. You can "trick" InDesign into creating a more pleasing look.

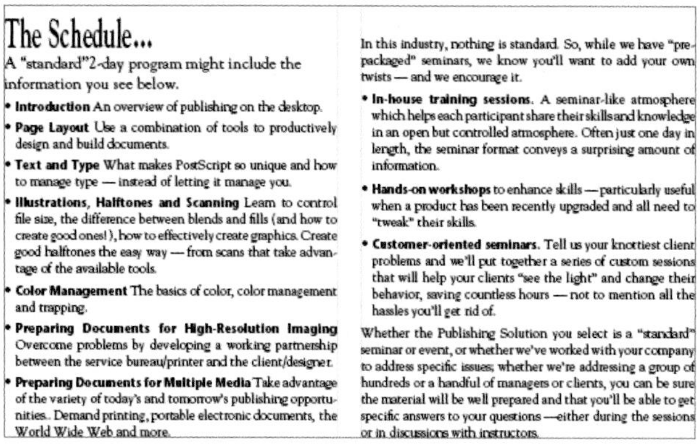

**FIGURE 3.12**

**10** With the Type tool, select the first two bulleted items in the second column ("In-house training sessions" and "Hands-on workshops"). In the Paragraph palette, set the Space After field to 0 pt.

This sets off the bulleted list from the text in this column.

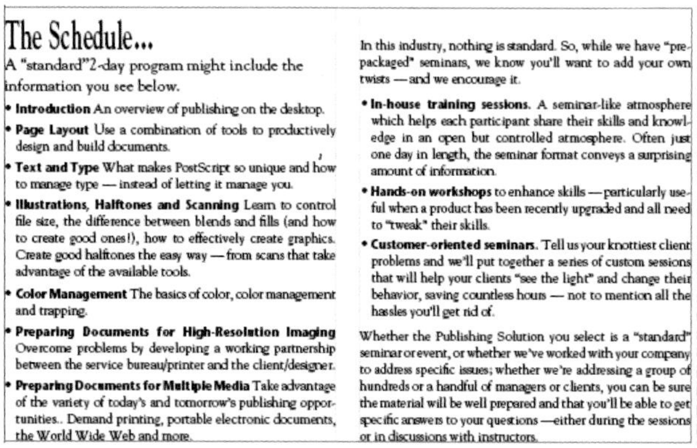

**FIGURE 3.13**

**11** Select the "Who Should Participate" frame. In the Text Frame Options dialog box, add 6-pt. insets at the top and left.

**12** Select the yellow angled text frame near the bottom of the page and add top, left, and right insets of 4 pt.

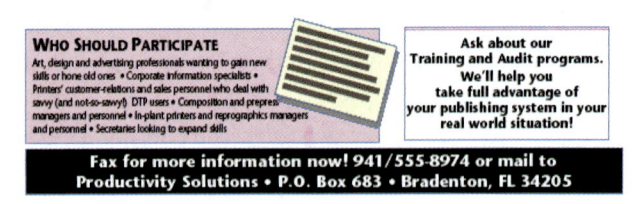

**13** Select the bottom text frame (with the reversed type) and change the Vertical Justification menu to Center.

FIGURE 3.14

**14** Save the document and close the file.

## LESSON 2  Applying Hyphenation Parameters

When composing a document, you must consider column width and point size to ensure the best possible look and fit. The nature of the document — and specific elements within the document — affects the hyphenation parameters you apply. For example, you would not want to hyphenate headlines, and hyphens should be kept to a minimum in ads. Even some types of books, such as those for very young children, should be hyphen-free.

Hyphenation is defined on a paragraph-by-paragraph basis. You can define the minimum number of letters that remain alone on a line at the beginning or the end of a hyphenated word. As a rule of thumb, there should be at least two letters before a hyphen and three after a hyphen; more than three hyphens in a row is almost always considered unacceptable. You can adjust hyphenation settings from the Paragraph palette (or its equivalent in the Control palette) or you can define hyphenation as part of a paragraph style.

The Hyphenation Zone — the distance from the right margin or indent in which hyphenation can occur — only affects non-justified text composed by the Adobe Single-line Composer. When using the Adobe Paragraph Composer, the Better Spacing option creates more hyphens; the Fewer Hyphens option gives the Composer fewer options in composing a paragraph.

### Apply Hyphenation Parameters

**1** Open the document ds_ch1.indd.

This is a Russian novel translated into English; the text is formatted in Adobe Garamond Pro.

**2** Select all the text with the Type tool. Because this text is a British translation that uses British spelling, select English: UK in the Language menu in the Character palette.

This choice affects hyphenation behavior (or behaviour) and spelling checks, if you perform the latter. It does not, however, check for punctuation differences between UK and US grammar rules.

**3** Change the point size to 9 pt.

**4** Zoom in on the page and apply leading values of 10, 11, 12, 13, and 14 pt. to a selected paragraph. For each value, deselect the text to get a better view, print it to examine the line spacing, read the passage and turn the page upside-down to consider the "color" of the type. Apply the leading that appears best to you.

The object is to determine which settings look best in terms of readability, separation of ascenders and descenders, and height of caps. You'll probably find that 11–12-pt. leading is the best compromise between legibility and story length.

**5** Select all the text and choose Hyphenation from the Paragraph palette Options menu. Set the After First and Before Last fields both to 3; set the Hyphenation slider two ticks from the left, and uncheck the Hyphenate Capitalized Words box.

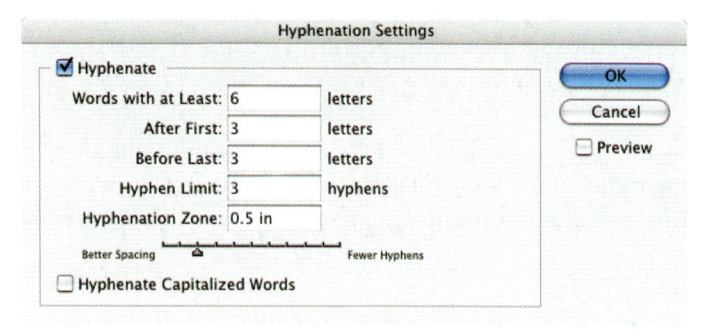

**FIGURE 3.15**

**6** Save the document and leave it open for the next exercise.

### If You Have Problems

If English: UK is not a choice in the Language menu, you need to install the extra dictionaries that come with InDesign, but that aren't installed by default. If you need to do so, quit InDesign, locate your InDesign installation CD, run the installer application, then choose Custom Installation. Deselect InDesign and SVG Viewer, select Dictionaries, and then proceed with the installation. This doesn't affect any of your preferences or other settings. If you can't install the dictionaries, continue anyway.

## LESSON 3  Justifying Text

In addition to considering how you hyphenate a document, you should also think about the justification options — for example, the "flush left" setting results in an irregular right margin; if you choose the Justified Left setting, all of the lines in a paragraph will align to both margins except the last line, which will align only to the left. Generally speaking, shorter lines look best with a flush-left alignment, and wider columns (such as in a book) can handle full justification.

Rules set in the Justification dialog box take effect when text is justified to both margins. You can choose these options from the Paragraph palette (or its Control palette equivalent), or define them as part of a paragraph style.

The Justification options control the word spacing, letter spacing, and glyph (character) scaling that is used to justify a paragraph. The Minimum and Maximum fields let you specify the spacing and scaling values to use when setting justified text.

Non-justified text, which is any text set to align flush left, center, or flush right, does not require any word spacing, so InDesign ignores any values in the Word Spacing fields. In most cases, it's best to avoid using letter spacing, because extra space between letters results in loose-appearing text. It is simpler to adjust tracking of letters rather than letter spacing.

Glyph scaling shrinks or enlarges the font-defined character width, and altering the shapes of letters is generally a bad idea. Used in small amounts (typically no more than ±3%), however, glyph scaling can solve copyfitting problems without visibly changing type appearance.

### Use Justification Controls

**1** Continue in the open document, ds_ch1.indd.

**2** Examine each page closely. If there is a single line from the following paragraph at the bottom of a page, or if a single line occurs alone at the top of a page, you will need to force the paragraph before to more or less spacing.

When confronted with this sort of copyfitting problem, you should not change leading, font size, glyph scaling, or any other attribute that's not applied to the entire story. Instead, use H&Js to help solve a fit problem. Fine-tune on a paragraph-by-paragraph basis. As a last resort, try small amounts of positive or negative tracking applied to the entire paragraph. Only as a last resort should you consider glyph scaling in the problem section.

**3** As you examine the pages, you also want to get rid of unwanted hyphenation.

A word that hyphenates at the bottom of a verso (left) page is not desirable, but it is acceptable. A word that hyphenates at the bottom of a recto (right) page needs to have the paragraph adjusted so it does not hyphenate.

**4** Click with the Type tool in any problem paragraph (or in the preceding paragraph, if you need to force a line of text to the next page). Choose Justification from the Paragraph palette Options menu and adjust the Minimum and Maximum Word Spacing fields until you achieve the result you need.

With the settings at 9/12 Adobe Garamond Pro, you can fix a problem on Page 2 (only one line of text from the last paragraph on the preceding page flowed over) by setting a minimum word spacing of 80% and a maximum word spacing of 120%.

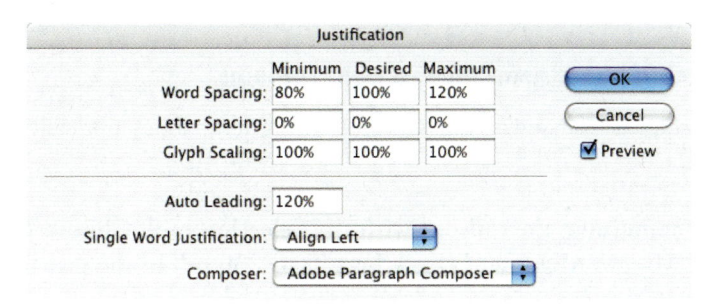

**FIGURE 3.16**

**5** Click OK to accept the new justification settings, then examine the paragraph for any bad spacing between words. Continue through the book, making corrections to copyfitting problems as you find them.

Fortunately, the author of the text used in this exercise, 19th-century Russian novelist Nikolai Gogol, was fond of huge paragraphs, so there aren't many opportunities for widows and orphans to occur. In most cases, you won't be so lucky.

**6** The document shrank considerably during composition, so delete any unused pages.

**7** Save the file and close it.

## LESSON 4  Aligning Margins Optically

Closely related to paragraph controls but wider-reaching in scope is Optical Margin Alignment, also called *hanging punctuation*. Although this feature can be used effectively for long-running text, it is best used for accent features such as call-outs. Optical Margin Alignment affects all text frames in a threaded story.

Optical Margin Alignment causes punctuation and the edges of some letters to "hang" outside the text frame, giving the paragraph a more even appearance. It is accessed by choosing Type>Story, then clicking the Optical Margin Alignment box. You can enter the desired amount of *escapement* in the text field, or select it from the menu. The escapement amount determines how far outside the frame InDesign will hang punctuation or the edges of letters. In theory, to achieve best results, this number should be equal to the point size. In practice, because typefaces differ dramatically, you'll want to experiment to find the solution that works best for the typeface you are using.

Another feature that affects the appearance of lines of ragged (having at least one unjustified edge) text is the Balance Ragged Lines option. This feature automatically equalizes the length of unjustified text and is most effective in headlines and call-outs.

## Use Optical Margin Alignment

**1** **Open the document advice.indd and look it over carefully, noting widows, orphans, and spacey lines.**

**2** **Go first to the call-out that spans the two right columns.**

This call-out is isolated in its own text frame. Aligning its margins optically will not affect anything else in the article.

**3** **Click the frame containing the call-out with the Selection tool. Choose Type>Story, then activate the Optical Margin Alignment check box. Type "30 pt" in the text field.**

The quotation marks hang into the left margin, and the quote is compressed onto only three lines of text. This looks awkward, because the quotation marks hang beyond the rule above the callout.

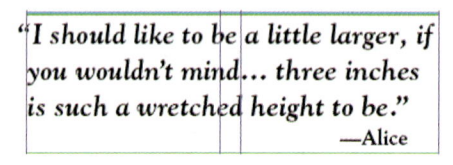

*"I should like to be a little larger, if you wouldn't mind... three inches is such a wretched height to be."*
—Alice

**FIGURE 3.17**

**4** **With the Type tool still in the text, apply a left indent of 0.3 in. from the Paragraph Control palette.**

It could still look much better — next you'll try balancing the lines.

**5** **From the Options menu in the Paragraph Control palette, choose Balance Lines.**

All lines are made as equal in length as possible.

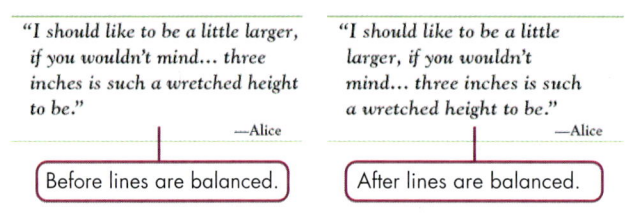

*"I should like to be a little larger, if you wouldn't mind... three inches is such a wretched height to be."*
—Alice

Before lines are balanced.

*"I should like to be a little larger, if you wouldn't mind... three inches is such a wretched height to be."*
—Alice

After lines are balanced.

**FIGURE 3.18**

**6** **Change the left indent of the paragraph to 0.5 in. to improve its look.**

**7** **Select all of the body text in the document.**

This is a two-page document, so clicking in the body text and pressing Command/Control-A is the most expedient way to select the text. Note that the type is 10 pt.

Project 3   Applying Advanced Typesetting Functions   117   LEVEL 2

**8** If the Optical Margin Alignment palette is not available, activate it (Type>Story). Set the Align Based on Size amount to 10.

All punctuation that abuts a margin is hung.

**9** Go back into the document and fix any widows, orphans, or bad breaks, using the H&J methods you learned in the previous lessons.

**10** Save the document and close it.

## LESSON 5  Copying Text Attributes

Working on documents that do not contain style sheets can be inefficient because it can be time-consuming to copy attributes from one passage of text to another. The manual way to do this is to look up the text characteristics in the Character and Paragraph palettes, write everything down, then apply those same settings to the new text.

InDesign's Eyedropper tool makes it possible to copy text attributes directly from existing text; you can even apply a color from an imported image to text. In this lesson, you will experiment with using the Eyedropper tool.

### Copy Attributes from Text and Images

**1** Open the documents balihai_new.indd and balihai_old.indd and position them on the monitor so you can see both documents.

The text for the new ad is correct (although it could stand some tweaking), but you need to apply the headline style used in the preceding ad.

**FIGURE 3.19**

**2** **Be sure no element of the ad is selected and select the Eyedropper from the Tool palette.**

The Eyedropper may be hidden under the Measure tool; you can access it by pressing "I" when another tool is active.

**3** **Click in the headline of balihai_old.indd.**

The Eyedropper picks up the properties of the headline.

**4** **With the loaded Eyedropper, highlight the line near the bottom of the page in balihai_new.indd, "Relax…without a care in the world."**

The old heading's properties (including font, size, and color) are transferred to the highlighted text. The ad still doesn't look quite right — the color doesn't really work with this new layout.

**5** **Click the Eyedropper outside any text or image area to clear it.**

**6** **Be sure the Stroke icon is set to None and the Fill icon is in front of the Stroke icon. Click the Eyedropper in the light blue portion of the old Bali Hai logo.**

You see a warning that you have selected a color from a low-resolution image proxy of a vector graphic. Because the logo is comprised of flat colors, the color will be accurate. Dismiss the warning.

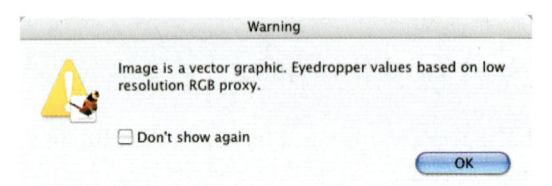

**FIGURE 3.20**

**7** **With the loaded Eyedropper, highlight the headline to transfer the color.**

The text takes on the color of the logo.

**8** **Save and close balihai_new.indd. Close balihai_old.indd without saving.**

**FIGURE 3.21**

Project 3  Applying Advanced Typesetting Functions    119   LEVEL 2

# LESSON 6  Creating Custom Glyph Sets

Many common characters are not easily accessible from the keyboard. On the Macintosh platform, for example, the dagger (†) symbol often used in footnotes is accessed by typing Option-t. On a Windows system, however, you need to type Alt-0134 on the numeric keypad. Memorizing numeric combinations — or even keyboard combinations — is somewhat daunting, so InDesign makes it unnecessary to do so.

If you often use special characters, you might want to create custom glyph sets. For example, you might have a client that regularly uses the multiplication symbol (×), usually referred to as the ***mult***. Even though the mult is in standard font character sets, you can't access it on a Macintosh unless you use a pi font such as Symbol. If you put the mult in a custom glyph set instead, you will always be able to access it regardless of the font you are using, and the weight will match the rest of the text. Creating and adding to a custom glyph set is easy — and can significantly streamline project workflow.

## Create and Use a Custom Glyph Set

1. Create a new document with a master text frame. Accept the default margins. Choose Adobe Caslon Pro as your active font.

2. Choose Type>Glyphs, and select New Glyph Set from the Options menu.

3. Name the new glyph set "[your initials]_glyphs" and click OK.

**FIGURE 3.22**

4. Expand the Glyphs palette so you can see all glyphs in the Adobe Caslon Pro font and click the mult to highlight it.

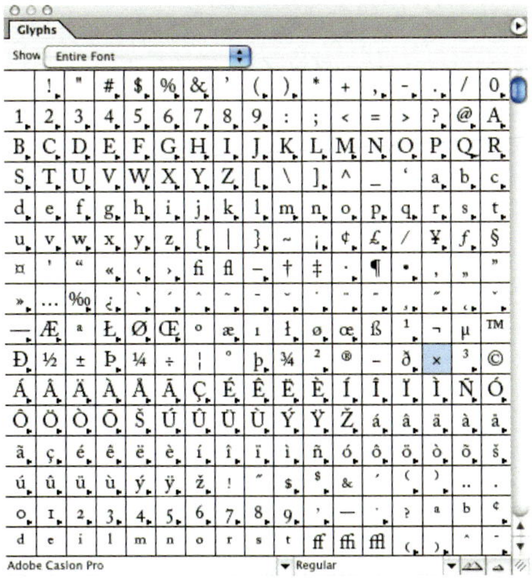

**FIGURE 3.23**

**5** Choose Add to Glyph Set from the Options menu, and choose your custom glyph set. Do not check the Remember Font with Glyph box.

The glyph is added to the set. Because you want the mult to change weight with the font that is selected, you do not link this glyph to any one font.

**6** Access the ATC Symbol font and click the foot mark ('). Add the glyph to your custom set.

This is not a symbol found in most character sets; together with the inch mark, though, it is used frequently.

**7** From ATC Symbol, add the inch mark (") to your glyph set.

**8** From the Options menu, choose Edit Glyph Set and select your glyph set.

The mult is highlighted when the Edit menu appears.

**9** Uncheck the Remember Font with Glyph box for the mult; leave it checked for the other two characters. Click OK when you are finished.

A "U" appears in the palette next to the mult. This indicates that the glyph is not linked to the font from which it originated. While most commercial fonts include the mult, some (such as the ATC fonts) do not. If a glyph is used in the document and you change to a font that does not include the glyph, InDesign will indicate that the font is missing.

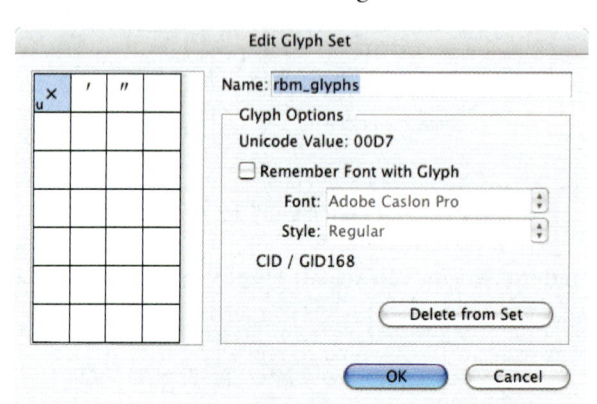

FIGURE 3.24

**10** Select Adobe Garamond Pro as your active font and, with your glyph set open, type "2″ × 4″". Double-click the glyphs to insert them.

**11** Close the document without saving.

# LESSON 7  Nesting Styles for Productivity

To properly plan your documents, you should first create every style you will use, then make a dummy paragraph that uses the style (the easiest way to do this is to create a frame of the proper size and choose Type>Fill with Placeholder Text). When you see the styles displayed, you can see that some paragraph styles include character attributes nested inside the paragraph. For example, you may want the drop cap for a chapter opener not only to drop three lines, but also to change font and color, and you may want the first three words to be small caps. You can create such effects using nested styles.

You can add more than one attribute to nested styles. If you do, the attributes will be applied sequentially — this can create some exotic effects. When you nest styles, you will save yourself many repetitive actions, allowing you to work faster and reducing the opportunity for the errors that occur when character styles are applied.

## Create and Use Nested Styles

**1**  **Open the document forge_fwd.indd.**

This is the text of the 1896 novel *The Forge in the Forest* by Charles G. D. Roberts; the novel is in the public domain. We have created paragraph styles and character styles for you.

**2**  **From the Paragraph Styles palette, double-click the Body Text 1 paragraph style.**

**3**  **Open the Drop Caps and Nested Styles pane.**

In this pane, you can define your drop cap and any styles you choose to nest within the Body Text 1 paragraph style.

**4**  **Define a 3-line, 1-character drop, using the Drop Cap character style.**

This character style is maroon in color, and will use any swash characters in the font. A swash character is part of the expanded character set; it is more decorative than the standard capital letter.

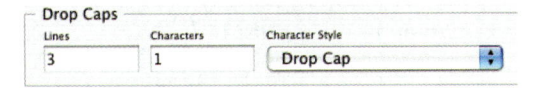

FIGURE 3.25

**5**  **Click the New Nested Style button and choose the Small Cap character style.**

**6** Click the word "Words" and choose End Nested Style Character from the menu that appears. Click OK.

The entire paragraph becomes maroon small caps. Using this strategy makes it easy to apply the nested style to different numbers of words, depending on the context.

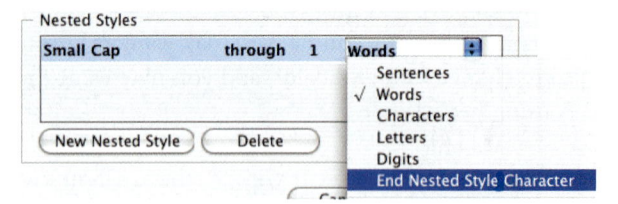

**FIGURE 3.26**

**7** Place the Type tool after the word "flow" and choose Type>Insert Special Character>End Nested Style Here.

The maroon small caps end where you positioned the marker. If you choose Type>Show Hidden Characters, you will be able to see the End Nested Style character in the text.

**8** Save the document and close it.

## LESSON 8  Setting Type on a Path

From time to time, you will want to set type on a curved path, rather than on a straight line. Only one line of type can be set on any path, so if you want type to run around the top of a circle, then appear right-side up on the bottom, you need to impose a second circle to create the path for the balance of the type.

You can create the path with the Pen or Pencil tool or with any of the shape or frame tools. Type set on a path behaves like regular type in a frame — you can apply most paragraph attributes and any character attributes. Any text that exceeds the length of a path is treated as overset, and can be threaded to a text frame or onto another path by clicking the red "+" symbol in the out port.

The brackets at the start, middle, and end of a path containing type are used to position the type along the curve. You can align the path with the type's baseline, center, ascenders, or descenders. You can apply five effects to type on a path:

- The Rainbow effect is the default; the baseline follows the path.
- The Skew effect keeps the sides of the characters consistent, but skews them horizontally to follow the path.
- The 3D Ribbon effect skews the characters vertically in proportion to the curvature of the path.
- The Stairstep effect doesn't rotate any characters; it puts the edge of each character's aligning point on the path.
- The Gravity effect locks the center of a character's baseline on the path and keeps each vertical edge in line with the path's center point; the flatter the curve, the greater the distortion.

## Create Type on a Path

**1** Create a new document using the default settings.

**2** Show the document grid, and enable the Snap to Grid feature (both are in the View menu). Zoom into the center of the page at 200%.

**3** Select the Pen tool and position it at the intersection of 2 in. horizontal and 3 in. vertical. Click once to set a starting point. Move the pen to 3 in. horizontal and 2 in. vertical and click again, then Shift-drag to draw handles out one inch.

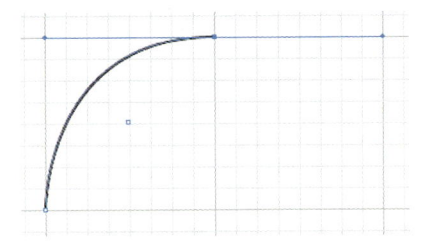

**FIGURE 3.27**

**4** Click once at 4 in. horizontal, 1 in. vertical. Make the resulting line 1-pt. black so it will be easy to see. Hide the document grid, and turn off the Snap to Grid option.

A smooth path is constructed, and you are ready to add text.

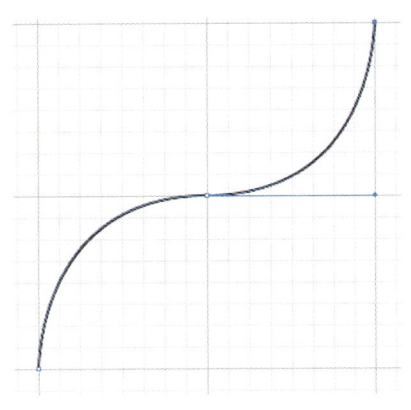

**FIGURE 3.28**

**5** Choose the Type on a Path tool by clicking and holding the Type tool in the Tools palette.

You can also activate the Type on a Path tool by simply pressing Shift-T.

**6** Move the Type on a Path tool over the path until a small "+" symbol appears next to the tool icon.

The plus symbol indicates that you've "found" the path with the tool.

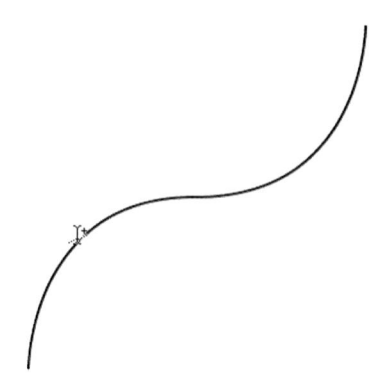

**FIGURE 3.29**

**7** Click once to position the tool on the path. A blinking text cursor appears at the start of the path. Type your name, then select it.

**8** Apply any typeface you wish to your name. Increase the size to 24–30 pt. Click the Center icon in the Paragraph palette to center the type on the path.

You can also press Command/Control-Shift-C to center type on a path. ATC Maple is the typeface used in the example below. Notice that the curves of the path can jam some characters together. You can fix this problem by kerning the type.

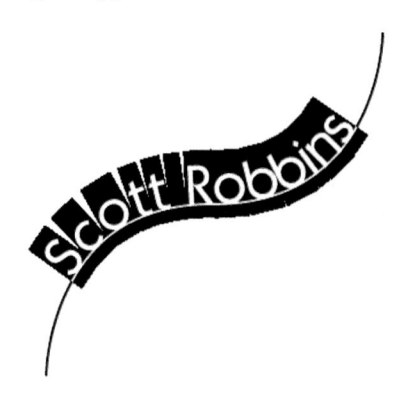

**FIGURE 3.30**

**9** Double-click the Type on a Path tool to open the Type on a Path Options dialog box. Select the Preview check box if it's not already active. Select the Flip check box and watch the type flip to the other side of the path.

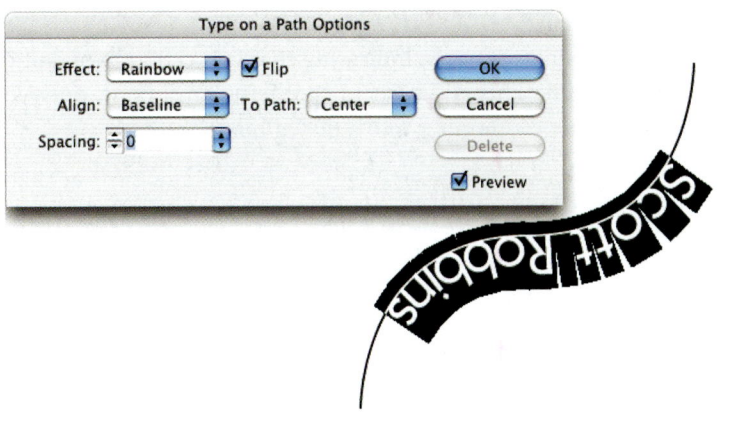

FIGURE 3.31

**10** Deselect the Flip check box. Experiment with all the options in the Effect menu. When you are finished experimenting, return to Rainbow.

The default Rainbow effect is probably the most legible; the Gravity effect results in unreadable text.

**11** Try the different alignment options in the Align menu, then set this option back to Baseline.

**12** Review the Top and Bottom options in the To Path menu, then set the menu back to Center.

If you change the weight of the line to a larger point size, you will immediately see the effect of changing the To Path option.

**13** Choose –12 from the Spacing menu and notice how the type is affected at different locations along the curve. Experiment with different spacing values to find a value that works with the font you chose and the letter shapes involved. Our example looks best with a Spacing value of 6.

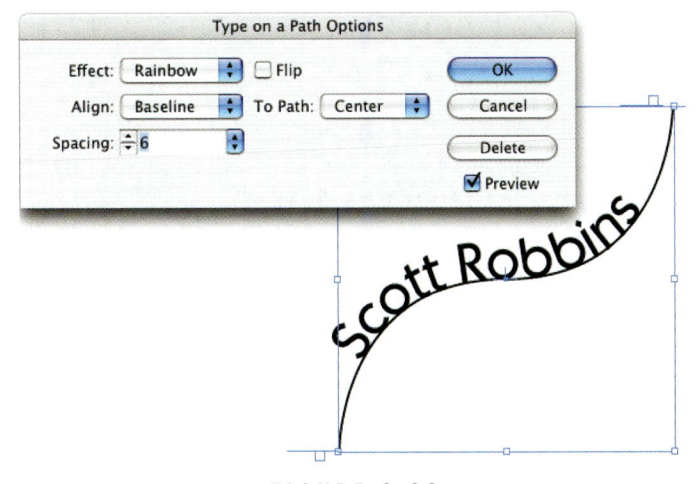

FIGURE 3.32

**14** Save the document as "curve_practice.indd" and keep it open.

## Modify Type on a Path

**1** **Continue in the open document. Move the Selection tool over the end bracket at the top right of the bounding box and watch it closely.**

Next to the pointer, a small icon appears, indicating that you can grab one of the brackets and slide it toward the center of the path. This is similar to specifying an indent, only you can move it interactively, instead of having to type a number into a dialog box.

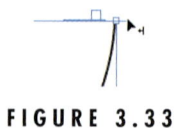

FIGURE 3.33

**2** **Slide the end bracket toward the center.**

The text moves to the left.

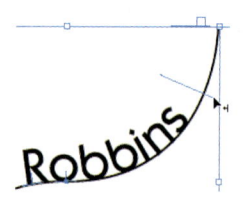

FIGURE 3.34

**3** **Drag the start bracket toward the middle.**

The text moves to the right.

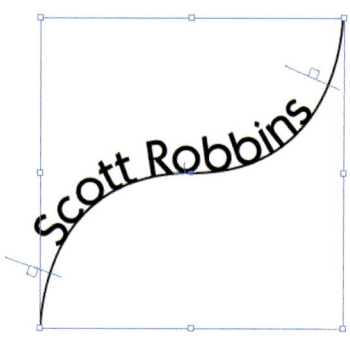

FIGURE 3.35

Project 3   Applying Advanced Typesetting Functions    **127**   LEVEL 2

**4**   **After you move the end brackets, you can adjust the center bracket. Zoom in until it's easily visible, click and hold the center bracket, and move the mouse to slide the text.**

The center bracket allows you to slide all the text along the path.

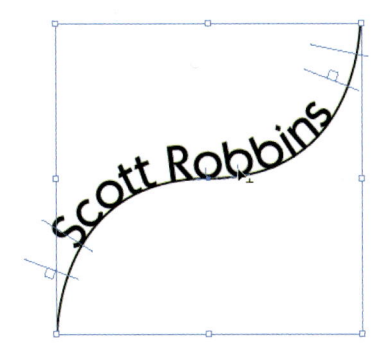

FIGURE 3.36

Be careful when moving the center bracket. If you move it below the path, the text flips to the other side of the path. If this happens, grab the center bracket and move it back above the path.

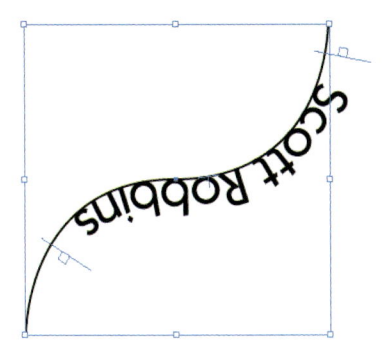

FIGURE 3.37

**5**   **Switch to the Type on a Path tool and select the first letter of your first name on the path and set a baseline offset of –6 pt. Repeat for the first letter of your last name.**

This tool works just like the normal Type tool, so you can select text by dragging, double-clicking to select a word, or triple-clicking to select the entire line.

FIGURE 3.38

**6**   **Save the file and close it.**

# SUMMARY

Setting attractive, readable text can be a real challenge for a designer, but InDesign makes it easier to do so. You can customize H&J settings, position type along a path of virtually any shape, and create custom glyph sets to allow you to more easily add symbols to your documents. You can format paragraphs of text by simply dragging character attributes from one element of text to another. InDesign's state-of-the-art Optical Margin Alignment feature allows you to produce electronic documents that simulate the appearance of painstakingly detailed hand-set type.

# KEY TERMS

| | | |
|---|---|---|
| 3D Ribbon | glyph scaling | Optical Margin Alignment |
| Adobe Paragraph Composer | Gravity | paragraph spacing limit |
| Adobe Single-Line Composer | hanging punctuation | Rainbow |
| Balance Ragged Lines | hyphenation | Skew |
| carding | hyphenation zone | Stairstep |
| custom glyph set | inset spacing | text inset |
| Eyedropper tool | justification | text on a path |
| feathering | letter spacing | vertical justification |
| first baseline | mult | word spacing |
| fixed column width | nested style | |

# CHECKING CONCEPTS AND TERMS

## MULTIPLE CHOICE

**Check the letter of the correct answer for each of the following:**

1. What occurs when you check the Fixed Column Width box?
   a. The text frame is locked — it cannot be enlarged or shrunk.
   b. The text frame can be altered vertically but not horizontally.
   c. The text frame can be expanded or shrunk only in increments of the column width plus the gutter width.
   d. The gutters become wider or narrower when the frame is adjusted.

2. How does InDesign manage vertical justification within a frame?
   a. It inserts space between paragraphs.
   b. It inserts space between lines.
   c. It aligns text to the top, bottom, or center of the frame.
   d. All of the above.

3. What is the Hyphenation Zone?
   a. The points in a word where hyphenation is acceptable
   b. The number of hyphens you allow to occur in successive lines
   c. The minimum length of a word that you can hyphenate
   d. The maximum distance from the end of a line in which a hyphen can occur

4. What parameter should be avoided whenever possible when justifying text?
   a. Word spacing
   b. Letter spacing
   c. Glyph scaling
   d. Hyphenation

5. What is "hanging punctuation"?
   a. A punctuation mark that extends outside the text frame
   b. An instance in which a punctuation mark, such as a dash, begins a line
   c. An occurrence of three hyphens in a row, also known as a "ladder"
   d. A means of balancing ragged lines

6. Which of the following can you apply with the Eyedropper tool?
   a. Indent and spacing attributes
   b. Size and leading attributes
   c. Style and color attributes
   d. All of the above.

7. When would you not want to link the originating font to a character in a custom glyph set?
   a. When the character is common to most fonts
   b. When using an OpenType font
   c. When the character comes from a font you always have active on your computer
   d. Never

8. What parameters define a nested style?
   a. Font name, style, and color
   b. Basic character format, character color, and indent amount
   c. Character style, duration, and ending parameter
   d. None of the above

9. In what way is type on a path different from normal text?
   a. There are no in and out ports.
   b. You cannot specify a justification parameter.
   c. You can have only one line of text.
   d. It cannot be threaded with other text.

10. When setting text that is aligned left (ragged right) what H&J parameters are applied?
    a. Minimum, Desired, and Maximum word spacing
    b. Variable letter spacing
    c. Glyph scaling
    d. Hyphenation limit

## DISCUSSION QUESTIONS

1. Discuss a variety of ways in which you could use nested styles.

2. Discuss types of glyph sets you could create that would make working on documents easier.

# SKILL DRILL

Skill Drills reinforce project skills. Each skill reinforced is the same, or nearly the same, as a skill presented in the lessons. Detailed instructions are provided in a step-by-step format. You should perform Skill Drills 2 and 3 in the order they are presented. Drills 1 and 4 may be performed in any order.

## 1. Apply Text Control

The ad for the not-for-profit account Music in Education is the only thing holding up your magazine from going to press. Although the ad was assigned to another designer, she had a family emergency after beginning production, so you are under the gun to finish the ad quickly. Fortunately, the only thing that remains to be done is to finish the placement of text. The client is moderately fussy, so any necessary modifications that you make will have to be subtle. All of the type has been specified, so you can't change any of the type sizes.

1. Open the file art_in_ed.indd and check it over. There's clearly a problem with the main headline, and the body text will require some work as well.

2. Select all the text in the frame holding the headline, access the Justification dialog box and change to Adobe Single-Line Composer to give yourself the most control over the document.

3. Experiment with the minimum word spacing to bring all the text into the frame.

    That's the most you can do with the Justification options. You'll need to use kerning and tracking to adjust the lines further. You can track the lines unequal amounts, if necessary. Your goal is to achieve a balance between the two lines.

4. Click the frame containing the body text with the Selection tool and access Type>Story. Activate the Optical Margin Alignment utility, and set the amount to the same size as the text.

5. Open the Text Frame Options dialog box.

6. Experiment with the First Baseline Offset setting to achieve a pleasing result; we chose 0.35 in. When you're satisfied with the result you achieve, click OK.

7. Double-click the Body Text paragraph style. Set its Hyphenation parameters to a minimum of two characters before a hyphen and a minimum of three characters after a hyphen.

8. Depending upon where you chose to position the first line of text in this frame, you may want to increase the leading 0.25 – 0.5 pt. Adjust as you see fit.

9. Add space above the "Call now…" line, as appropriate.

10. Review the ad and make any adjustments you think are appropriate. You might want to change the text wrap around the trumpet player if you don't like the way the text is falling.

11. Save and close the document.

FIGURE 3.39

## 2. Nest Styles

Your company is reprinting Oscar Wilde's *The Portrait of Dorian Gray*. Your company is doing the production, so you get production credits on the first page of the document. Rather than painstakingly working through each line, you're going to use nested styles to automatically style these elements.

1. Open the document dgray.indd and go to Page i, if the document does not open to that page.
2. Double-click the Credits paragraph style.
3. Open the Drop Caps & Nested Styles pane of the Paragraph Style Options dialog box.
4. Click the New Nested Style button.
5. Choose the Caslon Semi Ital character style.
6. Leave the default setting (Through 1), and choose En Spaces as the concluding element. Click OK.
7. Select the entire block of positions and names in the lower left of the page and assign them the Credits style.
8. Save the document and leave it open for the next exercise.

FIGURE 3.40

## 3. Set Hyphenation and Justification Parameters

In this continuation of the previous Skill Drill, you need to vertically justify your pages, set your hyphenation parameters (Wilde was Irish, so you'll use UK English), and set the justification.

1. Continue in the open document dgray.indd and go to the third page (Page 1).
2. Double-click the Body Text paragraph style and open the Advanced Character Formats pane. Choose English: UK from the Language menu.
3. Open the Hyphenation pane. Change the Before Last field to 3, change the Hyphen Limit field to 2, and uncheck the Hyphenate Capitalized Words box.
4. In the Justification pane, Word Spacing should be set to Minimum: 80%, Desired: 100%, Maximum: 133%. Letter Spacing and Glyph Scaling should be set to 0% and 100%, respectively. Set the Single Word Justification menu to Align Left, and accept the default of Adobe Paragraph Composer.
5. In the Keep Options pane, keep the first and last two lines of the paragraph together. Click OK.
6. Select the large text frame and choose Story from the Type menu. Turn Optical Margin Alignment on and set the value to 11 pt.
7. With the large text frame on Page 1 still selected, choose Object>Text Frame Options. Click the Preview button so you can see what is happening to the page.
8. Change the Vertical Justification menu to Justify. Note how the lines "feather" until they are equal at the bottom of the page.
9. Change the Paragraph Spacing Limit field to 3.25 pt., which is half the value of the Space After defined by the Body Text style.
10. Repeat Steps 7 and 8 for the remaining pages in the document. Do not justify the last page; instead, manually drag the frame up to balance the columns.
11. Get rid of any unacceptably short lines by judiciously tracking the paragraphs. When you are finished, save and close the document.

## 4. Apply Formatting

You have been assigned to produce a theater poster for the popular *The Music Man* by Meredith Willson. We have started the poster for you, and put all text and images in place. Using methods you have learned in this project, you will finish the poster.

1. Open the document music_man.indd and look over the page. As is often the case with a poster such as this, there are no styles; everything has been done interactively.

2. Select the two tan text frames on the right just under the picture and adjust their vertical justification to align center.

3. Select the two outlined text frames on the right at the bottom of the poster and adjust their vertical justification to align top, with an offset based on leading.

4. With the Eyedropper tool, click the "Music, Lyrics & Book by" line.

5. Select the top line in each of the succeeding two frames ("Staged by" and "Choreographed by") to apply the style.

6. Click outside the page to clear the Eyedropper, then click the "Meredith Willson" line.

7. Apply the style to the words "Morton Da Costa" and "Oona White", and to "Meredith Willson" and "Frank Lacy" in the line below the boxes. Setting these names in the same size fulfills a requirement common to play contracts.

8. Make similar changes to the text in the boxes at the bottom of the page.

9. Adjust the leading in the third frame so everything fits attractively. If you feel you must adjust the leading of the top line, you should adjust the leading to the top line in every frame so the words align.

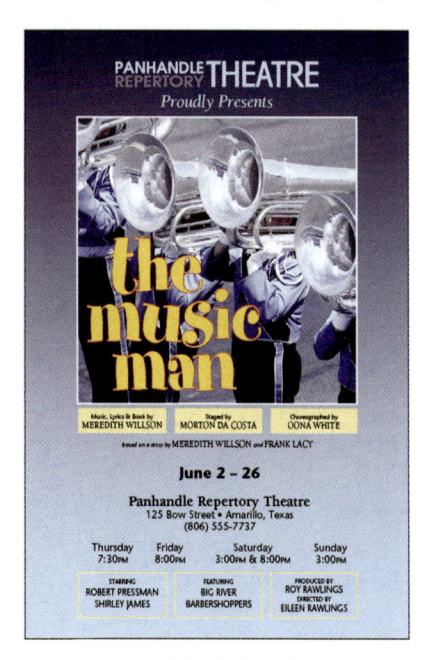

**FIGURE 3.41**

10. Save and close the document.

# CHALLENGE

Challenge exercises expand on, or are somewhat related to, skills presented in the lessons. Each exercise provides a brief introduction, followed by instructions presented in a numbered-step format that are not as detailed as those in the Skill Drill exercises. You should perform the first two and the last two of these exercises in the order in which they appear.

## 1. Create Custom Glyphs

You are the designer for a bookstore that is creating a series of bookmarks. They want a "touch of class" and have selected the Adobe Caslon Pro family of type. They want to use ornaments in the corners and a dingbat at the end of the verses on the bookmarks. The easiest way to accomplish this is to create a set of custom glyphs that can sit on the desktop and be applied at will.

1. Change the font to Adobe Caslon Pro Italic.
2. Open the Glyphs palette, show Ornaments, and choose New Glyph Set from the Options menu. Name the glyph set "Caslon Ornaments".
3. Click the acorn dingbat to select it and choose Add to Glyph Set>Caslon Ornaments. You may want to change the size of the display in the Glyphs palette by clicking the sizing icon in the lower right.
4. Add two sets of corner dingbats to the Caslon Ornaments palette, so your bookmarks will have some variety.
5. Add the right-pointing hand to your palette.
6. Choose Entire Font and scroll down until you see the alternate swash characters.
7. Add the "Th" ligature and all swash capital letters, since you may be using drop caps for your bookmarks.
8. Choose Options>View Glyph Set>Caslon Ornaments to view your new Glyphs palette.
9. Leave the palette open for the next Challenge.

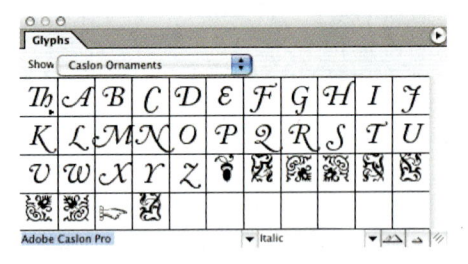

**FIGURE 3.42**

## 2. Use Custom Glyphs

Now that you have created your glyph set, you need to apply the glyphs to your client's product. You'll discover that it's relatively easy; you should be able to apply what you have learned in this project to complete this Challenge relatively quickly.

1. Open the document bookmark.indd. You will notice that the characters "DB" occur in a number of places. This is where you will place the dingbats you copied into your custom Glyphs palette.
2. Open the custom Glyphs palette, if it is not already open.
3. Highlight the first "DB" and double click one of the upper-left dingbats you chose.
4. Add the upper-right glyph. They're probably a little small. Change the size to one that looks good to you.
5. Add the lower glyphs.
6. Alternating between your choices of glyphs, add the corner characters to all six bookmarks.
7. Use the Eyedropper tool to make all the corner glyphs the same size.
8. Apply the acorn glyph to the ending DB on each of the bookmarks.
9. In the first paragraphs of each entry on the Irish Philosophy bookmarks, apply the Drop Cap style.
10. In the "Erin Gae Bragh" bookmark, replace the "DB" at the beginning of the saying with the pointing hand dingbat. Use the Balance Ragged Lines option to create the best overall look, and remove any hyphenation. Adjust lines and add interparagraph spacing as you feel appropriate.
11. Save the document and close it.

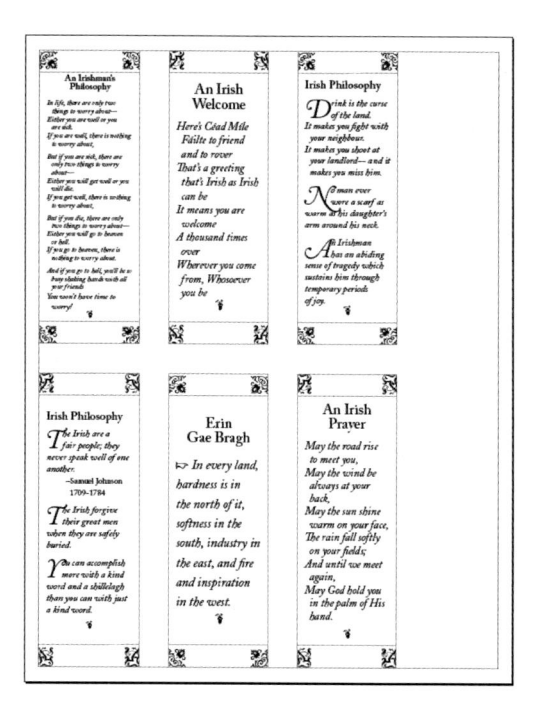

**FIGURE 3.43**

## 3. Use Type on a Path

Type on a path can be arbitrary, or it can illustrate something you are trying to show, such as a hilly terrain or the flight of a bumblebee. In this project, you will use type on a path to illustrate the trail that leads up a mountain. This could be used in a presentation, or could be part of a book cover.

1. Open the document hill_climb.indd.
2. Choose a drawing tool and draw a path from the edge of the trees to just below the summit of the mountain.
3. In 18-pt. ATC Oak Bold Italic, type "CLIMB YOUR WAY TO THE TOP OF THE HILL". If it doesn't fit on your line, reduce the point size.
4. Center the type on the line.
5. From the Type on a Path Options menu, align the baseline to the center of the path.
6. Change the weight of the rule to 18 pt. and assign round endcaps.
7. Change the color of the rule to yellow, or another color of your choosing.
8. This looks like a smooth, easy climb. Change the Effect to Stairstep, so it's obvious that the going gets tougher as you approach the top.
9. Save the file and leave it open for the next Challenge.

**FIGURE 3.44**

## 4. Add to and Edit Type on a Path

No matter how complete the directions are when the job comes in, the one thing you can count on is changes. Now the client wants to add some text, and wants to join paths together.

1. Re-insert the Type tool into the path and continue typing: "…don't let life send you around and around in circles when you'd really like to achieve your goals."

2. With the Text on a Path tool, click the spiral on the page; this establishes the path as a text frame.

3. With the spiral path active, hold the Shift key and click the "Climb your way…" frame.

4. Click the Overset Text icon, then click the Autoflow Text icon on the spiral path when the cursor changes to a Thread icon.

5. With just the text on the spiral selected, access the Text on a Path Options dialog box.

6. Check the Flip box to reverse the text on this path.

7. Save and close the document.

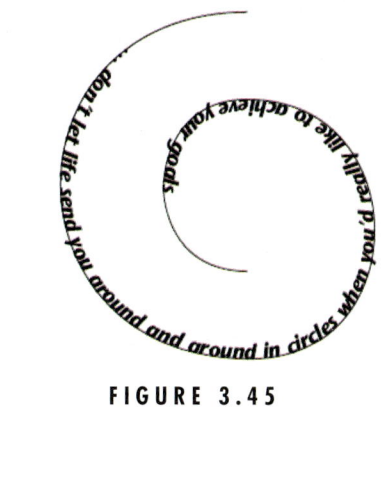

**FIGURE 3.45**

# PORTFOLIO BUILDER

## Build an Enticing Children's Book

You have already worked with *Alice in Wonderland* text, both in this project and in *Essentials for Design: InDesign Level 1*. Here is an opportunity for you to work with the complete, original e-text from Project Gutenberg (a group dedicated to making electronic books available for free online) and the illustrations that were designed to go with the book. The files are located in the Project_03>Alice Adventures folder; the artwork is in the Art folder within the Alice Adventures folder. You can create your book in any size you wish, with any number of columns.

To complete this project, use the following techniques:

- Design an attractive cover. Don't forget to give the author credit.

- Treat the book as a children's book — make the type somewhat large, and be sure it's easy to read.

- Use call-outs, illustrations, and captions.

- Wrap text around the illustrations, and be careful with the text wraps, so that if text wraps to both left and right of an illustration, the wraps look consistent. NOTE: Text becomes harder to read if it skips horizontally over an illustration — not what you want in a children's book.

- Work with InDesign's automated features to create a book that is typographically excellent.

- Create the document as a single document with sections, or as a book, whichever you prefer.

# PROJECT 4

## LEVEL 2

# Working with Tables

## OBJECTIVES

*In this project, you learn how to*

- Create tables
- Import tables from other programs
- Convert text to tables and tables to text
- Format tables and cells
- Adjust rows and columns
- Merge and split cells
- Apply strokes and fills to table elements
- Manage cell contents
- Insert graphics and nested tables

# WHY WOULD I DO THIS?

Not all text is produced as running text, or even as text on a path. In *Essentials For Design: InDesign Level 1*, you learned to set tabular text, which has many uses. Sometimes, though, you may want to include a graphic, or you might need to include several lines in a tab section. Instead of creating new lines and pressing the Tab key multiple times, in such instances, you can turn to InDesign's table-building features.

Tables consist of rows and columns of cells, much as information is presented in a spreadsheet such as Microsoft Excel. A table **cell** acts like a miniature InDesign frame; it can contain text, graphics, or even other tables. In many respects, tables behave like standard text; they can flow from one frame to another, and move in position if text is added above them. A single text frame can contain both tables and ordinary text.

A table behaves like a single character. If you type Return/Enter above it, it moves down; if you click the text cursor to the right of it and press the Delete/Backspace key, it is deleted. If you don't want the table to interact with the rest of the text on the page, you can set it in its own frame. Table controls are located on the Table menu and the Table palette.

You can still create effective table-like effects by using the tab features, as you have done before. If, however, you have tabular material that requires heavy formatting, inline graphics, or visual table cues such as shading and borders, you'll probably find it more efficient to use the Table function. Although you could create many of the same effects with tabs and paragraph styles, it would require a tremendous amount of unnecessary work.

InDesign tables are very flexible; you have a high degree of control over their appearance. You can easily insert, delete, and resize rows and columns. You can define cells to remain at a fixed size, or you can allow them to grow dynamically to accommodate their contents. You use the Character and Paragraph palettes, or the Character and Paragraph Styles palettes to format the text in a table. You can align cell contents vertically (to the top, bottom, or center, or justified to fill the cell) just as you align text vertically in a frame.

Project 4    Working with Tables    **141**    LEVEL 2

# VISUAL SUMMARY

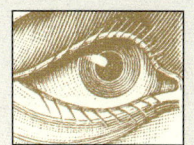

When you create tables in InDesign, you use the Table menu and the Table palette. Many of the options are similar to those in word-processing programs such as Microsoft Word. When you create a new table, you define the number of rows (horizontal) and columns (vertical). Text in the table defaults to the typeface in use when you create the text frame into which the table is placed.

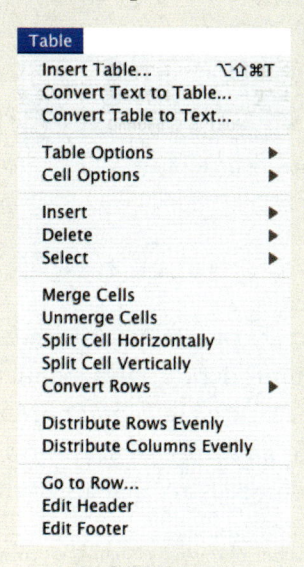

**FIGURE 4.1**

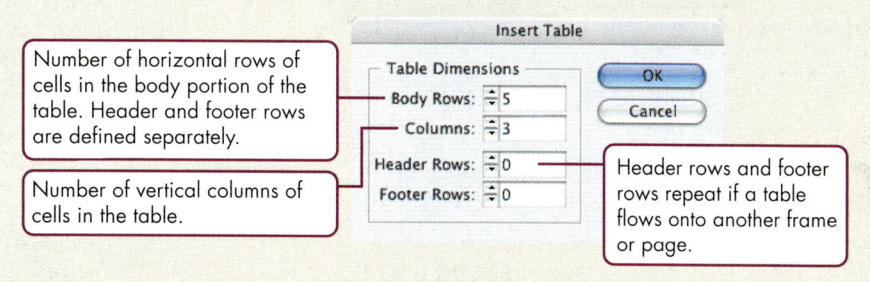

Number of horizontal rows of cells in the body portion of the table. Header and footer rows are defined separately.

Number of vertical columns of cells in the table.

Header rows and footer rows repeat if a table flows onto another frame or page.

**FIGURE 4.2**

In addition to typing data directly into a table, you can import tables from other programs, such as FileMaker, Microsoft Word, or Microsoft Excel. Imported tables are placed into InDesign in the same way as text and graphics are — with the File>Place command (or its shortcut, Command/Control-D). When importing files from programs such as Excel, you can specify which worksheet to place, and even the cell range.

You have several options when importing a spreadsheet. If you import an unformatted table, then InDesign's default formatting is applied to the text. If you import a formatted table, then the formatting defined in the spreadsheet program is applied; you can, however, specify a cell alignment of your choice after you import a formatted table. Importing a table as unformatted tabbed text results in tabular text. If you are not importing from an Excel spreadsheet or a Word table, you can import the information as tab-delimited text. Once the text is in place, you can quickly change it to a table using the Convert Text to Table command.

FIGURE 4.3

Once you have defined the basic structure of a table, it is easy to adjust its individual elements. You can resize the column widths and column depths, and stipulate that the width and depth be either variable or fixed. You can also resize the entire table, and universally or individually change text specifications. Individual cells can contain anything that a normal frame can contain, including text, graphics, or even other tables. Text and images are managed within the table using the Table palette.

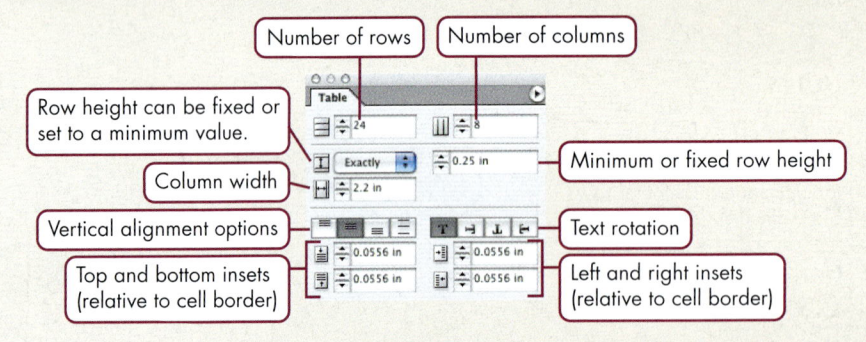

FIGURE 4.4

There are several ways to change the number of rows and columns in an existing table. You can add or remove rows or columns using the Insert Row, Insert Column, Delete Row, or Delete Column commands that appear on both the Table menu and palette, or you can simply change the number of rows or columns in the Table palette fields.

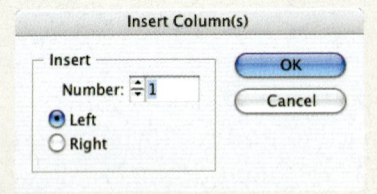

FIGURE 4.5

The Table>Merge Cells and Table>Split Cell Horizontally/Vertically commands allow you to combine or divide cells to create custom tables. The selected cells are either merged into a single cell or split into two cells of equal height or width.

Although tables have 1-pt. black rules as default boundaries, you can remove, color, or change the width or patterns of any rule. Similarly, you can fill cells with colors and patterns. InDesign allows you to define patterns of alternating fills and strokes.

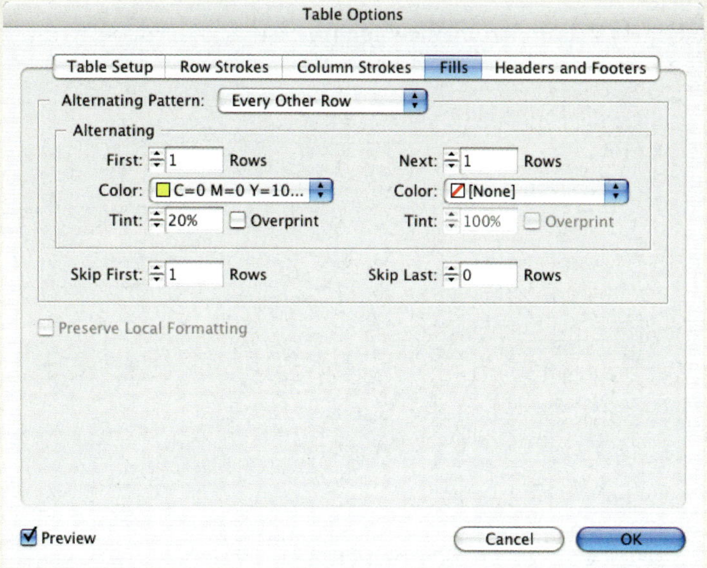

**FIGURE 4.6**

## LESSON 1  Creating Tables

To create tables in InDesign, you use the Table menu; to format them, you can use either the Table menu or the Table palette. Basic tables are easy to create; you can make them more complicated (and more interesting) as you need to. A table may consist of three parts: the ***header***, the ***body***, and the ***footer***. When you define cells as header or footer text, they repeat when the table spans more than one frame.

Although tables may look similar to tabular text or columns on a page, they behave much differently. Tabbed text flows in a horizontal direction only; text columns flow in a down-and-up fashion from one column to another. Table columns do not flow, unless the table itself flows to another text column or frame.

You can navigate through tables using the Tab key and the arrow keys. To move to the next horizontal cell, simply press the Tab or Right Arrow key. To move to a cell immediately below the cell in which the cursor appears, press the Down Arrow key. If you're in the last cell of a row, use the Tab key to move to the first cell of the next row.

InDesign treats table cells as independent items; any text formatting applied to text before or after a table is not applied to the text in the table. Instead, all text typed into a table is styled with the default settings in the Character palette, or the typeface in use when the text frame was created. You can select any cell, row, column, or the whole table, to change the character formatting applied in that area.

## Create and Navigate a Simple Table

**1** Create a new document with the following settings:

> Facing Pages: Off
> Master Text Frame: Off
> Page Size: Letter-Half
> Margins: 0.5 in. (all sides)
> Columns: 1
> Frame Edges: Visible (from View menu)

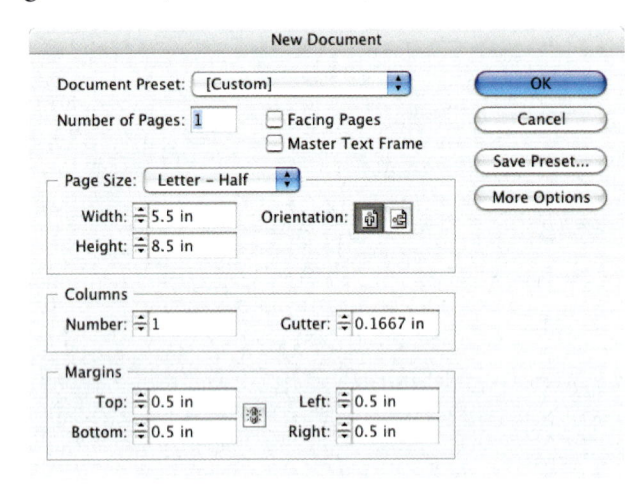

**FIGURE 4.7**

**2** Using the Type tool, draw a text frame within the margins of the page.

**3** Choose Table>Insert Table, and create a table with five rows and three columns.

When the Insert Table dialog box appears, you have the option of defining body, header, and footer rows. Since this example will only be a short table, you don't need header and footer rows, which repeat if a table is forced into additional frames.

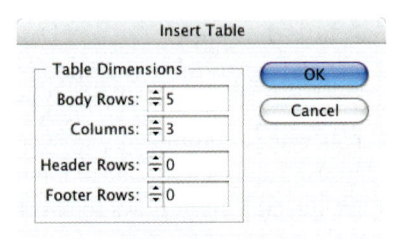

**FIGURE 4.8**

The new table fills the width of the frame. The height is determined by the number of rows that you specified. The actual height of the rows can vary, but it is never less than the value specified in the Row Height field of the Table palette. The default row height accommodates 12-pt. text.

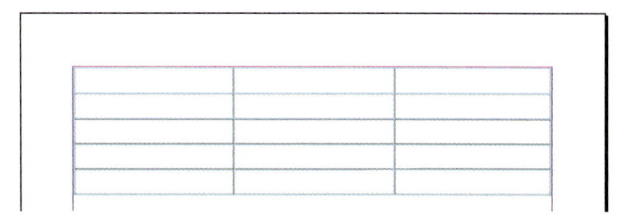

**FIGURE 4.9**

**4** **The text cursor should be active in the first cell. If it is not, click once in the cell. Type "Film". Press Tab to move the cursor to the next cell to the right. Type "Studio", then press Tab once more to move to the upper-right cell. Type "Producer" and press Tab.**

When you get to the end of a row and press Tab, the cursor advances to the first cell in the next row.

**5** **Press Shift-Tab to go back to the last cell, automatically selecting the word "Producer." Type "Starring" to replace this word.**

**6** **Press Shift-Tab twice to return to the first cell. Press the Down Arrow key twice to move the cursor to the next row, which is empty. Press the Right Arrow key three times.**

The cursor returns to the first cell of the same row when you use the Left or Right Arrow keys and reach the other end. If there is any text in the cells, the cursor moves one letter at a time until it gets to the end of the text, then it jumps to the previous or next cell.

**7** **Use the Up and Down Arrow keys to move the cursor between rows.**

The Up Arrow key moves from the end of a word to the beginning of a word or, if at the beginning of a word or in an empty cell, to the row above. The Down Arrow key moves from the beginning of a word to the end of a word or, if at the end of a word or in an empty cell, to the row below.

**8** **Close the document without saving.**

## LESSON 2 Importing Tables from Other Programs

If you save an Excel, FileMaker, or other database file as a text-only file, you can create delimiters, which act to separate each field and record. A tab character is commonly used as a field delimiter, and a return character used as a record delimiter (creating a new row). Exporting delimited text from a database is one way of getting tabular data into InDesign; you can also import Microsoft Excel or Word files that contain tables as InDesign tables.

If you are importing an Excel file, you can specify the number of rows and columns to place in the document. This is convenient if you need just a portion of the data in an Excel spreadsheet. If you import a text-only file, it is not converted to a table. Instead, you have to place it as text, then convert it to a table, as you will do in the next lesson.

## Import a Table

**1** Create a new document with no facing pages, keeping the default margins.

**2** Set the font to ATC Elm Normal, then use the Type tool to draw a text frame within the margins of the page.

**3** With the cursor placed in the frame, open the Place dialog box. Make sure the Show Import Options box is checked. Highlight the file renwear.xls and click Open.

The Microsoft Excel Import Options dialog box opens. There is more information in the renwear.xls file than you need for the document you are creating.

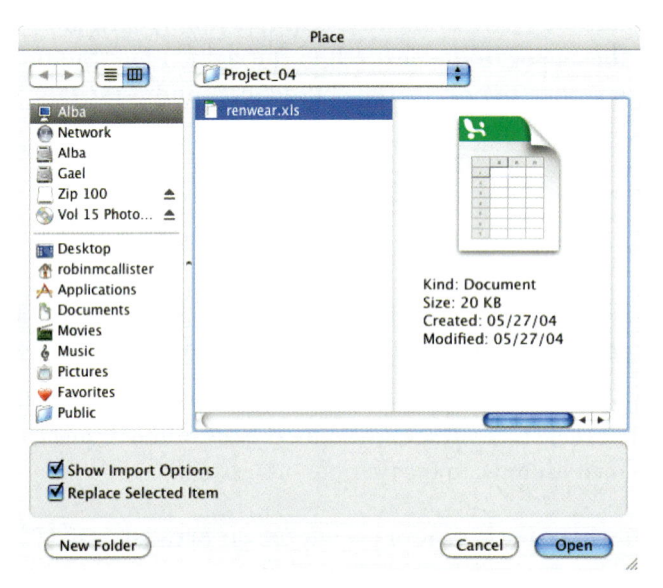

**FIGURE 4.10**

**4** Choose Inventory from the Sheet menu, then type "A1:H24" in the Cell Range field. Set the Table menu to Unformatted Table. Set the Number of Decimal Places to Include field to 0, and check the Use Typographer's Quotes box. Click OK.

This is an inventory, so there are no decimal places in the file. If you receive any warnings about missing fonts, ignore them; you will change fonts later.

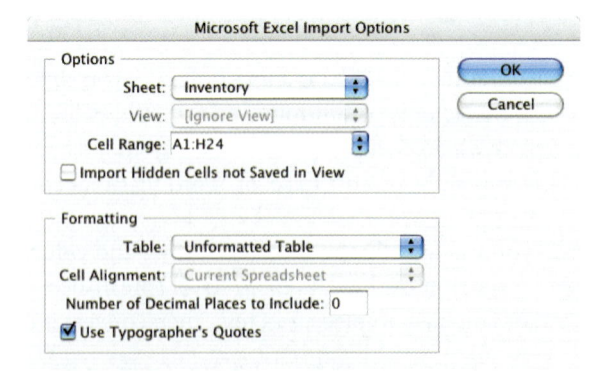

**FIGURE 4.11**

The selected cell range is placed as an InDesign table, which is only as wide as necessary. Notice the contrast to creating a new, blank table, which fills the width of the text frame. When you import data from an Excel file, InDesign uses the relative column width set in Excel to determine the column widths.

There is now a very tall blinking cursor to the left of the table. Remember that InDesign treats a table as a giant character, so this blinking cursor is the same height as the table.

**5** **To further demonstrate how InDesign treats tables as large characters, press the (forward) Delete key (not the Delete/Backspace key on the main keypad).**

The table disappears.

**6** **Undo the deletion. Press the Right Arrow key once, and the tall cursor jumps to the other side of the table. Press Return/Enter and notice how the cursor returns to its usual size underneath the table.**

**7** **Press Return/Enter once more to make a blank line.**

**8** **Save this file as "table_practice.indd" and leave it open for the next exercise.**

| Item # | Description | Colors | | | | |
|---|---|---|---|---|---|---|
| | | Purple | Red | Blue | Black | |
| 64123-S | Maiden Dress | 4 | 2 | 1 | 3 | 2 |
| 64123-M | Maiden Dress | 25 | 3 | 2 | 3 | 2 |
| 64123-L | Maiden Dress | 6 | 3 | 2 | 3 | 1 |
| 64301-P | Maiden Dress | 3 | 2 | 1 | 3 | |
| 64142-FS | Flare Sleeve Victorian Dress | | 2 | | | |
| 64142-P | Flare Sleeve Victorian Dress | | 1 | | | |
| 64124-M | String Dress | 2 | 3 | | | |
| 64124-L | String Dress | 3 | 4 | 1 | | |
| 64148-S | Maiden Blouse | 2 | 1 | 2 | 1 | 3 | 1 |
| 64148-M | Maiden Blouse | 4 | 3 | 3 | 2 | 2 |
| 64148-L | Maiden Blouse | 3 | 2 | 3 | 1 | 1 | 2 |
| 4229-S | Crepe Lace-up Blouse | 2 | 1 | 2 | 1 | 2 |
| 4229-M | Crepe Lace-up Blouse | 4 | 3 | 3 | 5 | 2 |
| 4229-L | Crepe Lace-up Blouse | 2 | 2 | 2 | 2 | 1 |
| 5025-FS | Crepe Skirt | 4 | 2 | 2 | 3 | |
| | | Pink | Purple | Red | Aqua | Black | Natural |
| 63212-FS | Angelica Flare Blouse | 2 | 1 | 2 | 2 | 3 | 5 |

**FIGURE 4.12**

## LESSON 3  Modifying Tables and Text

InDesign allows you to either convert text to a table format or convert an existing table to text. InDesign only imports Excel files and Word tables into InDesign tables, so if you import plain, delimited text files from other sources, you need to convert that text into a table. You can use this function to convert any tabular data (not just imported data) into a table.

When converting text to a table, InDesign begins a new row when it encounters a return character, and a new column when it encounters a tab character. You must make sure text is properly formatted with tabs between fields and returns separating records (lines) before converting to a table.

Conversely, when you convert a table to text, InDesign removes the gridlines, sets tabs at each column, and ends each row with a return. You might want to convert an InDesign table to text if, for example, you need a client (or anyone who doesn't use InDesign) to edit the text. Having the versatility to work with either text or tables is very useful.

### Convert Text to a Table

**1**  **Open the document (table_practice.indd) that you created in the previous exercise.**

The cursor should be one line below the table you imported.

**2**  **Place the file renwear.txt; uncheck the Show Import Options and Replace Selected Item boxes.**

The text imports as a tab-delimited document, containing more information (including the columns you didn't place previously) than that shown in Figure 4.12.

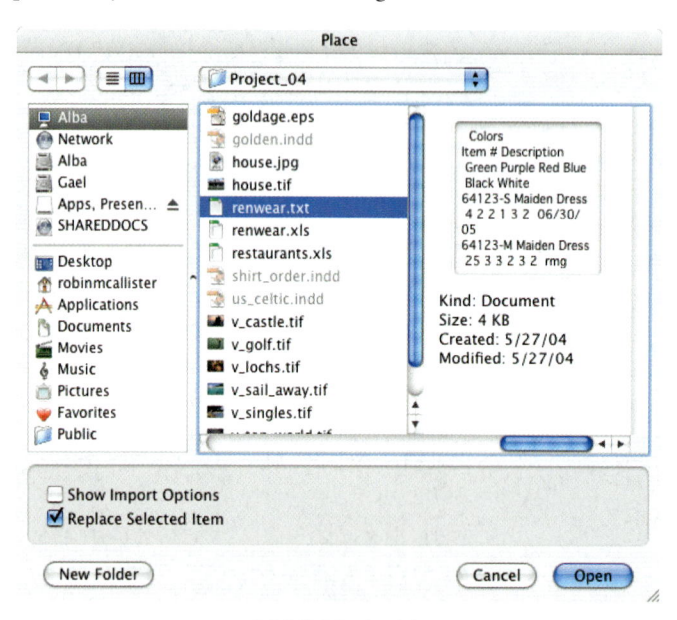

**FIGURE 4.13**

**3**  **With the cursor immediately in front of the text you just placed, press the Enter key to force the type to the next frame, then create a second page, and link the text to the second page.**

**4** Using the Type tool, select all the imported text, then choose Table>Convert Text to Table. Accept the default column separator (Tab) and row separator (Paragraph). Click OK.

The new table fills the width of the text frame with equal-width columns, as opposed to the variable width of imported tables. A plain text file contains no information about fonts or column widths, so the new table uses the default font and column width settings.

| Item # | | Colors | | | | | | |
|---|---|---|---|---|---|---|---|---|
| | | Green | Purple | Red | Blue | Black | White | |
| 64123-S | Maiden Dress | 4 | 2 | 2 | 1 | 3 | 2 | |
| 64123-M | Maiden Dress | 25 | 3 | 3 | 2 | 3 | 2 | rmg |
| 64123-L | Maiden Dress | 6 | 3 | 2 | 2 | 3 | 1 | |
| 64301-P | Maiden Dress | 3 | 2 | 1 | | 3 | | |

**FIGURE 4.14**

**5** Highlight all text in the table, then choose Table>Covert Table to Text; accept the default column and row separators. Click OK.

The table is converted back to tab-delimited text.

**6** Save the file and leave the document open for the next exercise.

## LESSON 4  Formatting Tables and Cells

InDesign offers several methods for selecting cells, rows, columns, and entire tables. The Type tool must be active in the table for any of these selection methods to work.

The simplest way to select table elements is to click the text cursor in a cell, then drag through the cells you wish to select. You can drag vertically to select cells in the same column, horizontally to select cells in the same row, or diagonally to select a range of cells across rows and columns.

To understand table formatting, you need to differentiate the content of a table from the table itself. To format cell contents, you must use the Character and Paragraph palettes, the Character and Paragraph Styles palettes, or the Type menu. To modify the table itself, you must use the Table palette, Table menu, or contextual Table menu. Many Table menu functions are duplicated on the Table palette Options menu.

You can resize a table interactively by clicking the Type tool at the lower-right corner and dragging. You can also drag any row or column boundary line. If you expand a column in a table that fills the width of the text frame, the table will extend beyond the frame edge.

Instead of dragging, you can achieve greater precision by using the numeric controls in the Table palette, Table menu, and contextual Table menu. You can define a fixed-size row height by choosing Exactly in the Row Height menu of the Table palette, or you can allow the height to change as needed (the default) to accommodate cell contents.

## Adjust Table Elements

**1** Continue in the open document from the last lesson, table_practice.indd. Be sure the Type tool is active and choose Table>Select Table to select the table on Page 1.

FIGURE 4.15

**2** Choose Window>Type & Tables>Table to open the Table palette.

**3** Set the Row Height menu to Exactly, and type "0.25" in the associated text field. Press Return/Enter to accept these settings.

All rows become 0.25 in. (18 pt.) in height, and some overset text results. The Column Width field is empty because the table has varying column widths.

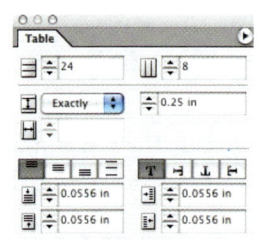

FIGURE 4.16

**4** Click with the Type tool in the table to deselect it.

In the lower-right corner of some cells, a small red dot indicates that the text in the cell is now overset. You need to fix the overset-text condition.

**5** Select the second column and set its width in the Table palette to 2 in.

The entire table becomes wider.

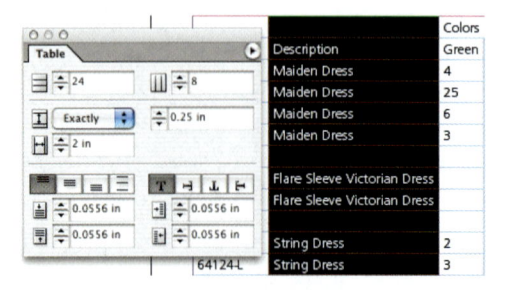

FIGURE 4.17

**6** Select the entire table and change the font to ATC Oak Normal, 12 pt., auto leading.

This causes several different cells to become overset.

**7** Click the Type tool on the right-hand boundary line of the second column and drag to the right to expand the cell enough to allow the text to fit.

**8** Change the width of each of the Colors columns to 0.7 in.

Although these columns did not have to be changed to fit the text, the table looks neater if similar cells are the same size.

**9** Set the vertical alignment of the cells to Center by selecting the table, then clicking the Align Center button in the Table palette.

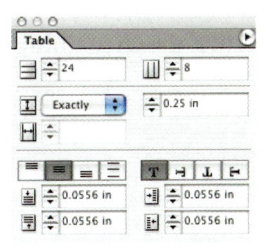

**FIGURE 4.18**

**10** To improve the look of the table, click above the third (Green) column and drag to the right to highlight all the colors cells. Click the Center button in the Character Control palette.

**11** Save the file and leave it open for the next exercise.

## *To Extend Your Knowledge...*

### EXPANDED SELECTION TECHNIQUES

To quickly select a row with a single keystroke, you can click the cursor in any cell in that row and press Command/Control-3. To select a column, click in that column and add Option/Alt to the shortcut. Pressing Command/Control-A selects the contents of a single cell. Pressing Command-Option-A or Control-Alt-A selects all the cells in the table.

You can also make selections with the mouse. To select a column, move the cursor just above the top of the column and click when the cursor changes to a downward-pointing arrow. To select a row, move the cursor to the left end of the row (just outside the table) and click when it turns to a right-pointing arrow. To select all cells in the table, move the cursor to just outside the upper-left corner until the cursor changes to an arrow pointing diagonally down and to the right, then click.

## LESSON 5 Working with Rows and Columns

Many table-editing functions are placed on both the Table menu, which has several submenus, and the Table palette Options menu. These functions are available only when a cell, row, column, or entire table is selected.

When you choose Insert Row or Column, you can specify the number of rows or columns to add, as well as where to insert them in relation to the currently selected row or column, in the dialog box that appears.

Just like a regular text story, you can thread a table to another frame by clicking the red "+" symbol in the out port of the first table text frame, then clicking the in port of the second text frame.

### Manage Rows and Columns

**1** Continue in the open document, table_practice.indd.

**2** With the Type tool, select the first two rows of the table and choose Table>Convert Rows> To Header.

These rows will repeat in any succeeding frames into which the table extends.

**3** Highlight the type in the header rows and style it as 11-pt. ATC Oak Bold.

**4** Highlight the text in the remainder of the table and style it as 11-pt. ATC Oak Normal.

**5** Click the lower-right corner of the frame, and drag to the left to reduce the frame size.

When you release, be sure there is no overset text.

| Item # | Description | Colors | | | | | |
|---|---|---|---|---|---|---|---|
| | | Green | Purple | Red | Blue | Black | White |
| 64123-S | Maiden Dress | 4 | 2 | 2 | 1 | 3 | 2 |
| 64123-M | Maiden Dress | 25 | 3 | 3 | 2 | 3 | 2 |
| 64123-L | Maiden Dress | 6 | 3 | 2 | 2 | 3 | 1 |
| 64301-P | Maiden Dress | 3 | 2 | 1 | | 3 | |
| | | | | | | | |
| 64142-FS | Flare Sleeve Victorian Dress | | | 2 | | | |
| 64142-P | Flare Sleeve Victorian Dress | | | 1 | | | |
| | | | | | | | |
| 64124-M | String Dress | 2 | | 3 | | | |
| 64124-L | String Dress | 3 | | 4 | 1 | | |
| | | | | | | | |
| 64148-S | Maiden Blouse | 2 | 1 | 2 | 1 | 3 | 1 |
| 64148-M | Maiden Blouse | 4 | 3 | 3 | | 2 | 2 |
| 64148-L | Maiden Blouse | 3 | 2 | 3 | 1 | 1 | 2 |
| | | | | | | | |
| 4229-S | Crepe Lace-up Blouse | 2 | 1 | 2 | | 1 | 2 |
| 4229-M | Crepe Lace-up Blouse | 4 | 3 | 3 | | 5 | 2 |
| 4229-L | Crepe Lace-up Blouse | 2 | 2 | 2 | | 2 | 1 |
| | | | | | | | |
| 5025-FS | Crepe Skirt | 4 | | 2 | 2 | 3 | |
| | | Pink | Purple | Red | Aqua | Black | Natural |
| 63212-FS | Angelica Flare Blouse | 2 | 1 | 2 | 2 | 3 | 5 |

**FIGURE 4.19**

Project 4 Working with Tables 153 LEVEL 2

**6** Click in the Black column and choose Table>Insert>Column. Insert one column to the left. Label the Column "Yellow"; above the Angelica Flare Blouse (next to "Aqua") name the color "Citron".

Note that adding a column did not affect the merged cells above the header row.

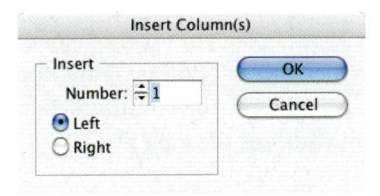

FIGURE 4.20

**7** Drag the bottom edge of the text frame containing the table up just above the Maiden Blouse entries.

The overset text flows into the next frame. If this does not happen for you, create a text frame on the bottom of the page and thread the text into it.

**8** Examine the text frame into which the balance of the table has flowed.

The header rows from the table on the first page are duplicated.

| | | Colors | | | | | | |
|---|---|---|---|---|---|---|---|---|
| Item # | Description | Green | Purple | Red | Blue | Yellow | Black | White |
| 64148-S | Maiden Blouse | 2 | 1 | 2 | 1 | | 3 | 1 |
| 64148-M | Maiden Blouse | 4 | 3 | 3 | | | 2 | 2 |
| 64148-L | Maiden Blouse | 3 | 2 | 3 | 1 | | 1 | 2 |
| 4229-S | Crepe Lace-up Blouse | 2 | 1 | 2 | | | 1 | 2 |
| 4229-M | Crepe Lace-up Blouse | 4 | 3 | 3 | | | 5 | 2 |
| 4229-L | Crepe Lace-up Blouse | 2 | 2 | 2 | | | 2 | 1 |
| 5025-FS | Crepe Skirt | 4 | | 2 | 2 | | 3 | |
| | | Pink | Purple | Red | Aqua | Citron | Black | Natural |
| 63212-FS | Angelica Flare Blouse | 2 | 1 | 2 | 2 | | 3 | 5 |

FIGURE 4.21

**9** Return to Page 1. Click the first number under the Purple Maiden Dress and drag down the column to select all four numbers, and copy them.

**10** Click in the first cell for the Yellow Maiden Dress and paste the numbers.

You see only an overset mark because the numbers were pasted into the cell as a mini-table.

**11** Undo the paste. Now click the first frame and drag, highlighting all four cells for the Yellow Maiden Dress. Paste.

Each number is pasted into its own cell.

**12** Save the document and close it.

# LESSON 6 Merging and Splitting Cells

As you saw in the lessons you just completed, you will sometimes encounter a table that has columns or rows spanned by other columns or rows that indicate a grouping of some sort. To create this effect, you need to merge cells, or in some instances split cells, to present your data most effectively.

You can merge two or more cells, or even an entire row or column, into a single cell with the Merge function in the Table menu. A merged column becomes a single, tall cell that extends the full height of the table; a merged row becomes a single cell the full width of the table.

You can select any adjacent cells in a row or column (or both) to create a single merged cell as large as the selected cells. You can't thread a table to another frame if the part of the table you want to thread contains a merged column. You also can't merge a row across a column that's already been merged (and vice-versa).

Splitting a cell is the opposite of merging — you can divide one or more selected cells horizontally or vertically into clones of the original cells. You can keep splitting cells until you reach the minimum cell width or height of 3 pts. (0.0417 in.). If you split one or more cells horizontally without splitting the entire row, the unsplit cells grow to the height of the split cells.

## Merge and Split Cells

**1**    **Open the document us_celtic.indd.**

In this document there is a table and a list of Celtic festivals. The festivals will be grouped by region, then by state, then by date.

**2**    **Click inside the table (the headline is not part of the table) and select all rows in the table; from the Table palette, set the row height to at least 0.1389 in.**

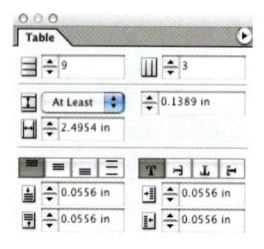

FIGURE 4.22

**3**    **Select the cells in front of the six New England states (Connecticut – Vermont) and choose Table>Merge Cells. Type "New England" in the merged cell.**

**4**    **Select the cells in front of New Jersey, New York, and Pennsylvania, merge them, and type "Northeast" in the merged cell.**

**5** **Select the cell to the right of Connecticut and select Table>Split Cell Horizontally twice, so you have three cells.**

Only one cell should be selected when you make the second split; if both cells are selected, you will end up with four cells. Because these cells are all set to be at least 0.1101 in. high, the Connecticut row becomes deeper. Notice that the minimum cell height automatically changed when you split the cells.

| Celtic Festivals in the United States | | |
|---|---|---|
| New England | Connecticut | |
| | | |
| | | |
| | Maine | |
| | Massachusetts | |
| | New Hampshire | |
| | Rhode Island | |
| | Vermont | |
| Northeast | New Jersey | |
| | New York | |
| | Pennsylvania | |

FIGURE 4.23

**6** **Repeat Step 5 for all the states, creating as many divisions as there are dates.**

**7** **Fill in the dates of all the festivals. Where there are multiple festivals on the same day, split the cell vertically and type each festival on its own line.**

| | | |
|---|---|---|
| New York | 03/26 - Ellenville | |
| | 05/07 - Chatham | |
| | 06/04 - Mumford | |
| | 07/09 - Mt. Morris | |
| | 07/30 - Frankfort | |
| | 08/13 - Liverpool | |
| | 08/20 | Amherst<br>Hunter |
| | 08/27 - Westbury | |
| | 09/03 - Altamont | |
| | 09/11 | Cortland<br>Wilmington<br>Turin |
| | 09/17 | Olcott Beach<br>Patchoque<br>Staatsburg |
| | 11/05 - Staten Island | |

FIGURE 4.24

**8** **Add a row at the top of the table and merge all the cells. Be sure the type rotation is at 0°, and cut and paste the heading into the merged cell.**

**9** **With the Type tool, click the right boundary line of the first column and drag it to the left, to about the 1.5-in. mark.**

**10** **Drag the right boundary of the second column to approximately the 3-in. mark.**

**11** **Save the file and leave it open for the next lesson.**

## LESSON 7 Working with Strokes and Fills

Cell borders are stroked by default when you first create or import a table. Rows and columns can also contain fills. You can turn the border strokes off, and create alternating fills in rows and columns to improve readability. You can also create alternating strokes between rows or columns.

When you choose to apply a stroke, you need to define its attributes in the Table Options dialog box. You can define the stroke weight, its type (pattern), color or tint, and whether the stroke will overprint.

When you apply fills, you can affect the color, tint, and overprint settings. If you apply alternating fills, the option affects the entire table. To remove the effect from specific cells, you need to select those cells and edit their fills and strokes after applying the alternating settings.

### Use Strokes and Fills

**1** Continue in the open file, us_celtic.indd.

**2** Select all rows in the table, then choose Table>Table Options>Alternating Fills.

The Fills pane of the Table Options menu appears. You can also open this dialog box from the Table palette.

**3** Set the Alternating Pattern menu to Every Other Row. In the Alternating section, enter "1" in the First Rows field. Set the Color menu to Bright Yellow, and specify a 20% tint. Leave the Next Rows field set to 1, and the Color menu at its default of None. Enter "1" in the Skip First Rows field. Check the Preview box.

This is almost the final state of this relatively complex table. Using this as a starting point, you will now adjust individual cells.

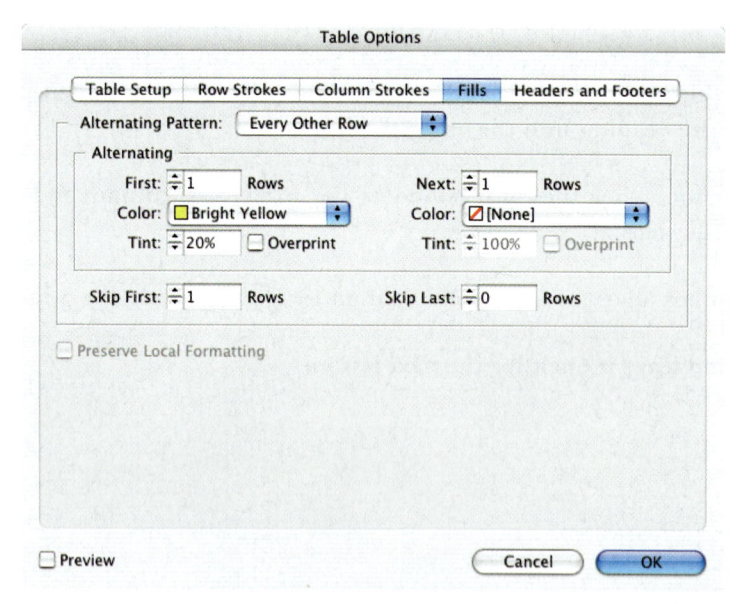

**FIGURE 4.25**

Project 4 Working with Tables  157  LEVEL 2

**4** Click OK.

**5** Position the cursor in the New Jersey cell and choose Table>Cell Options>Strokes and Fills. Make the cell fill 20% Bright Yellow to match the rest of the fills and click OK.

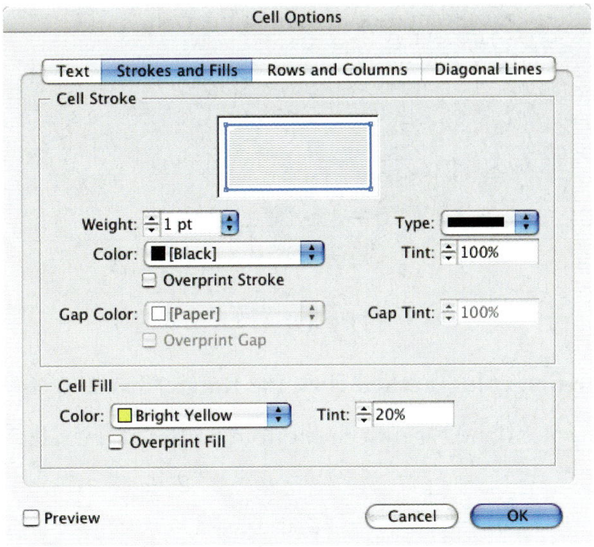

**FIGURE 4.26**

**6** Apply the same fill to the Pennsylvania cell.

**7** Click the New England cell and drag to select the Northeast cell as well. From the Cell Options>Strokes and Fills pane, make both cells 100% Deep Blue.

**8** Save the table and leave it open for the next lesson.

## LESSON 8  Managing Cell Contents

There is quite a difference between managing cells and managing their contents. Managing cells is similar to managing frames, but managing their content is virtually identical to managing text and graphics within containing frames.

Table cells can contain tabular material, text, or graphics. You can cut and paste cell contents to other cells, or delete it completely without affecting the structure of the table. As you saw in Lesson 6, you can allow text frames to expand when you insert text. When you fix the cell height, the text will overset, as you experienced in Lesson 4.

In this lesson, you will manipulate and color text, and change its orientation. You will also learn how to insert tabs and modify cells and their contents.

## Manage Cell Content

**1** In the open file, us_celtic.indd, highlight every cell in the table, then click the Align Center button in the Table palette.

All text is aligned to the vertical center of its containing cell.

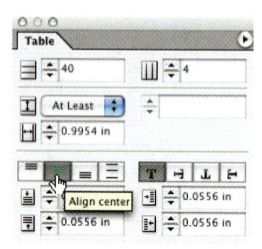

FIGURE 4.27

**2** Select the text in the first column, then click the Rotate Text 270° button in the Table palette.

The text rotates and is positioned against the bottom border of the cell.

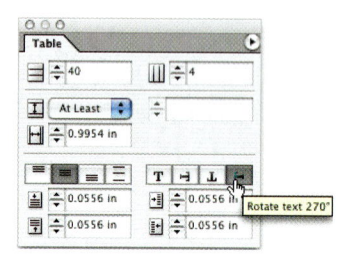

FIGURE 4.28

**3** With the text still selected, style the text as 12-pt. ATC Laurel Bold, Centered in the Control palette.

**4** Click the Formatting Affects Text button in the Swatches palette, ensure that the Fill icon is on top, and color the text in these cells Paper.

FIGURE 4.29

**5** Highlight the third column (the one containing dates and cities).

**6** Choose Type>Tabs and insert a tab stop at 1.25 in.

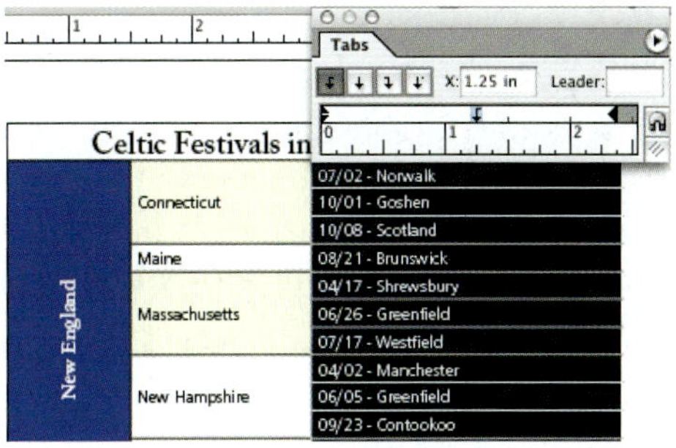

**FIGURE 4.30**

**7** In the first entry (07/02 – Norwalk), delete the hyphen and the spaces around it, and press Option-Tab (Macintosh) or Right-click>Insert Special Character>Tab (Windows) to insert a tab character into the column.

This could be a tedious operation, but InDesign has some features to speed it up. The Find/Change command works within tables just as it does in standard text frames.

**8** Open the Find/Change dialog box. Enter "[space]-[space]" in the Find What field and "^t" in the Change to field. Click Change All, dismiss the message that reports how many changes were made, then click Done.

All the dates and cities change to tabular information.

**9** Save the document, and close it.

## LESSON 9  Inserting Graphics and Nested Tables

As you know, cells act as little frames, so in addition to text, they can contain any images or graphics that InDesign supports (including those created in InDesign), as well as other tables.

When you insert such an item, the cell expands to accommodate its size; if you specify that the cell remain an exact size, it will clip the inserted item. You can use the Selection and Direct Selection tools to resize inserted graphics or images. You can resize inserted tables interactively by moving the cursor over a corner of the table until it changes to double-headed diagonal arrows, then clicking or Shift-clicking and dragging. You can't reduce a table beyond a certain size until you reduce the size of its text content.

Graphics or images are frequently much larger than the cell in which they're inserted. Although a cell can expand to hold inserted content, it can't expand beyond the edge of the text frame that contains the table; large images, however, can extend beyond the cell boundaries. You can use the Selection tools or Transform palette to resize the content to fit the cell.

## Insert Graphics and Nested Table

**1** **Open the document golden.indd.**

The document contains a text frame, a table, and some text. You're going to assemble a real estate form. These could be printed or copied four-up on a page for easy reference.

**2** **Click in the empty text frame and insert a table with 4 body rows and 1 column.**

The top and bottom cells of this table will hold graphics, and the third one will hold a frame, so they need to have their indents removed.

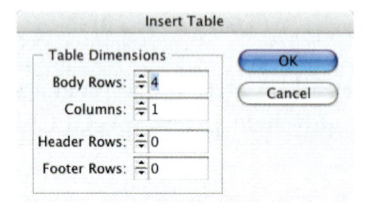

**FIGURE 4.31**

**3** **Click the Type tool in the top cell of this table and, from the Table palette, change all the inset fields to zero.**

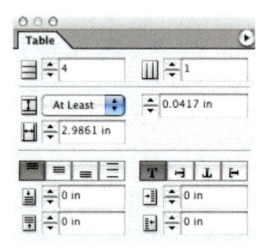

**FIGURE 4.32**

**4** **Apply the same inset to the third and fourth cells.**

**5** **With the cursor in the top frame, place house.tif.**

The frame of the house image extends beyond the table and its text frame.

**FIGURE 4.33**

**6** With the Selection tool, drag the right side of the image's frame to the right edge of the table. It should be 3 in. wide. Use the Direct Selection tool to adjust the position of the house image in the frame until you are happy with it.

**7** Copy and paste the text ("This single family property…") into the second frame.

The built-in offsets are necessary when you insert text into a cell.

**8** With the Type tool, highlight all the text in the table, copy it, and paste it into the third cell of the table featuring the house.

The entire table is pasted into place.

**9** Place goldage.eps into the bottom cell, as you did house.tif in the top cell.

**10** Add some spacing back into the top offsets of the bottom two cells, so it looks attractive to you.

**11** Select the entire large table, and from the Control palette, assign a Stroke of None.

**12** Select the text frame that contains the table and assign a 1-pt. stroke.

**13** Remove all extraneous items from the page. Save and close the document.

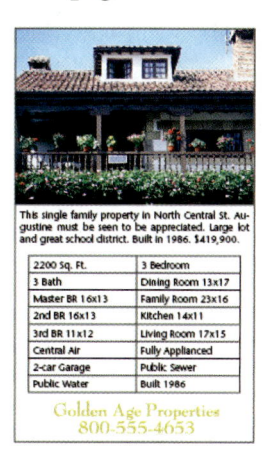

**FIGURE 4.34**

## SUMMARY

In this project you created tables, imported them from other applications, and converted text to tables. You learned how to select table elements such as rows and columns, how to resize these elements, and how to format table contents. You discovered that rows defined as headers or footers are duplicated if the table flows into another frame. You split and merged cells, and inserted and deleted rows and columns from tables. You also learned to manage the content of a table regardless of its content.

## CAREERS IN DESIGN

### MANAGING TEXT

It's easy to think of text as "unglamorous" because there's so much of it. As you've discovered — and will continue to appreciate throughout your graphics career — the appearance of text in your documents is extremely important. As you work with InDesign's text management, open your mind to the possibilities that each feature offers.

Selecting the best font for a job is indeed an art. Almost everyone has a favorite font or two (an old printer's maxim is "when in doubt, use Baskerville"), but no font is perfect for every job. Think about the different fonts you would choose for a children's reading book versus a children's workbook, or for an ad versus a product specification sheet.

Now that OpenType is available, you have all the options that the designers of the typefaces originally intended, including small caps, the full sets of ligatures, and, in many cases, alternate characters. As a designer, you must be able to decide when it is best to use such options; for example, if you were composing a textbook or workbook for primary school students, you would want to turn ligatures off, to avoid confusing young students with unfamiliar letter shapes.

In addition to *designing* with type, graphic artists *produce* with type. Although perhaps not as glamorous as design, composition can be every bit as profitable — especially when you have developed proficiencies with a program that allow you to produce a large amount of work in a short period of time.

You can control text both manually and with InDesign's automatic controls. In some cases, you could automate production using nested character styles and balanced text. In the majority of your higher-end work (such as producing ads, brochures, and newsletters), you will probably use the Adobe Single-line Composer instead of the automated Paragraph Composer to gain the most control over text.

InDesign also allows you to determine whether particular information would better be presented more effectively in a table. This is frequently the best option for presenting information with repetitive subject matter; you created several tables in Project 4.

As you manage and work with the text in your documents (regardless of their nature or complexity) remember that the fundamental principal of publishing is not about the process, or the programs, or how "cool" the design is — it's about producing effective documents that serve their creators and those who read them.

# KEY TERMS

| | | |
|---|---|---|
| border | footer row | shading |
| boundary line | header row | split |
| cell | merge | tab-delimited |
| cell range | row | table |
| column | row height | text rotation |

# CHECKING CONCEPTS AND TERMS

## MULTIPLE CHOICE

Check the letter of the correct answer for each of the following:

1. What are the three primary components of a table?
   a. Graphics, text, and lines
   b. Rows, columns, and cells
   c. Frames, rules, and images
   d. Tabs, headers, and footers

2. Header rows differ from body rows in what way?
   a. Header rows repeat in successive frames.
   b. Header rows cannot be imported.
   c. Body rows can have a fill applied to them.
   d. Body rows cannot be the first line in the table.

3. When you import a table from WordPerfect…
   a. You can import it as a table.
   b. You must import it as delimited text.
   c. You cannot make it into text.
   d. It retains its format.

4. What happens when you make a column wider?
   a. The columns to its left become smaller.
   b. The columns to its right become smaller.
   c. The table becomes wider.
   d. You can't make a column wider.

5. How do you progress from cell to cell?
   a. Press the Tab key.
   b. Press the Right Arrow key.
   c. Click in the cell with the mouse.
   d. All of the above.

6. If you don't need all the data in an Excel file, what do you do?
   a. Import it all and remove the columns you don't need.
   b. Import it all and remove the rows you don't need.
   c. Define the cells you want to import in the Cell Range field.
   d. Import it as a formatted table.

7. How do you convert a table to text?
   a. Cut and paste each cell into a text frame.
   b. Copy the entire table and copy it into a text frame.
   c. Use the Convert Table to Text option.
   d. Delete the table and re-import as tab-delimited text.

8. When you copy content from one row of a table to another…
   a. You should copy cell-by-cell.
   b. Highlight the text you want to copy, then highlight the same number of cells in the target row.
   c. Highlight the text you want to copy, then copy it into the first of your target cells.
   d. Copy the entire row, then delete anything you don't want.

9. How do you center text vertically in a cell?
   a. Click the Align Center button in the Table palette.
   b. Assign it enough Space Before in the Paragraph palette.
   c. Adjust it using the Inset Top controls in the Table palette.
   d. Adjust the height of the row.

10. How do you make an image completely fill a cell?
    a. Use the Direct Selection tool and enlarge it to fit.
    b. Enlarge it to fit using the Scale tools.
    c. Set all cell insets to 0 in the Table palette, then adjust the image as needed.
    d. All of the above.

## DISCUSSION QUESTIONS

1. When would you choose to import an entire Excel file to make a table, rather than selecting only the range of cells you need?

2. What advantages are offered by using tables instead of tabular text? When would you choose to use each method?

# SKILL DRILL

Skill Drills reinforce project skills. Each skill reinforced is the same, or nearly the same, as a skill presented in the lessons. Detailed instructions are provided in a step-by-step format. You must perform Skill Drills 1 and 2 sequentially. Drills 3 and 4 should also be completed sequentially.

## 1. Create a Calendar

You have just been assigned the job of creating a desktop calendar. In this exercise you will create the basis — the grid and the dates — for a calendar that a specialty company will sell. The calendars will be glued onto a base that will have the client's information foil stamped. There will not be much room on the calendar for clients to make notes.

1. Create a new one-column document, 5.5 in. × 3.5 in. with 0.25-in. margins. It should not have a master text page. Save it as "calendar_2006.indd".
2. Choose Adobe Caslon Pro as your typeface and create a text frame that fully fills the space within the margins.
3. Type the word "January" at the top of the page and style it Adobe Caslon Semibold, 18 pt., centered. Press the Return/Enter key.
4. Insert a table with 7 rows and 7 columns.
5. Highlight the bottom 6 rows and change their height to exactly 0.417 in.
6. Highlight the top row and assign its cells Adobe Caslon Pro Semibold, 9 pt., centered. Type the days of the week in these cells.
7. When you have typed "Saturday" press the Tab key to advance to the next line. Interestingly, 2006 begins on a Sunday. Type "1".
8. Advancing through the calendar by pressing the Tab key, type the date in each cell, accepting default size and placement.
9. Add 3 pt. below the name of the month.
10. Save the document and leave it open for the next Skill Drill.

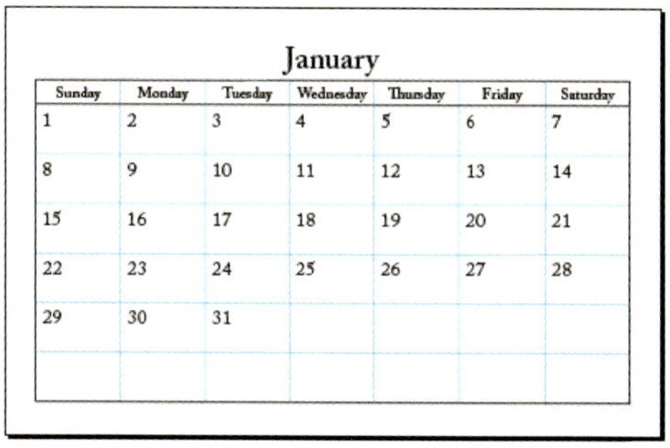

January

| Sunday | Monday | Tuesday | Wednesday | Thursday | Friday | Saturday |
|---|---|---|---|---|---|---|
| 1 | 2 | 3 | 4 | 5 | 6 | 7 |
| 8 | 9 | 10 | 11 | 12 | 13 | 14 |
| 15 | 16 | 17 | 18 | 19 | 20 | 21 |
| 22 | 23 | 24 | 25 | 26 | 27 | 28 |
| 29 | 30 | 31 | | | | |
| | | | | | | |

FIGURE 4.35

## 2. Add Color to Rules and Fills

Although the basics for the document are in place, this calendar looks pretty boring and gives only minimum information. In this exercise, you will add some color and mark the holidays for the month.

1. Continue in the open document.
2. Select the table with the Type tool, then choose Table>Table Options>Alternating Row Strokes and set the following specifications:

   Alternating Pattern: Custom Row
   Alternating First: 5 Rows, Weight: 0.5 pt., Color: Cyan
   Next: 0 Rows
   Skip First: 1 Row

3. Click the Column Strokes tab and set the following specifications:

   Alternating Pattern: Custom Column
   Alternating First: 7 Columns, Weight: 0.5 pt., Color: Cyan
   Next: 0 Columns
   Skip First: 0 Columns
   Click OK.

4. Select the cells that have no numbers in them (you will have to do this in two parts, because you can't select all the cells at once). Select Table>Cell Options>Strokes and Fills and assign a cell fill of 20% cyan.
5. In each cell that represents a holiday, use 7-pt. Adobe Caslon Pro Regular to add an en space, an Indent to Here character, then type the name of the holiday. January 1 is New Year's Day; January 19 is Martin Luther King Day; you'll need to abbreviate this holiday to "MLK Day" to make it fit.
6. Accent the holidays still more by assigning a 20% yellow fill to these cells.
7. Save the document and close it.

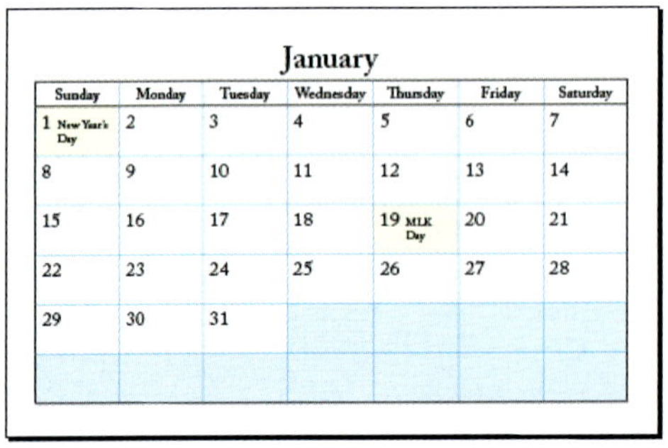

January

| Sunday | Monday | Tuesday | Wednesday | Thursday | Friday | Saturday |
|---|---|---|---|---|---|---|
| 1 New Year's Day | 2 | 3 | 4 | 5 | 6 | 7 |
| 8 | 9 | 10 | 11 | 12 | 13 | 14 |
| 15 | 16 | 17 | 18 | 19 MLK Day | 20 | 21 |
| 22 | 23 | 24 | 25 | 26 | 27 | 28 |
| 29 | 30 | 31 | | | | |
| | | | | | | |

FIGURE 4.36

## 3. Convert and Style a Table from Text

You have been hired to produce an order form for a T-shirt designer. Like calendars, order forms lend themselves to tables. We have already imported the text into a text frame for you. The goal of a form is to make it as easy as possible to record information, because most customers prefer to phone in orders, in case there are specials or if certain styles are backordered.

1. Open the document shirt_order.indd.
2. Select all the text and choose Table>Convert Text to Table. Accept the default column and row separators.
3. Highlight the four right-hand columns and assign them a width of 0.375 in.
4. Drag the right boundary line for the first column to the right until the table extends the width of the text frame.
5. Select the first two rows in the first column and merge the cells.
6. Select the unmerged cells in the first row and merge them.
7. Select the first two rows and convert them to header rows.
8. Style the word "Designs" as 12-pt. ATC Oak Bold and the words "T-Shirts $21.00" as 10-pt. ATC Oak Bold.
9. Center "Designs" vertically in its cell.
10. Center "T-Shirts $21.00" and the sizes under it horizontally in their cells.
11. Save the document and leave it open for the next Skill Drill.

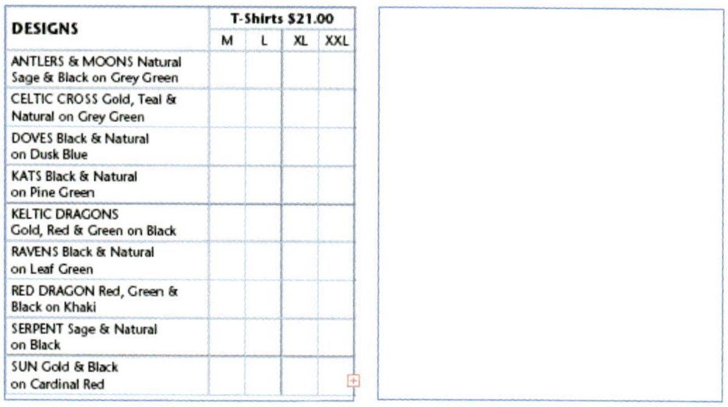

**FIGURE 4.37**

## 4. Thread a Table and Enhance Its Appearance

The table is well on its way, but it needs to be threaded to a second frame and "prettied up." You have the skills to do it with a minimum number of steps.

1. Continue in the open document, shirt_order.indd.
2. With the Selection tool, click the Text Overset icon and thread the table to the next text frame.
3. Click in the Total Quantity cell, which has two lines of text and should span two rows. Select all cells in this row and split the cells horizontally. Cut and paste the words "Total $" into the newly created cell just below the Total Quantity cell.
4. Click in a cell that is two lines deep and change the Row Height from "At Least" to "Exactly." Enter this measurement as the row height for the two "Total" rows.
5. Center the text in these rows vertically and align it right.
6. Merge the cells in the last row and center the text.
7. From Table Options, select Fills. Set the Alternating Pattern to Every Other Row. The First: 1 Row should be a 20% tint of green and the Next: 1 Row should be a 20% tint of cyan. Skip Last: 3 Rows.
8. Shorten the text frame holding the first table so Red Dragon is the last shirt listed.
9. Make any other enhancements you wish, then save and close the document.

| DESIGNS | T-Shirts $21.00 | | | |
|---|---|---|---|---|
| | M | L | XL | XXL |
| ANTLERS & MOONS Natural Sage & Black on Grey Green | | | | |
| CELTIC CROSS Gold, Teal & Natural on Grey Green | | | | |
| DOVES Black & Natural on Dusk Blue | | | | |
| KATS Black & Natural on Pine Green | | | | |
| KELTIC DRAGONS Gold, Red & Green on Black | | | | |
| RAVENS Black & Natural on Leaf Green | | | | |
| RED DRAGON Red, Green & Black on Khaki | | | | |

| DESIGNS | T-Shirts $21.00 | | | |
|---|---|---|---|---|
| | M | L | XL | XXL |
| SERPENT Sage & Natural on Black | | | | |
| SUN Gold & Black on Cardinal Red | | | | |
| TREE OF LIFE Gold, Black & Natural on Pine Green | | | | |
| TRISKELION Blue, Sage, Black & Natural on Black | | | | |
| WORLD TREE Sap Green, Teal & Green on Black | | | | |
| TOTAL QUANTITY | | | | |
| TOTAL $ | | | | |
| XXL Shirts $1 Additional | | | | |

FIGURE 4.38

# CHALLENGE

Challenge exercises expand on, or are somewhat related to, skills presented in the lessons. Each exercise provides a brief introduction, followed by instructions presented in a numbered-step format that are not as detailed as those in the Skill Drill exercises. You should perform these exercises in the order in which they appear.

## 1. Import a Table

The Seacoast Region Chamber of Commerce annually publishes a *Guide to the Seacoast* that promotes local tourism. An important part of this publication is its restaurant guide, which is presented in table form. All restaurants that are members of the Chamber are listed, and may purchase additional ad space if they so desire.

1. Create a new 6.5 × 8.5 in. document with 0.25-in. margins.
2. With the active font set to 7/8 ATC Oak Normal, create a text frame the width of the margins positioned slightly below the bottom margin.
3. Place the file restaurants.xls as an unformatted table. Be sure the Use Typographer's Quotes box is checked.
4. Reduce the entire table so it fits within the text frame.
5. Place the cursor in the third column, and adjust the column width until the text in the body of the table is no longer overset. Adjust the column width of the fourth column until "B/L/D" fits on one line. Don't worry about the overset text at the top of the table — you'll fix that later.
6. Reduce the first column until the table again fits within the frame.
7. Select all the text in the second row and center it vertically.
8. Select all the text in the body of the table except the first column and center it horizontally and vertically.
9. Center the text in the first column vertically, leaving it left aligned.
10. Select the second through the last columns in the second row and rotate the text 270°.
11. Create a new character style named "Name" defined as ATC Oak Bold. Apply it to the first line in each listing. If text overflows onto the second line, track it or apply a small amount of glyph scaling to force the line to fit.

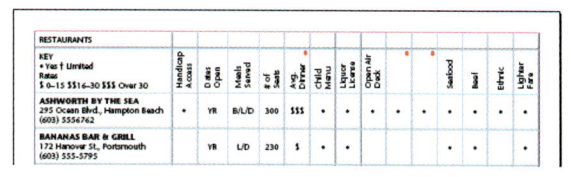

**FIGURE 4.39**

12. Save the document as "restaurants.indd" and leave it open for the next Challenge.

## 2. Manage the Table

You will now give the table some character by managing its structure.

1. Continue in the open document.
2. Select all the cells in the first line (Restaurants) and merge them.
3. With the word "Restaurants" highlighted, change the font to ATC Oak Bold.
4. Position the cursor on the lower boundary of the second row and drag vertically until the table fills the text frame to the bottom margin.
5. Select the six right-hand cells in the header area and split them horizontally.
6. Copy the text remaining in each of the cells to the lower of the two cells you just created, cell-by-cell.
7. Drag the bottom boundary line of the upper cells up until you can see all the text in the lower cells.

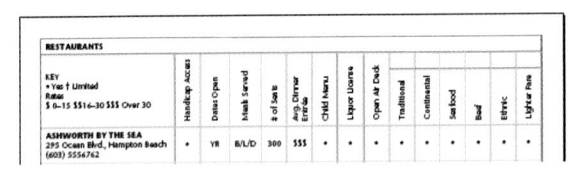

**FIGURE 4.40**

8. Merge the top group of six cells.
9. Make the first 3 row strokes 1-pt. red and the next 15 rows 0.5-pt. black.
10. Define column strokes of 1-pt. black for the first column and 0.5-pt. black for the next seven.

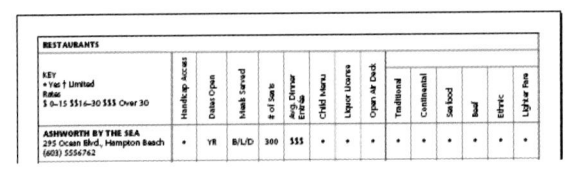

**FIGURE 4.41**

11. Save the document and leave it open for the next Challenge.

## 3. Enhance the Table's Readability

Although the table is functional, you can improve it by making it more readable. Alternating lines of tint will accomplish this effectively, as will a headline.

1. Continue in the open document.

2. Fill every other column with a tint of 20% red, skipping the first column.

3. In the open cell in the upper right, type the word "CUISINE" in 9-pt. ATC Oak Bold, centered, with a color of Paper. Rotate the text to 0°.

4. Select the CUISINE cell and change its overprint to 100% red.

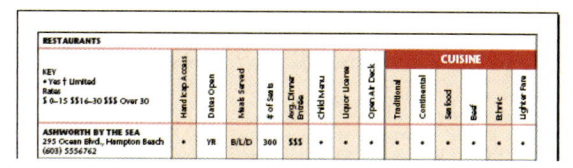

**FIGURE 4.42**

5. In the first column, change the top and bottom cell insets to zero.

6. Add some space between the Key and Rates information.

7. Make any other modifications necessary to eliminate text oversets.

8. Save and close the document.

**FIGURE 4.43**

## 4. Create a Travel Promotion

You work for a travel agency that produces a brochure that features abbreviated descriptions of their featured vacations. The vacation descriptions are extracted from an Excel spreadsheet and inserted into a table in the brochure.

1. Create a new, one-column, 8.5 × 11-in. document with 0.5-in. margins.
2. With ATC Oak Normal as the active font, create a text frame to fill the space between the margins.
3. Place the Summer sheet of the vacations.xls file as an unformatted table in the text area.
4. Adjust the second column so it is two inches wide. Leave the height at the default setting.
5. Change the insets for the cells in this column to zero.
6. Place the photos that match the vacations. All the photos for this flyer begin with "v_".
7. Make the titles of all the vacations ATC Oak Bold and the descriptive text Adobe Garamond Pro. Leave the size at 9/11 and vertically center all text in its cells.
8. Change all row and column strokes to 0.5 pt.
9. Make any other adjustments you feel are necessary or appropriate. (We used the Eyedropper tool to pick up a color from the image and apply it to that image's cells, tinting it if necessary.)
10. Save the document as "vacations.indd" and close it.

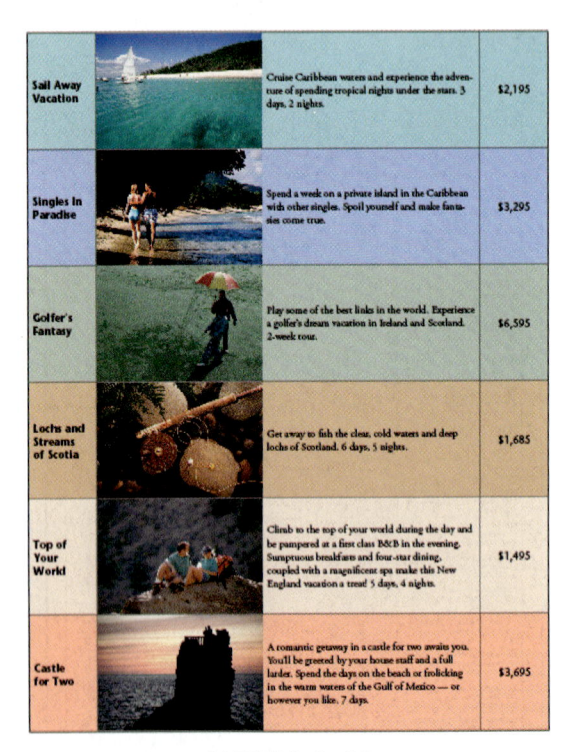

**FIGURE 4.44**

# PORTFOLIO BUILDER

## Build a Day-Seminar Schedule

Tables can be put to all sorts of uses, and some may be unique. Your assignment is to use the information in an Excel spreadsheet to produce the day's schedule for Publishing Productivity Seminars. We have provided the original Excel file (workshop.xls) and several related text files in your Project_04 folder. The final document should be a two-color, six-page advertising piece, 8.5 × 11-inch, with 0.625-inch margins.

To complete this project, use the following techniques:

- Import the Excel spreadsheet into a table and determine a type size and face that will be attractive and fit on the page.
- Use color appropriately in the cells.
- Make sure the cell borders are as you want them.

# PROJECT 5

## LEVEL 2

# Working with Color

## OBJECTIVES

*In this project, you learn how to*

- Build colors using the CMYK model
- Create tints from spot colors
- Mix spot and process inks
- Apply transparency to objects
- Create realistic drop shadows
- Feather objects
- Flatten transparent objects for printing
- Import color from other documents
- Manage color for printing

# WHY WOULD I DO THIS?

Throughout *Essentials for Design: InDesign Level 1* and this book, you have been working with color. Color enhances documents — study after study shows that ads and whole documents printed in color are more effective than similar black-and-white documents. In previous projects, you used color that has been supplied and added colors from the PANTONE Matching System's library. In this project, you will create color for process-color printing using the CMYK model or for display on the monitor using the RGB model.

The CMYK model is referred to as a **subtractive** color model because removing all the **subtractive primaries** (cyan, magenta, and yellow) produces white. In theory, adding the three subtractive primaries produces black. In fact, it produces a dirty brown. Black (K) is added to the mix to achieve a robust black color, and for printing type. By default, black **overprints** other colors, rather than abutting, or **trapping** to them. The CMYK model is also called **process color**.

The RGB model is referred to as an **additive** color model because all three **additive primaries** (red, green, and blue) at full intensity produces white. The RGB model is used for display on a monitor or to print to some inkjet printers, many of which use inks in addition to the standard CMYK set to produce more vibrant color.

For some jobs, you might want to combine process colors with spot colors, or mix spot colors to achieve a specific effect. Although you can do this with InDesign, the results are not predictable, so you should proceed with caution. Before making a final color decision, you should obtain a sample of the ink mix from the company that will print your job. It's always best to ask the final producer of the job what they prefer for color definitions. Most printers want you to provide final job files in CMYK color space. Digital printers convert RGB colors to the CMYK colors that are appropriate for that device.

With InDesign, not only can you mix colors in the traditional sense, you can also add transparency to images. Transparency allows you to create realistic shadows and to fade the edges of objects, much as they appear in real life, and to include "see-through" effects.

It is, however, not enough to simply use color. You must also be able to manage it. The color on your monitor should be a reasonable representation of the color you will print. To that end, you will find the ability to calibrate and profile your monitor invaluable. Because this course is about InDesign, we do not provide details about calibrating color. If you choose to pursue color management and color science on your own, however, Against The Clock's *Color Companion for the Digital Artist* is a good resource.

# VISUAL SUMMARY

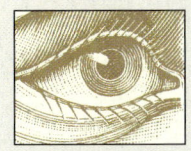

Color as it exists in nature covers a range from invisible infrared to invisible ultraviolet, with the virtually limitless visible color spectrum in between. When we attempt to produce color for print or the Web, we are constrained by the colors we can mix, called color spaces. InDesign can work in four different color spaces:

- Spot colors are pre-mixed pigments that you can select from special color libraries.

- RGB is the additive color model; when you build RGB colors, you can combine up to 256 parts each of red, green, and blue light.

- CMYK is the subtractive or process color model; when you build CMYK colors, you combine percentages of cyan, magenta, yellow, and black inks.

- L*a*b* includes both RGB and CMYK color spaces, plus colors that can be displayed in neither color space; you should never build colors in L*a*b*, because the color space cannot be accurately printed or displayed on the monitor. Because it includes both color spaces, L*a*b* provides a device-independent color space for translating from RGB to CMYK.

RGB color definition, with swatch name defined by color value

CMYK color definition, with user-defined swatch name

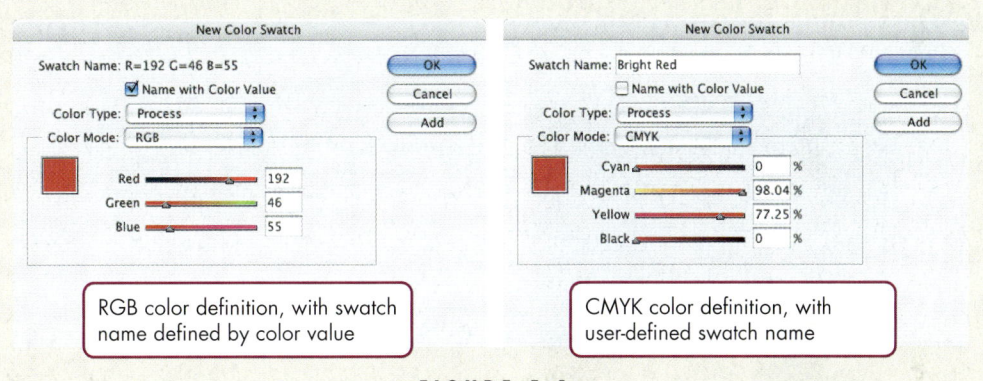

**FIGURE 5.1**

InDesign's Swatches palette provides a wealth of information about the makeup of the colors in the document. You can determine in what mode the color is created, whether it is spot or a mix of colors, and whether you can remove the color from the palette. The CMYK indicator to the right of the spot-color indicator gives the CMYK equivalents, if spot is converted to process.

Slashed icon indicates colors cannot be removed from Swatches palette.

No color

Registration colors

Process color

RGB color

CMYK color named by color mixture

Spot color

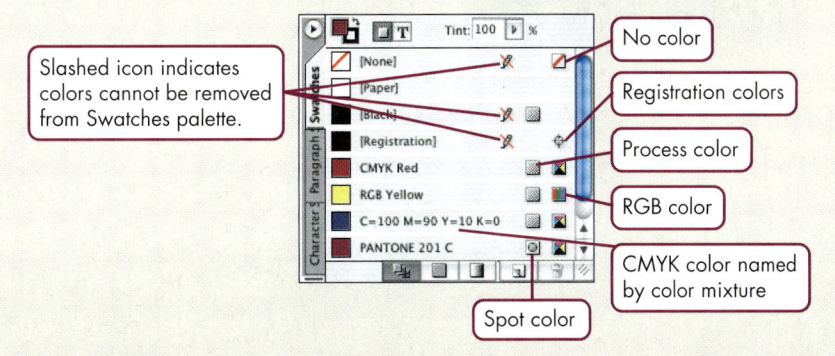

**FIGURE 5.2**

In addition to creating colors and tints in a single color space, you can also use InDesign to create mixed-ink colors — combinations of spot and process colors, or mixtures of two spot colors. You can create a single mixed-ink swatch, or a mixed-ink group if you need to use several tints of the mixed-ink swatch. If you create mixed spot-color inks, you should definitely obtain printed samples of the resulting ink color (and tints).

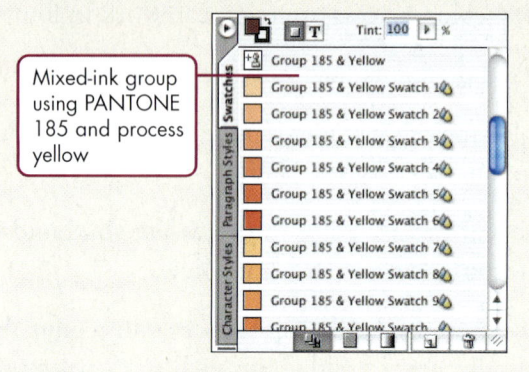

**FIGURE 5.3**

With InDesign's transparency features, you can create the illusion of transparent objects, add realistic drop shadows, and feather the edges of images.

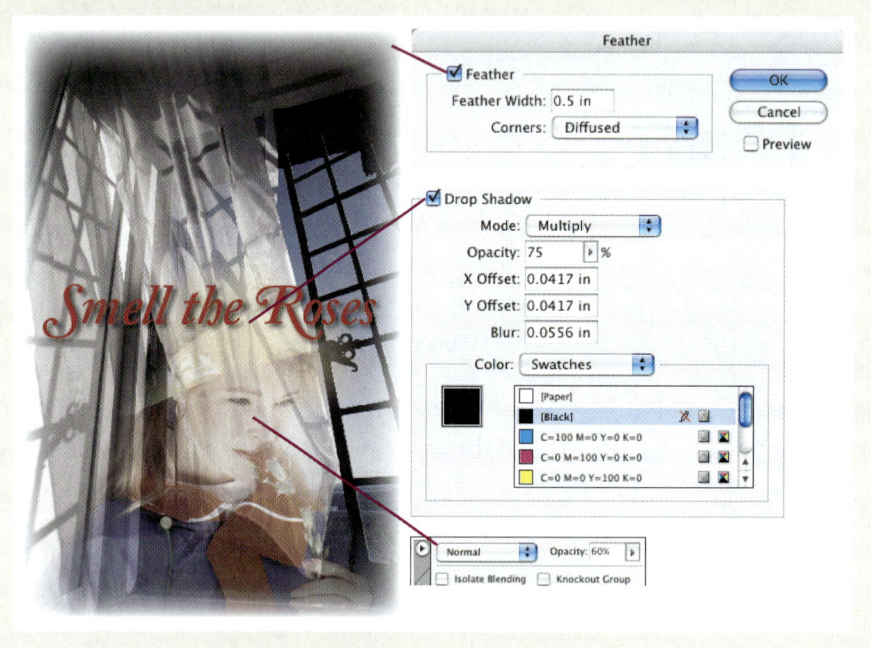

**FIGURE 5.4**

You must flatten any documents that contain objects with transparency. ***Flattening*** removes complexity from an object so it can be more easily printed. You can select InDesign's Transparency Flattener presets or create your own printer-specific preset. The standard presets are for Low-, Medium-, and High-Resolution printers. When creating your own presets, the Raster/Vector Balance is used to select the highest setting to keep as much artwork as possible as vector data. Line Art and Text Resolution should be set to the resolution of printers up to 600 ppi or to half the resolution of imagesetters. Gradient and Mesh Resolutions should be set no higher than 300 ppi, because quality will not increase, although printing time and file size (complexity) will.

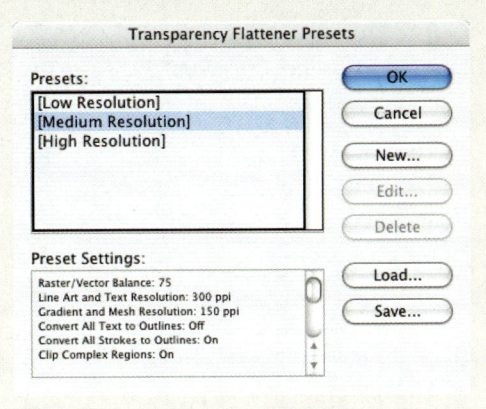

**FIGURE 5.5**

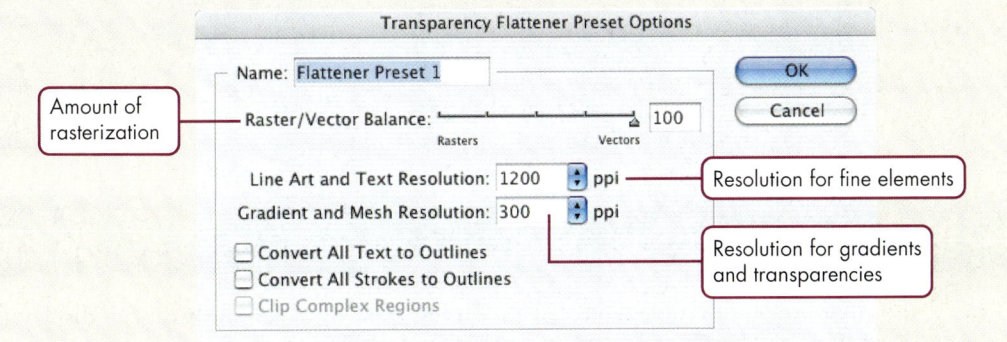

**FIGURE 5.6**

InDesign's color-management capabilities allow you to make sure the colors in images captured digitally (for example, with a scanner or digital camera) will reproduce as accurately as possible both on the screen and when printed. InDesign makes it easy to convert colors from RGB space (in which most images are captured) to their nearest equivalents in CMYK space (in which most printing takes place).

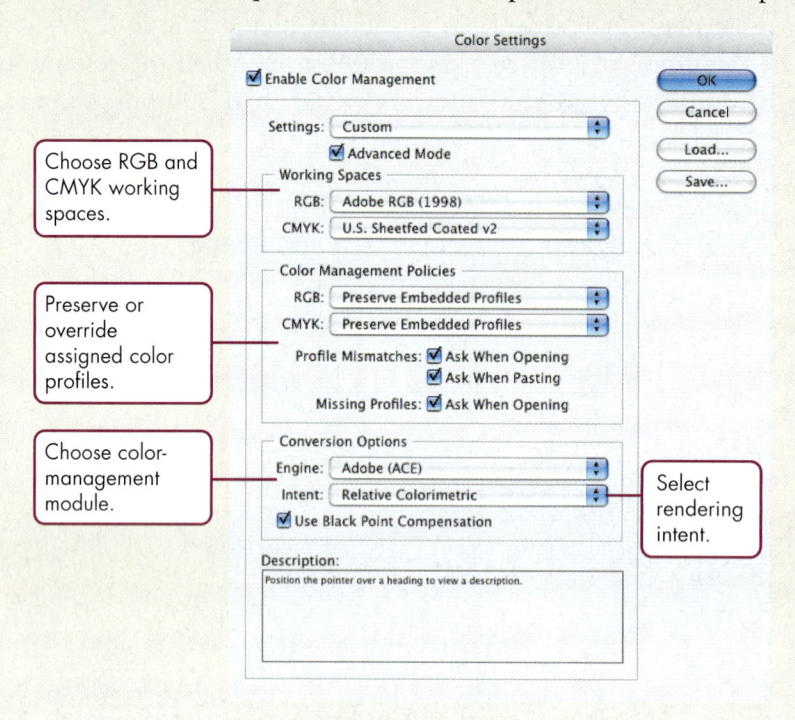

**FIGURE 5.7**

## LESSON 1 Building RGB Colors

The RGB space, the color model of visible light, has the largest *gamut*, which means it can display the widest range of the color spectrum. (The L*a*b* model is purely theoretical, and is not used to display colors.) When mixing RGB colors, you must forget the rules you learned in grade school for mixing paints. The ***additive primaries*** are red, green, and blue. When they overlap at full intensity, they create the ***subtractive primaries*** — red and green make yellow, red and blue make magenta, and green and blue make cyan. When all three additive primaries combine at full intensity, white results.

Because it is the model of light, RGB is used by monitors, television sets, scanners, and digital cameras. Most modern imaging devices are capable of performing an internal conversion from RGB to CMYK, but you should not rely on this for offset printing because you may not like the conversion. It is, however, the preferred color model for inkjet printing, including printing to wide-format devices, because the inks they use are different from the CMYK inks used in the printing process; many even use inks in addition to the four process colors.

***Indexed color*** is a subset of RGB used to create GIF files, which are generally images with areas of flat color (as opposed to photographs). An indexed-color image can contain up to 256 colors. This color model is unsuitable for print, but is very useful for images intended for monitor displays.

## Build an RGB Palette

1. Create a new document with default margins.

2. Remove all the color swatches except None, Paper, Black, and Registration.

3. From the Swatches palette Options menu, choose New Color Swatch.

4. Set the Color Type menu to Process and the Color Mode menu to RGB. Uncheck the Name with Color Value box.

5. Enter "255" in the field next to the Red slider and name the swatch "Red". Click Add.

   A message box warns you that this color will not be accurately printed when using process-color inks.

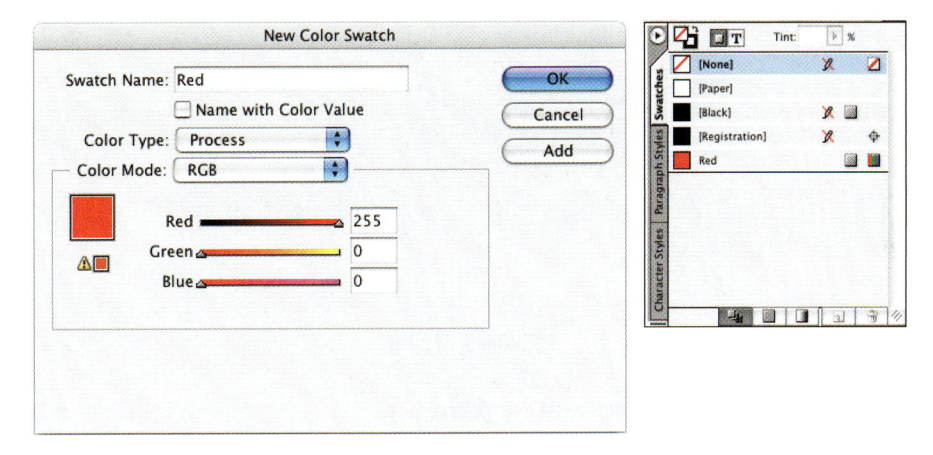

   **FIGURE 5.8**

6. Repeat Step 5 to create green and blue swatches.

7. Create a yellow swatch by setting both the Red and Green fields to 255; name the swatch "Yellow RGB".

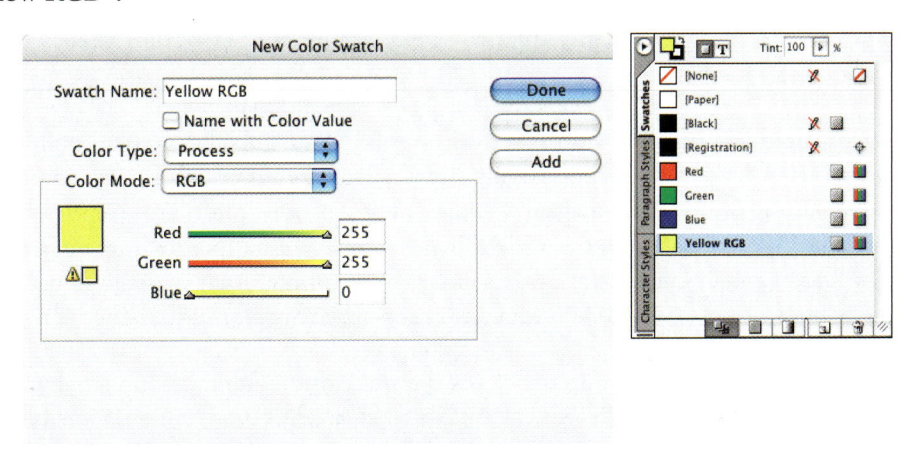

   **FIGURE 5.9**

**8** Create a swatch named "Cyan RGB" by setting both the Green and Blue fields to 255. Create a swatch named "Magenta RGB" by setting both the Blue and Red fields to 255.

The names "Cyan", "Yellow", and "Magenta" are reserved for the process inks; adding the "RGB" suffix indicates that these colors were created in the RGB space.

**9** Create a swatch named "Neutral Gray" by setting all three color fields to 128. Click Done to add this swatch to the palette and close the New Color Swatch dialog box.

As you probably noticed, higher values of the three primary colors produce lighter colors; lower values produce darker colors. If all three colors are set to zero, the result is black.

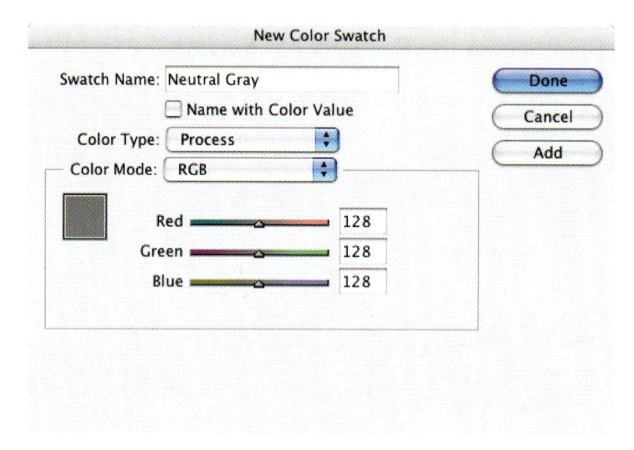

**FIGURE 5.10**

**10** Save the document as "rgb_color.indd" and close it.

## LESSON 2 Building CMYK Colors

The RGB model explored in Lesson 1 is based on the emission and transmission of light; the CMYK model, in contrast, is based on the absorption and reflection of light. A portion of the color spectrum is absorbed when white light strikes ink-coated paper (or any pigment-coated material). The color that is not absorbed is reflected to the eye.

The CMYK model is also called ***process color***. It is used to print documents that contain multiple distinct colors or color photographs. A pattern of dots in varying sizes (called a ***rosette***) fools the eye into thinking that it sees continuous tones instead of tiny cyan, magenta, yellow, and black dots. The density of these dots, when used in the printing process, is described in lines per inch. If there are 150 lines per inch, there can be as many as 22,500 distinct dots in a one-inch square area. The resolution of the printer itself is usually about 2,400 spots per inch, giving it the capability to place 5,760,000 miniscule spots for each color in that one-inch square.

***Color separation*** is the process of converting the colors specified on the monitor into varying amounts of the four process colors. Any colors defined in RGB or L*a*b* space must be separated into their closest CMYK components before they can be printed; separation can occur at the output device, or by the computer's software.

## Create Custom CMYK Colors

**1** Create a new document with default margins.

**2** Remove all the color swatches except None, Paper, Black, and Registration.

**3** From the Swatches palette Options menu, choose New Color Swatch.

**4** Set the Color Type menu to Process and the Color Mode menu to CMYK. Uncheck the Name with Color Value box.

**5** Set the sliders (or type the numbers) as follows: C:25, M:10, Y:0, K:10. Name the color "Wedgwood Blue" and click OK.

You have defined a soft blue, similar to that used for Wedgwood china. The color is added to the palette and becomes the active color.

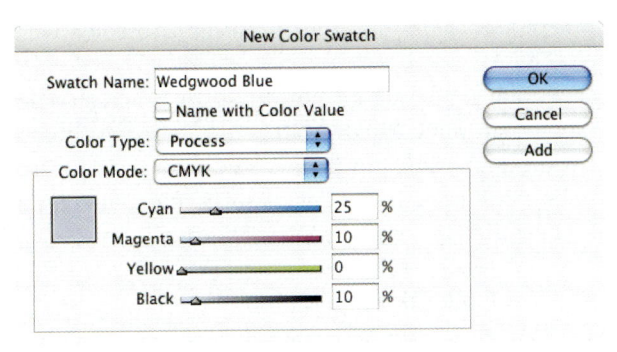

**FIGURE 5.11**

**6** In the Swatches palette, double-click the Wedgwood Blue swatch to bring up the Swatch Options dialog box.

**7** In the Swatch Options dialog box, change the Color Type menu to Spot. Click OK.

The icon in the Swatches palette changes to indicate that the color is spot, not process; the CMYK icon indicates that it was created in CMYK mode.

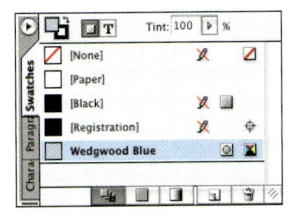

**FIGURE 5.12**

**8** Now you need to create another color compatible with the color scheme. Open the New Color Swatch dialog box.

9. Name this swatch "Medium Blue", with a Process color type and the CMYK color mode.

10. Use the sliders or type the following percentages into the color fields: C:50, M:30, Y:0, K:20. Click OK.

11. Save the document as "color_work.indd". Leave the document open for the next lesson.

## LESSON 3  Building Tints from Spot Colors

There are several swatch libraries built into InDesign. These can be broken down into three types: spot, process, and RGB. Spot libraries include PANTONE Coated, PANTONE Uncoated, Toyo Color Finder, DICColor, and the four HKS libraries. Process libraries are PANTONE Process Coated, TruMatch, and Focoltone. Process libraries are similar to spot libraries, except they contain pre-built formulas for specific colors that can be printed in CMYK rather than specific ink numbers and mixing proportions. The RGB libraries are the Macintosh and Windows system colors, and the optimized 216-color Web palette.

PANTONE is the most popular color-matching system in North America. The PANTONE Process library uses a different numbering system than the Coated, Matte, and Uncoated libraries do, and the process-color numbers do not correspond to the spot-color numbers. TruMatch and Focoltone are rarely used in North America — both are more common in Europe. HKS is a complex system used primarily in Germany; Toyo and DICColor (Dainippon Ink and Chemicals) are used primarily in Japan and other Asian countries.

A *tint* is a lightened derivative of a solid ink color that is produced on paper by creating a halftone screen of the color at the chosen percentage. You can create tints using the Swatches palette. You could technically create tints from process-color builds, but the results would be somewhat unpredictable.

### Create Spot Colors

1. With the document color_work.indd still open, choose New Color Swatch from the Swatches palette Options menu and select PANTONE Solid Coated in the Color Mode menu.

2. Type "185" in the PANTONE field, then click Add.

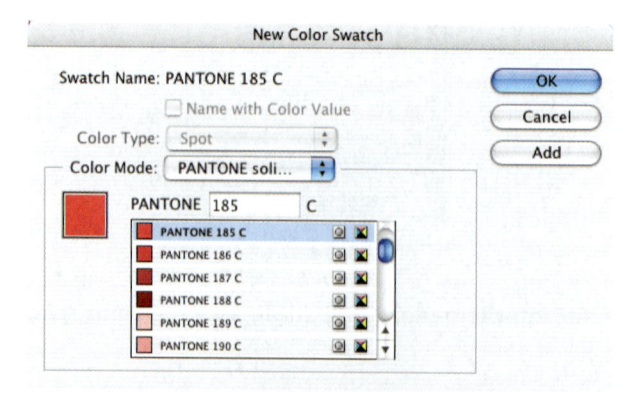

FIGURE 5.13

Project 5   Working with Color    **185**   LEVEL 2

**3** Repeat the process and choose PANTONE 286.

**4** Make a third spot-color swatch with PANTONE 320 and click OK.

**5** Save the document and leave it open.

## Create a Tint

**1** With the document color_work.indd open, highlight PANTONE 185C in the Swatches palette.

**2** Choose New Tint Swatch from the Swatches palette Options menu.

**3** Move the slider so the Tint percent reads 50% (or type "50" in the Tint field), then click OK.

The tint is added to your Swatches palette.

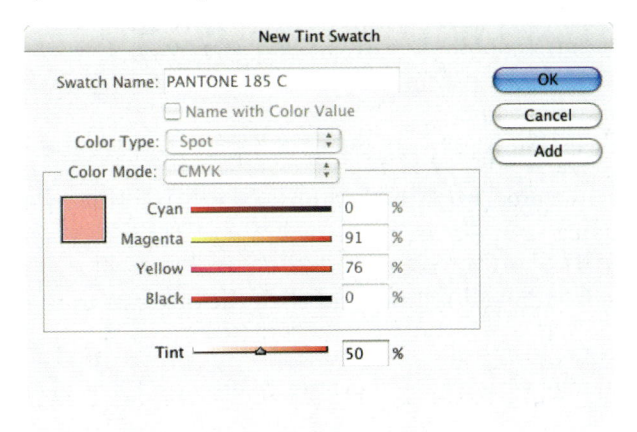

**FIGURE 5.14**

**4** Click the tint with the Selection tool, and drag it up so it is just below the PANTONE 185C swatch.

This has no effect on the way InDesign handles colors — it's simply easier to find things that are grouped in a logical order.

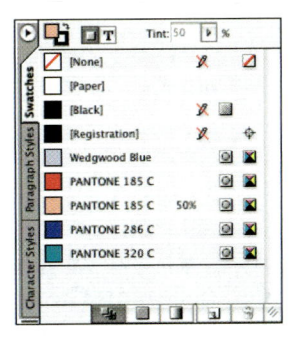

**FIGURE 5.15**

**5** Save the document and leave it open for the next exercise.

## LESSON 4  Creating Mixed Inks

In addition to mixing process colors and using premixed spot colors, you can mix two or more spot inks or you can mix spot and process inks to create unique colors. By mixing colors, you can create more interesting documents with only two colors. This is especially useful when you're on a budget.

You can create a single *mixed-ink swatch*, or you can create a *mixed-ink group*, which contains several related colors generated from incremental percentages of the process and spot colors used in the mixed-ink swatch. When you specify a mixed-ink group, you define the initial percentage, the number of steps, and the increment value. InDesign then creates swatches for each step. For example, you could create a group using 5 steps of Yellow and 4 steps of PMS 185, for a total of 20 swatches in the group.

The biggest problem associated with creating mixed inks is that, unlike process inks, spot inks are created to be used by themselves. It might be difficult to obtain the result you are attempting to achieve. Before you mix spot colors, it's best to see how they interact. You may be able to get samples from your printer, or refer to special printed books that show color interactions.

### Create Mixed Inks

1. In the open document, color_work.indd, choose New Mixed Ink Swatch from the Swatches palette Options menu.

2. Name the new swatch "185 and Yellow" and click the boxes in front of Process Yellow and PANTONE 185C.

    You see a representation of what mixing these two colors with 100% of each color will create.

3. Click OK to both add the new color and close the palette.

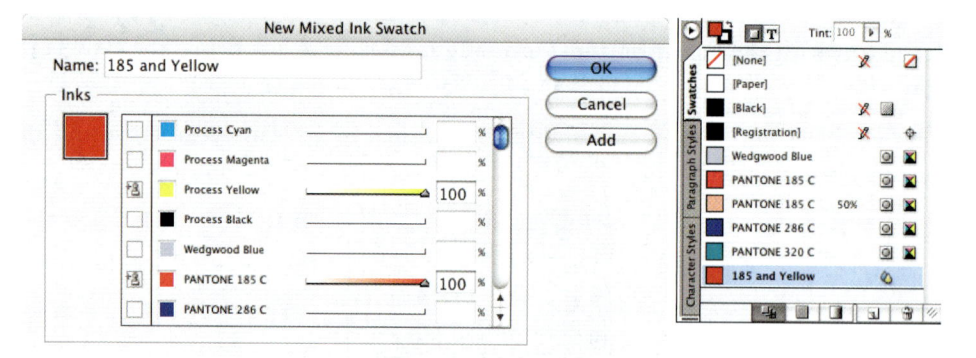

FIGURE 5.16

4. Experiment with a mix of the colors PANTONE 185C and Process Cyan. Drag the pointers up and down to apply equal amounts of each color. Create a final mixed-ink color named "Maroon" defined as 100% PANTONE 185C and 50% Process Cyan.

    The colors are almost directly opposite one another on the color wheel. When equal amounts of both colors are applied, the resulting color is nearly a neutral gray.

**5** Choose New Mixed Ink Group from the Swatches palette Options Menu and name the group "Group 185 & Yellow".

Note that the mixed inks are not available as components of the mixed-ink group.

**6** Enter the following values:

| Color | Initial | Repeat | Increment |
|---|---|---|---|
| Process Yellow | 20% | 4 | 20% |
| PANTONE 185C | 20% | 5 | 15% |

**7** Click the Preview Swatches button.

Thirty swatches are generated.

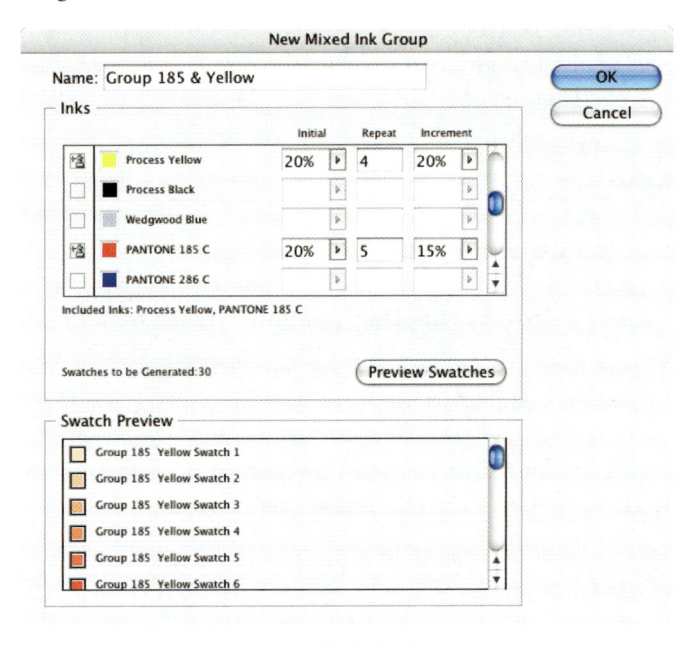

**FIGURE 5.17**

**8** Scroll through the list to see the available swatches.

**9** Save and close the document.

## LESSON 5 Creating Transparency

InDesign's transparency feature is based on technology developed for two other products in the Adobe Creative Suite. It is a fairly simple concept: an object's opacity defaults to 100% (completely solid), but you can adjust this value as low as 0% (completely transparent). Any objects underneath a transparent object are visible to the extent allowed by the transparency setting. This impressive feature enables you to create effects using transparency, drop shadows, and feathering that previously you could do only in Photoshop.

You can apply transparency to one or more selected objects — or grouped objects — from the Transparency palette. To change the transparency level of a selection, simply change the value in the Opacity field by typing a new value or moving the slider.

Transparency affects grouped objects differently than ungrouped objects. Transparency is applied to multiple, selected, ungrouped objects relative to each object's stacking order. Overlapping areas amplify the transparency effect. When transparency is applied to grouped objects, the group is treated as a single object, and transparency is not applied to any overlapping areas.

### Create Transparency

1. **Open the document transparency.indd.**

2. **Open the Transparency palette by choosing Window>Transparency.**

    The Transparency palette is in the same palette bay as the Stroke, Color, and Gradient palettes. Windows users can also press Shift-F10 to access the Transparency palette.

3. **At the top of the page are four similar sets of images. In the leftmost one, click each of the squares and apply 60% opacity from the Transparency palette.**

    Elements below one another are visible to a greater or lesser extent, depending on the hue of the object. This works the same whether you change the opacity one image at a time, or select all three objects at once.

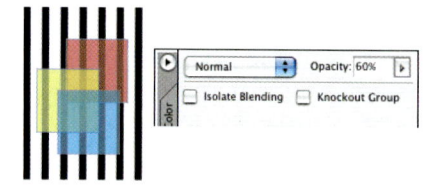

    **FIGURE 5.18**

4. **Click the next set of rectangles.**

    These rectangles have been grouped.

Project 5   Working with Color   **189   LEVEL 2**

**5**   **Apply 60% opacity to the grouped rectangles.**

Notice the contrast to the ungrouped images. The background shows through evenly, and transparency does not affect overlapping areas.

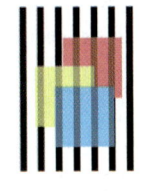

**FIGURE 5.19**

**6**   **Select the next set of rectangles and apply 60% opacity, then group the rectangles.**

The grouped rectangles look just like the ungrouped rectangles because transparency was applied prior to their being grouped.

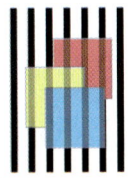

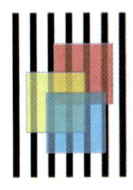

**FIGURE 5.20**

**7**   **With the recently grouped rectangles selected, check the Knockout Group box.**

The rectangles now function the same as the rectangles that were grouped before transparency was applied.

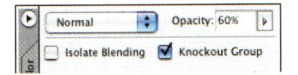

**FIGURE 5.21**

**8**   **Click the woman in the lower photograph and assign 60% opacity.**

This gives her a somewhat ghostly effect — perhaps she is thinking about warmer, balmier days.

**FIGURE 5.22**

**9**   **Save the document to your WIP_05 folder and leave it open for the next lesson.**

## LESSON 6  Creating Realistic Drop Shadows

In the past, creating drop shadows was a manual operation, and the shadows didn't look at all realistic — they had hard edges instead of feathering out to nothingness. InDesign's drop shadow feature allows you to simulate a shadow cast by an object; you can even specify the direction from which the object is illuminated. You can also customize the "softness" of shadow edges by defining the final transparency setting (0 to 100%) of the edge, and the distance over which the edge fades to that setting.

The default shadow color is black, but you can choose any color from the Swatches palette. Opacity defaults to 75%, which is usually acceptable. The X and Y Offset values specify how far the shadow is moved from the casting object; the Blur value sets the size of the shadow. Small Blur values make smaller, denser shadows; larger Blur values make longer, more diffuse shadows.

You can apply shadow effects, like transparency, to images imported into InDesign, objects drawn in InDesign, and type. You can apply shadows to one or more objects simultaneously.

### Create Realistic Drop Shadows

1. Continue in the open file, transparency.indd.

2. With the Selection tool, select the text frame containing the "Smell the Roses" text.

3. Choose Object>Drop Shadow and check the Drop Shadow box. If it is not already on, check the Preview box so you can see the effect of the shadow on the image.

   The default values produce a satisfactory, realistic, soft shadow, which looks very good over a photograph such as this one.

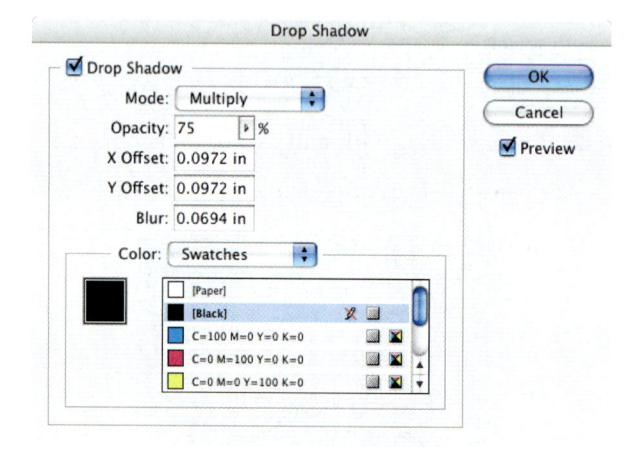

FIGURE 5.23

**Project 5   Working with Color**   191   **LEVEL 2**

**4**  **Change the X and Y offsets to 0.0417 in. and the blur to 0.0556 in.**

The shadow moves closer to the text and becomes darker, since the blur distance is shorter.

**5**  **Change the color of the shadow to the dark blue color in the Swatches palette.**

The shadow actually looks better, but it looks unnatural because of the other shadows in the image.

**6**  **Switch back to black, then click OK to apply the shadow.**

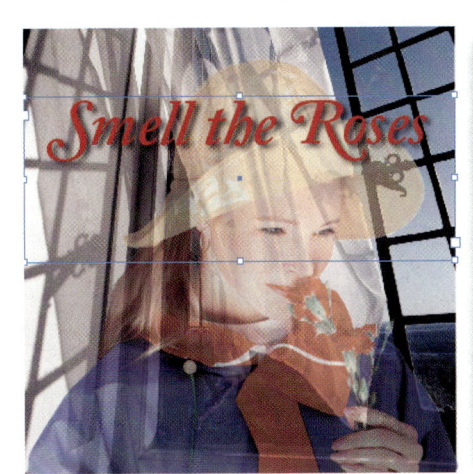

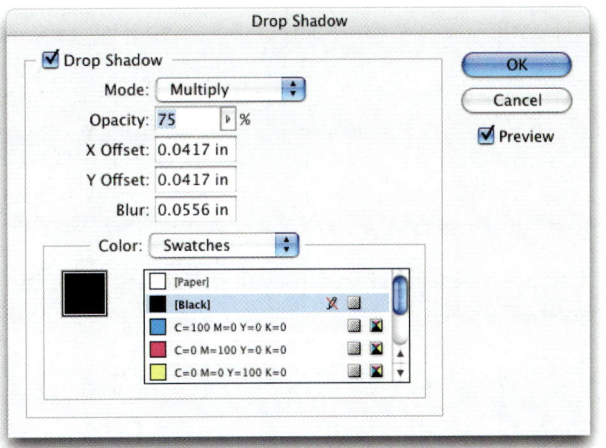

**FIGURE 5.24**

**7**  **Save the document and leave it open for the next lesson.**

## LESSON 7   Feathering Objects

Feathering an object softens its edges, blending them into the background. The Feather Width value determines the length of the feathering effect. The default value is 0.125 in.

You define how feathering applies to objects with sharp corners (such as rectangles) in the Corners menu:

- ***Diffused*** is the default setting; the feather is inset at the corners, so they appear approximately even with the edges.

- ***Rounded*** corners use a denser feather; the corners, while diffused, have a definite rounded appearance.

- ***Sharp*** extends the solid area out at the corners, giving them a pointed appearance.

## Feather Images

**1** Continue in the open document, transparency.indd.

**2** With the Selection tool, click the background photograph to select it.

**3** Choose Object>Feather (there is no keyboard shortcut), and check the Feather box.

The Feather dialog box opens.

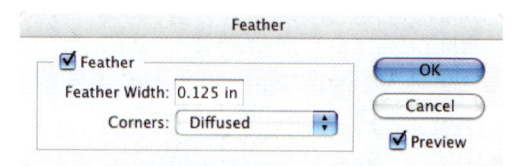

**FIGURE 5.25**

**4** Change the feather width to 0.5 in. With the Preview box checked, watch what happens to the picture.

You may have to click the Preview box on and off. Only the background picture is affected.

**5** Experiment with the Rounded and Sharp Corners options, and select the one you like best.

Sharp   Rounded   Diffused

**FIGURE 5.26**

**6** With the image still selected, apply a different corner option.

Only the new option is applied. The corner options are discrete, not cumulative.

**7** Now click the foreground photograph (the woman) and apply the same corner option that you just applied to the background photo.

The feather effect is applied to the foreground photo. You could have applied both effects at the same time.

**FIGURE 5.27**

**8** Save the document and leave it open for the next exercise.

## LESSON 8  Flattening Transparent Objects for Printing

When transparency is applied to an object to create any of the effects described above, some pixels are removed and replaced with the pixels of the background object. When sending files containing transparent objects to a printer, a process called *flattening* is required.

When a Photoshop document is flattened, the objects are all reassembled into a single layer. This allows virtually any printer to image the file. InDesign objects, however, are flattened only during the process of exporting to PDF or while printing. They remain layered in the InDesign document.

You can use colors in transparency, drop shadows, and feathering, but they should use the same color space — it's best to use RGB colors for drop shadows applied to RGB images and CMYK colors for drop shadows applied to CMYK images. You can set a *blend space* that forces mixed RGB or CMYK colors to the color space of your choice.

## Flatten Transparent Objects

**1** Continue in the open document, transparency.indd.

**2** Choose Edit>Transparency Blend Space and choose Document CMYK from the menu.

You should use Document RGB for images that will be displayed on a monitor and Document CMYK for images that you will print.

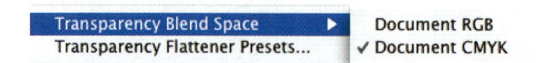

FIGURE 5.28

**3** Choose Edit>Transparency Flattener Presets and select Medium Resolution. Click OK.

This is an appropriate setting for most color proofing. You could create a new preset especially for your desktop printer, but it's not necessary.

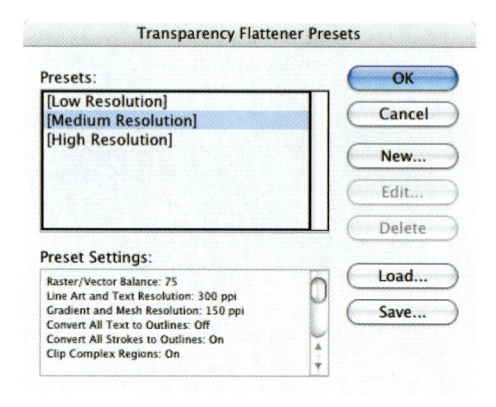

FIGURE 5.29

**4** Choose File>Export and export to your WIP_05 folder as PDF using the Print preset.

You can ignore the warning that appears.

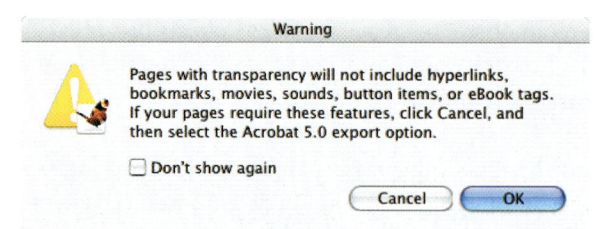

FIGURE 5.30

**5** Click OK to dismiss the warning.

The PDF file is created.

**6** Save the file and close it.

## LESSON 9  Managing Color

A thorough understanding of color reproduction is a valuable asset for any design professional. Color management in InDesign is a software-controlled system based on the specifications of the International Color Consortium (ICC). Color-management systems aren't limited to software, however; printers have used a number of processes and controls to achieve consistent color for decades. Because this book is about InDesign, we have kept this section concise, but color management and color science are complex topics you should research on your own. Against The Clock's *Color Companion for the Digital Artist* is a valuable aid to help you understand color-management systems more fully.

A color-management system (CMS) is intended to preserve color fidelity and ensure predictability and consistency throughout the color-reproduction process. Unless you have configured InDesign's (and all other programs that deal with color) color-management options correctly, you can't be certain that the colors displayed on your computer screen will match the colors that are printed.

Every device used in design work has a unique method for reading, interpreting, or displaying color. In our discussion of color-managed workflow, we refer to three different categories of color space:

- *Input* (or source) *space* refers to the RGB color space of a particular image-capture device, such as a scanner or digital camera.

- *Working space* is a standardized color space used for portability of color. A working space is device-independent because its gamut is based on a theoretical gamut that can be easily reproduced on any color system using the L*a*b* model.

- *Output* (or destination) *space* refers to the RGB or CMYK model used by an output device, such as a monitor, film recorder, printer, or color-separation device.

When working with color in InDesign, you can specify the rendering intent of the image when you assign the ICC profile. An intent is simply a table of numbers used by an application's CMS to manage the color-conversion process. You can choose from four different rendering intents, each of which defines a unique conversion method to accommodate various types of images.

- *Perceptual* intent causes gamut compression, preserving the visual relation between colors while compressing the entire tonal range and gamut of the source space to map within that of the destination space.

- *Relative Colorimetric* intent doesn't alter colors common to the source and destination gamuts; colors outside the destination gamut are mapped to the closest in-gamut color. This intent is better for most photographic images because it usually results in a closer match.

- *Absolute Colorimetric* intent preserves the white point of the destination and is used only for proofing.

- *Saturation* intent attempts to preserve apparent color saturation at the expense of hue accuracy in conversion. It is useful for business graphics where color accuracy is not critical and should not be used for photographic images.

Depending upon which operating system — and version of that system — you are using, there are a number of ways to calibrate and profile your monitor. You should ensure that your monitor is properly calibrated before proceeding with the following exercise.

## Set Up Color Management in InDesign

**1** With InDesign open, choose Edit>Color Settings and check the Enable Color Management box. Select U.S. Prepress Defaults from the Settings menu.

The default CMYK working space, U.S. Web Coated (SWOP) v2, is a CMYK color specification used for web-offset printing on coated paper; it's the standard color space of most magazines. You can visit www.swop.org for more information about this specification.

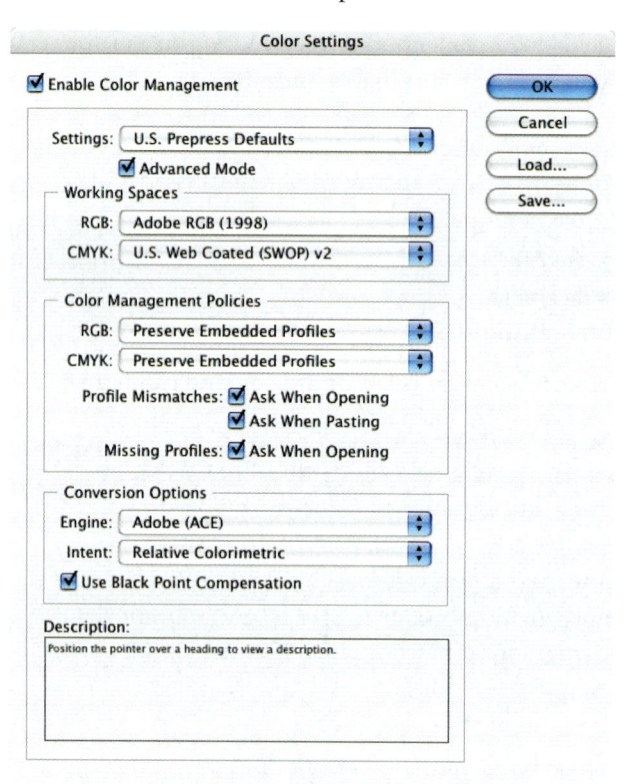

**FIGURE 5.31**

**2** In the Working Spaces area, change the CMYK menu to U.S. Sheetfed Coated v2.

The Settings selection changes to Custom.

**3** Click OK to save the settings.

The settings are saved under the name "Custom" in the list of color settings.

## Apply Color Management

**1**  Create a new letter-size document, using the default settings. Choose Edit>Color Settings. Make sure that color management is enabled and that the Color Settings dialog box uses the settings established in the previous exercise, then click OK.

**2**  Open the InDesign preferences, access the Display Performance pane, choose High Quality, then click OK.

**3**  Place oranges_cmyk.tif; when placing it, check the Show Import Options box in the Place dialog box.

The oranges image is in a CMYK device space, doesn't have an embedded profile, and has already been pre-separated for a specific output (in this case, to a printing press). You don't want to color-manage it for output.

**4**  Click the Color tab in the Image Import Options dialog box, and uncheck the Enable Color Management box.

This turns off color management for this particular image, although color management remains activated for the entire document.

**5**  Place the image anywhere on the page.

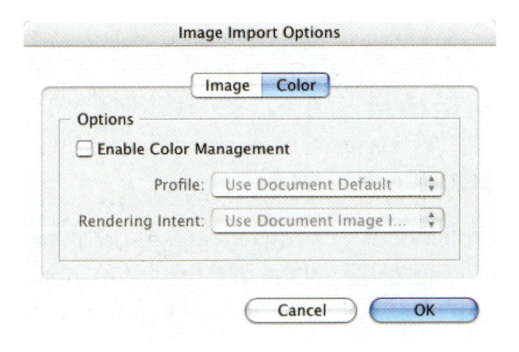

FIGURE 5.32

**6**  Place strawberries.tif, but uncheck the Show Import Options box in the Place dialog box. Place the image anywhere. Place grapes.tif and onion.tif with Show Import Options off, and arrange the images on the page so you can see all of them.

**7**  Select the strawberries image and choose Object>Image Color Settings.

This RGB image was saved without an embedded profile, so it was converted to the Adobe RGB (1998) working space by default when imported. That's OK. Remember, the default InDesign behavior for dealing with RGB images that lack embedded profiles is to use the document's RGB working space — which in this case happens to be Adobe RGB (1998) — and the document's default rendering intent.

**8** Click OK to close the dialog box.

**9** The grapes and onion images have embedded Adobe RGB (1998) profiles, so leave them alone.

**10** Choose Edit>Color Settings and turn off color management for the entire document, then click OK.

The colors on the screen change. What you're seeing is a generic image-data conversion for display purposes, which doesn't give a good representation of what the images will look like when they are printed.

**11** Turn color management back on.

**12** Select the oranges image and choose Object>Image Color Settings. Position the dialog box so you can see the image. Check the Enable Color Management box, and use the defaults. Click OK. Watch the image preview, which was originally a little over-saturated.

This image was separated in Photoshop from RGB to CMYK using the U.S. Sheetfed Coated profile, which matches your document CMYK working space. You can see what happens when you convert very bright, saturated RGB colors such as those originally used in this image to CMYK. This doesn't, however, give you an idea of what this image (or any image) will look like when printed, because this preview doesn't account for the color of the paper.

**13** Leave the document open for the next exercise.

## *To Extend Your Knowledge...*

### CHANGING AN IMAGE'S SOURCE PROFILE

Changing an image's source profile does not convert image data from the original source space; it merely reassigns the image's existing color values to those in the new source profile. This can cause drastic color changes. If an image already has an embedded profile, you should use it unless you are certain that it is incorrect. If an image lacks an embedded profile, it is safe to assign a working space; doing so merely gives the image a definable gamut — it doesn't change the colors.

### WORKING IN CMYK WORKFLOWS

If you use a CMYK workflow, you really don't need to use InDesign's color management for anything other than an accurate screen preview. Make sure you have the correct CMYK profile (the same one that was used to convert the images from RGB) assigned as the CMYK working space in the InDesign Color Setup dialog box.

## Soft-Proof the Document

In this exercise you will set InDesign to provide an on-screen simulation of your images' printed appearance. This process is called *soft proofing* because you view the images on your monitor instead of on an actual ("hard") printed proof.

**1** Choose View>Proof Setup>Custom. In the Profile menu, select U.S. Sheetfed Coated v2, then check the Paper White box.

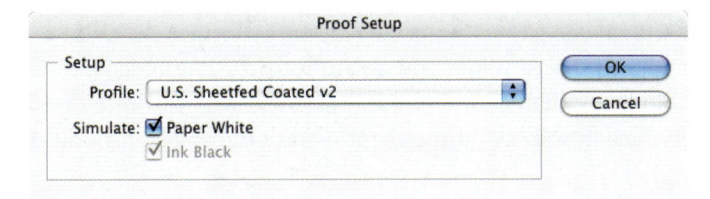

FIGURE 5.33

**2** Click OK and watch the white area of the page.

The white area turns a light yellowish-gray, because white paper isn't truly white. Image colors should only change slightly.

**3** To return to a non-proofing view, choose View>Proof Colors to deselect the option.

The option is automatically activated when you close the Proof Setup dialog box.

**4** Leave the document open for the next exercise.

## *To Extend Your Knowledge...*

### BLACK AND SOFT PROOFS

Black appears as a very dark gray when an InDesign document is color-managed, regardless of whether you are viewing a soft proof. Remember, color management shows you a simulated view of ink on paper — and black ink isn't absolutely black when printed. To return to a non-gray view of black, turn color management off.

## Manage Colors

**1** In the Swatches palette Options menu, choose New Color Swatch.

**2** Change the Color Type menu to Process, and the Color Mode menu to RGB. Check the Name with Color Value box.

**3** Enter the following into the appropriate fields: R: 255, G: 0, B: 25.

This color recipe sets off the gamut alarm, which tells you that the color is outside the gamut of the current CMYK working space. When you create RGB or L*a*b* colors when color management is turned on, each color is evaluated to determine whether it is within the gamut of the current CMYK working space. If your job won't be printed and will only be used for online viewing, you can ignore the gamut alarm.

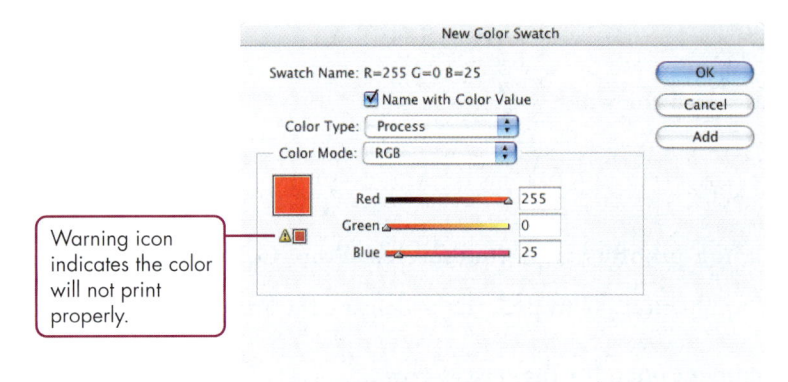

*Warning icon indicates the color will not print properly.*

**FIGURE 5.34**

**4** To fix this problem, click the little color swatch next to the gamut alarm icon.

InDesign uses an RGB>CMYK calculation to determine the best match within the CMYK working space for the swatch you just defined.

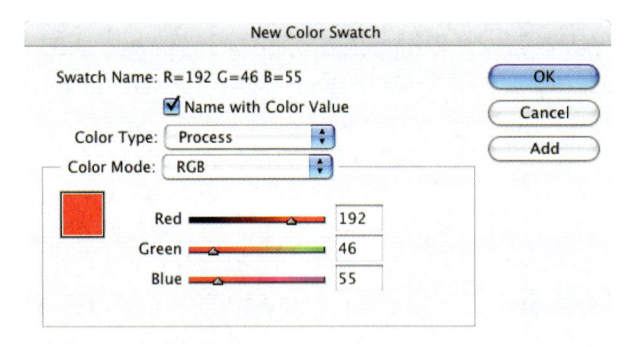

**FIGURE 5.35**

**5** Click OK.

**6** Close the document without saving.

# SUMMARY

Color theory, science, and management are advanced topics that we encourage you to investigate further on your own. People obtain doctoral degrees in color science, which is a subject of continuous research in academia and industry. A thorough understanding of how color reproduction works and how to apply this knowledge in your work will certainly give you an advantage. We explained the basics of color theory and how the various models relate to the graphic arts, specifically to the RGB and CMYK color spaces that you will work with daily. You learned about the limitations of each space, and about the gamuts that can limit their ability to reproduce color. We described how to apply color management in InDesign. Finally, you gained experience applying ICC profiles to imported images, and setting up InDesign's color-management options.

# KEY TERMS

| | | |
|---|---|---|
| additive model | intent | saturation |
| additive primaries | L*a*b* | shadow |
| CMYK | mixed ink | soft proof |
| color management | opacity | spot color |
| colorimetric | overprint | subtractive model |
| diffuse | PANTONE | subtractive primaries |
| feather | perceptual | tint |
| flatten | profile | transparency |
| indexed color | RGB | trapping |
| input space | rosette | working space |

# CHECKING CONCEPTS AND TERMS

## MULTIPLE CHOICE

**Check the letter of the correct answer for each of the following:**

1. What is the additive color model?
   a. Using RGB to mix colors
   b. Using CMYK to mix colors
   c. A means of creating tints
   d. All of the above

2. Which is true of the subtractive color model?
   a. If all colors are removed, white results.
   b. The primary colors cyan, magenta, and yellow are used to mix colors.
   c. If all colors are present, black results (theoretically).
   d. All of the above.

3. What is the L*a*b* color model?
   a. A color space that includes both RGB and CMYK color space
   b. A color space that builds colors using 256 parts of each color
   c. A necessary color space for building transparency
   d. Color space that results when you flatten images

4. Transparency is used to create…
   a. See-through images
   b. Realistic shadows
   c. Feathered edges
   d. All the above

5. What does color management do?
   a. Converts RGB images to CMYK
   b. Allows you to see on-screen just how the printed document will look
   c. Converts input color space to monitor color space to output color space
   d. Assigns color profiles to images

6. When should you build an RGB color palette?
   a. When your document's primary distribution is print
   b. When your document's primary distribution is on-screen
   c. When using subtractive primaries
   d. When you need to introduce transparency

7. What is the preferred color space if you intend to produce a tint from the color?
   a. Process
   b. Spot
   c. RGB
   d. L*a*b*

8. If you create a mixed ink, you should…
   a. Also create a mixed-ink group.
   b. Use only process color.
   c. See a sample of the ink mix.
   d. Use RGB and spot colors.

9. What happens when transparency is applied to grouped objects?
   a. Transparency is applied to the entire group.
   b. Transparency is applied to each element of the group as though it was ungrouped.
   c. The top element in the group becomes transparent.
   d. Nothing. You can't apply transparency to grouped objects.

10. When should you use InDesign's color management?
    a. When images are in a CMYK device space
    b. When you want to change an image's source profile
    c. When your entire workflow is CMYK
    d. When working in RGB and CMYK color spaces

## DISCUSSION QUESTIONS

1. What purpose does L*a*b* have in InDesign, and why should you not use the color space when defining colors?

2. Discuss the advantages and disadvantages of using mixed inks in documents.

# SKILL DRILL

Skill Drills reinforce project skills. Each skill reinforced is the same, or nearly the same, as a skill presented in the lessons. Detailed instructions are provided in a step-by-step format. The drills should be performed in the order in which they are presented.

## 1. Build a Custom Color Palette

Your client, a national hotel chain, has very strict rules about use of its corporate colors, when using process color and when printing with spot color. You have been given the responsibility of creating a document that will hold all the colors. When printing two-color documents to coated paper, PANTONE 201 is used; when printing on uncoated paper, PANTONE 207 is used to achieve the same appearance. The process colors are similarly created. A 35% tint is used when the logo is placed against a dark background. Occasionally, a darker tone is used; this color is created as a mixed ink, when the job is printed using two colors.

1. Create a new document and accept its defaults.
2. Remove all colors from the Swatches palette except the four permanent colors.
3. Add the first spot color, PANTONE 201, from the PANTONE Solid Coated library to the Swatches palette.
4. Add the second spot color, PANTONE 207, from the PANTONE Solid Uncoated library.
5. Create the first process color, named "Process 201", as C:0, M:100, Y:60, K:40 and add it to the Swatches palette.
6. Create the second process color, named "Process 207", as C:0, M:96, Y:32, K:32 and add it to the Swatches palette.
7. Create the two tints from PANTONE 201 and PANTONE 207. For each, click the ink in the Swatches palette, choose New Tint Swatch from the Options menu, and assign a 35% tint.
8. Create two mixed inks named "PANTONE 201 Shaded" and "PANTONE 207 Shaded" by adding 28% process black to PANTONE 201 and 207.
9. Create matching shaded process colors named "Process 201 Shaded" and "Process 207 Shaded" by adding 16% black to Process 201 and Process 207.
10. Save the document as "ultrasuite_colors.indd" and close it.

## 2. Import and Apply Colors and Shadow

In addition to creating a container for the colors, you will produce a number of shell ads for individual hotels to place in their local media. You will use some of the colors you created in the previous Skill Drill for this process-color ad.

1. Open the document ultrasuite_ad.indd. This is a full-color ad that will be printed on coated paper.
2. From the Swatches palette Options menu, choose Load Swatches and select the swatches from the file ultrasuite_colors.indd.
3. Apply the Process 201 color to the logo.

4. Color the headline Paper.

5. Switch to the Selection tool and choose Object>Drop Shadow.

6. Turn the drop shadow on and leave the Mode at Multiply and the Opacity at 75%. Change the X and Y Offset fields to 0.05 in. and the Blur field to 0.07 in. Select Process 201 Shaded as the color and click OK to apply the shadow.

7. Click the photograph with the Selection tool, then choose Object>Feather. Turn feathering on; set the Feather Width field to 0.5 in and the Corners menu to Diffused, then click OK.

8. Choose Edit>Color Settings and enable color management.

9. Set the RGB working space to ColorMatch RGB and the CMYK working space to U.S. Web Coated (SWOP) v2. Preserve all embedded profiles. Click OK.

10. Save the document and leave it open.

**FIGURE 5.36**

## 3. Prepare an Ad Using Spot Color

When you set up the colors, you set them up for both process and spot color. Spot-color ads could be used for newspaper reproduction, as you will do in this Skill Drill. You will use many of the same skills as in the process-color ad, but there are some subtle differences.

1. Open the document ultrasuite_ad_2c.indd. This two-color ad will be printed on newsprint.

2. Load the swatches from the ultrasuite_colors.indd file.

3. Apply the PANTONE 207 color to the logo.

4. Switch to the Selection tool and choose Object>Drop Shadow.

5. Turn the drop shadow on and leave the Mode at Multiply and the Opacity at 75%. Change the X and Y Offset fields to 0.05 in. and the Blur field to 0.07 in. Select PANTONE 207 Shaded as the color and click OK to apply the shadow.

6. Click the photograph with the Selection tool, then choose Object>Feather. Turn feathering on; set the Feather Width field to 0.5 in. and the Corners menu to Diffused, then click OK.

7. Choose Edit>Color Settings and enable color management.

8. Set the RGB working space to ColorMatch RGB and the CMYK working space to U.S. Web Coated (SWOP) v2. Preserve all embedded profiles. Click OK.

9. Save the document and leave it open.

## 4. Soft-Proof and Compare Documents

You need to compare both printed documents. You will notice that they are quite different on-screen, but more similar when they are actually printed.

1. In the process-color ad, choose View>Proof Setup>Custom. Choose U.S. Sheetfed Coated v2 and check the Paper White box.

2. Click OK and watch the white area of the page turn a yellowish gray.

3. In the spot-color ad, choose View>Proof Setup>Custom. Choose U.S. Web Uncoated v2 and check the Paper White box.

4. Click OK and watch the white area of the page turn a medium gray.

5. Print both documents if you have a color printer available.

6. In both documents, return to the View menu and click Proof Colors to turn the proofing option off.

7. In both documents, return to the Edit menu and turn color management off.

8. Save and close the document.

# CHALLENGE

Challenge exercises expand on, or are somewhat related to, skills presented in the lessons. Each exercise provides a brief introduction, followed by instructions presented in a numbered-step format that are not as detailed as those in the Skill Drill exercises. You should perform these exercises in the order in which they appear.

## 1. Add and Apply Color to a Document

You have been assigned to produce an ad for the House of Rose Bed and Breakfast. The photo has been selected for you, and the copywriters have done their job well. It is up to you to take the basics they have given you and produce the best-looking ad you can.

1. Open the document bb_ad.indd. You're going to add color to the subhead and the drop cap.

2. With the Fill icon active, click the Eyedropper tool on one of the purple roses in the photo.

3. Click the icon and drag the color into the Swatches palette.

4. Double-click the swatch and alter its values to whole numbers. We used C:30, M:100, Y:75, K:35. Name the color "Purple".

5. Apply the color to the subhead and to the drop cap.

6. Create a new color based on this one to use as a drop shadow. Name it "Purple Shadow" and increase the Black value to 55%.

7. Save the document and leave it open for the next exercise.

## 2. Apply Transparent Elements

It's the little things that count — and you're expert enough to recognize that applying a little transparency to elements in the ad will make it more effective. Drop shadows and feathering effects will make a world of difference to this document.

1. Continue in the open document, bb_ad.indd.

2. Apply a drop shadow to the main headline with X and Y offsets of 0.06 in. and a blur set to 0.07 in. Use the Purple Shadow color for the headline.

3. Select the Peaches image and apply feathering and rounded corners to this image. We selected a feather width of 0.3 in., but you should use your best judgment.

4. Select the House of Rose image and apply a purple drop shadow. Experiment with the opacity, offsets, and blur. We preferred a blur that was considerably longer than the offsets.

5. Move the House of Rose image so it is appropriately positioned.

6. Save the document and leave it open for the next exercise.

FIGURE 5.37

## 3. Flatten Transparent Objects for Printing and Examine Links

You should recognize that transparent objects can create problems for imaging devices, which is why they need to have some complexity removed through the flattening process. In this Challenge, you will prepare the document for printing.

1. Continue in the open document, bb_ad.indd.
2. Set the Transparency Blend Space to Document CMYK.
3. Select High Resolution from the Transparency Flattener Presets.
4. From the Links palette, double-click the b&b.tif listing. Note this image's color space and profile.
5. Click the Next button to successively check the color space and profile for the houseofrose.tif and peaches.tif images.
6. Save the file and leave it open.

## 4. Color Manage Your Document

You now know enough about the content of the document to successfully color-manage it. You need to turn on color management and either manage — or not — the images within the document.

1. Continue in the open document, bb_ad.indd.
2. Enable color management.
3. Set the RGB working space to Adobe RGB (1998) and the CMYK working space to U.S. Sheetfed Coated v2. Preserve all embedded profiles and use the Relative Colorimetric rendering intent.
4. From Proof Setup, choose U.S. Sheetfed Coated v2, which matches your color management, and check Paper White.
5. Return to non-proofing mode.
6. Export a color-managed PDF to your WIP_05 folder, using the Press setting.
7. Close and save the document.

# PORTFOLIO BUILDER

## Create Thumbnails of Your Work

You have already discovered the value of building a portfolio in which to present your work. In addition to placing your full-sized works in a folder, it is useful to create thumbnails of each document as references. You can use them as a visual table of contents, or place them on a Web page with hyperlinks to PDF versions of your documents, or to downloadable InDesign documents. You can complete this project with no additional resource files.

To complete this project, use the following techniques:

- Create a document with enough pages to hold thumbnails of your portfolio pieces. You can make the thumbnails any size, but they should be large enough to show reasonable detail.

- Add colors and gradients as appropriate. Drop shadows will help make your thumbnails stand out.

- Write descriptive captions for each of the entries in your portfolio.

- Include your name and contact information on each page that contains thumbnails.

PROJECT **6**

LEVEL **2**

# Controlling and Editing Documents

## OBJECTIVES

*In this project, you learn how to*

- Convert text to outlines
- Create compound paths
- Use the Pathfinder
- Group and ungroup objects
- Align and distribute objects
- Nest objects and create inline elements
- Import and create clipping paths
- Create a variety of wraps
- Wrap text to drop caps

# WHY WOULD I DO THIS?

Although InDesign is not primarily a graphics program, you can use it to create both simple and complex graphics for use in an InDesign document. You can create paths from text, merge paths together to form compound paths, and split compound paths apart. You can also change the direction of a path, create nested objects, and embed a graphic into a line of text so it will flow with the text. In addition, you can force text to wrap around objects, even if they're irregularly shaped.

When you create outlines from text — which is practical only if you are using very large type — the text is converted to a graphic and you can use fonts that the recipient of the document doesn't have. In addition, you can give the text special treatment; for example, you can place an image inside the outlines or you can alter the shape of the outline.

You can also change the direction of a path. Where compound paths intersect, they create inside and outside paths. To change the fill of an object, you can reverse the path's direction by selecting one point on the path. You may also need to reverse the direction of a subpath to achieve a specific transparency effect that you want.

In addition, you can group objects or nest objects inside one another so they are treated as a single unit. You can align objects with reference to each other and distribute them evenly based on their dimensions. These features enhance your control over objects within a document.

Inline objects are those that you place or paste into a text story, where they act as any other characters. You can place any object into a text frame as an inline object, as long as there is room within the text frame. The benefit to using inline objects is that they flow with the text; this is very useful for longer documents where images and drawings need to remain with material that refers to them. All the images and drawings in this series are inline objects, because we require that images and graphics flow with the text in case sections or pages are added or removed.

In addition to cropping images, as you have previously done, you can use an image's clipping path to show and hide parts of an image. If an image doesn't have a clipping path, you can create one either manually in InDesign, or with InDesign's automatic clipping-path generation utility. A clipping path can be used to silhouette an object, so the background will not show.

Text can wrap around any other object on a page. When you create a text wrap, InDesign creates a boundary around the shape that holds text away from the shape at a specified distance. Text wraps can follow an object's bounding box or clipping path. You can also create inverted wraps — for example, you could fill a glass with type by using the Object Shape wrap. There are also several techniques for wrapping text around a drop cap.

# VISUAL SUMMARY

You have learned a number of ways to control the content of your document. In this project, you learn to control the interaction of elements on your page.

On certain occasions, you will need to convert text to outlines. You may be using an unusual typeface that you don't want to include with the document, or you may want to apply special treatment (such as filling it with a photograph) to the type. The process is as simple as selecting the type you want to convert, then choosing Type>Create Outlines.

**FIGURE 6.1**

Compound paths are created when type is converted to outlines, or when objects overlap and one object *knocks out* (removes) a part of the other. You can access Compound Paths commands from the Object menu or the Pathfinder palette, new to this version of InDesign.

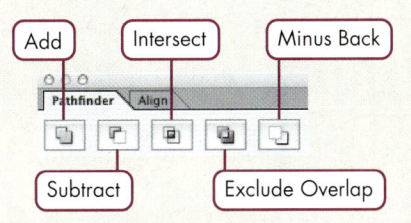

**FIGURE 6.2**

In addition to creating compound objects, you can group and ungroup objects. You can use the Align palette to arrange objects in relation to one another and to distribute space between them.

Vertical alignment options: Align Left Edges, Align Horizontal Centers, Align Right Edges buttons

Horizontal alignment options: Align Top Edges, Align Vertical Centers, Align Bottom Edges buttons

Distribute Vertical Top, Center, and Bottom buttons

Distribute Horizontal Left, Center, and Right buttons

Distribute Spacing Vertically button

Distance between distributed objects; negative numbers result in overlaps

Distribute Spacing Horizontally button

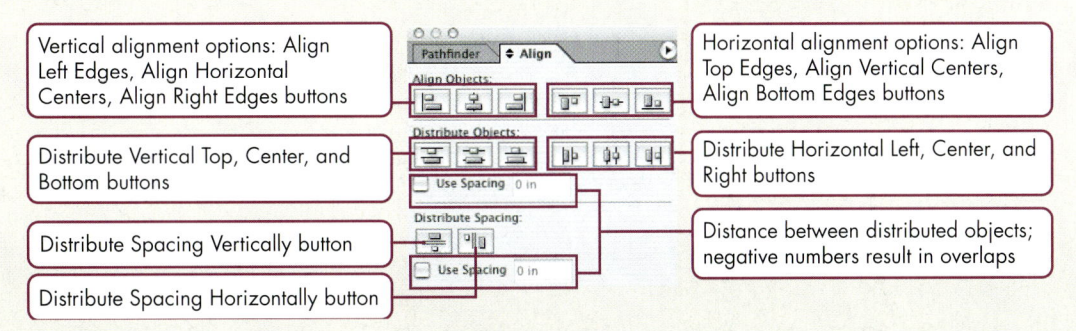

**FIGURE 6.3**

You can use the Paste Into command to nest objects inside one another; you can then drag them into position relative to the frame into which they have been placed. You can also insert objects into text as inline objects that flow with the text. This can be useful if you choose to use a graphic as a bullet, or if you wish to insert graphic elements into the text — the images will not be separated from the editorial content regardless of any changes that you make. Once you place an object as an inline object, it is treated much the same as text. To create Figure 6.4, we used the Rectangle tool to create the boxes and the Pencil to make the checkmarks; we then grouped them and pasted the group as an inline graphic at the beginning of each line.

☑ Integrity
☑ Reliability
☑ Honesty
☑ Capability

**FIGURE 6.4**

When you don't want the background of an object to show, you create a mask, or clipping path, that allows only the desired portion of the object to be visible. You can import clipping paths with an object, or create them automatically with InDesign's Detect Edges utility. The best solution is to use or clipping paths created in the originating graphic program, such as Photoshop. You can also use a Photoshop path or alpha channel to define a clipping path.

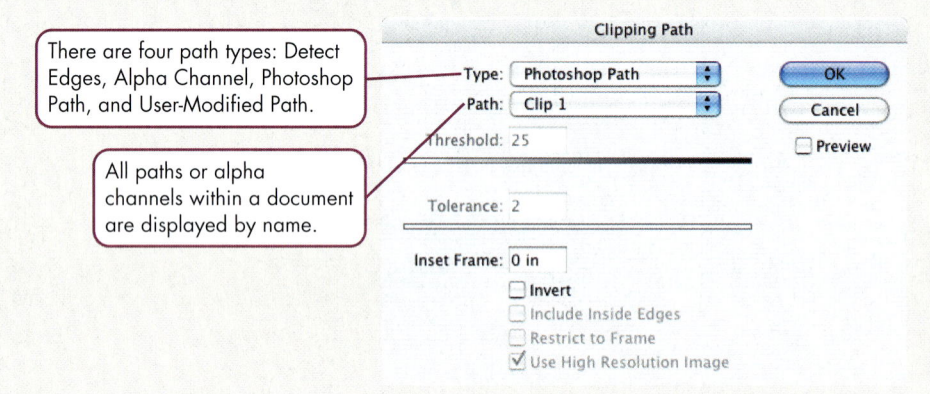

There are four path types: Detect Edges, Alpha Channel, Photoshop Path, and User-Modified Path.

All paths or alpha channels within a document are displayed by name.

**FIGURE 6.5**

In addition to hiding parts of an image, clipping paths are often used to define text wraps. The most common text wrap option forces text to wrap around a bounding box, but there are also other possibilities. Text can wrap to the object's shape, which can be the shape of a vector graphic, or a defined clipping path. Text can also jump the object, which means that no text will appear beside the image, or it can jump to the next column or frame after the one in which the image appears.

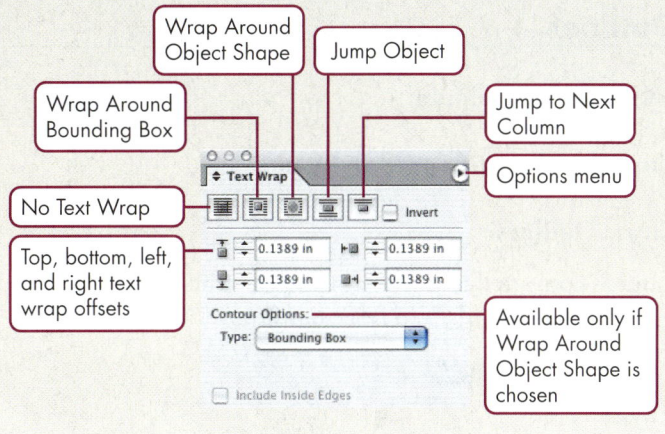

**FIGURE 6.6**

## LESSON 1 Converting Text to Outlines

You can convert any letter or other text character to its component outlines, or ***paths***, by selecting it and choosing Type>Create Outlines (or pressing Command/Control-Shift-G). You can convert every character within a frame to a single object using the Selection tool to select the frame, then converting. You can convert individual characters or groups of characters by selecting them with the Type tool, then converting.

After the conversion process, the original text disappears; if you want to retain it, you need to hold the Option/Alt key while using the menu command or the keystroke command. In this case, the outlines are created above the original type, so you can move the paths without affecting the original text.

After conversion, you can treat a character or character group like any other frame or path. You can place images or text inside, you can apply various strokes and fills, and you can change its shape with the Direct Selection tool. If you select single letters, each will be treated as a frame; if you select a group of letters, it will be treated as a single frame. Figure 6.7 shows the difference between applying a gradient fill to grouped and single (ungrouped) letters — the "Group" letters were converted to outlines as a unit, and the "Single" letters were converted individually.

**FIGURE 6.7**

The default stroke and fill colors of the new path are those that you assigned to the letter before conversion; by default, this is a black fill with no stroke. To place any object into the path created from text, you can select the path with either of the selection tools, then choose File>Place. If you want to use the paths as masks for an image that's already been placed in the document, you can copy or cut the image, select the paths, then choose Edit>Paste Into.

## Convert Text to Outlines

**1** Open the document conversion.indd.

**2** With the Selection tool, click the upper text frame.

**3** Choose Type>Create Outlines.

All type in the frame is converted to outlines, which are filled with black and have no stroke. You can also press Command/Control-Shift-O to create outlines.

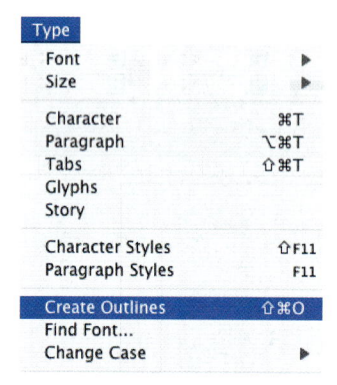

FIGURE 6.8

**4** In the middle text frame, highlight "HEI" with the Type tool and choose Type>Create Outlines.

The three characters are converted to a compound path.

**5** In the middle text frame, select the "G" and create outlines, as you did in Step 4. Repeat this process for the "HTS" letters.

The space between the three separate frames is eliminated. The characters are still contained in the text frame; you cannot move them because InDesign treats them as inline graphics. If you want to restore their spacing, you can add kerning of about +75 between the "I" and the "G" and between the "G" and the "H."

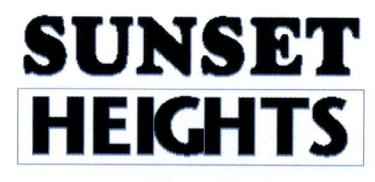

FIGURE 6.9

**6** With the Selection tool, click the word Sunset. Place sunset_mtn.tif into this frame.

The image fills all the letters as a single unit.

**7** Place the same image in the three frames that make up the word "Heights."

You need to place the image in each frame separately. The image appears in its entirety in each frame, rather than appearing as a single unit across all three frames.

**8** With the Direct Selection tool, adjust the images as you would like them to appear.

We kerned the letters (as described after Step 5) prior to adjusting the position of the images within the frames.

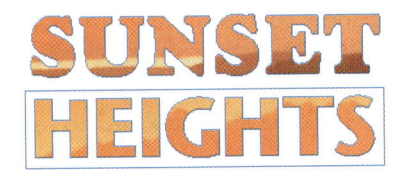

**FIGURE 6.10**

**9** Save the document and leave it open for the next lesson.

## LESSON 2 Making and Releasing Compound Paths

With compound paths, you can create objects with transparent holes in them. You can also combine existing paths into a single compound path. This is helpful when you want multiple paths to act as a frame for a single imported graphic or for a gradient; any content placed within a compound path spans across all the compound subpaths. You worked with compound paths in the previous lesson.

To create a compound path, you need to select two or more paths (which can be open or closed) or frames, then either choose Object>Compound Paths>Make or press Command/Control-8. To separate a compound path back to individual ones, you can either choose Object>Compound Paths>Release or press Command-Option-8/Control-Alt-8.

Where compound paths intersect, they create inside and outside paths. To change a path from inside to outside, you need to reverse its direction. To change a path's direction — and thus its fill — you use the Direct Selection tool to select one point on the path, then choose Object>Reverse Path. You may need to experiment when reversing different subpaths of a compound path.

### Make and Release Compound Paths

**1** Continue in the open document, conversion.indd.

**2** Click the third frame "A Mature Adult" with the Selection tool and convert the type to outlines.

**3** With the frame still selected, choose Object>Compound Paths>Release.

The "holes" in the middle of the letters are filled in, and each letter is a separate entity.

**A MATURE ADULT**

FIGURE 6.11

**4** Zoom in to about 400% and, with either the Selection or Direct Selection tool, drag a marquee to select the entire first letter "A."

**5** Hold the Shift key and click the stem to deselect it, then, with the Direct Selection tool, click one of the anchor points of the triangle in the upper center of the letter.

When you deselect the stem, the only part of the letter that should remain selected is the triangle that makes up the hole in the letter.

**6** Choose Object>Reverse Path. Hold the Shift key and select the rest of the letter, then choose Object>Compound Paths>Make.

The hole reappears in the character.

**A MATURE ADULT**

FIGURE 6.12

**7** Save the document and leave it open for the next lesson.

## LESSON 3 Using the Pathfinder

InDesign provides an additional sets of tools for working with compound paths in the Pathfinder palette. As you might deduce from its name, the purpose of the Pathfinder palette is to take some of the guesswork out of reversing paths, thereby allowing the computer to make that decision for you. InDesign's Pathfinder palette contains a number of the same features found in Adobe Illustrator's Pathfinder palette.

There are five buttons in the Pathfinder palette:

- **Add** combines selected objects into one shape, even if the objects do not touch one another (such as letters in a word).

- **Subtract** removes objects in front of the backmost object; if objects completely cover the backmost object, this option will not function.

- **Intersect** removes all parts of the objects except those where the objects overlap; in this case the remaining shape takes on the fill of the frontmost object.

- **Exclude Overlap** removes only the overlapping parts of the objects; you must be careful when working with more than two objects.

- **Minus Back** removes the objects behind the frontmost object.

You can access the Pathfinder via the menu (Object>Pathfinder), or from the Pathfinder palette. If you're going to be using this tool much, it's much easier to work with the palette, then put it away when it is not in use.

## Use the Pathfinder

1. Continue in the open document, conversion.indd.

2. Choose Window>Pathfinder to activate the Pathfinder palette.

3. Select the second "A" dragging the Selection tool over it and marqueeing the letter.

4. Click the fourth button in the Pathfinder palette, Exclude Overlap.

   The area of overlap, where the opening in the A exists, is removed.

   **FIGURE 6.13**

5. Select the "R" in the same manner as you selected the "A."

6. Click the fifth button in the Pathfinder palette, Minus Back.

   The area at the back of the stack is removed.

7. Using either method you have learned, convert the "A" and "D" to compound paths.

8. Save the file and close it.

## LESSON 4  Grouping and Ungrouping Objects

One way to manage documents and work with them effectively is to group elements within the document. You can group multiple objects — even of different types — into one large object. The bounding box of a group accommodates all objects in the group. Grouped objects retain their original stacking order, and the entire group possesses its own stacking order relative to other objects. If you group objects from different layers, the resulting group ends up on the topmost layer that contained one of the grouped objects. You can even create groups that contain other groups, resulting in *nested groups*. You can select and modify any individual object in a group with the Direct Selection tool, but you cannot change the stacking order within the group. To group objects, you simply select them and choose Object>Group or press Command/Control-G. To ungroup objects, you select the group with the Selection tool and choose Object>Ungroup or press Command/Control-Shift-G.

## Group and Ungroup Objects

**1** Open the file manage.indd.

**2** Move the photograph to the top center of the page.

The easiest way to do this is to select the top-center reference point and enter the desired X position, 4.25 in.

**3** Select the text block below the photograph and, using the top-center reference point, position it at X: 4.25 in., Y: 4.8 in.

**4** Click both objects and choose Object>Group.

The photo and the block of text are grouped with a single bounding box.

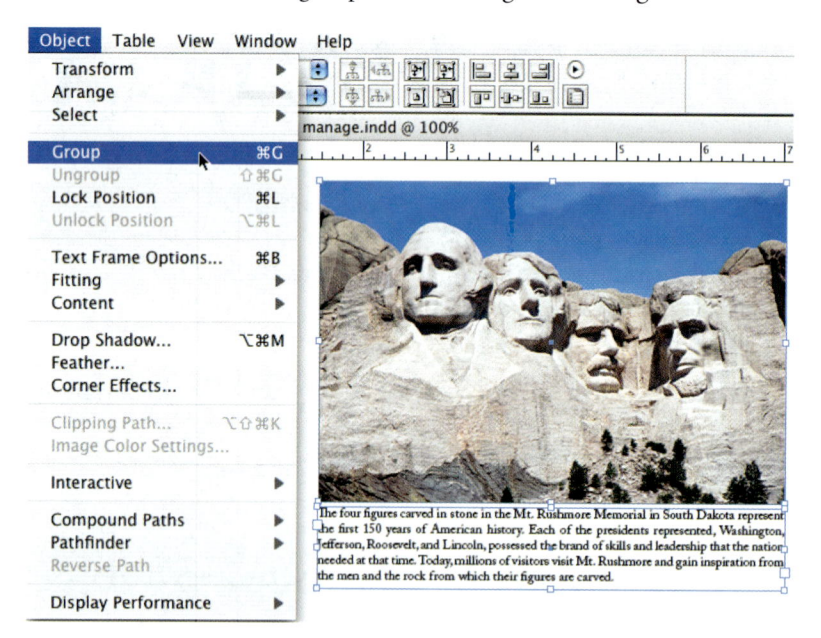

**FIGURE 6.14**

**5** Click any part of the grouped object with the Selection tool and move it left or right.

The photo and the type act as a single unit.

**6** With the Direct Selection tool, click the block of type. Using the Down Arrow key, move it two points down the page.

You can use the Direct Selection tool to move the block of type independently from the photo.

**7** Switch to the Type tool and click in the paragraph. In the third line, change "brand of" to "specific".

You can still edit the text, even though it is part of a group.

**8** Switch back to the Selection tool and click the grouped frame. Choose Object>Ungroup.

The frames are ungrouped and each displays its own bounding box. You can also press Shift-Command/Control-Shift-G to ungroup objects.

**9** Save the document and leave it open for the next exercise.

## LESSON 5 Aligning and Distributing Objects

You can align the tops, middles, or sides of objects manually, using the Control or Transform palette. In addition, you can use an Excel spreadsheet (or a piece of paper) to do the math to distribute objects with relation to one another. But InDesign has an easier way — the Align palette.

From the Align palette, you can control the position of objects in reference to each other. You can align objects either vertically (so the left or right edges are even) or horizontally (so the top or bottom edges are even). If you specify left alignment, for example, the left edges of all the selected objects align with the leftmost object. Center alignment aligns the exact centers of each object.

When you use the distribution options, InDesign automatically adds space between objects to maintain an equal distance between their edges or center points. InDesign also offers a distribute-by-object spacing method, which helps to evenly distribute different-shaped or -sized objects. To use these functions, you simply select the desired objects, open the Align palette (Window>Align, or press F8), then choose the desired alignment or distribution method.

In addition to InDesign's automatic object-distribution options, you can distribute objects by putting the same amount of space between objects, add a specified amount of space between facing edges of objects, or place a specified amount of space between specified edges. When you specify a Use Spacing value, you can use either positive or negative values, if you desire images to overlap.

### Align and Distribute Objects

**1** Continue in the open document, manage.indd.

**2** Choose Window>Align to open the Align palette.

**3** Select the green circle, red square, and yellow triangle.

**4** Click the Align Vertical Center button in the Align palette.

All the objects align horizontally, based on their vertical centers. Because they are all the same size, their tops and bottoms align as well.

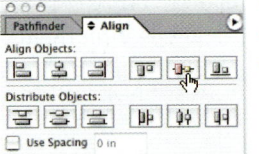

**FIGURE 6.15**

**5**    **Click the Distribute Horizontal Center button (immediately below the one you clicked in Step 4).**

The objects distribute their space between the center of the circle and that of the triangle, based on the center position of each element — the square moves left just a little.

**6**    **Click the Show Options button in the upper right of the palette to make the Distribute Spacing options visible.**

**7**    **Select the three objects below those you have worked with and click the Distribute Horizontal Space button.**

Equal space is inserted between each item.

**8**    **Check the Use Spacing box and set the field to –0.1 in. Click the Distribute Horizontal Space button again.**

The objects infringe on one another's space by 0.1 in.; the leftmost object becomes the anchor for the line.

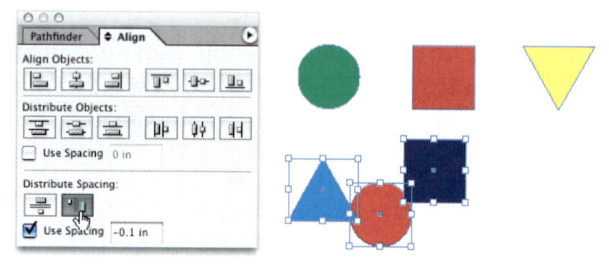

**FIGURE 6.16**

**9**    **With the objects selected, align their horizontal and vertical centers to place them on top of one another.**

**10**    **Save and close the document.**

## LESSON 6   Creating Nested and Inline Elements

In addition to creating grouped objects, you can created ***nested objects*** by placing one frame inside another. A single frame can contain only one other frame, but that frame can contain another and so on, to infinity, or until the frames are physically so small that you can't create a smaller frame. The outer frame can't contain any other objects, but you can apply a fill and stroke to it.

If you scale or rotate a frame that contains another frame, any nested frames scale and rotate too. You can transform nested objects independently of their containing frames by selecting them with the Direct Selection tool, switching to the Selection tool, and then manipulating the nested frame. (You can use the same technique to select an object that's part of a group.)

An *inline element* is any object that is inserted into the text flow; it could be a rule, an image, or even another text frame. You might, for example, want to insert a small table in a line of running text.

While inline images are very versatile and help create more compelling copy, you should use them with care — especially larger inline images. You cannot adjust the bounding box of an inline image, so it is more difficult (but not impossible) to affect its interaction with surrounding text.

## Add Nested and Inline Elements

**1**     **Open the document antiques.indd.**

**2**     **With the Selection tool, click the text frame at the left of the page and cut it, then select the ad frame and choose Edit>Paste Into.**

The text frame is nested at the top of the frame into which you pasted it, almost invisible against the photo.

**3**     **Click the text frame with the Direct Selection tool and, with the upper-center proxy reference selected, position it at X: 2.125 in., Y: 3.6 in.**

This centers it in the 4.25-in. frame. When frames are nested, they take their position from the position of the frame in which they are nested, not the page. Note the "+" sign that appears following the X and Y in the Control panel.

**FIGURE 6.17**

**4**     **Place the image point.eps anywhere on the page. Manually adjust the bounding box so it fits tightly around the hand.**

The hand image is too small to use the Fit Frame to Content option.

**5** Choose the Selection tool and cut the graphic. Switch to the Type tool, highlight the first bullet and paste the graphic.

It replaces the bullet, and will remain inline as though it were text.

**6** Replace the remaining two bullets with hands.

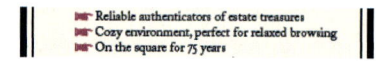

**FIGURE 6.18**

**7** Using the same method, replace the words "Mastercard," "Visa," and "Amex" with the images m_card.eps, visa.eps, and amex.eps. Reduce the images to 40% before you place them inline.

You could place them into the text stream, then reduce the images, but that would require manual alteration.

**8** Highlight the word "Logo" with the Type tool and place the file tr.eps.

If there will be few modifications to a file, you can place it inline as though it were text, rather than placing it elsewhere in the document, then cutting and pasting.

**9** Place the Type tool in the line containing the credit card images; in the Paragraph palette, assign 0.125-in. Space Before and Space After.

The images behave exactly as if they were text.

**10** Save the document and close it.

**FIGURE 6.19**

# LESSON 7  Importing and Creating Clipping Paths

*Clipping paths* are drawn with a series of Bézier curves to follow the edge of an image. Anything outside the path is masked (not visible); anything inside the path is visible. Clipping paths, sometimes called ***silhouettes***, are often compound. If an image has a clipping path, adjusting its frame doesn't affect the path's effects, although it can crop part of the visible image if you cover it with the edge of the frame.

You can manually create a clipping path in InDesign by carefully tracing the object you want to silhouette with the Pen tool, creating a close-fitting, irregularly-shaped frame. After you create all the necessary paths, you can select them all with the Direct Selection tool and combine them into a single compound path. After you have done so, you can select the image, cut it, select the clipping path, then choose Edit>Paste Inside. You can then zoom in and fine-tune the clipping path, if necessary.

InDesign can create clipping paths automatically for images that don't have them. If an image already contains a clipping path, InDesign's automatic clipping path replaces the original one. To create a clipping path, InDesign looks for abrupt transitions in light and dark areas. If an image doesn't have nice hard edges, it may be a poor candidate for automatic clipping-path generation. In such cases, you're better off manually creating a clipping path.

InDesign's automatic clipping-path generation relies on a number of elements:

- **Threshold** is the point of lightness or darkness in the image where the clipping path should start. Generally speaking, the automatic clipping path should be used to mask out lighter backgrounds.

- **Tolerance** specifies how closely a pixel in the image must match the threshold value. If the tolerance is too low, you may end up with a clipping path containing thousands of anchor points; if it is too high, you will end up with a sloppy path.

- **Inset Frame** moves the entire path closer or farther from the object.

- **Invert** reverses the visible and invisible parts of the image.

- **Include Inside Edges** creates a compound path that includes areas within the image that match the masked areas outside the image.

- **Restrict to Frame** creates a clipping path only for the visible area within the frame.

- **Use High Resolution** Image should always be used.

If your image includes a Photoshop-generated clipping path or an alpha channel that reveals the desired parts of the image, you should almost always use that path. You can't change the threshold or tolerance of a Photoshop path, but you can specify an inset and invert the path. If you use an alpha channel, you can adjust the threshold and tolerance settings.

## Create Clipping Paths in InDesign

**1** **Open the document clipping.indd.**

This is a four-page document with text on all pages, and two images pre-placed on Page 1.

**2** **Select the Pen tool, and carefully trace around the ring case in the top image.**

Take your time creating this clipping path. Use as few points as you need to make the path simple, but don't aim for simplicity over accuracy.

FIGURE 6.20

**3** **Select the ring image and cut it, then select the frame you drew and choose Edit>Paste Into. Tweak your frame as necessary, using the Pen and Direct Selection tools.**

Text flows around the frame you have created. You will tweak the wraparounds in the next lesson.

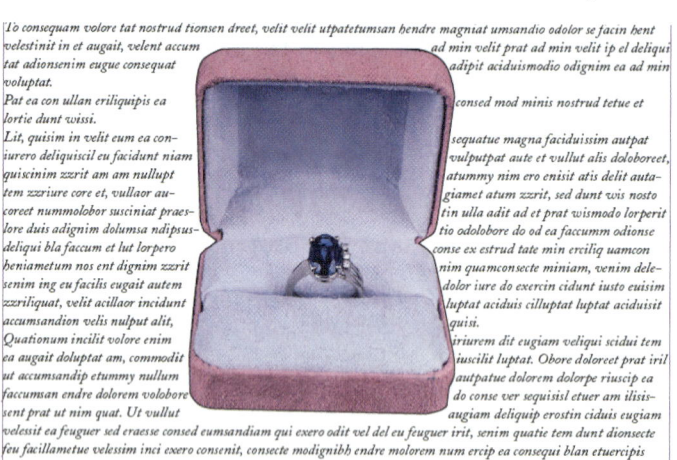

FIGURE 6.21

**Project 6  Controlling and Editing Documents**  **225**  **LEVEL 2**

**4** Click the image at the bottom of the page.

**5** Choose Object>Clipping Path, and set the Type menu to Detect Edges. Make sure the Preview box is checked.

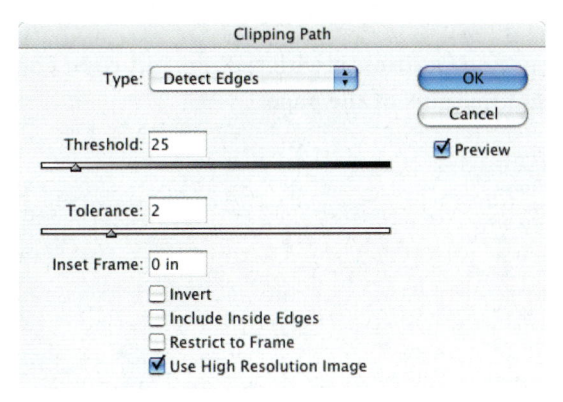

FIGURE 6.22

**6** Adjust the Threshold value until all of the sky disappears.

The lighter parts of the sky disappear first. Although you might want to get rid of the haze around the trees in the background, it is not practical to do so using this method.

**7** Move the Tolerance value up and down. Accept the default of 2 for this image.

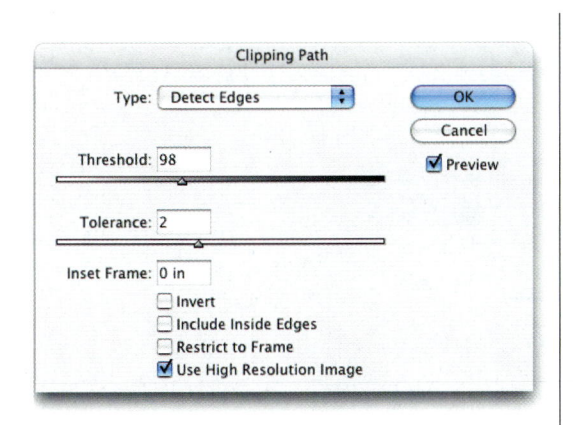

FIGURE 6.23

**8** Save the document and leave it open for the next exercise.

## Import Clipping Paths

**1**    **Continue in the open document, clipping.indd, and go to Page 2.**

This is a page filled with nonsense text, as is the third page.

**2**    **Place the image chef.eps and position it with the top and right edges of the bounding box against the top and right margins of the page.**

FIGURE 6.24

**3**    **With the image still selected, choose Object>Clipping Path, and choose Photoshop Path in the Type menu. Click OK.**

InDesign automatically sets the Path menu to Clip.

FIGURE 6.25

**4** Switch to the Direct Selection tool and click the chef image.

You can view and edit the Photoshop path, just as if it were created with the Pen tool in InDesign.

**FIGURE 6.26**

**6** Navigate to Page 3; place waiter.tif in the upper left of the page.

**7** Choose Object>Clipping, then choose Alpha Channel in the Type menu and Alpha 2 in the Alpha menu.

The type flows around the image erratically, but you will fix that in the next lesson.

**8** Save the document and leave it open for the next lesson.

## LESSON 8  Creating Text Wraps

You have already seen that text wraps and clipping paths are closely related. Text can wrap around regular (rectangular) and irregular-shaped images. The options to set a text wrap are located in the Text Wrap palette.

The Text Wrap palette contains five icons, each representing a different type of wrap. The first represents no wrap. The remaining four, in the order of their icons, are:

- **Bounding Box**, the most basic wrap; the default boundaries are determined by the object's bounding box.

- **Object Shape** creates a wrap based on the shape of the object. If the object is an image in a frame, then the Contour Options menu becomes available. All four of the text-wrap inset fields are identical if you choose this option.

- **Jump Object** prevents text from appearing to the right or left of the object's frame in the column containing the frame. If the object's frame straddles two or more columns, text is forced away in each column.

- **Jump to Next Column** forces the paragraphs affected by the wrap to jump to the next column or text frame.

If you want to wrap text accurately around the shape of an image, you should first create a clipping path in Photoshop, then choose Apply Photoshop Clipping Path when you place the image. To prevent text from wrapping around the boundaries set in the Text Wrap palette, you can select Ignore Text Wrap in the Text Frame Options dialog box. Text frames inside a group ignore text wraps applied to the group itself.

The Object Shape option works with vector art as well as raster images. InDesign generates this type of wrap based on any existing clipping paths or alpha channels, or it tries to use automatic edge detection if a path or channel is absent. For accurate wraps, it's best to create clipping paths or alpha channels in Photoshop. If the image contains multiple clipping paths or alpha channels, you can specify which to use.

When the Object Shape option is selected, you can choose from six (self-explanatory) wrap types in the Contour Options area: Bounding Box, Detect Edges, Photoshop Path, Alpha Channel, Graphic Frame, or Same As Clipping. You can use one Photoshop path to mask part of the image and another to define the text wrap.

If you invert a wrap, text fills the wrap area instead of flowing around it. If you invert a Bounding Box wrap, the text fills the bounding box, not the object's shape. The Include Inside Edges option allows "holes" within a clipping path to be filled with type.

Text wraps can be useful for creating dropped initial caps. Instead of using the automatic drop cap utility, you can manually cut the character, place it into its own frame, move it into position, apply an Object Shape wrap, then adjust the shape of the outer object-shape path with the Direct Selection tool to achieve a pleasing effect. Unfortunately, you cannot create the frame as an inline object because you can't apply wraps to inline objects.

## Wrap Text to Images

**1** Continue in the clipping.indd document and return to Page 1.

**2** Choose Window>Type & Tables>Text Wrap to view the Text Wrap palette.

**3** Click the ring box, then click the Wrap Around Bounding Box button (the second icon in the Text Wrap palette). Set the left and right offsets to 0.125 in.

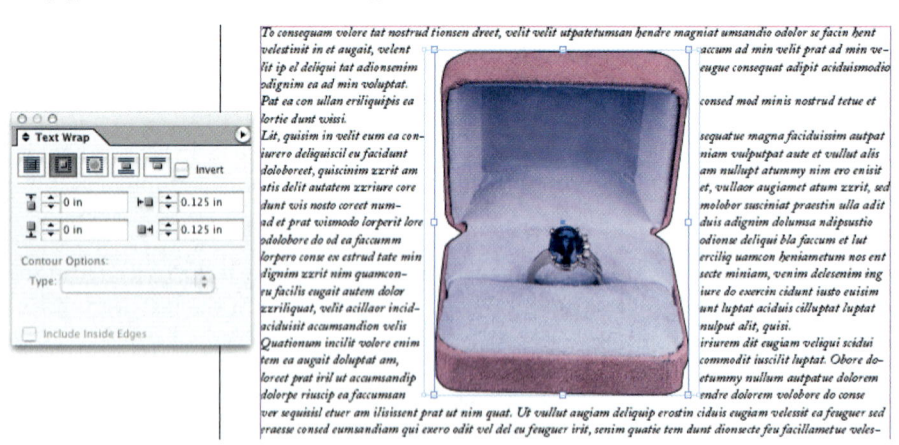

**FIGURE 6.27**

**4** Click the picture at the bottom of the page.

**5** Select Wrap Around Object Shape, and choose Same As Clipping in the Contour Options Type menu.

The text flows into the top of the image. Note that only one offset is used when text is set to wrap around the object shape.

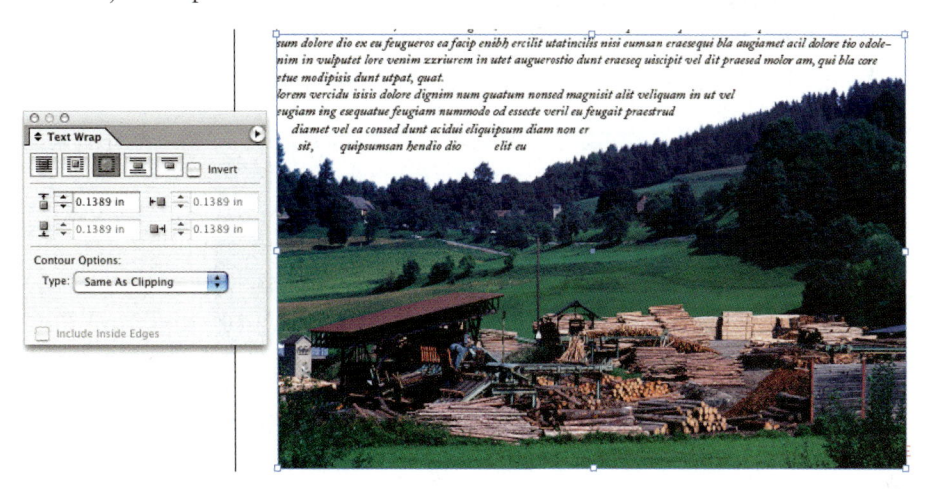

**FIGURE 6.28**

**6** On Page 2, click the chef image.

**7** Leave the text wrap set to Wrap Around Object Shape, and choose Photoshop Path in the Contour Options Type menu; leave the offsets at the default values.

The text flows around the image; it even fills several areas from which you'll remove the type later.

**FIGURE 6.29**

**8** On Page 3, click the waiter image.

**9** Leave the text wrap set to Wrap Around Object Shape and choose Alpha Channel in the Contour Options Type menu, and Alpha 2 in the Alpha menu; accept the default offset.

**10** Save the document and leave it open for the next exercise.

## Edit Text Wraps

1. In the open document, clipping.indd, return to Page 1.

2. With the Direct Selection tool, click the bottom image.

3. Click the blue anchor points and drag them away from the bottom line of text so it flows together. Clean up any extraneous clipping points (brown anchor points).

   You'll probably see some clipping in the mid-left edge of the image, which you'll want to remove.

   FIGURE 6.30

4. On Page 2, click the chef image.

5. With the same technique used on Page 1, use any of the Pen tools to remove all text to the right of and inside the image by manipulating the shape of the wraparound.

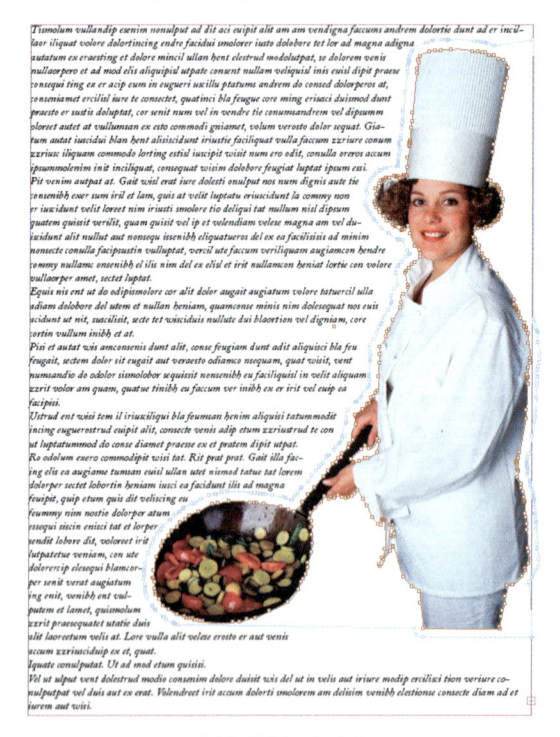

   FIGURE 6.31

Project 6   Controlling and Editing Documents   **231**   LEVEL 2

**6** Continue to Page 3. Use the same techniques to remove all text on the waiter's left and between his body and the towel.

FIGURE 6.32

**7** Save the document and leave it open for the next exercise.

## Wrap Text to Drop Caps

**1** Continue in the open document, clipping.indd, and go to Page 4.

The first paragraph contains an InDesign-generated drop cap. You will create your own drop cap for the second paragraph using a different method. Because of the shape of the letter, the drop cap doesn't flow well with the paragraph.

**2** In the first paragraph, place the Type tool immediately in front of the first letter "s" and kern –100.

The characters from all three lines affected by the drop cap move left. A few adjustments will fix this.

**3** Place a soft return at the end of the second line, then put an en space (Type>Insert White Space>En Space) immediately before the word "the" in the third line.

This is an effective, quick way to force the characters to "wrap" to the dropped character. You would normally have kerned more, but there must be a visual space between the word "A" and "speckled."

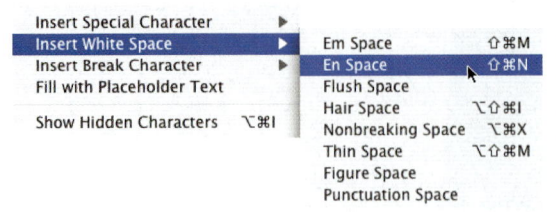

FIGURE 6.33

**4** In a separate frame, create an "A," three lines deep, in ATC Laurel Book.

Through experimentation, we determined that this letter should be created as 56-point type. If you choose to use this method of creating drop caps with wraps, we recommend that you keep a log of the appropriate size, based on the type size and leading of the original type.

**5** Delete the first letter "A" from the paragraph, and drag the frame so the baseline of the A sits on the third line.

**6** Using the Direct Selection tool, adjust the runaround box to achieve the wrap you want. You can use the Add Anchor Point tool, if you think you will create a better wrap that way.

You must experiment to find the right size for your drop cap when you use this method. Its greatest failing is that the drop cap will not flow with the text.

FIGURE 6.34

**7** Save the document and close it.

## To Extend Your Knowledge...

### ISSUES WITH DROP CAPS

While both methods described above will produce drop caps, both have problems. In the first instance, you must insert a soft return between lines; if you edit any of the lines in which you have forced a return, chances are you will have to rework your wrap. In the second instance, the drop cap will not flow with the text, so you would need to reposition the text if the line breaks change. You should decide which is the lesser of two evils on a document-by-document basis.

## CAREERS IN DESIGN

**MANAGING COLOR AND GRAPHICS**

Reading one-color publications isn't exactly boring, but it lacks the excitement of interacting with documents laced with color. In late 1982, *USA Today* introduced the color publication as a part of daily life, and turned the graphics world upside down. Suddenly, color became mandatory, and designers had to learn to manage color. When color finally came to the desktop, graphic designers had to learn to control what they had previously simply ordered from technicians. Technology has simultaneously made our jobs both easier and more complex.

You have learned to use InDesign's tools for color management and control. At the same time, you have considered a number of caveats, including those dictating the length of gradients, and pitfalls of improperly defining tints built from process colors. It should be evident that the more expert a color manager you become, the more valuable you will be to your employer and clients.

By this time, you know how to manage InDesign's color effects, and you know how the internal color-management system works. You have also learned the value of building documents primarily intended to act as style libraries; while this is a small matter, it speeds production.

In addition to learning about managing color in InDesign, you have become proficient in managing the interaction between objects and between type and objects. While many users manually adjust the relationships among objects, you are able to do so automatically — and to automatically wrap type around images, using a variety of methods. The more expert you are at using advanced text and object-management tools, the more quickly you will be able to complete the design and layout of complex documents.

## SUMMARY

Learning the intricacies of object manipulation can be difficult, yet having these skills enhances your creativity when designing pages. You created paths from type, and manipulated and transformed paths to produce compound paths. The Align and Distribute functions are essential in the production of precise, professional layouts. You positioned objects inline with text, and altered their appearance. Clipping paths are powerful tools for creating masks to hide the background of an image, or to isolate a part of an image. You created a clipping path with InDesign's Pen tool, used different types of text wraps, and created a complex text wrap based on a clipping path.

## KEY TERMS

| | | |
|---|---|---|
| align | distribute | Photoshop path |
| alpha channel | group | text wrap |
| bounding box | inline | threshold |
| clipping path | nest | tolerance |
| compound path | Pathfinder palette | ungroup |

# CHECKING CONCEPTS AND TERMS

## MULTIPLE CHOICE

**Check the letter of the correct answer for each of the following:**

1. When you convert text to outlines, what are you creating?
   a. Text within frames
   b. Compound paths
   c. Outlined letters
   d. Uneditable text

2. How can you change the fill of an object?
   a. By using the Pathfinder
   b. By clicking the Change Fill button
   c. By reversing the path's direction
   d. By creating a clipping path

3. What happens when an object is nested within another?
   a. It becomes uneditable.
   b. It becomes grouped.
   c. It is centered in the frame.
   d. It must be selected with the Direct Selection tool.

4. What always happens when objects are distributed?
   a. The objects are spaced evenly within the bounding box.
   b. There is equal space between each object.
   c. The objects align horizontally.
   d. The objects align vertically.

5. What is an inline object?
   a. An object that aligns with other objects
   b. An object created with the Pen or Line tool
   c. An object that flows with text
   d. An object pasted with the Direct Selection tool

6. What does a clipping path do?
   a. Creates a text wrap
   b. Masks part of the image
   c. Reverses the path direction of an object
   d. Allows text to wrap to inline images

7. What happens if you release compound paths from text converted to outlines?
   a. It becomes editable text again.
   b. You can fill the letters with an image.
   c. The open letters fill in.
   d. Nothing.

8. When would you use inline objects?
   a. When using graphics as bullets
   b. When you want the text to flow around the graphics
   c. When you have converted text to outlines
   d. When you have nested the text frame in another frame

9. What is an inverted wrap?
   a. A wrap around a concave contour
   b. A wrap that includes areas within the clipping path
   c. A wrap that surrounds the clipping path
   d. A wrap that fills the clipping path

10. What is the most common text wrap?
    a. Wrap around bounding box
    b. Wrap around object
    c. Jump object wrap
    d. Inverted wrap

## DISCUSSION QUESTIONS

1. How can you most effectively use compound paths created in InDesign? In what situations would you be likely to use them?

2. How important to good design are clipping paths and text wraps? What skills are particularly important to develop if you are going to use these features effectively?

# SKILL DRILL

Skill Drills reinforce project skills. Each skill reinforced is the same, or nearly the same, as a skill presented in the lessons. Detailed instructions are provided in a step-by-step format. You must perform the Skill Drills in order.

## 1. Convert Text to Paths

You have been assigned to create a poster for a new event at the Ringling Center for the Cultural Arts. The event will run for one week in March. You will apply a number of the skills you have learned in this project in the course of building the poster, which has the type elements already in place for you.

1. Open the document irish_eyes.indd.
2. Select the first block of type and create outlines, then deselect.
3. With the Direct Selection tool, click each of the four lines of type to select them.
4. With all four lines selected, make compound paths.
5. With the compound path selected, place the image irish_eyes.tif.
6. Choose the Rotation tool and rotate the image –9°. With the Direct Selection tool, enlarge and position it so it fits the area as you wish.

**FIGURE 6.35**

7. Click the next block of type and create outlines.
8. Deselect, save the file, and leave it open for the next Skill Drill.

## 2. Add Art and Create Compound Paths

The poster looks pretty stark. You need to add some color and art to make it more interesting.

1. Continue in the open document.
2. Place the art shamrock.eps in the upper left of the page and choose Object>Arrange>Send to Back.
3. Rotate the shamrock 13° and enlarge it to 115%.
4. Draw a circle 3.4 inches in diameter. Position it at X: 4.25 in., Y: 4.45 in., using the top-center proxy. Send it to the back.
5. Give the circle a fill of C:100, M:0, Y:75, K:0 and a stroke of None.
6. Click the top line of converted type "A Musical Tour" with the Direct Selection tool. Switch to the Selection tool, hold the Shift key, and click the circle.
7. Choose Object>Compound Paths>Make.

**FIGURE 6.36**

8. Repeat Steps 6 and 7 for the next three lines of type.
9. Save the document and leave it open for the next Skill Drill.

## 3. Align and Distribute Objects

Although you could manually adjust objects, it's much easier to use InDesign's automated features, especially if you're under a production deadline.

1. Continue in the open document.
2. Choose Window>Align to activate the Align palette.
3. Select the top headline and the shamrock. In the Align palette, choose Align Horizontal Centers, then choose Align Vertical Centers.

4. Group these two items, then position the top center at X: 4.25 in., Y: 0.3 in.

5. Select the names of the four performing groups and align their top edges.

6. If the Distribute Spacing option is not visible, choose Show Options from the Align palette.

7. Click Distribute Horizontal Space.

8. Make any adjustments you feel are necessary, including adding any color.

9. Save and close the file.

**FIGURE 6.37**

## 4. Work with Nested and Inline Objects

You have been hired by a publisher to compose a workbook for *Type for the Digital Artist*, a companion book to this series. The designer has specified that check boxes and "write-on" lines should have a weight of one-half point, and that the rules should be a minimum of 1.5 inches and a maximum of 3 inches in length, depending upon the answer to be supplied.

1. Open the document type_workbook.indd.

2. Cut the Type Categories text frame and paste it into (Edit>Paste Into) the graduated tint frame in the upper right of the page, nesting it.

3. Using the center reference point, position the center of the nested frame at X: 1.5 in., Y: 2 in. using the Direct Selection tool.

4. Select the Line tool and draw a half-point horizontal line 1.5 in. long.

5. Cut the line with the Selection tool, then, using the Type tool, paste wherever the word [LINE] appears in the running text.

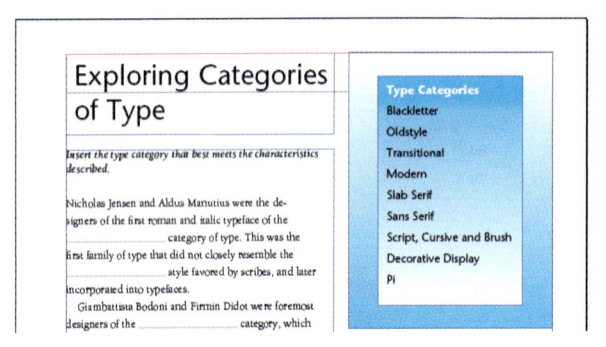

**FIGURE 6.38**

6. Select the Rectangle tool and draw a 0.1458-in. square. Assign it a black stroke and a fill of none.

7. Cut the box, then switch to the Type tool.

8. Paste the box into the text frame in the lower right using the Type tool. Replace all instances of square [ ] brackets with the box you created.

9. Save the document and close it.

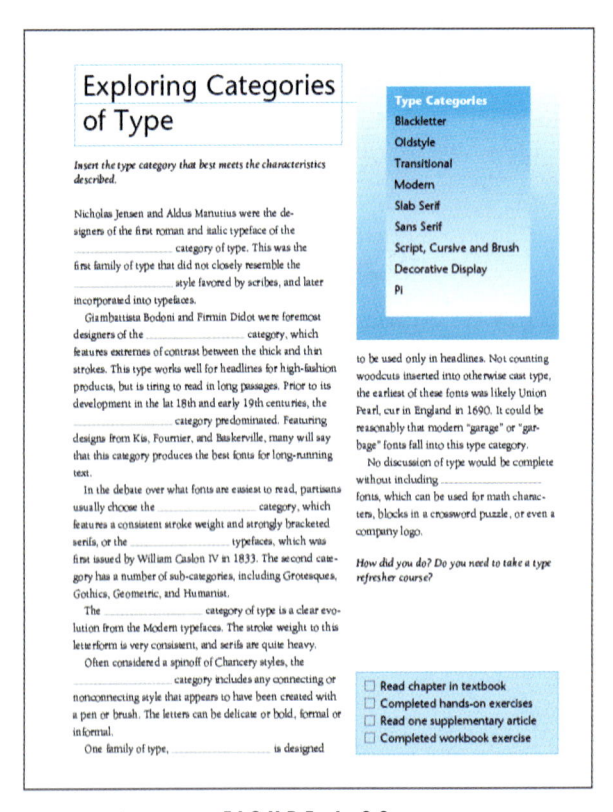

**FIGURE 6.39**

# CHALLENGE

Challenge exercises expand on, or are somewhat related to, skills presented in the lessons. Each exercise provides a brief introduction, followed by instructions presented in a numbered-step format that are not as detailed as those in the Skill Drill exercises. You should perform these exercises in the order in which they appear.

## 1. Convert Type to Paths

The Center for Technology Training has both online and on-campus courses. While they don't give out much information at job fairs, they do produce a flyer designed to attract the interest of prospective students. Most CTT students are working adults who, for one reason or another, bypassed the opportunity to obtain a degree immediately following high school. In this Challenge, you will prepare the main headline; you will complete the flyer in succeeding Challenges.

1. Open the document tech_train.indd.
2. Select the main heading and create outlines from the text.
3. Select all three lines of type and create a single compound path.
4. Place the image tech_train.psd in the compound frame.
5. Reduce the image and move it around to give the best result.
6. Assign a drop shadow to the headline to give it some definition. We chose an X and Y offset of 0.04 in., with a blur of 0.03 in.
7. Save the document and leave it open for the next Challenge.

**FIGURE 6.40**

## 2. Import an Image and Create a Clipping Path

From time to time you will need to use an image that does not have a built-in clipping path. The best solution is to use Photoshop to create the path, but it may not always be possible to do so. In this Challenge you create a clipping path in InDesign.

1. Continue in the open document, tech_train.indd.
2. Import the image woman_computer.tif.
3. Zoom into the photo and, with the Pen tool, carefully trace around the woman, desk, and computer, eliminating the window shade background. Don't forget the inside spaces, such as the space inside her left arm and between her arm and the desk. When you're finished, you will have three separate paths.

4. Select all the paths and create a compound path.

5. Cut the photo and paste it into the compound path you've made.

**FIGURE 6.41**

6. Because one of the areas did not mask the photo, you'll have to reverse the path for that area.

7. Tweak your paths until they're as good as you can make them.

8. Using the upper-left reference point, position the photo at X: –0.125 in., Y: 4.4 in.

9. Save the document and leave it open for the next Challenge.

**FIGURE 6.42**

## 3. Import and Position an Image with a Clipping Path

When you receive images containing clipping paths, it makes your job much easier. Although you are relieved of the task of painstakingly drawing a path, you must still deal with the details of making sure the clipping path is applied to the photo.

1. Continue in the open document, tech_train.indd.

2. Import the image data.eps and click it with the Direct Selection tool.

3. If you look closely at the image, you will see some imperfections in the Photoshop-generated clipping path. Clean up the imperfections using InDesign's editing tools.

4. Assign the clipping path as User-Modified Path.

5. Position the right edge of the photo against the bleed line and at Y: 7.35 in., using any of the top reference points.

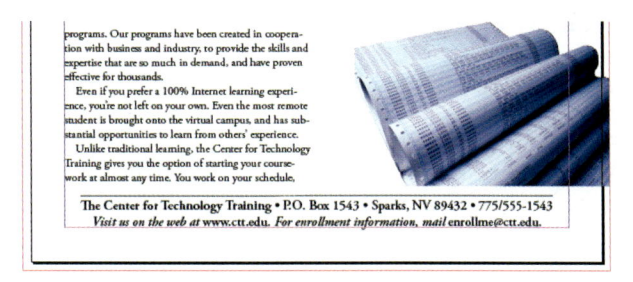

**FIGURE 6.43**

6. Save the document and leave it open for the next Challenge.

## 4. Create Text Wraps

Now that clipping paths are built and tweaked, you can wrap your text around them. Wrapping text around images enhances the interest of the page overall. Since the text looks somewhat bland, you will give it some energy by creating a colorful drop cap.

1. Continue in the open document, tech_train.indd. Be sure the Text Wrap palette is open.

2. Select the woman at the computer image and wrap the text around the object shape.

3. Define a 0.125-in. offset.

4. Create the text wrap for the data image, with the Contour Options Type menu set to Same As Clipping and an offset of 0.125 in.

**FIGURE 6.44**

5. Change the Y position of the woman image to close up some of the space between the text below.

6. Rework the text wrap (and rework the text, if necessary) to achieve a pleasing text flow. (You will find it easier if you switch to the Adobe Single-Line Composer.)

7. Check the entire document for bad hyphenation, bad line breaks, and widows or orphans. Fix them, as appropriate.

8. In ATC Oak Bold, create a free-standing capital letter "F" to act as a drop cap for the first paragraph. Be sure to delete the letter from the first word in the paragraph.

9. Pick up an orange color from the woman's blouse and apply it to the letter.

10. Adjust the wraparound of the "F" so the fourth line of text abuts the left margin. There should be more space between the "F" and abutting words on the second and third lines than between the "F" and the rest of the first word ("rom").

**FIGURE 6.45**

11. Save and close the document.

# PORTFOLIO BUILDER

## Create a Series of Ads

Some of the most complex documents, from a design standpoint, are those in which text and graphics must interact. These are the documents that tend to win awards. In addition to knowing which buttons to push, working with interactive text and graphics usually requires both artistic and technical skills.

Using freely distributed images, images from any of your RF folders, or images that you already own, construct at least three ads for a single client with the skills you have learned in this project. Pay special attention to the interaction of text and images.

To complete this project, use the following techniques:

- Be consistent. While the ads should each have a unique look, they should be easily recognizable as a single series.
- Convert text to outlines and fill it with an image or images.
- Use text on a path.
- Create clipping paths in Photoshop or InDesign.
- Pay careful attention to the interaction of text and graphics; make sure you eliminate all widows, orphans, and unattractive text wraps.

# WHY WOULD I DO THIS?

Outputting a file for professional reproduction is far more complex than simply printing to a desktop printer. When documents are printed on a press, they are subject to inescapable mechanical variables, including vibration and paper stretch. The industry has developed several techniques for overcoming these variables, and to ensure that errors are not introduced into the printing process.

The process of *trapping* entails altering the intersections of colors that print on separate plates to correct visually for minor (and unavoidable) press misregistration. By deliberately introducing minor distortion into artwork, colors can be slightly expanded into each other so blank paper doesn't show through. Properly applied trapping is not noticeable, although you can sometimes detect traps on close examination of the printed piece. Bad trapping is worse than no trapping at all.

InDesign allows you to define multiple trap styles and apply them to specific pages or ranges of pages within a document; you should assign trapping only to pages that need it. The effects of trapping are not visible on your monitor. InDesign can specify comprehensive trap settings that work with imaging devices that support Adobe's in-RIP trapping system. It can also perform its own host-based trapping without using any special equipment or extra software. InDesign's built-in trapping engine traps elements created in InDesign, but not placed elements. Always check with your service provider before applying trapping. You will find a more in-depth discussion of trapping in *Color Companion for the Digital Artist*.

As for trapping, you should work in close collaboration with your service provider when specifying bleeds and slugs. They can tell you what to include, and what may cost you more money (for example, a large slug could force the job to be printed on a larger sheet of paper and on a larger press).

While InDesign uses the same basic process for printing regardless of the output device, you need to consider some special issues when you output files to a press. For example, you can control which side of the film you print on (emulsion up or down), whether the image is positive or negative, the screen ruling, and the angle of screening for colors. The Print dialog box contains eight different function panes.

Exporting pages as Encapsulated PostScript (EPS) is useful if you want to place a completed page into another InDesign document, or into another application. You can also open and edit EPS files in Adobe Illustrator, or import and rasterize them in Photoshop.

You can preview color separation, ink coverage limits, and overprinting using the Separations Preview palette. This allows you to see how varnishes have been applied, identify areas where a **rich black** (process black mixed with other inks to achieve a darker color) has been applied, determine if ink coverage exceeds press limits, and preview how blending, transparency, and overprinting (one ink on top of another) will appear.

***Preflighting*** is the process of verifying that all of a document's fonts, images, and ICC profiles are present. Although commercial utilities such as Markzware's FlightCheck can more thoroughly check a document, InDesign's built-in function is free and adequate for most jobs. Once a job is preflighted, it can be packaged for a GASP (Graphic Arts Service Provider).

Jobs prepared for print do not incorporate advanced PDF features such as hyperlinks, sounds, and bookmarks, but you can include any of these elements in electronic documents. Because such features can make online presentations more interesting, learning to manage this form of output is important to add to your skills.

# VISUAL SUMMARY

The process of printing documents at high resolution or for publication online is complex. When separating colors for offset printing, you must ensure that there will be no unsightly gaps where colors abut one another. If the image will print to the edge of the page, it must extend far enough off the page to allow for mechanical variances. If files are exported, settings must be correct or the document may print incorrectly. Files exported to PDF can contain interactive features to make them more interesting to those "reading" the document.

Each page of a document can be assigned a separate trap preset, or no trap at all. If there are no abutting colors on a page, or if all abutting colors have common components, there is no point in assigning a trap preset for that page.

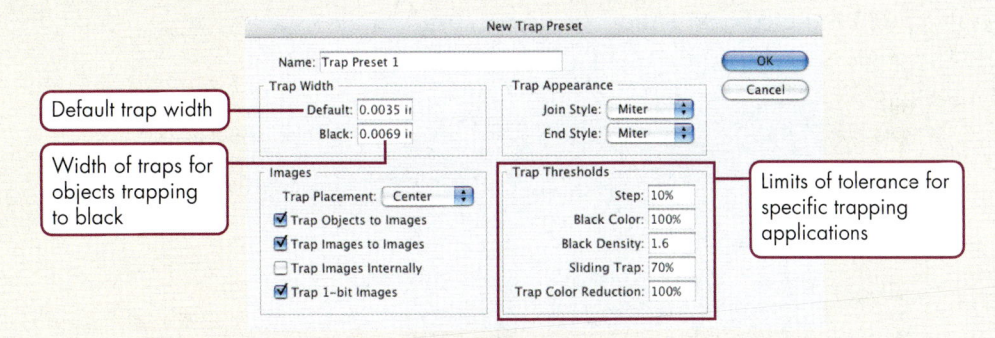

**FIGURE 7.1**

If your document will bleed, or if you provide a slug so your client can sign off on a document, you will need to print on a larger sheet of paper, which can add cost to the project. The bleed amount should always be coordinated with your printer, and you will likely want to turn slugs off after you have proofing approval. InDesign allows you to choose which printer's marks will print.

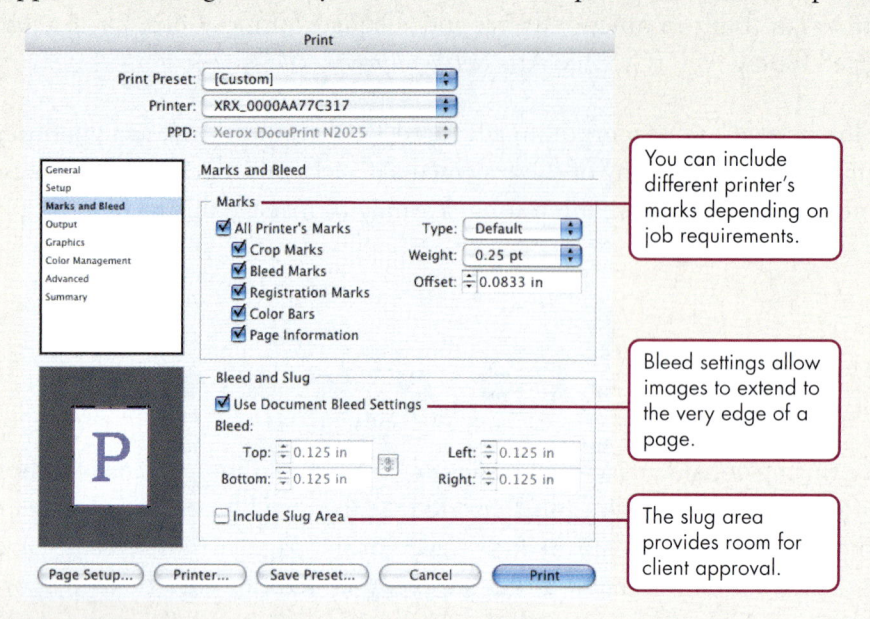

**FIGURE 7.2**

When preparing final output, you can turn on color separations and define trapping specifications. If you're preparing a PostScript file for a GASP, you should find out the correct preferences to use, since many use third-party trapping programs. Some output devices accept Adobe in-RIP trapping. In such cases you can define whether the document is to be printed positive or negative, emulsion up (for contact printing to another piece of film) or down. You can also specify the screen ruling, ink frequency, and the angle of each color.

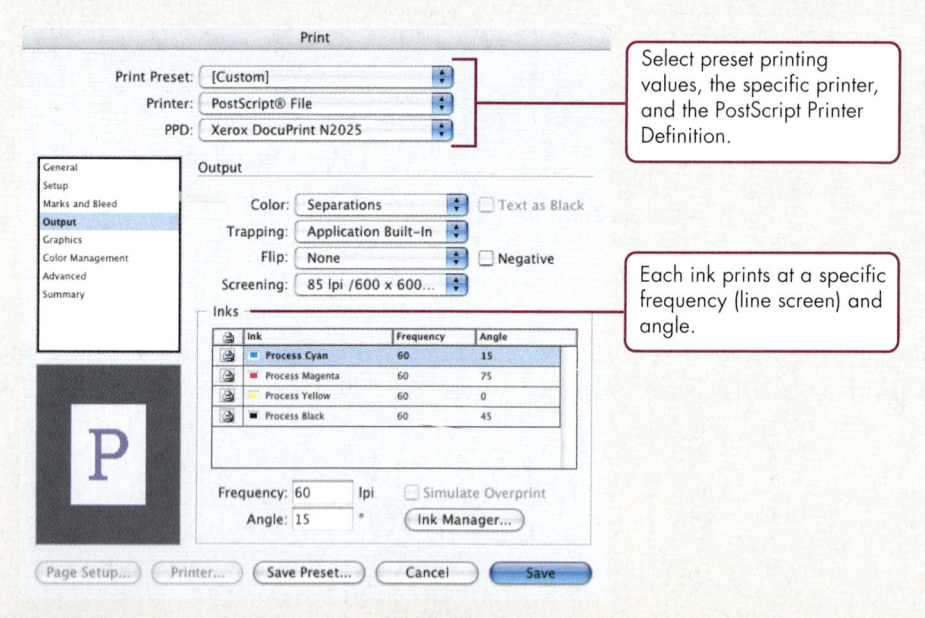

**FIGURE 7.3**

In addition to defining the frequency and angle at which each ink will print, InDesign allows you to specify the printing order of inks. When printing with spot inks, you can define the printing order and screen angle based on the **neutral density** of the inks. Neutral density (ND) is the value that the selected trapping engine uses to determine the precise placement of traps.

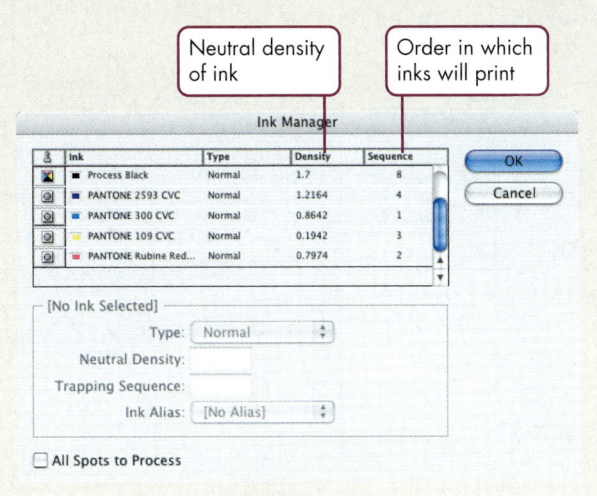

FIGURE 7.4

Although PDF is becoming the standard workflow for an ever-increasing number of printers, EPS (Encapsulated PostScript) is still important. Pages and even entire documents can be exported as EPS files for inclusion into other publications. This can be very handy for ads and catalogs.

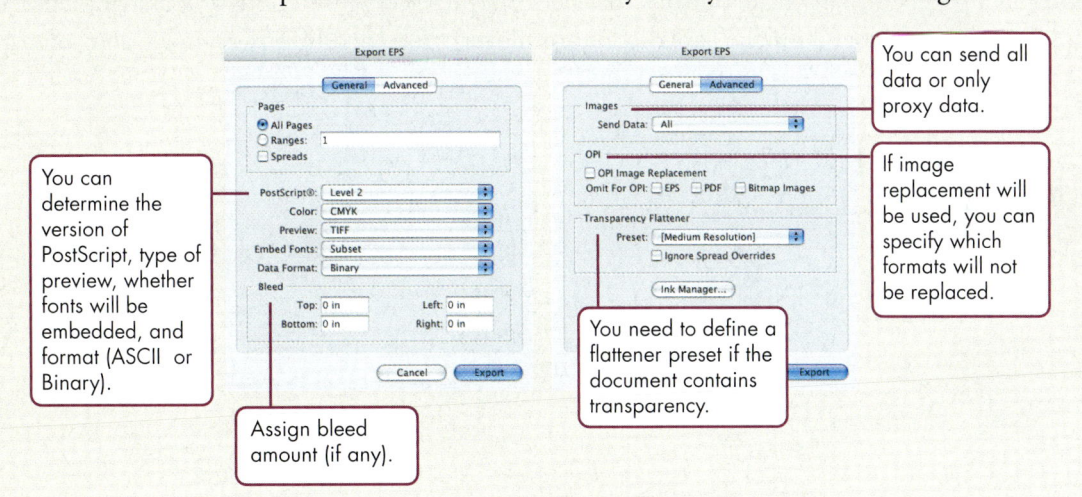

FIGURE 7.5

Before you export your document or send it to a GASP, you should check it carefully to ensure that ink densities are within the limits specified by your printer; you can use the Separations Preview palette to check this. You should also preflight the document to catch problems that are not immediately visible. When you know the job is correct and complete, you should use the Package routine to collect all components before sending them away.

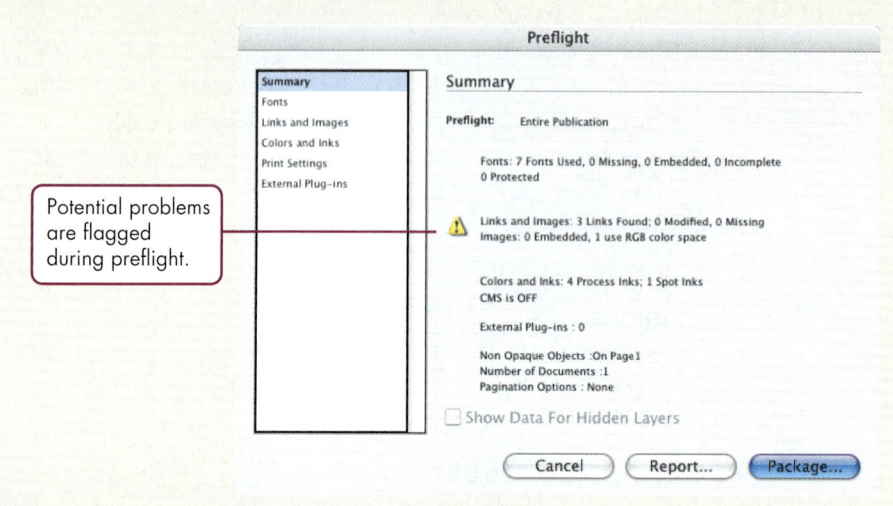

Potential problems are flagged during preflight.

**FIGURE 7.6**

When you export a PDF for use electronically, you can hyperlink pages and even create jumps to specific positions on a page. You can create buttons that perform preselected functions and assign them a different look for each state they can take (up, down, or rollover). You can also insert movie and sound files.

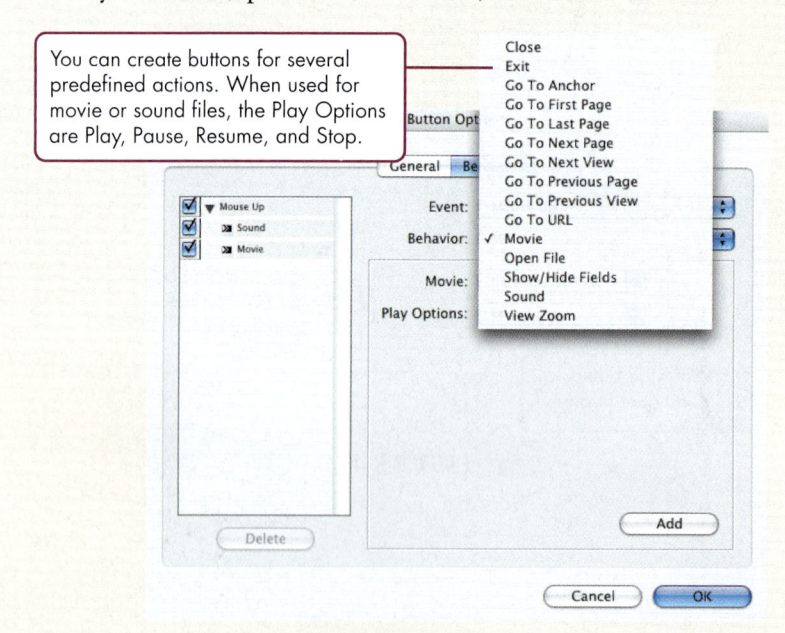

You can create buttons for several predefined actions. When used for movie or sound files, the Play Options are Play, Pause, Resume, and Stop.

**FIGURE 7.7**

## LESSON 1  Trapping Images

In a perfect world, all printing presses would be in perfect registration, which means that all ink colors would print perfectly in relation to each other. In reality, no press is ever in perfect register because the paper shifts slightly as it travels through the press.

While trapping is a complex subject about which many books have been written, its concepts are easily understandable. The first concept necessary for understanding trapping is the difference between **background** and **foreground** colors. The background color is that of the hindmost object, the one furthest back in the stacking order. The foreground color is that of the object in front of the background object. The foreground object is the one to which a trap is applied.

The rule to remember is that lighter colors always become larger. If the foreground color is darker than the background, you apply a **choke**, usually by overprinting a stroke of the lighter color around the darker color (Figure 7.8).

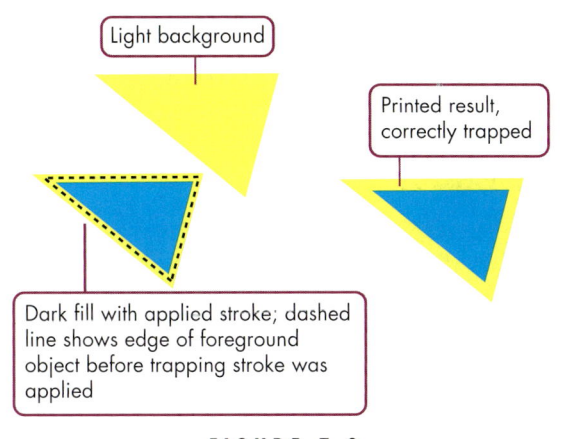

**FIGURE 7.8**

When the foreground color is lighter than the background color, you apply a **spread**, usually by overprinting a stroke of the lighter color around the lighter foreground (Figure 7.9).

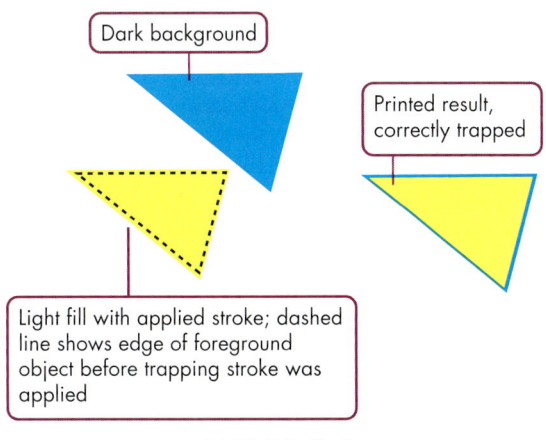

**FIGURE 7.9**

When the stroke overprints the darker color, it creates a composite of the two colors that is often even darker than the dark color. Under most circumstances, you can't see this third color, because the width of the overprint is only approximately 0.25 pt. (about 1/288 in.).

You can define several trapping preferences using the Trap Presets palette:

- Trap width can be up to 8 pt. for in-RIP trapping, and up to 4 pt. for host-based trapping.
- With the trap appearance options, you can select Miter, Round, or Bevel join and end styles.
- You can define how to trap vectors against raster images.
- The thresholds indicate the degree to which components of abutting colors must vary before InDesign creates a trap.

## Use Built-in Trapping

**1** **Open the document banks.indd.**

You may recognize this as the first page of a document you worked with in *Essentials for Design: InDesign Level 1*.

**2** **Choose Window>Trap Presets.**

The Trap Presets palette opens. Only the Default preset is available for use.

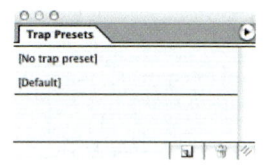

**FIGURE 7.10**

**3** **From the Trap Presets palette Options menu, choose New Preset.**

The New Trap Preset dialog box appears.

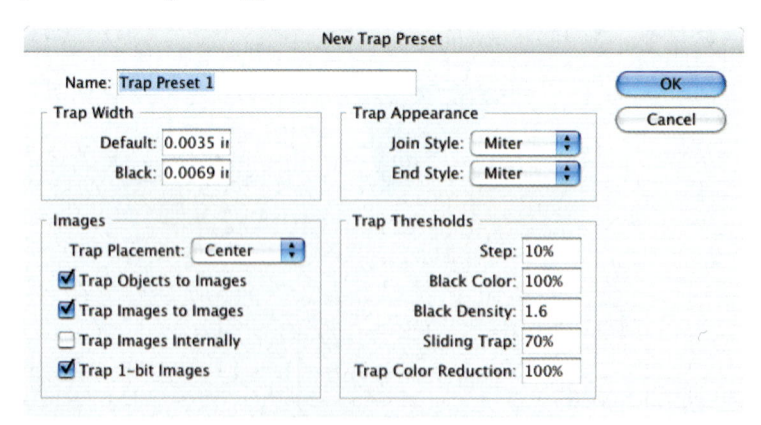

**FIGURE 7.11**

**4** **Accept the default name and set the Default Trap Width field to 0.0278 in.**

This is a huge trap — the default 0.0035-in. (1/4-pt.) trap is common to the industry, and will be acceptable for most offset printing. The trapping value you entered above will allow you to see what happens (albeit on a much smaller scale) when you apply trapping. You should always consult with your GASP to ascertain their preferences before assigning trapping.

**5** **Click OK.**

**6** **From the Trap Preset palette Options menu, choose Assign Trap Presets.**

The Assign Trap Presets dialog appears.

**7** **Choose Trap Preset 1 from the menu; leave the Pages option at the default (All), and click Assign.**

This assigns the preset to the page (the only page in the document). You can assign different presets to different sections of a document that contains multiple pages.

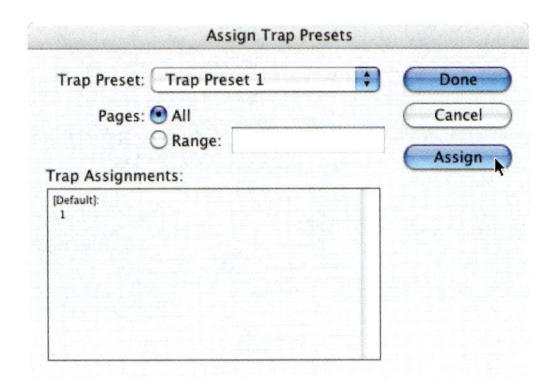

**FIGURE 7.12**

**8** **Click Done to close the Assign Trap Presets dialog box.**

**9** **Save the document and close it.**

## LESSON 2  Setting Up Bleeds and Slugs

Mechanical realities make it impossible to print exactly to the edge of a page; if you want an object to ***bleed*** off a page, you need to create it so it extends beyond the page edge, into the area of the paper that will be trimmed off. While we have used 0.125-in. bleed as a standard throughout this book, some printers may prefer a little more or a little less. It is always best to ask the printer's requirements before beginning any project.

The ***slug*** typically contains job details, and provides room for client approvals prior to printing; it's a valuable tool for the graphic designer. When you create a slug, it should contain all of, and only, the information you need — it should be useful, but compact.

Depending on quantity and size, your document may be printed one, two, or more at a time. For example, if you're printing 20,000 two-sided, letter-size flyers on a sheetfed press, they will probably be run two-up or four-up, depending on press size. If you include a large slug on the bottom of the document, you may double the time it takes to print your job — and add substantially to your cost. You may prefer to include the slug information only on your proof, but not in the final printed document.

## Set Up Bleed and Slug Values

**1**     **Create a new document. If Bleed and Slug options are not visible, click the More Options button. Uncheck the Facing Pages box and leave the Page Size, Columns, and Margins settings at their defaults.**

**2**     **Set the Bleed Top field to 0.125 in.**

**3**     **Click the chain link icon at the right of the four Bleed fields.**

This button sets all four Bleed fields to the same value; in this case, it copies the 1/8-inch bleed you stipulated into the Bottom, Inside, and Outside fields.

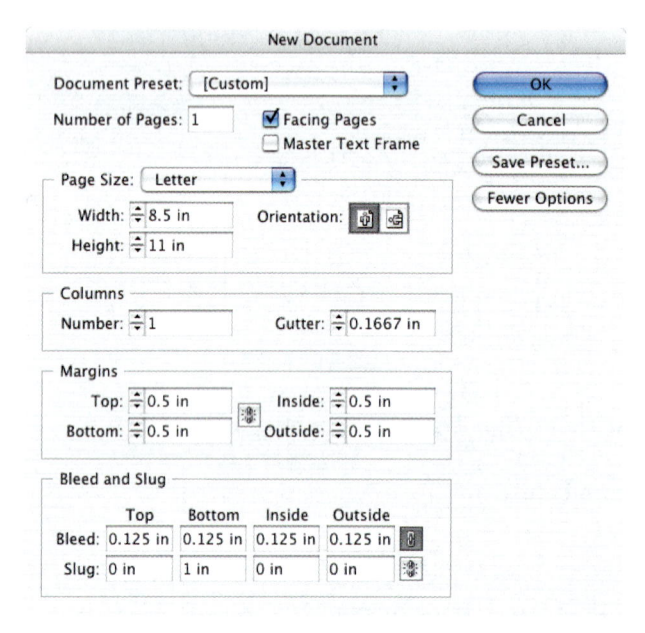

FIGURE 7.13

**4**     **Set the Slug Bottom field to 1 in. Do not click the chain link icon. Click OK.**

InDesign does not fill in the other fields. You need space only at the bottom of the document for the slug.

**5** **Go to the master page.**

The page is set up with bleed and slug areas.

**FIGURE 7.14**

**6** **Open slug_lib.indl.**

**7** **Drag the 1 Approval slug into the slug area on the master page.**

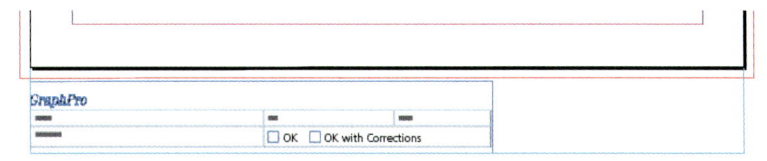

**FIGURE 7.15**

**8** **Save the document as "bleed_slug.indd" and close it.**

## LESSON 3  Printing Your Document

InDesign uses the same basic process for printing all documents, regardless of whether you are printing documents on a desktop laser printer or imaging them on high-end prepress equipment. In every case, InDesign requires a means of communicating with a printer or imaging device, such as a network connection, and a language with which to describe the pages and their contents.

**PostScript**, invented by Adobe Systems, is a specialized programming language designed specifically to describe a page to a device that can render the page; PostScript is a page-description language, or PDL. PostScript desktop printers include an internal computer (called the **raster image processor** or RIP), so they're often more expensive than standard printers. Imagesetters and platesetters use a powerful server, usually a separate piece of equipment, as their RIPs.

You define the printer driver and the printer's characteristics when you install a new printer for use on your computer system. Each printer, imaging device, or digital press that will receive PostScript files from your computer needs to have its own PostScript Printer Description (PPD) file. A PPD contains specific information about that device, such as media sizes, different media inputs, color capabilities, and separation and trapping capabilities.

In *Essentials for Design: InDesign Level 1*, you used the General and Setup panes of the Printing dialog box. In the Marks and Bleed pane you can select which printer's marks to include in your file, depending on the number of colors in your document and the media to which you are printing. If, for example, you're printing process color to a letter-size document with no bleed and the target printer is a Xerox Docutech, you don't need any printer's marks. For a job printed on an offset press, however, you would probably include all the printer's marks.

The selections you make in the Output pane determine how InDesign sends color information to a printer or a PostScript file. You can choose one of the composite options to convert a document to the chosen color space, or one of two color-separation options. You can choose from three trapping options, flip a file, specify whether it prints positive or negative, and select from the screening options available to your printer. In the Inks list, you can change the line-screen frequency or screen angle for each ink, but we don't recommend doing so. You may, however, need to change angles if you are imaging spot colors. In a two-color spot-ink job, for example, you need to set the darkest ink to a 45° angle and the lightest ink to a 75° angle. You can use the Ink Manager to edit the density, type, and printing sequence of all inks in the document.

In the Graphics pane, you determine which images you send to the printer, and how they are sent. You can also specify whether and how (as a complete set or a subset of characters) to include fonts with the job. You determine the PostScript level; if the PPD supports it, Level 3 is best because of its advanced imaging features. Finally, you determine whether you will send the data in ASCII (slow but reliable) or Binary (fast, but error-prone) format.

In the Color Management pane, you determine the source space. You only have options if you are printing a proof with composite output. If you choose either of the separation methods, the Proof option is disabled and the Print Space menu is preset to Document CMYK. The Print Space options allow you to tell InDesign the color space of your printer.

There are two options in the Advanced pane. OPI (Open Prepress Interface) was developed when disk space was expensive and networks were slow. It creates low-resolution versions of large, high-resolution images, which are then available to users who connect to the server. The low-resolution proxy images are swapped out when the file is imaged. Although current technology makes OPI less critical, it is still used by many companies. The transparency flattener options allows you to choose a flattener style; you can also force InDesign to override any transparency styles applied to spreads in the document.

## Output a Complex Job

This job uses a messy mix of RGB images, spot-color swatches, transparency, and feathering. You will learn to create a usable PostScript file from this document, but we can't tell you how to print it because we can't predict what printing or imaging equipment you have available. This exercise uses the Adobe Distiller PPD file in place of a high-end prepress imaging device. After finishing this exercise, try printing it using what you've learned in this chapter.

**1** Quit InDesign if it is running. Copy the distiller.ppd file to the location indicated for your operating system:

- Mac OSX. System/Library/Printers/PPDs/Contents/Resources/en.lproj *or* [Home Directory]/Library/Printers
- Windows XP. C:\Windows\system32\spool\drivers\w32x86\3
- Windows 2000. C:\WINNT\system32\spool\drivers\w32x86\3

**2** Start InDesign and open travel.indd.

**3** Update links if necessary. Turn color management on (Edit>Color Settings). Click OK.

This document uses embedded ICC profiles.

**4** Open the Print dialog box. Set the Printer menu to PostScript File, and the PPD menu to any printer except Device Independent. Leave the default settings in the General pane.

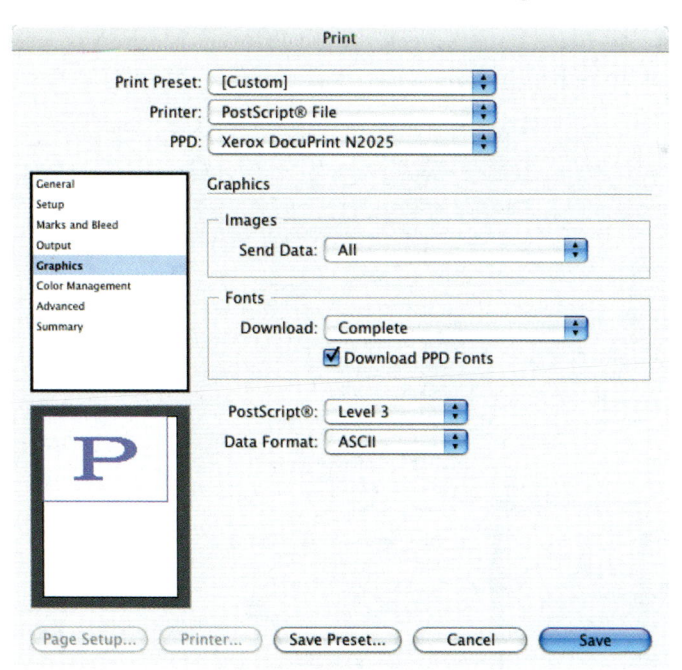

**FIGURE 7.16**

**5** **Open the Setup pane. In the Paper Size area, the Width and Height menus are blank.**

Some printers don't support specific features, in which case those options aren't available. You will use the default settings in this exercise.

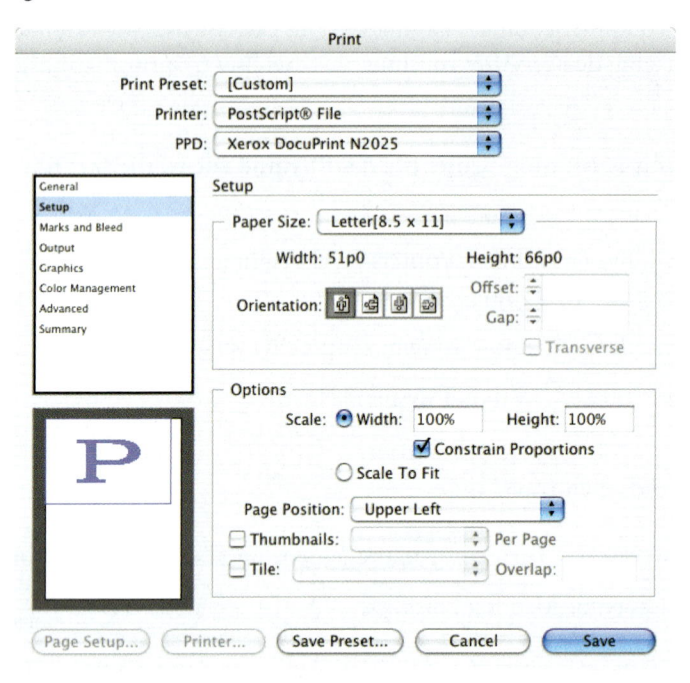

FIGURE 7.17

**6** **Open the Marks and Bleed pane. Check the All Printer's Marks box, accept the default offset, and set a bleed of 0p6 on all sides.**

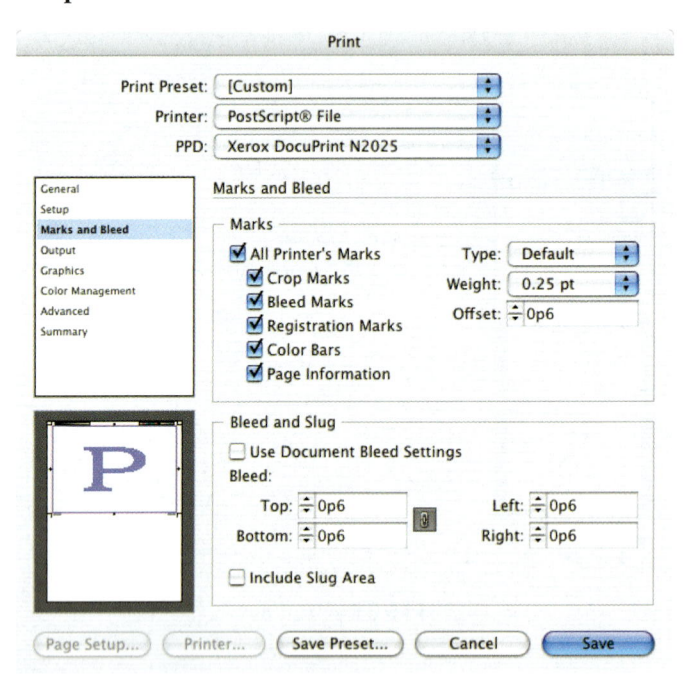

FIGURE 7.18

Project 7   Managing Output   **259**   LEVEL 2

**7**   **Open the Output pane. Choose Separations from the Color menu, Application Built-in from the Trapping menu, None from the Flip menu, and 150 lpi/2400 dpi from the Screening menu.**

If high-resolution screening options are not available to you because you are using a desktop printer, select the highest options you have available. The imagesetter you choose may have a different screening option.

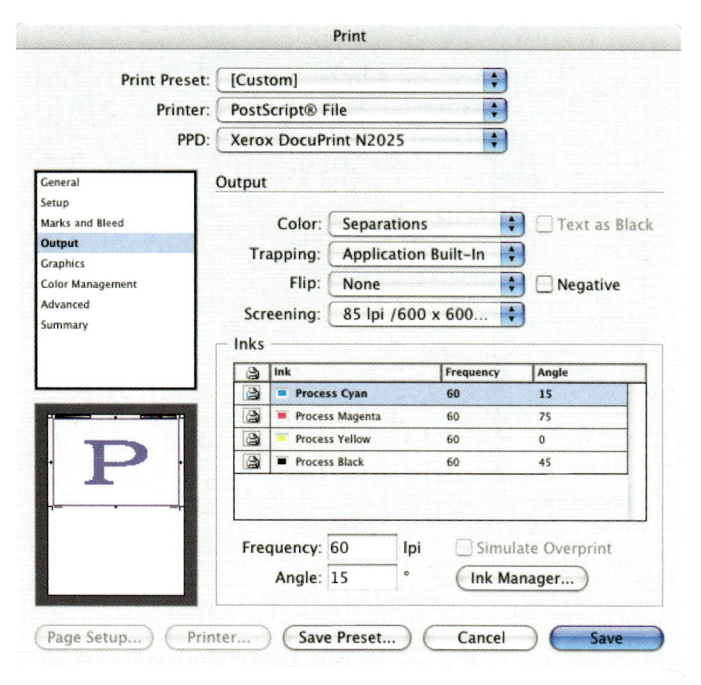

FIGURE 7.19

**8**   **Click the Ink Manager button and check the All Spots to Process box, then click OK.**

This document uses spot colors, which need to be converted to process colors.

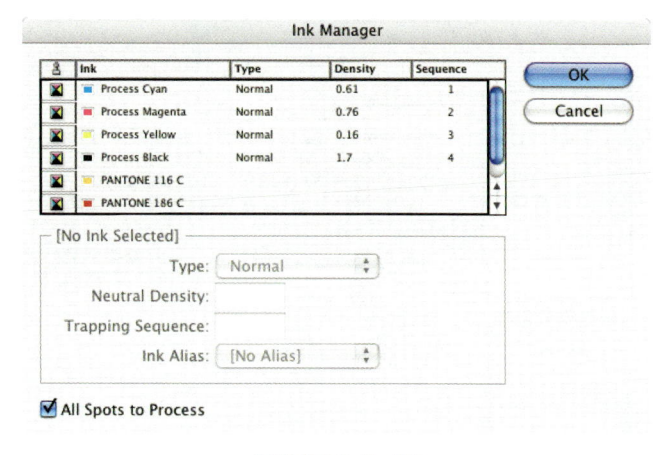

FIGURE 7.20

9. **Open the Graphics pane. Ensure that the default settings are selected (Send Data: All, Download: Complete, PostScript: Level 3, Data Format: Binary).**

   If you have an older imaging device, the PPD you selected may not support PostScript Level 3.

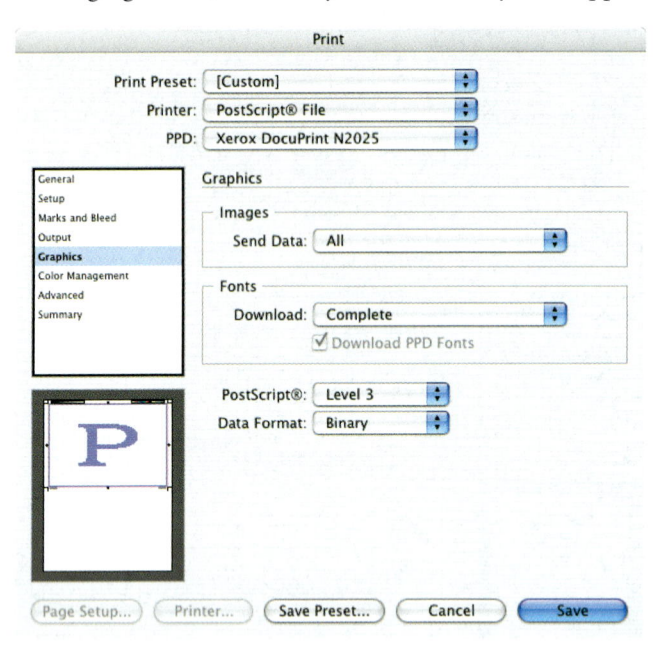

   **FIGURE 7.21**

10. **Open the Color Management pane. The Profile menu should be set to Document CMYK – U.S. Sheetfed Coated v2.**

    Because you're making separations, the Source Space options aren't available.

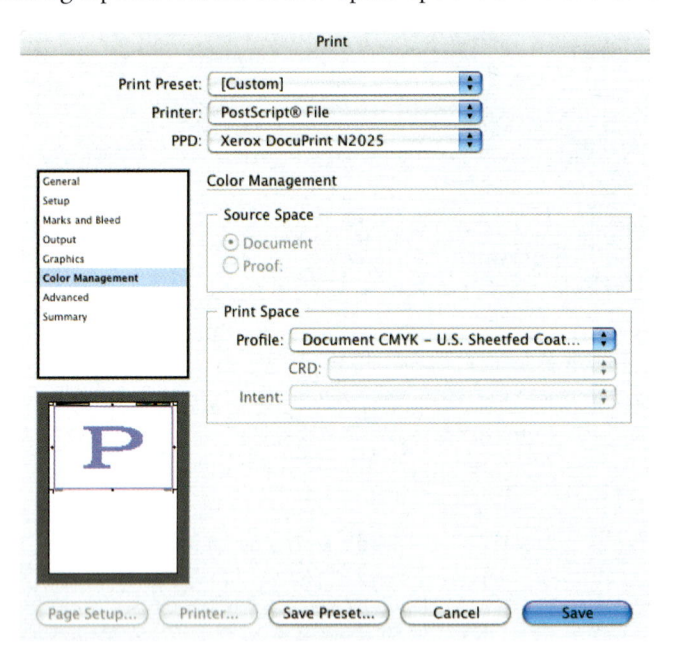

    **FIGURE 7.22**

**11** Open the Advanced pane. Set the Transparency Flattener Preset menu to High Resolution, and check the Ignore Spread Overrides box.

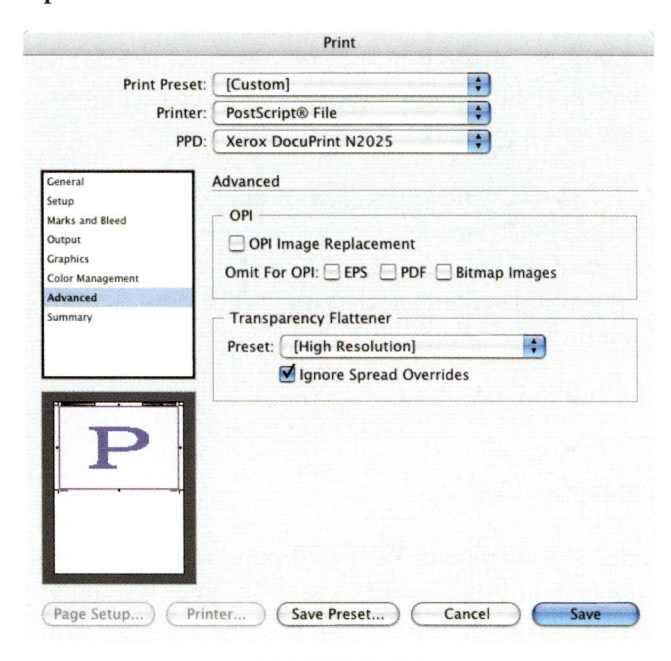

**FIGURE 7.23**

**12** Click Save to write the PostScript file to disk.

A Save PostScript File dialog box appears; accept the default file name, and save the file. InDesign shows a progress bar as it flattens, traps, and separates the document. The time it takes to complete this process depends on the speed of your computer.

**13** Close the document without saving.

If you have Adobe Acrobat installed on your computer, run the resulting PostScript file through Acrobat Distiller using the Press job options, then open the resulting PDF document in Acrobat. You will see a color-separated file.

## LESSON 4  Exporting EPS Files

EPS (Encapsulated PostScript) files are single-page files that you can export from nearly any graphics application and import into other applications as graphics. They are particularly useful if you want to place a resolution-independent page into another document; a publisher, for example, might want to include images of book covers in a catalog. There is no need to choose a PPD, and there is no support for color management as there is when printing a PostScript file.

When you export a file to EPS, each page (you can print all or a range of pages) is exported to its own file; spreads, however, can be exported as single pages if you check the Spreads box.

You need to choose the PostScript language level that will be used to generate the file. Modern applications and output devices can interpret Level 3 PostScript, but there are enough older devices remaining in use to make exporting as Level 2 PostScript a safer alternative. In selecting a color space, you should typically choose CMYK for print and RGB for electronic display. RGB images are converted to CMYK using color management if you've enabled it in the document, and spot colors are preserved. To prevent unwanted color shift, you should avoid using the Device Independent color option.

You should select a TIFF preview; PICT images are useful only on Macintosh computers, and even some Macintosh applications cannot use PICT previews. As a general rule, you should always embed fonts to ensure that the EPS file can be imaged anywhere, even remote sites that don't have those fonts installed. You must enter a bleed margin value, or objects that bleed off the page will be cropped during the export process (which might be an effect that you want).

## Export as EPS

**1** Open the document musiced.indd.

**2** Choose File>Export. Navigate to your WIP_07 folder, name the export file "musiced_ad.eps", choose EPS from the Format (Macintosh) or Save As Type (Windows) menu, then click Save.

You can also press Command/Control-E to begin the export process.

**FIGURE 7.24**

Project 7  Managing Output  **263**  LEVEL 2

**3**  In the General tab of the Export EPS dialog box that appears, make the following selections in the menus:

| | |
|---|---|
| PostScript | Level 2 |
| Color | CMYK |
| Preview | TIFF |
| Embed Fonts | Subset |
| Data Format | Binary |
| Bleed | 0.125 in. on all sides |

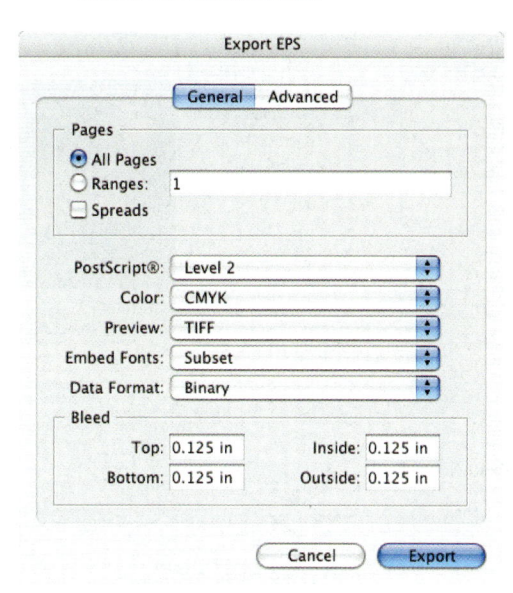

**FIGURE 7.25**

**4**  In the Advanced tab, accept the default settings.

There isn't any transparency in the document, so you don't need to change the flattener setting.

**FIGURE 7.26**

**5** **Click Export.**

InDesign saves the file to disk. You may receive a message about updating images; if you do, allow InDesign to update the images.

**6** **Close the document without saving.**

The ad is now ready to incorporate into another layout.

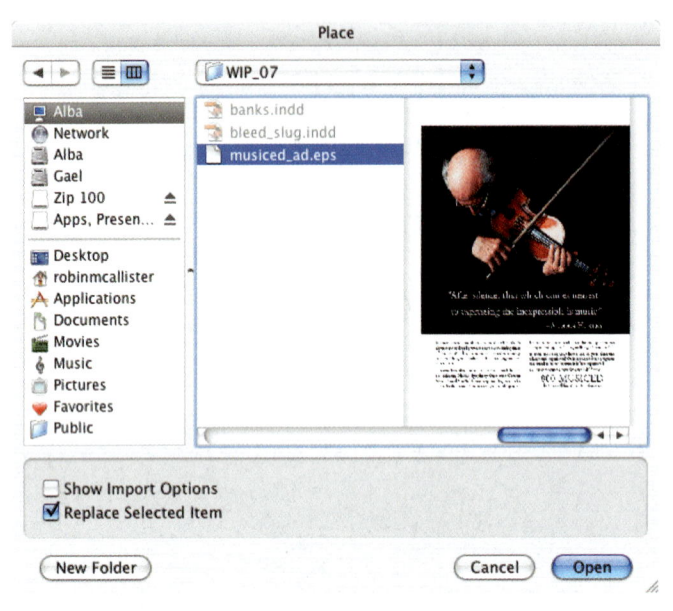

**FIGURE 7.27**

**7** Create a new tabloid document using the defaults. Place the musiced_ad.eps file you just made on the document page.

**8** Close the file without saving.

## LESSON 5   Using the Separations Preview Palette

You can use InDesign's Separations Preview palette to preview color separation, ink coverage, and overprinting, thereby avoiding costly mistakes before committing your file to film. Previewing separations on the monitor can help you detect problems without the expense of printing separations, but you can't preview trapping, halftone screens, or resolution. You should work with your GASP to verify these settings using "hard" proofing techniques. Objects on hidden layers are not included in the on-screen preview.

The Separations Preview palette can also help you resolve several ink issues, including those related to varnishes (which are transparent and difficult to preview on-screen), rich blacks (which are combinations of process-black ink and other color inks for richer color and increased opacity), and ink coverage (your printer can tell you how much is too much). You can also preview how blending, transparency, and overprinting will appear in color-separated output.

Project 7   Managing Output    **265**   LEVEL 2

When you preview separations, a single color separation appears black on the monitor, as if you were looking at a piece of positive film. When you preview two or more colors at once, they appear in color, simulating what you would see if you were viewing color overlays. Varnishes are treated just as other colors.

## Preview Separations

**1** **Open the document strawberry_fest.indd.**

This is a process-color document with varnish as an additional color.

**2** **Choose Window>Output Preview>Separations.**

The Separations Preview palette opens.

**3** **In the View menu, choose Separations.**

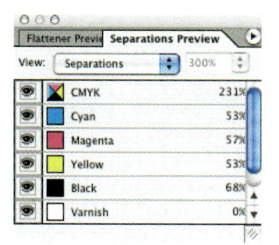

FIGURE 7.28

**4** **Click the word Cyan (not the Eyeball icon next to it).**

The cyan components in the images appear as tints of black. All other colors become invisible.

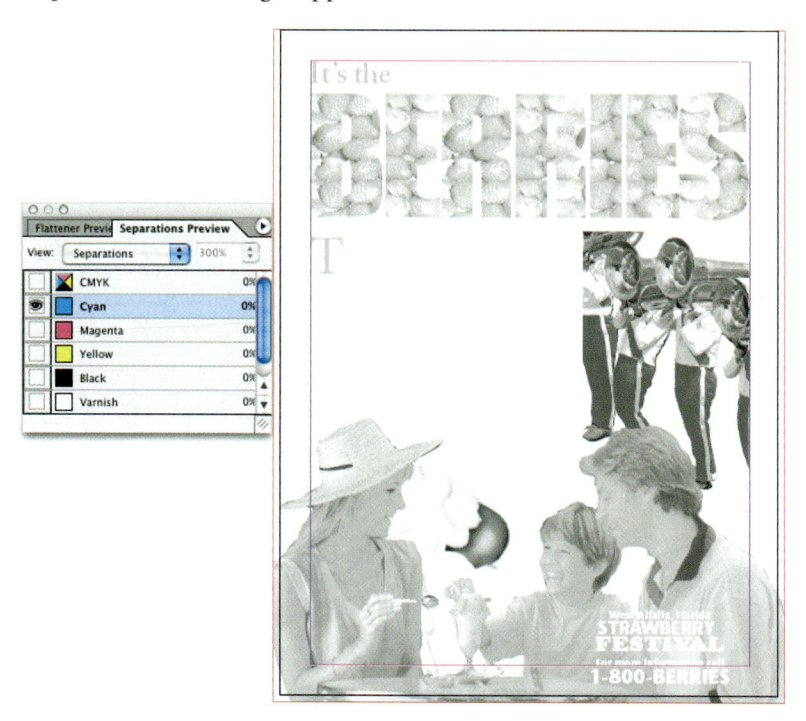

FIGURE 7.29

**5** **Click the empty block to the left of the Yellow swatch.**

You can see how the cyan and yellow inks combine.

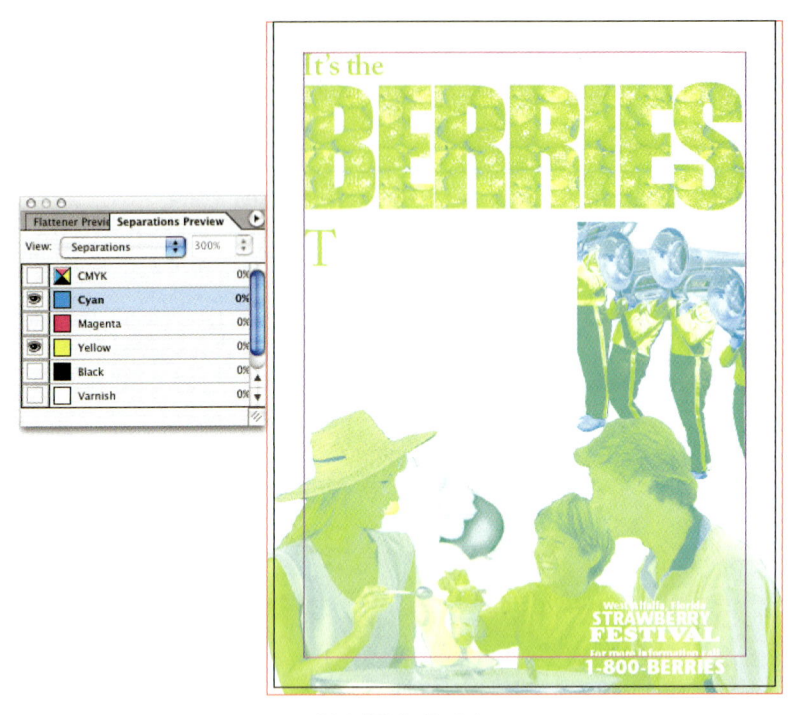

**FIGURE 7.30**

**6** **Click the word Varnish.**

The word BERRIES appears in solid black, showing where the varnish has been applied.

**7** **Click the word CMYK.**

This shows all four process colors combined.

**8** **Choose Ink Limit from the View menu.**

The default ink limit is 300%. The ink limit is the maximum allowable ink percentages in a color, based on the specifications of the printing press. For example, if you create a reddish brown color as C:22, M:58, Y:93, K:09, the sum of the four ink percentages is 182%, well below the ink limit. You should ask your printer for the correct ink limit for the press on which your job will be printed. Areas that exceed the maximum ink coverage are shown in red. Higher values result in a darker shade of red.

**9** **Move the cursor around the page.**

The percentages of each ink are listed in the palette as the cursor passes over different areas of the document.

**FIGURE 7.31**

**10** **Leave the file open for the next lesson.**

## LESSON 6  Preflighting Documents

To refresh your memory from *Essentials for Design: InDesign Level 1*, **packaging** is Adobe's term for gathering all the fonts, images, ICC profiles, and text files used in a document into a single location (usually a new folder) for compact delivery to a print provider. If your provider wants you to submit InDesign files rather than PostScript or PDF files, then you will find this function very useful. Before packaging a document, however, you should always perform a preflight to confirm that all the necessary electronic elements are available. To preflight an open document, you can either choose File>Preflight or press Command-Option-Shift-F (Macintosh) or Control-Alt-Shift-F (Windows).

The Fonts pane of the Preflight dialog box lists all fonts used in the document that have a status of Embedded, including any used in placed EPS, PDF, and Illustrator files. Missing fonts are labeled Missing in the status column, and incomplete (or subset) fonts within placed files are labeled Incomplete. Fonts that have an internal flag set to prohibit embedding have a Protected status of Yes. If a document contains protected fonts, you can still print or export a PostScript file, but you can't embed those fonts into an exported PDF file.

The Links and Images pane lists all linked files included in the document. The file names and link types are listed, along with their status (Linked, Embedded, or Missing). The ICCProfile column simply shows whether a linked file has an embedded ICC profile or not. If you need to update links, you can do so from the Current Link/Image area.

The Colors and Inks pane lists all separations that are required by the document. This is an easy way to catch excess spot colors. If you want to convert these to process colors, you just click Cancel, then convert them by editing their swatches, or by choosing All Spots to Process in the Ink Manager. The Colors and Inks pane also tells you if the document uses color management (CMS is ON/OFF).

The Print Settings pane lists all current print settings for the document. Print settings are carried along with the document, and may not be useful on another computer that has different PPDs installed. The External Plug-ins pane lists any third-party plug-ins that have features used by the document. Service providers may not be able to print or even open your document if it uses non-Adobe plug-ins. If you use them, you may need to export the document to a PostScript or PDF file before sending it to a service provider.

## Preflight a Document

**1** Continue in the open document, strawberry_fest.indd.

**2** Choose File>Preflight.

The Preflight dialog box summarizes all the potential problems with the document. One image is in the RGB color space.

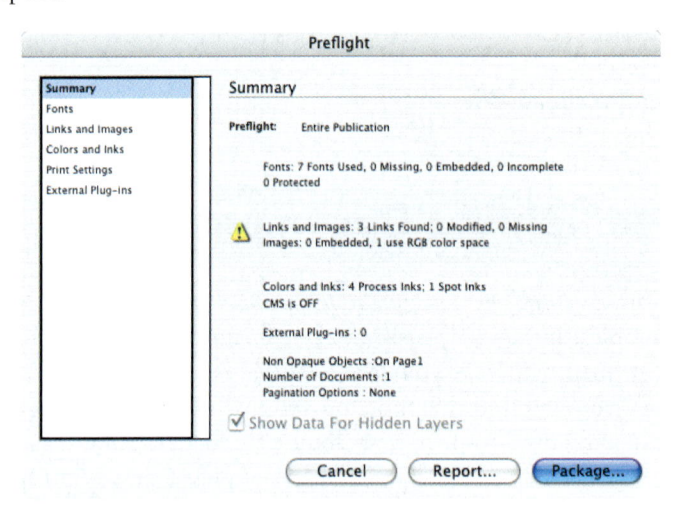

**FIGURE 7.32**

3. **Open the Links and Images pane.**

   You can see that the berries.psd image is a Photoshop RGB file with no embedded profile. The other images are EPS CMYK files that contain no embedded profiles.

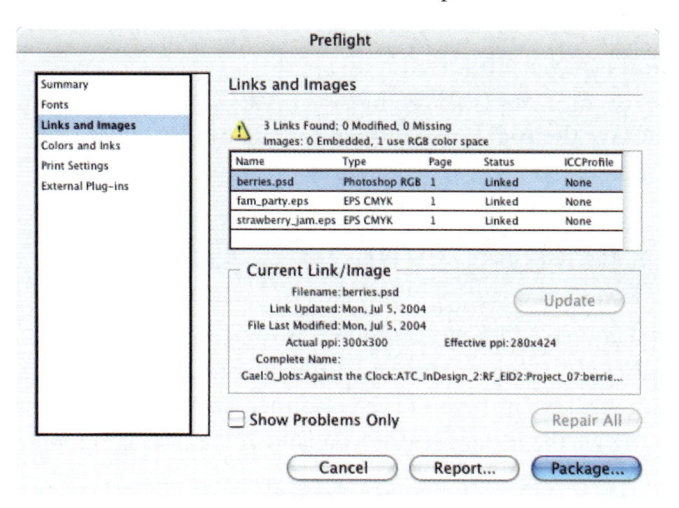

   FIGURE 7.33

4. **Open the Colors and Inks pane.**

   The four process colors are listed. Varnish is listed as a spot ink.

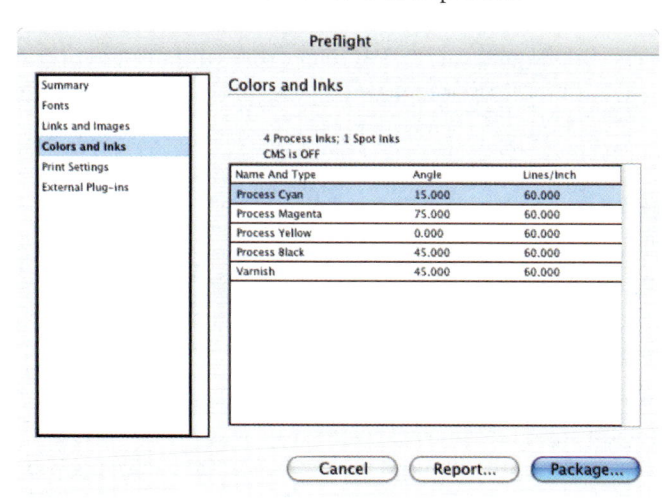

   FIGURE 7.34

5. **Click Cancel. In the Links palette, click the berries.psd image, then click the Relink button.**

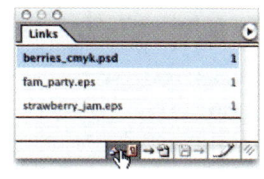

   FIGURE 7.35

**6** Select berries_cmyk.psd.

InDesign changes the link to the CMYK file.

**7** Choose File>Preflight again.

You receive no warnings; your file is ready.

**8** Click Cancel, and save the file. Leave it open for the next exercise.

## LESSON 7  Exporting Files to a GASP

Most designers must eventually send files out-of-house for imaging and printing. Because of this, after preflighting a file, you must package it to ensure the service provider receives everything they need. Before you can package a file, though, you must save it. If you have performed any functions following the most recent save, InDesign will prompt you to save the file again after you launch the packaging routine.

Before you package, you fill out printing instructions to include in the folder that is sent to the GASP. When you package the document, you decide what you want to include. You should include the fonts, in case the GASP doesn't have the same versions you do (you'll receive an alert that reminds you of your need to comply with copyright law). You also need to copy linked graphics and update the links to those graphics. If you fail to update the links, InDesign won't know where to look for the images when it is on a foreign computer.

During the packaging process, InDesign creates a job folder that contains a report (the printing instructions), the InDesign document itself, a subfolder that contains all the fonts, and another subfolder that contains all the linked images.

### Export Files to a GASP

**1** Continue in the open document, strawberry_fest.indd.

**2** Choose File>Package.

InDesign preflights the document automatically, then either displays a window prompting you to save the document, or continues to the next screen. You can also press Command-Option-Shift-P (Macintosh) or Control-Alt-Shift-P (Windows) to begin the packaging process.

**3** If you are prompted to save the document, click Yes.

The Printing Instructions dialog box appears.

**4** Complete the printing instructions as follows, then click Continue:

    Filename:    strawberry_fest.txt
    Contact:     Your name
    Company:    Your company
    Address:     Your address

Phone & Fax: Your numbers
Email: Your e-mail address
Instructions: Image to film. 150 line screen. 2400 ppi. RRED

**FIGURE 7.36**

5. Navigate to your WIP_07 folder, then check the Copy Fonts, Copy Linked Graphics, and Update Graphic Links in Package boxes. Name the package "strawberry_fest folder" and click the Save button.

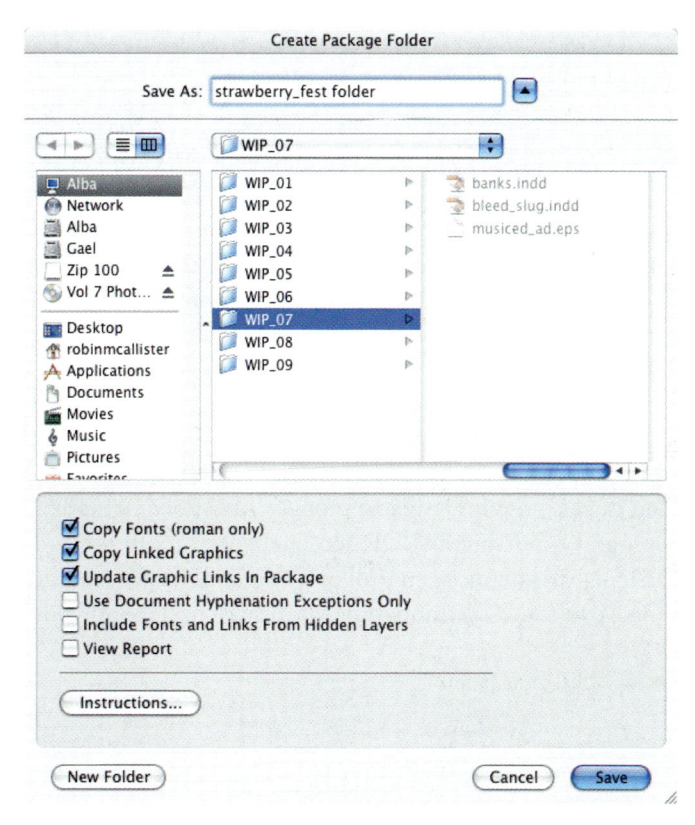

**FIGURE 7.37**

**6** **Open the strawberry_fest folder you just saved to your WIP_07 folder and examine the contents.**

All of the job's fonts are included in the Fonts folder; all linked files (images) are in the Links folder. The report and InDesign files are in the main folder.

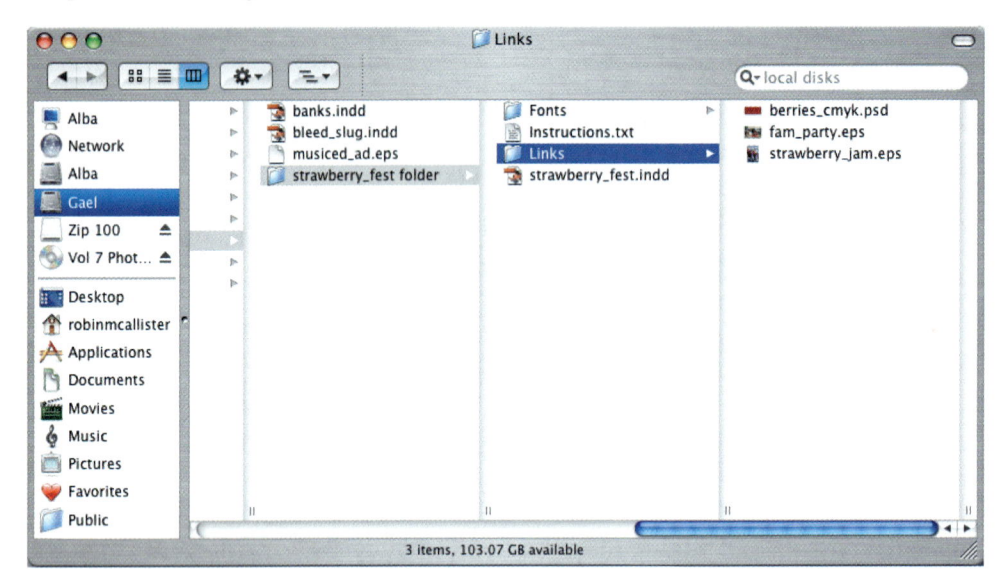

**FIGURE 7.38**

**7** **Save and close the document.**

## LESSON 8 Using Advanced PDF Features

When you export a PDF file from InDesign, you have the option of including eBook tags, which provide the document with structure and enable it to be accessible, reusable, and viewable in numerous display formats. Without tags, a PDF file is considered to be unstructured — useful for commercial printing or proofing, but not acceptable for electronic distribution. Including tags, and therefore a structure, in an exported PDF file can be as simple as checking the Include eBook Tags box in the General pane of the Export PDF dialog box.

You can also include bookmarks, hyperlinks, and interactive elements such as movies or sound files. These not only add more interest to the file, but also make it more navigable. In this way, you can publish one document for multiple applications. You can also use InDesign to produce such documents as slide presentations, creating the presentation in InDesign and exporting as PDF, rather than switching to a dedicated program such as Microsoft PowerPoint. InDesign gives you more control over text and images than do presentation programs — and the fewer programs you have to learn, the more time you'll have to develop your expertise on the programs you use.

## Add Hyperlinks within a Document

**1** Open the document idea_conf.indd.

**2** Choose Window>Interactive>Hyperlinks.

The Hyperlinks palette opens.

**3** Choose New Hyperlink Destination from the Hyperlinks palette Options menu.

The New Hyperlink Destination dialog box appears.

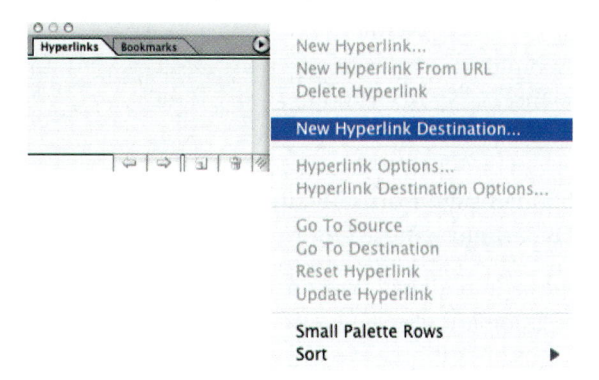

FIGURE 7.39

**4** Choose Page from the Type menu, type "Daily Schedule" in the Name field, set the Page field to 2, and leave the Zoom Setting menu at Fixed. Click OK.

The destination does not appear in the Hyperlinks palette. It will appear only after it is linked to a source.

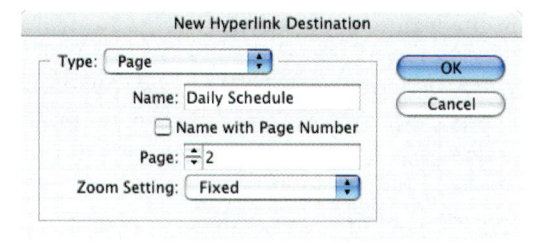

FIGURE 7.40

**5** Click with the Type tool in the main headline on Page 3.

**6** Choose New Hyperlink Destination from the Hyperlinks palette Options menu. Choose Text Anchor in the Type menu and name this destination "Learn". Click OK.

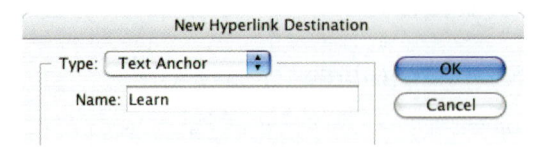

FIGURE 7.41

**7** Repeat the procedure in Step 6 to set three new destinations on Page 3:

| Destination | Name |
|---|---|
| The Important Stuff | Rates |
| Annual Conference… | Recreation |
| Registration Form | Register |

**8** With the Type tool, highlight the words "Daily Schedule" on Page 1, then choose New Hyperlink from the Hyperlinks palette Options menu. Set the Type menu to Page and click OK.

The first hyperlink appears in the Hyperlinks palette. Because you have only one Page hyperlink, the rest of the dialgo box is automatically filled in for you.

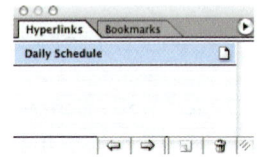

FIGURE 7.42

**9** Highlight "What You'll Learn" and choose New Hyperlink. Choose Text Anchor in the Type menu and Learn in the Name menu. Click OK.

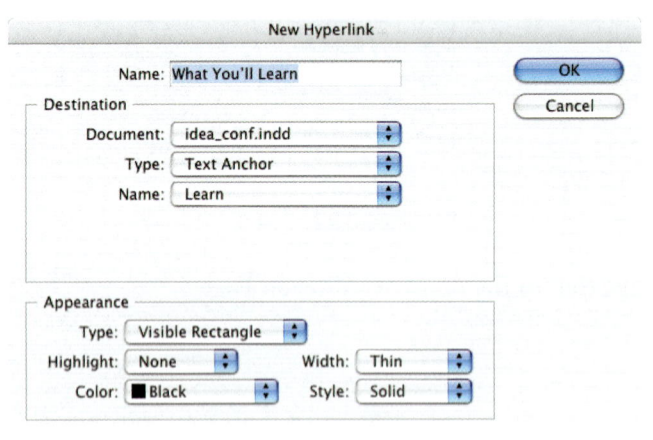

FIGURE 7.43

**10** Repeat Step 9 to assign the text "Fees and Details" to the Rates link, "Recreation" to the Recreation link, and "Register Here" to the Register link.

**11** Save the document and leave it open for the next exercise.

## Insert Interactive Files

**1** Continue in the open document, idea_conf.indd; you should still be on Page 1.

**2** Choose File>Place, then double-click the file gmta.wav.

Remember, you can also press Command/Control-D to place a file.

**3** Click with the loaded sound icon on the page just before the words "Register Here."

**4** Drag the frame so it encompasses the entire phrase.

FIGURE 7.44

**5** Choose Object>Interactive>Sound Options. Choose None in the Poster menu, and check the Do Not Print Poster and Embed Sound in PDF boxes. Click OK.

The final page will have no *poster* (a visual indicator of a sound or movie) telling readers that a sound will play when this hyperlink is clicked.

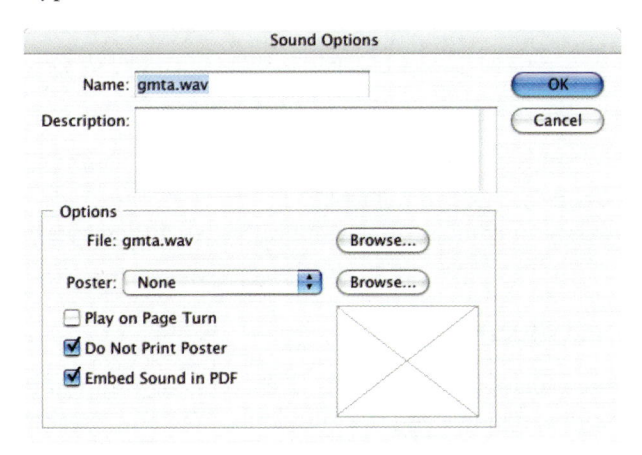

FIGURE 7.45

**6** Drag idea_intro.wav from the Project_07 folder to the upper-right corner of Page 1.

**7** With the object selected, choose Object>Interactive>Sound Options. Choose None in the Poster menu, and check the Play on Page Turn, Do Not Print Poster, and Embed Sound in PDF boxes. Click OK.

This sound will play when a user accesses the page.

**8** Save the document and choose File>Export. Choose the Adobe PDF format from the menu, and save to your WIP_07 folder.

**9** Choose Screen in the Preset menu. Set the Pages option to All. Check the Optimize for Fast Web View and View PDF after Exporting boxes (in the Options area) and the Hyperlinks and Interactive Elements boxes (in the Include area).

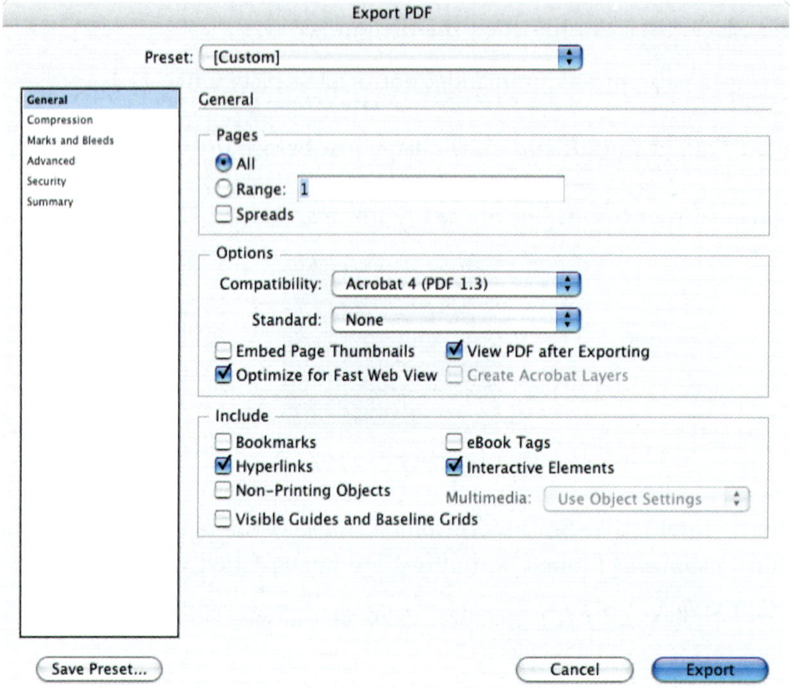

FIGURE 7.46

Notice that the Preset menu changes to Custom after you adjust the settings.

**10** Click Export.

You can ignore the two warning messages that appear. After all elements on the page appear, the music will begin.

**11** Open the PDF file and click the links.

Unfortunately, the music plays every time Page 1 is accessed. Wait until it's done playing, then click the first part of the Registration line and the sound file ("Ya know, great minds do think alike!") plays. Click the second part of the line to be taken to the link.

**12** Close the file.

## Add a Movie to a Page

**1** Open the document escape.indd.

**2** Place the file hotdogging.mov at X: 2.5 in., Y: 4.5 in.

**3** Choose Object>Interactive>Movie Options. Make sure the Embed Movie in PDF box is not checked. Choose None in the Poster menu and Play Once Then Stop in the Mode menu. Leave the rest of the boxes unchecked.

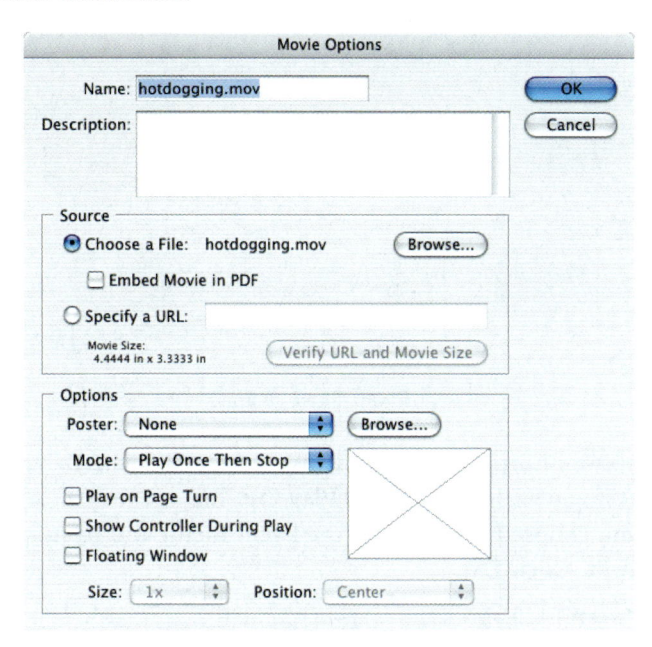

**FIGURE 7.47**

**4** Using the Button tool, draw three 1 × 0.4-in. frames. Position the first at X: 2.5 in., Y: 8 in. and distribute the other two across the width of the movie window.

The Button tool allows you to create a frame that contains additional data, such as navigation options or the ability to play, pause, resume, or stop movies or sound files. Otherwise it is virtually identical to any frame in a document.

**5** With the Selection tool, double-click Button 1 and name it "Play", then click the Behaviors tab.

**6** Choose Mouse Up in the Event menu, Movie in the Behavior menu, hotdogging.mov in the Movie menu, and Play in the Play Options menu. Click the Add button, then click OK.

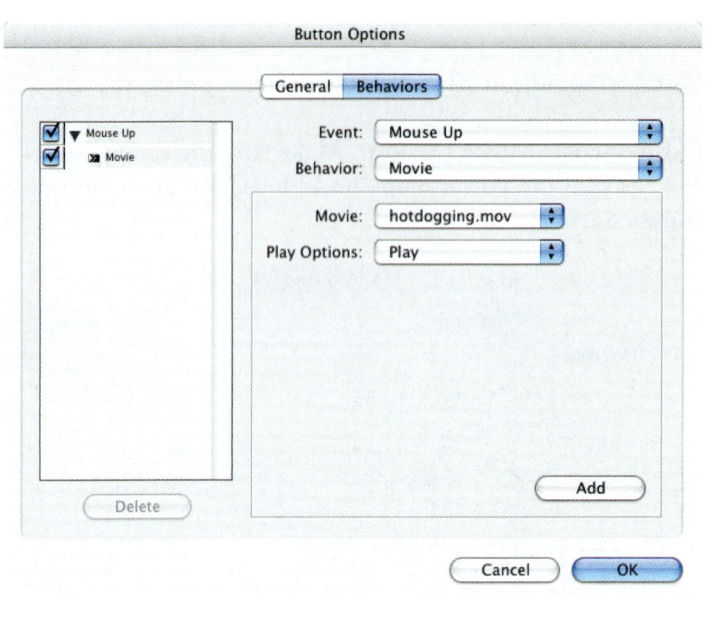

FIGURE 7.48

**7** Double-click the second button, name it "Pause", then click the Behaviors tab. Choose Mouse Down in the Event menu and Pause in the Play Options menu. Click Add. To add a second action to the button, choose Mouse Up in the Event menu and Resume in the Play Options menu, then click Add. Click OK.

When the mouse button is held down, the movie will pause. When it is released, the movie will resume.

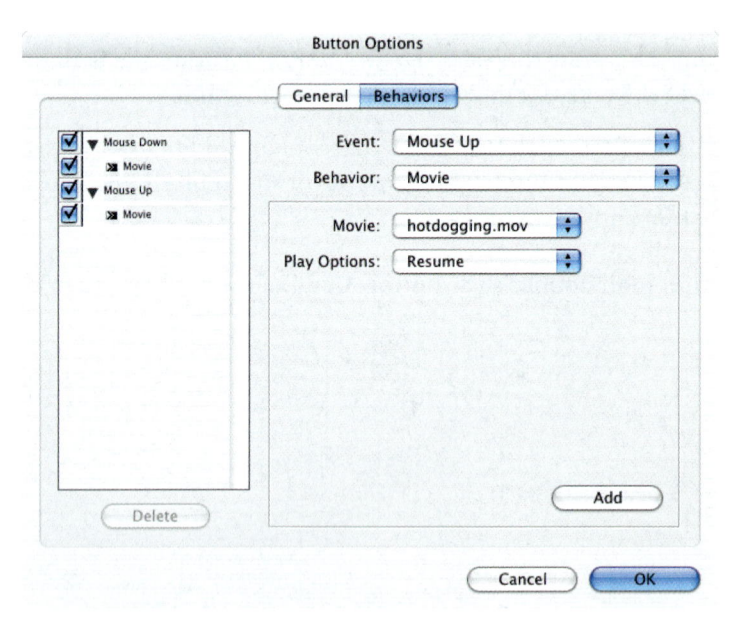

FIGURE 7.49

**8** Select the third button, name it "Stop", then click the Behaviors tab. Choose Mouse Down in the Event menu and Stop in the Play Options menu. Add the action, then click OK.

**9** Open the file buttons.indl. Drag each button "cap" onto the page, then cut them and paste them into their respective buttons.

**FIGURE 7.50**

**10** Export to PDF using the same parameters as in the previous exercise. Open the PDF document and click each button (remember to hold the mouse button to pause the movie) to confirm that they all work correctly.

**11** Save the document and close it.

# SUMMARY

In this project, you reviewed and learned new skills relative to exporting and printing your documents. You preflighted and packaged a document for a service provider, and learned how to check your documents for ink coverage. You also learned to print files to a high-resolution printer, and to export files as EPS for insertion in other documents.

In addition to learning skills that are specific to printed documents, you gained advanced skills for creating portable documents for electronic distribution. You inserted sound and movie files into documents purposed for PDF distribution. In addition, you created buttons that invoke specific actions within the document.

# KEY TERMS

| | | |
|---|---|---|
| Adobe in-RIP trapping | ink coverage limits | PPD |
| Application Built-In trapping | movie | preflight |
| background color | neutral density | printer's marks |
| bleed | OPI | rich black |
| bookmark | overprinting | RIP |
| button | package | screen angle |
| color separation | PDF | screen ruling |
| EPS | PDL | Separations Preview palette |
| foreground color | PICT | TIFF |
| GASP | plug-in | transparency |
| hyperlink | poster | trap |
| ink coverage | PostScript | |

# CHECKING CONCEPTS AND TERMS

## MULTIPLE CHOICE

**Check the letter of the correct answer for each of the following:**

1. What is the purpose of trapping?
   a. To catch all errors in a file
   b. To ensure that images that print to the edge of the page are not cut off
   c. To ensure that abutting colors do not have white gaps in between
   d. To collect all elements of a job for export

2. When exporting a job to EPS, which of the following is true?
   a. You can specify pages, color space, and OPI preferences.
   b. You can specify compression, color space, and font embedding.
   c. You can specify trapping, OPI preferences, and color space.
   d. You can specify printer's marks, pages, and trapping.

3. Which of the following is true of PDF?
   a. PDF files can contain hyperlinks.
   b. PDF stands for "Portable Document Format."
   c. You can display movies and sound in PDF files.
   d. All of the above are true.

4. Which of the following can you view using the Separations Preview palette?
   a. Neutral density
   b. Objects on hidden layers
   c. Ink limits
   d. RGB color space

5. What information does preflighting a document provide?
   a. Color space, missing fonts, missing images, misspellings
   b. Color management, missing fonts, missing images, external plug-ins
   c. Missing fonts, missing images, color management, update links
   d. Missing fonts, missing images, color space, bitmap images

6. When trapping an object, which of the following occurs?
   a. The foreground becomes larger with relation to the background.
   b. The background becomes larger with relation to the foreground.
   c. Darker colors get larger with relation to lighter colors.
   d. Lighter colors get larger with relation to darker colors.

7. When printing a file, which of the following is true?
   a. You should always turn on printer's marks.
   b. You should always send PostScript files in Binary because this format provides the fewest errors.
   c. You must select the correct PPD.
   d. Image downloads are controlled by the Optional Prepress Interface.

8. Which of the following can be specified for a PDF file?
   a. Hyperlinks, movies, and sounds
   b. Buttons, bookmarks, and URLs
   c. Object visibility, navigation, and events
   d. All of the above

9. When inserting a hyperlink, which of the following is true?
   a. A hyperlink can have only one destination.
   b. A destination can have only one source.
   c. A hyperlink can only function within the document.
   d. A hyperlink must be inserted with the Direct Selection tool.

10. In InDesign, what is a "poster"?
    a. Any document that is printed only on one side
    b. A document that is larger than 11 × 17
    c. A visual representation of a movie or sound file
    d. The command to show a movie

## DISCUSSION QUESTIONS

1. Why might you use InDesign to produce "slide" presentations, instead of using a dedicated program such as PowerPoint?

2. Discuss the advantages and disadvantages of trapping within InDesign.

# SKILL DRILL

Skill Drills reinforce project skills. Each skill reinforced is the same, or nearly the same, as a skill presented in the lessons. Detailed instructions are provided in a step-by-step format. Skill Drills 3 and 4 should be performed sequentially.

## 1. Work with Built-in Trapping

The smallest jobs require the same attention to detail as large, expensive jobs. Graphic designers are often called on to design and produce stationery projects, including business cards. It is important to our clients' business that these look absolutely perfect, even where colors overlap.

This file represents a typical three-color business card design, consisting of geometric shapes and type. The background is not colored. "Paper" has been redefined to approximate the buff paper stock that the job will be printed on.

1. Open the document business_cards.indd.
2. From the Swatches palette Options menu, choose Ink Manager.
3. In the Ink Manager dialog box, scroll down and compare the neutral densities (ND) of PANTONE 193 and 131.
4. Click each color and assign the PMS color with the higher ND a Trapping Sequence of 1. Assign the color with the lower ND a trapping sequence of 2. Leave the sequence of the other inks as they are; except for Black, they will not print. This ensures that Black will print on top of the other inks.
5. If it is not already open, open the Trap Presets palette.
6. From the Options menu, choose New Preset. The default parameters should be acceptable for this job. Close the dialog box.
7. Open the Print dialog box and access the Output pane.
8. Set the Color menu to Separations and the Trapping menu to Application Built-in.
9. Click Cancel and close the file.

## 2. Trap a Job for Screen Printing

Although screen printing uses a different process than offset printing, the principles for both processes are the same. One important difference between the two is that screen printing requires a heavier trap. This exercise features a four-color T-shirt design using only PANTONE colors.

1. Open the document space_t.indd. It is immediately obvious that the trapping of the blue type to the squiggle highlights is going to be affected by the frame of the EPS file. You must correct this before you can perform any trapping operations.
2. Using the Add Anchor Point, Convert Direction Point, and Direct Selection tools, adjust the bounding box around the graphic so it doesn't interfere with the InDesign elements.

**FIGURE 7.51**

3. Open the Print dialog box and access the Output pane.

4. Set the Color menu to Separations and the Trapping menu to Application Built-in.

5. Click the Ink Manager button and view the neutral densities of the colors used. Assign a printing sequence as follows: PANTONE 300: 1, PANTONE Rubine Red: 2, PANTONE 109: 3, PANTONE 2593: 4. Click OK.

6. Assign the printing angles as follows: PANTONE 2593: 45°, PANTONE Rubine Red: 75°, PANTONE 300: 15°, PANTONE 109: 0°.

7. Click the Save Preset button. Name the style "Screen Print", then click OK. Click cancel to close the dialog box.

8. From the Trap Presets palette Options menu, choose New Preset and name the preset "ScreenPrint".

9. In the Trap Width section, set the Default field to 8 pt. and click OK.

10. Choose Assign Trap Presets, choose ScreenPrint in the Trap Preset menu, then click Done.

11. Save and close the file.

## To Extend Your Knowledge...

### ASSIGNING PRINTING ANGLES

For inks to print correctly, they should print at different angles. Black (or the darkest spot color) is typically on a 45° angle. The second-darkest color (magenta, if process color is used) is at a 75° angle. The third-darkest color (cyan, if process color is used) is at a 15° angle. The lightest color (yellow, in process) is printed at a 90° or 0° angle.

Because only solid colors were used in the first Skill Drill, no screening occurred and you didn't have to be concerned with screen angles. The second Skill Drill, however, used screens of colors, so it was important to set the angles.

## 3. Add the Bleed and Slug to a Document

If you work on a document that was prepared with no bleed, but that now needs a bleed because of a design change, it is a simple matter to add it. In this Skill Drill, you simply need to modify the document so the bleed and slug will print.

1. Open the document lwi_soups.indd.
2. Choose File>Document Setup.
3. If the Bleed and Slug options are not visible, click the More Options button.
4. Set 18-pt. top and bottom bleeds and a 1p6 outside bleed.
5. Set a 72-pt. bottom slug. Click OK.
6. On each of the master pages, create two approval lines within the slug area. Use the Rectangle tool to create two check boxes, then add signature lines for "OK" and for "OK with changes" and short lines for the date.

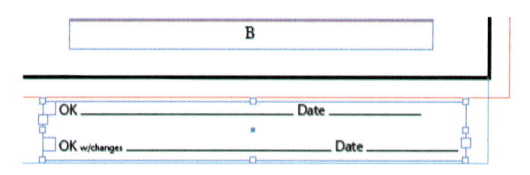

**FIGURE 7.52**

7. Save the document and leave it open for the next exercise.

## 4. Check and Print Documents

Before you print a document or send it to a service provider you should check it to ensure there are no errors. There is little sense in spending a great deal of time in document preparation if you do not check the file before you send it to be printed, or even print it yourself.

1. Continue in the open document, lwi_soups.indd.

2. Choose Window>Output Preview>Separations, and choose Ink Limit from the View menu. Note that no area is outside the ink coverage limit.

3. Change the View menu to Separations. Deselect everything but yellow. Notice there is some yellow in the word "Soups." Now make magenta visible as well. There is also magenta in the background, so it is unnecessary to apply a trap to the word "Soups."

**FIGURE 7.53**

4. Choose File>Preflight. Note that color management has not been turned on. Click Cancel.

5. Choose Edit>Color Settings. Click the Enable Color Management button and accept the defaults. Click OK.

6. Open the Print dialog box, then choose PostScript File as the printer and select an appropriate PPD.

7. In the Setup pane, set the Page Position menu to Centered.

8. In the Marks and Bleed pane, check the All Printer's Marks box, and the Use Document Bleed Settings and Include Slug Area boxes.

9. In the Output pane, set the Color menu to Separations with Trapping off.

10. In the Advanced pane, choose the High Resolution preset.

11. Click Save, then save to your WIP_07 folder. Dismiss any warning messages.

12. Save and close the document.

## 5. Create Buttons

When you're creating interactive documents, you can create buttons using rectangles or ovals, and change the appearance of buttons using custom graphics. You can also use InDesign's standard button designs and effects. In this exercise, you're going to create buttons and define their behavior. The movie poster in this file has been placed on top of a sound file. You will create buttons that will drive both movie and sound together.

1. Open the document buttons.indd.
2. Select the Button tool and click below the movie poster. In the resulting dialog box, define the Width as 1 in. and the Height as 0.5 in.
3. Create three additional identical buttons in a row below the movie poster.
4. With the Selection tool, double-click the first button to access the Button Options dialog box. Name the button "Play", and click the Behaviors button.
5. Set the Behavior menu to Sound, and the Play Options menu to Play. Click Add. Set the Behavior menu to Movie and click Add. Click OK.
6. Following the same procedures, name the remaining three buttons and assign the movie and sound Play Options as Pause, Resume, and Stop.
7. Choose Window>Interactive>States, and click the first button with the Selection tool. Change the Appearance to Glow. If Up, Rollover, and Down states are not available, select New State from the Options menu.
8. Select each of the three states of the button and type the word "PLAY" in ATC Oak Bold. Center it horizontally and vertically. Assign 100% Black to the Up and Rollover states, and 50% Black to the Down state.
9. Select each of the other buttons and type the appropriate name (Pause, Resume, or Stop) in each state of the button, as you did with the Play button.
10. From the Align palette, distribute the buttons across the width of the movie poster and export to PDF in your WIP_07 folder, using the Screen preset.

**FIGURE 7.54**

11. Test your buttons, then save the InDesign document and close it.

# CHALLENGE

Challenge exercises expand on, or are somewhat related to, skills presented in the lessons. Each exercise provides a brief introduction, followed by instructions presented in a numbered-step format that are not as detailed as those in the Skill Drill exercises. You should perform these exercises in the order in which they appear.

## 1. Preflight an Ad and Export as EPS

Many designers mistakenly believe that preflighting is only necessary for documents that will be sent to a GASP. Actually, you should preflight every document before sending it out of shop or imaging at high resolution. Advertisements are especially vital to a client's business — if an ad prints incorrectly, the newspaper or magazine will usually print a correction, but if the ad features an event, a poor turnout could be irreversible.

1. Open the document bay_brides.indd.
2. Run InDesign's Preflight routine. One warning message appears.
3. Cancel and replace the RGB image with bride_cmyk.tif.
4. Rerun the Preflight routine to ensure that everything is correct.
5. Click Cancel, then choose to export the file to EPS, the format the magazine wants the ad delivered in.
6. Use PostScript Level 2, specify the CMYK color space, embed a subset of the fonts, use Binary format, and turn the bleeds off. Export the file, accepting the default name.
7. Open the document magazine.indd and place the ad in the lower-right of the document page.

**FIGURE 7.55**

8. Save and close magazine.indd.
9. Save and close bay_brides.indd.

## 2. Export a Document to a GASP

There are several reasons you might need to send a document to a service provider. The most common is that you need to have the document printed on an offset press. In other cases, your document might be larger than your desktop printer can handle.

That is the case with the lobby posters for Seacoast Repertory Theatre. Only four of these 22 × 34 in. posters are produced, but they must be imaged on a wide-format printer. In this Challenge, you prepare a poster for imaging by a GASP.

1. Open the document all_in_the_timing.indd.
2. Run InDesign's Package routine. The first part of this routine is a preflight, such as you ran in the first Challenge.
3. Fill out the Printing Instructions form. In the Instructions section, enter "4 Encad prints. Trim to 22 in. × 34 in.", then click Continue.
4. In the Create Package Folder dialog box, check the Copy Fonts, Copy Linked Graphics, and Update Graphic Links in Package boxes, then save to your WIP_07 folder.
5. Click OK to dismiss the Fonts warning.
6. Close the document without saving.

## 3. Add Hyperlinks to a Document

Presentation software has become much more user-friendly, but if you're accustomed to working in InDesign, switching to another suite of programs isn't necessary. In this Challenge, you'll hyperlink the pages of a file so the speaker, who will be using a PDF file as a "slide" presentation, will be able to easily navigate from one page to the next. Although you could use buttons to do this, you're going to use image maps, instead. The image maps were prepared as part of the master pages, so you're going to have to release them on each page.

1. Open the document legal_ethical.indd.
2. Open the Hyperlinks palette.
3. In the document, go to Page 1.
4. Create a new hyperlink destination and accept the defaults.
5. Repeat the process for the rest of the pages in the document, then return to Page 1.
6. Release the image maps over the graduated tint bar at the bottom of Page 1.

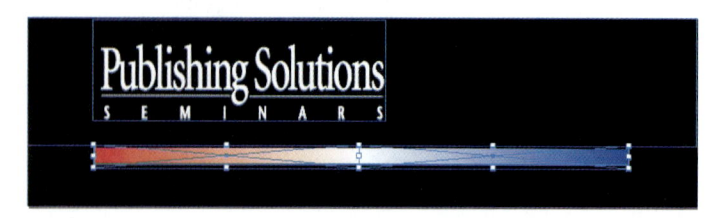

**FIGURE 7.56**

7. Click the right (blue) image map and choose New Hyperlink. Choose the Page 2 hyperlink.

8. Go to Page 2 and link the red image map to Page 1 and the blue image map to Page 3. Continue through Page 9, linking the red map to the previous page and the blue map to the next page. On Page 9, link the blue map to Page 1.

9. Create a PDF file, using the Screen preset.

10. Test the hyperlinks in your PDF file to ensure that you linked the pages properly.

## 4. Create a Multimedia Presentation

From kiosks to trade shows, interactivity is often the key to getting and holding potential buyers' attention. Of course, interactive presentations may carry the same message as your brochures (which the customer can take home with them), but there is nothing like engaging more than one of the senses, and getting the customer involved in the process.

Heather Glens is an upscale development near Kansas City. The developer has worked with others to bring all the amenities to the area, including a new home for the Wheatlands Repertory Theatre and the Big Bend Symphony Orchestra. At this year's Home Show, they are making a major pitch to sell both custom-designed homes and condominium living within the development.

1. Open the document heather_glens.indd.

2. Place the movie hg_waterfall.mov at X: 1 in., Y: 3.5 in.

3. Place the sound file hg_waterfall.wav below the Click Here to Enter text.

**FIGURE 7.57**

4. Double-click the movie poster to bring up the Movie Options dialog box. Choose None in the Poster menu.

5. Double click the sound poster to bring up the Sound Options dialog box. Choose None in the Poster menu and check the Embed Sound in PDF box.

6. Drag a button over the words "Click Here to Enter".

7. Define button behaviors — set the event for Mouse Up and the behaviors as Movie and as Sound. Set the Play Options as Play for each behavior. When the button is clicked both movie and sound will play simultaneously.

8. Export the document to PDF.

9. Open the PDF file and click the button to see and hear the movie.

10. Save the document and close it.

# PORTFOLIO BUILDER

## Multipurpose a Document for Print and Electronic Distribution

Multipurpose documents are commonplace today. Typically, documents are originally designed for print, then assigned interactive features that make them effective electronic documents. You will enhance your portfolio by developing an electronic version of it.

To complete this project, use the following techniques:

- Using appropriate music or movie files, add sound to your portfolio pages.
- Use the thumbnail pages to link to the portfolio pages. (If you create the thumbnails as inline graphics, they can be clicked just like text — and they can contain drop shadows.)
- Be sure to create links back to the thumbnail pages, or navigation links to other pages.
- Use buttons to allow viewers to play the interactive portions of your pages.
- Be innovative in your approach.

# PROJECT 8

## LEVEL 2

# Creating HTML and XML Documents

## OBJECTIVES

*In this project, you learn how to*

- Create hyperlinks
- Package documents for GoLive
- Export documents to SVG
- Export documents and elements to JPEG
- Tag document content for XML
- Assign XML structure
- Export and import XML
- Modify XML content

# WHY WOULD I DO THIS?

Repurposing — changing a document from one format to another — has become a widespread practice in the graphic design community. You can use InDesign's built-in features to convert a document originally designed for print to one that is appropriate for use on the Internet. Alternately, you can take data that originated in an XML database and import it into InDesign. You might also want to export an individual image or certain pages of a document to SVG or JPEG for easy Web viewing.

If your document must appear exactly as designed to every reader, then you should export it as a PDF file, which nearly anyone can view and print. (Anyone can download the Acrobat Reader application for free from Adobe's Web site.) If, however, you can be flexible about the formatting and image quality of your document, then HTML or XML might be a viable alternative. InDesign can export pages to Adobe GoLive for formatting in Hypertext Markup Language (HTML); it can also create pages in Extensible Markup Language (XML).

HTML is the language of the Web; it allows browsers such as Microsoft Internet Explorer to view your pages. Unlike other applications (and previous versions of InDesign), InDesign does not export directly to HTML. Instead, it packages all the items necessary for editing with Adobe GoLive or a similar application. Style sheets are converted to Cascading Style Sheets (CSS), images are converted to GIF or JPEG, a PDF preview page is created, and a number of XML files are readied for import into GoLive. XML is used mostly in data interchange and cross-media publishing, rather than as a method of displaying Web pages.

When you package a document to HTML or package it for GoLive (Adobe's Web-editing program), you should expect some file tweaking will be necessary. When you import an XML document, you will undoubtedly make some layout adjustments, as well.

## VISUAL SUMMARY

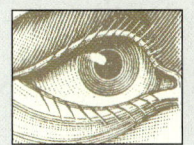

When creating pages that will be purposed for the Web, page-to-page navigation is vital. You can't just flip the pages of electronic documents. The process of creating hyperlinks seems backward — you first establish the destination, then link the starting point (the source) to that destination. The exception to this rule is when you define a URL address as a hyperlink; InDesign understands that the URL will link to the appropriate page on the Web, so you don't need to define a destination. You establish hyperlink destinations and set links from the Hyperlinks palette.

Callouts around the Hyperlinks palette:
- Page destination
- Text Anchor destination
- URL destination
- Delete Hyperlink
- Create New Hyperlink
- Go to Hyperlink Destination
- Go to Hyperlink Source

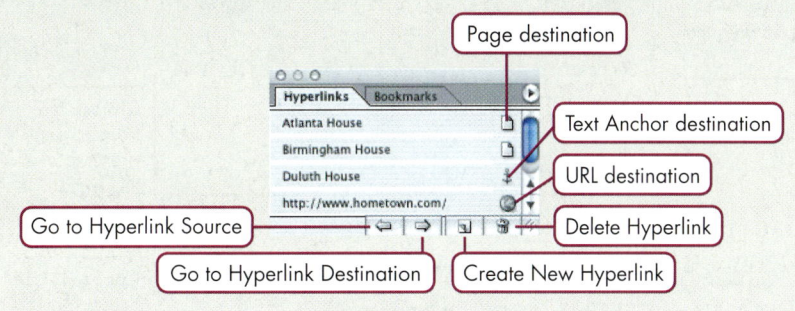

**FIGURE 8.1**

It is important that graphics are handled correctly when a file is packaged for conversion to HTML, especially if GoLive is your editing program. All images can be optimized for the Web, but if you select the Optimized Formatted Images option, all the cropping, scaling, and rotation you have performed in InDesign will be carried over, at a potentially great time savings in GoLive. The selections you make are not exclusive. You can, for example, select Original Images and select Optimized Formatted Images, so you will have the original in the folder to work with, if you wish.

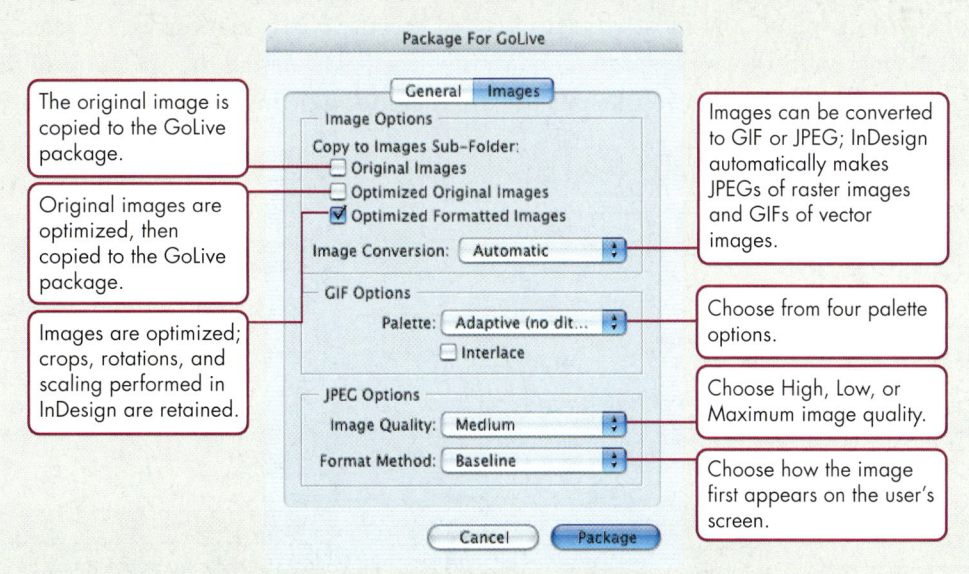

Callouts around the Package For GoLive dialog:
- The original image is copied to the GoLive package.
- Original images are optimized, then copied to the GoLive package.
- Images are optimized; crops, rotations, and scaling performed in InDesign are retained.
- Images can be converted to GIF or JPEG; InDesign automatically makes JPEGs of raster images and GIFs of vector images.
- Choose from four palette options.
- Choose High, Low, or Maximum image quality.
- Choose how the image first appears on the user's screen.

**FIGURE 8.2**

You can export InDesign documents to SVG or SVGZ (a subset of XML, short for Scalable Vector Graphics) format and to JPEG (a common graphics format). SVG contains the most options, because it may include fonts and transparency, which must be flattened.

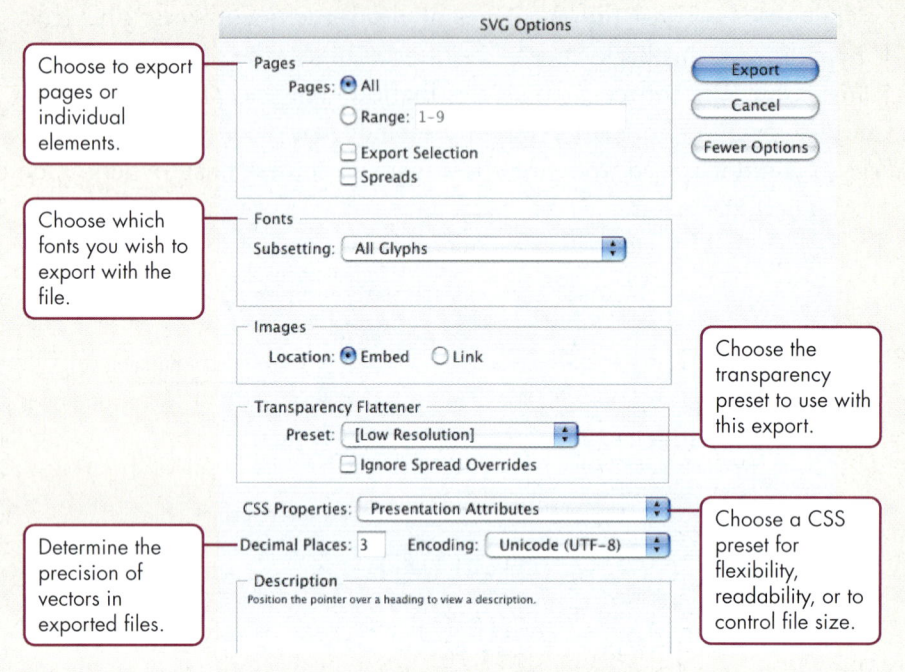

**FIGURE 8.3**

XML (Extensible Markup Language) is a language that solely defines content. XML tags are mapped to the styles applied in your document. You could, for example, use a "BT" XML tag and map it to a "Body Text" style in your document; all text marked with the BT tag would display the Body Text attributes of the document. The most efficient way to execute XML markup is to create document styles and XML tags with the same names. The more clearly you define the structure of your document, the better results you will have when exporting to and importing XML.

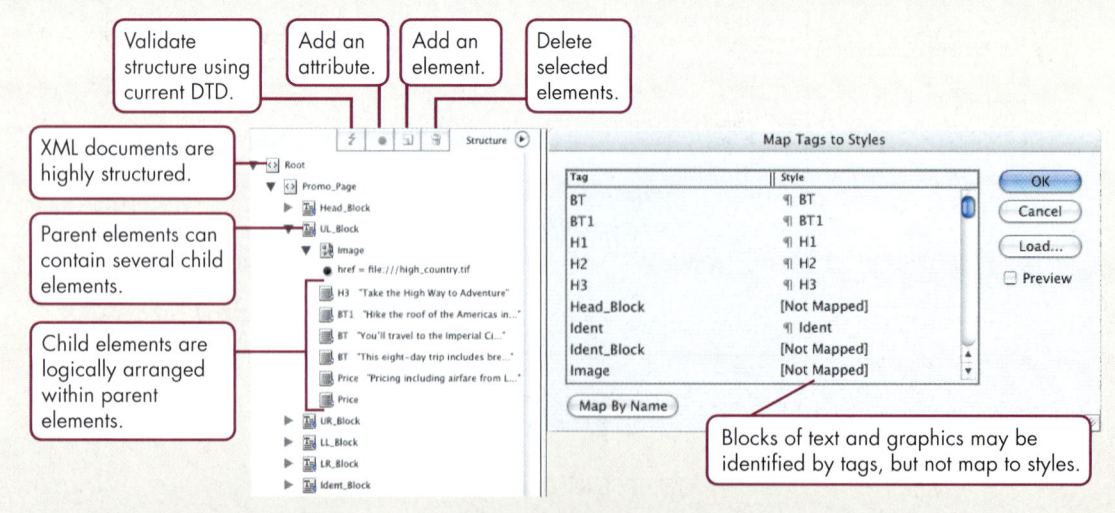

**FIGURE 8.4**

Project 8   Creating HTML and XML Documents

## LESSON 1  Creating Hyperlinks

Navigation tools are probably the most important tools you will use when preparing any document for the Web. Your readers have to be able to move from one page to another; hyperlinks allow them to jump from one element on a page to another location, which can be a different page within the same Web site, or a specific *text anchor* at a defined position in the current page, or any other URL that you specify.

In Project 7, you created hyperlinks for use in PDF files. Creating links for use on a Web page is a very similar process. To create a hyperlink, you first define the *destination*, the location to which the user is directed after clicking the link. You then define one or more *sources*, the objects tagged with the hyperlink. InDesign's Hyperlinks palette allows you to control and specify hyperlinks.

### Create Hyperlinks

1. **Open hometown.indd (fix any reported broken links) and make sure Page 1 is active.**

   The document should open to Page 1 automatically.

   **FIGURE 8.5**

   You're going to create hyperlinks that allow Web viewers to click the house pictures and jump to the page that describes that house. First, you need to set up the destinations.

2. **Open the Hyperlinks palette (Windows>Interactive>Hyperlinks).**

3. **Go to Page 4, then choose New Hyperlink Destination from the Hyperlinks palette menu.**

4. **Be sure the Type menu is set to Page and enter "Atlanta" in the Name field. Choose Fit in Window in the Zoom Setting menu, then click OK.**

**5** Repeat Steps 3 and 4 for the other two houses. The house on the left in Duluth is described on Page 3, and the middle house in Birmingham is on Page 8.

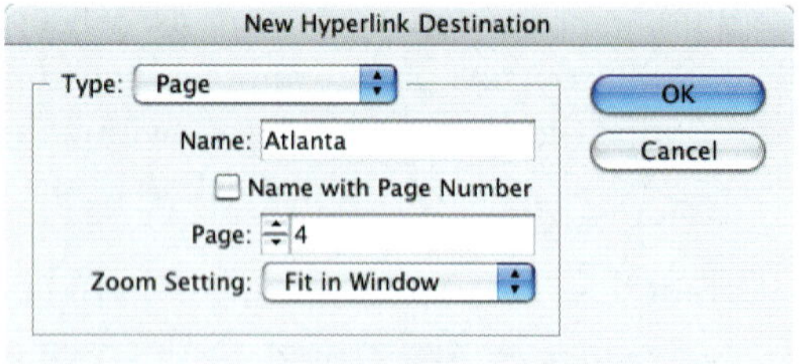

FIGURE 8.6

**6** Return to Page 1 and select the Duluth house (the one on the left). Choose New Hyperlink from the palette menu. Type "Duluth House" in the Name field at the top, choose Duluth from the Name menu in the Destination area, then click OK.

You can override destinations and the zoom setting in the New Hyperlink dialog box. This could be useful if, for example, you have a destination that is referenced by several points of origin; in most cases it appears at 100%, but you want it to appear at a larger size when it's accessed from a specific point of origin.

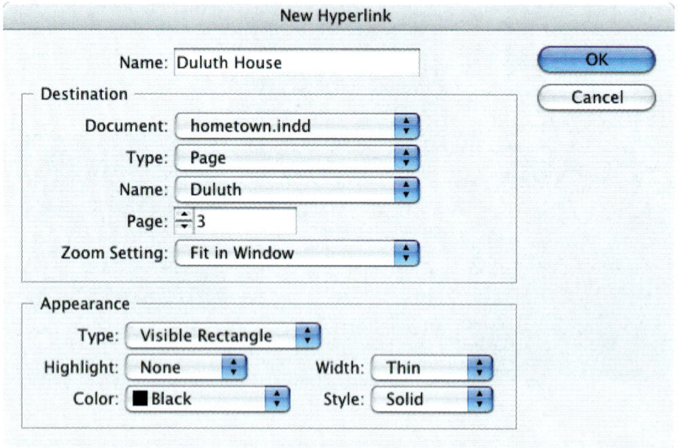

FIGURE 8.7

**7** Repeat Step 6 to set the appropriate destinations for the Birmingham and Atlanta houses. Verify each link by selecting it in the palette, then clicking the right-arrow icon (Go to Hyperlink Destination) at the bottom of the palette. Click the left-arrow icon (Go to Hyperlink Source) to return to the source.

**8** Save the document.

**9** Select the text "www.hometown.com" on Page 1 and choose New Hyperlink from URL to add this as a Web site hyperlink.

**10** Double-click the www.hometown.com entry in the Hyperlinks palette.

InDesign assumes that anything that starts with "www" uses the http protocol, but you still need to add the protocol to ensure that there are no problems with Web browsers that require it.

**11** Add "http://" to the beginning of the URL field, add a trailing "/" at the end, then click OK.

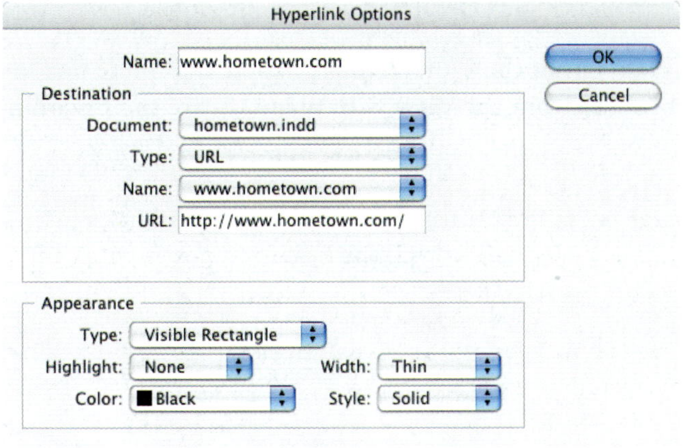

FIGURE 8.8

**12** Save the document and leave it open for the next exercise.

## LESSON 2  Packaging for GoLive

When you have finished creating all your hyperlinks, your InDesign document is ready to be packaged to send to GoLive, so it can be displayed on the Web as an HTML file. The export process can potentially generate hundreds of files, depending upon how your document is structured; InDesign renames all images and all objects exported as images with generic names such as image01.jpg. InDesign will automatically create a folder in which your package is placed.

You simply need to choose Package for GoLive from the File menu, then select the appropriate options. InDesign will create a PDF file that is an image of the entire page, a number of XML files, a cascading style-sheet file, files for each story in the document, a toc.html file, and folders for each photo. If you include both the original and optimized versions of an image, both will be placed in that photo's folder. The toc.html file provides a linked table of contents of the package, referencing the generic names to the real names of the images.

Once you export an InDesign document to GoLive, you are ready to create your HTML document. When you open the package in GoLive CS (not in earlier versions of GoLive), the preview opens in a separate window. You can drag objects from the preview window into GoLive. You cannot drag from the preview into other HTML editors.

## Package for GoLive

**1** Continue in the open document, hometown.indd.

**2** Choose File>Package For GoLive. Navigate to your WIP_08 folder and click Save.

The Package For GoLive dialog box appears.

**3** Click the General tab, check the View Package When Complete box, and choose either GoLive or your Internet browser from the View with menu. Leave the Encoding menu at its default of UTF-8.

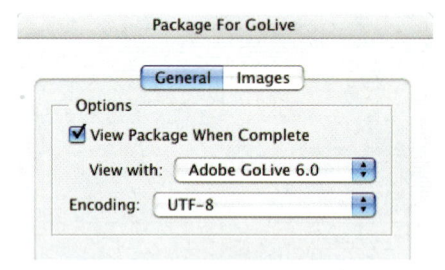

FIGURE 8.9

**4** Click the Images tab, and check only the Optimized Formatted Images box. Leave all other options at their defaults, then click Package.

If you choose Optimized Formatted Images, only the JPEG and GIF images resulting from the conversion from TIF and EPS images — not the original images — will appear in the exported folder. The Optimize Formatted Images option retains any modifications to the image, such as cropping and scaling, so you will not have to repeat them in GoLive. The Optimized Original Images option simply optimizes the images; you would have to modify them in GoLive.

FIGURE 8.10

The file toc.html appears in a new window in the application that you specified in Step 3.

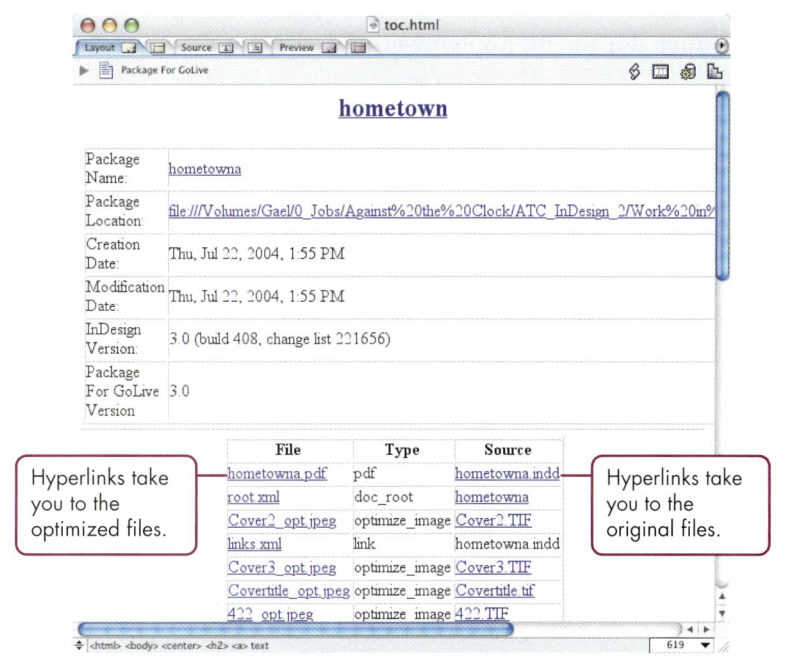

**FIGURE 8.11**

**5** Click the **PDF** and **JPEG** elements in the toc.html file.

Acrobat, your browser, or GoLive (depending on the file type and the choice you made in Step 3) opens the files so you can view them.

**6** Close the HTML document without saving, and leave the InDesign document open.

## LESSON 3  Exporting to SVG

SVG (Scalable Vector Graphics) format is an open-standard vector graphics format that lets you include high-resolution graphics in your Web pages. You can export a single object, a page, a spread, or an entire document in SVG format. If you choose to export an entire document or a range of pages, each page (or spread, if you checked that option) will be contained in its own file. You can choose to export documents using either SVG or SVG Compressed (SVGZ) format.

When you export to SVG, you need to use the transparency flattener, just as you would if exporting to PDF or printing a file. Since SVG files will, for the most part, be viewed on the Web at low resolution, you will almost always use the Low Resolution flattener preset.

SVG files can contain metadata, as can all files exported for use on the Web. They are image files intended to be inserted into Web pages; they do not contain hyperlinks and other files. If you want to link them, you must do so in an HTML-editing program.

## Export to SVG

**1** Continue in the open document, hometown.indd.

**2** Choose File>Export>SVG, and navigate to your WIP_08 folder and click Save.

**3** Select the following export settings:

| | |
|---|---|
| Pages: | All (do not check the Spreads box) |
| Fonts Subsetting: | Only Glyphs Used |
| Images Location: | Embed |
| Transparency Flattener Preset: | Low Resolution |

**Accept the default CSS Properties, Decimal Places, and Encoding.**

You might need to click the More Options button to access all of these options.

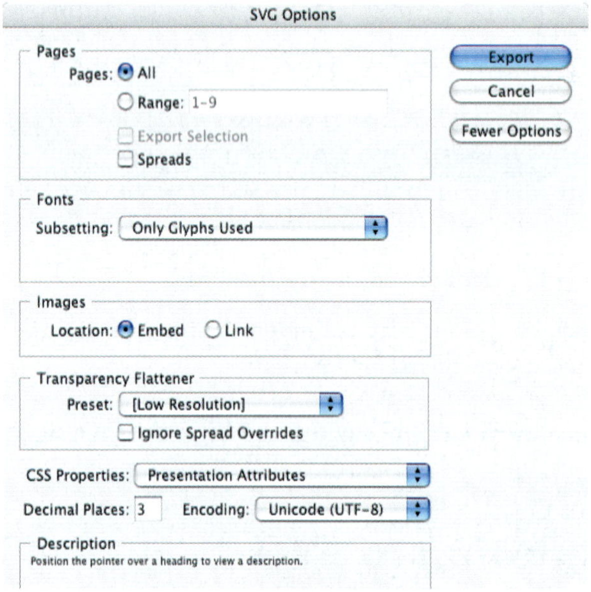

**FIGURE 8.12**

**4** Click Export, then check your WIP_08 folder.

Nine SVG files have been exported. They are named hometown.svg, and hometown2.svg through hometown9.svg.

**5** Click the house on Page 2 with the Selection tool.

**6** Choose File>Export>SVG, and save to your WIP_08 folder as "ht_house_1.svg".

**7** Check the Export Selection box and leave the rest of the settings at their defaults.

You can view the pages and the image in Microsoft Internet Explorer, and insert them into a GoLive document.

**8** Close any open SVG files and leave the document open for the next lesson.

## LESSON 4  Exporting JPEG

JPEG is a universally viewable format that uses image compression for display on the Web. It is a *lossy* compression mechanism; the more the image is compressed, the more data that is lost, so the more the image quality deteriorates. You can export individual images, pages, and spreads as JPEG files. Like SVG files, they are image files, and do not contain hyperlinks or other interactive features.

### Export a JPEG File

**1** Continue in the open document, hometown.indd.

**2** Choose File>Export>JPEG, navigate to your WIP_08 folder and click Save.

The Export JPEG dialog box appears.

**3** Choose to export Page 2 and check the Spreads box. Set the Image Quality menu to Low and the Format Method menu to Progressive. Click the Export button.

This tells InDesign to export the Pages 2–3 spread at a resolution of 72 dpi with a Progressive format, which gets data on the screen quickly, filling in the blanks until the image is up to its full resolution. This is adequate, since the image is only for viewing on-screen. The alternate method, Baseline, displays the image from top to bottom. Image Quality options are Low, Medium, High, or Maximum; for the Web, Low or Medium quality will always be adequate.

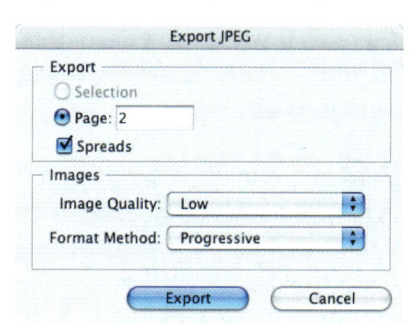

FIGURE 8.13

**4** Open the JPEG in a browser to view it, or place it in a Web-page layout program.

**5** Close the JPEG and InDesign files without saving.

## LESSON 5  Tagging XML Document Content

XML is a presentation-neutral markup language that solely defines content. In contrast to HTML tags, XML tags define the content between them, not the presentation of that content. You can define any XML tags that you need, as long as you follow the standard rules of tag syntax. For example, if you were creating a database or Web page about birds, you might create the following XML elements:

```
<bird_type>Large</bird_type>
<bird_color>Green</bird_color>
<bird_state>Active</bird_state>
<bird_beak_shape>Curved</bird_beak_shape>
<bird_beak_color>Gray</bird_beak_color>
<bird_volume>Loud</bird_volume>
```

Each of these XML tags is perfectly valid. You can program any application that understands XML to interpret those tags and extract meaningful information about their content. If you were creating a database about birds in a program that can interpret XML, you could program the database to read and interpret (or *parse*) the XML to create a database entry for that particular bird.

A program that interprets XML would encounter the first tag, store it, then interpret all the information before the closing tag as data. What the program does with that data and its associated tag definition depends on your instructions. It could build a database, import the data into a different format, or use the data in an e-commerce transaction to place an electronic order.

Applications can generate XML, interpret and execute XML, or both. InDesign can both export (generate) and import (interpret) XML, but it requires some intensive setup work to make this happen, especially if you want to create automatic layouts from XML. InDesign can interpret XML code to flow text and images into a pre-built template based on a set of simple rules. It takes a great deal of work and testing, but it is possible to create an InDesign template that can generate a complete layout in seconds, based on XML source data. Neither the creation of the template nor the XML coding is a trivial process.

Because you create your own tags in XML, you must tell an interpreter of XML what those tags mean and what to do when the tags are encountered. You can do this by creating a DTD (Document Type Descriptor) file that contains definitions of XML tags. For example, you could create a file named "bird attributes.dtd" that programs can search to learn what to do when interpreting the bird tags above. The XML specification doesn't require the use of a DTD, but many predefined XML tag sets require it.

You can create and apply structural tags to InDesign document elements with the options in the Tags palette. You can create tags one at a time, or load an entire set of tags from an XML file or a different InDesign document. Rather than creating tags from a document's existing styles, you can select each instance of a style, and apply an appropriate tag. Once you have defined a set of tags, you can use InDesign to map the tags to document text styles.

## Tag Document Content

**1**  Open bean_ad_xml.indd. Save the file with the same name to your WIP_08 folder.

**2**  Choose Window>Tags to open the Tags palette.

The only item in the palette is Root. We've created a set of tags for you already in another file.

**3**  Choose Load Tags from the Tags palette Options menu and load the file ad_tags.xml.

The Tags palette is populated with tags.

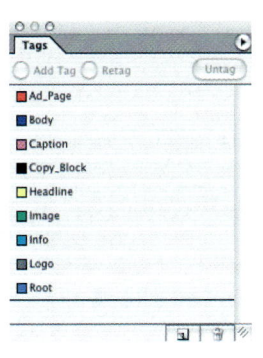

FIGURE 8.14

**4**  Choose Map Styles to Tags from the Tags palette menu. Map each paragraph style to the tag of the same name. Click OK when finished.

This process automatically tags all the styled text in the document.

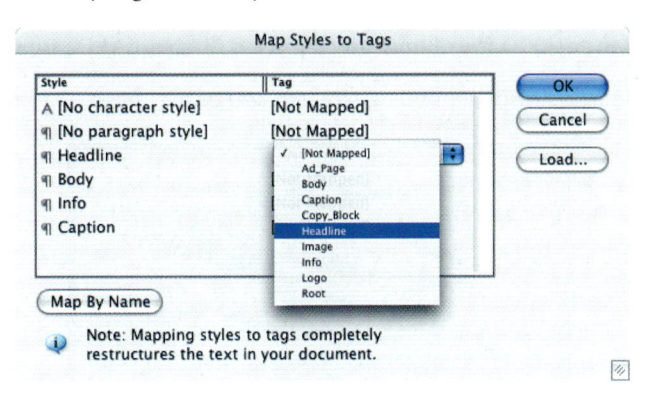

FIGURE 8.15

**5** **Choose View>Structure>Show Tag Markers.**

Tag markers are colored brackets that surround tagged text.

FIGURE 8.16

**6** **Choose View>Structure>Show Tagged Frames.**

Each tagged frame is colored with the color assigned to the tag; the text frame is assigned the automatically created Story tag.

FIGURE 8.17

**7** **Zoom out, if necessary. Select the frame containing the image of the beans, and click the Image tag in the Tags palette.**

This is how you tag any frame. The mapping shown in Step 4 only applies tags to styled text, not to frames.

**8** **Change to the Direct Selection tool and select the Center Market logo, which is in the frame that also contains the text "More Food. Better Food." Assign the Logo tag to the object.**

The two graphic elements display in green (Image) and gray (Logo).

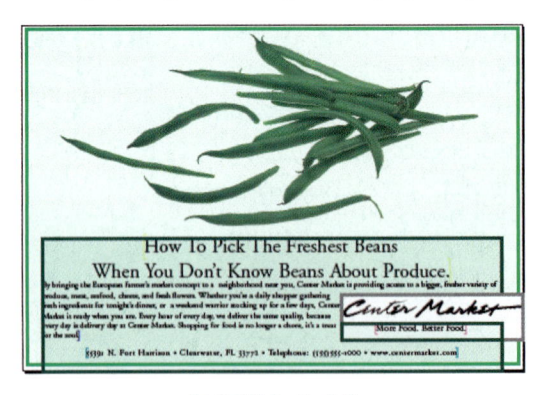

FIGURE 8.18

**9** **Choose View>Structure>Hide Tagged Frames and View>Structure>Hide Tag Markers to get rid of the distracting colors.**

**10** **Save the document and leave it open for the next lesson.**

## LESSON 6  Assigning Structure in an XML Document

An InDesign document has visual structure, but logically it's a random set of frames containing text or graphic information. Even if you know what it all means, InDesign can't interpret it until you define a logical structure for the document. Establishing document structure is a requirement when using XML with InDesign.

Setting up document structure is a two-part process. First, you need to determine the names and uses of the tags you will need, then add your tags to the Tags palette. Second, you need to assign tags to page elements. After you apply all the tags to a document, you can use the Structure view to modify the document's structure as needed.

"Root" is a special tag that defines the starting basis for any XML document; it always appears by default and is not used for tagging content. The document designer creates all the other tags. The relationship between a frame and its content is described as a parent/child relationship. Placed graphics are referenced as files on disk.

### Assign Structure

**1** Continue in the open document, bean_ad_xml.indd.

**2** Choose View>Structure>Show Structure to display the ad in Structure view.

You can also press Command-Option-1 (Macintosh) or Control-Alt-1 (Windows) to display the Structure view. The Structure view appears with two Story elements and two graphic elements named Image and Logo, which you tagged in the previous exercise.

**FIGURE 8.19**

**3** Click the triangles next to each Story element to expand them and show the child elements.

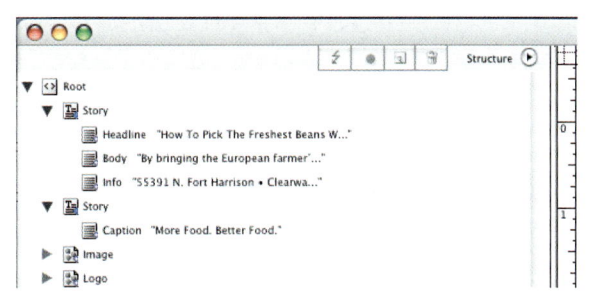

**FIGURE 8.20**

**4** Click the first Story element, then click the Copy_Block tag in the Tags palette.

This reassigns the frame marked with the automatically generated Story tag to the imported Copy_Block tag.

**5** Click the second Story element, then double-click the Story tag in the Tags palette. This allows you to change the tag's name. Rename it "Logo_Block" and press Return/Enter (or click OK) to save the change.

The Story element in the Structure view changes to Logo_Block.

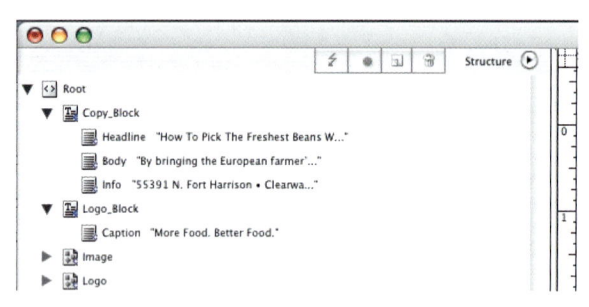

FIGURE 8.21

**6** Drag the Logo element up over the Logo_Block element. Release the mouse button when the Logo_Block element becomes highlighted.

This action turns the Logo image into a child of the Logo_Block element. If you click the triangle next to the Logo element, you can see how it is referenced in the file. Note that moving elements around and making them children of other elements doesn't affect their placement in the document; it only increases the level of structure in the document.

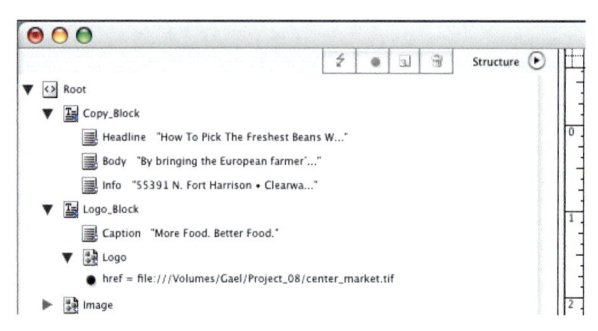

FIGURE 8.22

**7** Click the Root element in the Structure view, then click the Add an Element button above it. Assign this new element the Ad_Page tag, then click OK.

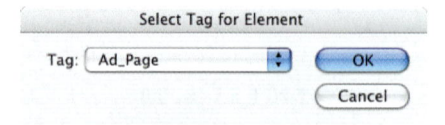

FIGURE 8.23

The new element appears at the bottom of the list.

Project 8   Creating HTML and XML Documents   **307**

**8**   Drag the Ad_Page element up to just below the Root element, then release the mouse button.

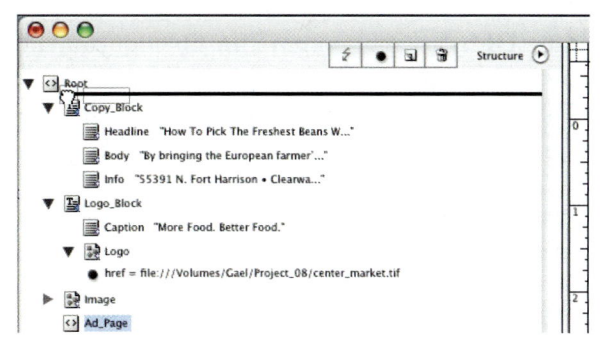

FIGURE 8.24

**9**   Shift-click all the elements below the Ad_Page element, and drag them to the Ad_Page element. Release the mouse button when the Ad_Page element becomes highlighted.

This step assigns all the document elements as children of the parent Ad_Page element. The document is now as structured as it's going to get. Every element is subordinate to the Ad_Page element.

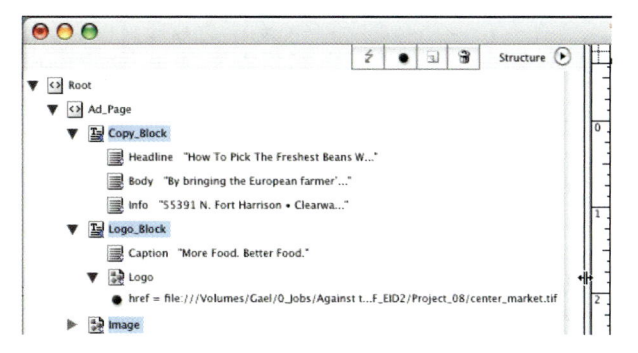

FIGURE 8.25

**10**   Save the document and continue.

## LESSON 7   Exporting XML

If an XML file is to be useful, you must export it in a meaningful way. As you noted in the last lesson, every image contains a path to its location on your computer. You should remove these paths, called ***absolute addresses***, because the recipient will most likely not have paths named identically to yours. If you do not remove the absolute address, the XML document will attempt to follow the path to the document on your computer.

The most efficient way to accomplish this is to use InDesign's Package feature, then edit the file attributes. While the file can be opened in a browser such as Internet Explorer, the browser can't interpret the file without a DTD, so it merely displays the content of the XML file.

## Export XML

**1** Use the Package routine (File>Package) to move the open document, hometown.indd, and all linked images to a new folder inside your WIP_08 folder. Accept the default folder name of "bean_ad_xml.indd Folder" in the Package dialog box. Do not include fonts. Ignore the warning generated during preflight about RGB images. Close the document, saving when prompted.

**2** Open the new folder and move all the files inside the Links folder to the main folder (the one containing the bean_ad_xml.indd file). Delete the Links folder and the bean_ad text file.

All elements are now at the same level; this simplifies the process of sending exported XML and document images to another user.

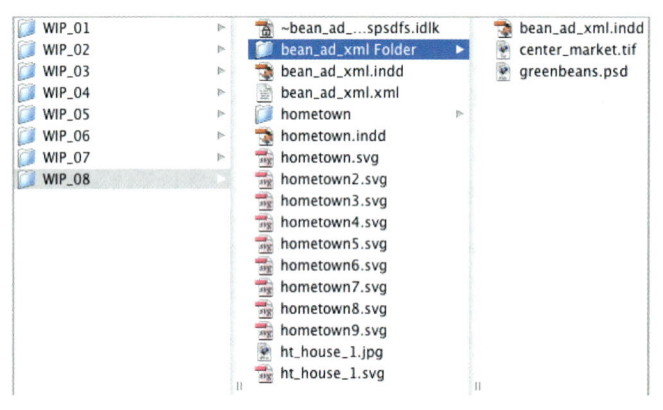

FIGURE 8.26

**3** Double-click the bean_ad_xml.indd file in the Finder or Windows Explorer to open it. Display the Structure view of the document. Expand the Root and Ad_Page elements by clicking the triangles next to their names. Click the triangle next to the Image element, and select the attribute that starts with "href=file///". Choose Edit from the Structure view menu.

**4** Drag in the URL to select everything between "file:///" and "greenbeans.psd", then delete it. The resulting URL should be simply "file:///greenbeans.psd". Click OK to change the attribute.

This procedure removes system dependencies from the URL. URLs without file paths assume the file is in the same directory as the InDesign document. By removing the file path from the URL, you ensure that InDesign can find the referenced file when importing XML as long as the file is at the same level as the InDesign document in the file system.

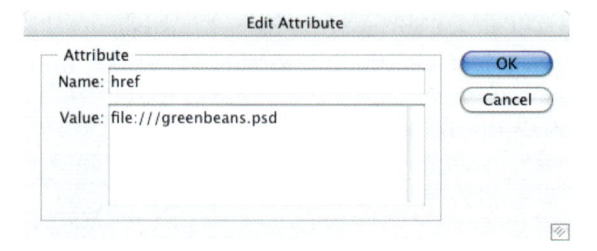

FIGURE 8.27

**5** Expand the Logo element within the Logo_Block parent and change its href attribute value as in Step 4.

FIGURE 8.28

**6** Save the document, then choose File>Export. In the Format (Macintosh) or Save As Type (Windows) menu, choose XML. Accept the default file name, and click Save to export to your bean_ad_xml.indd Folder.

FIGURE 8.29

**7** In the XML Export Options dialog box that appears, click the Images tab, then ensure that no boxes are checked. Click Export to continue.

The images should be where you want them. Because you are not exporting images, the Image Options Settings have no effect. If the images do not automatically update, go to the folder and link to the image.

**8** Hide InDesign and locate the file you just exported. It may be named bean_ad.xml or bean_ad_xml.xml, depending on your platform. Launch a Web browser and open this file by choosing File>Open in your browser, or by dragging the file onto your browser.

Note the structure defined by the tags. By imposing a structure, anyone can look at the XML and determine the type of content used in the original file. It's also very easy to change content as long as the tag structure is maintained; for example, you could create a series of food-related ads from this one XML file by altering the wording and the image file name specified in the image attribute.

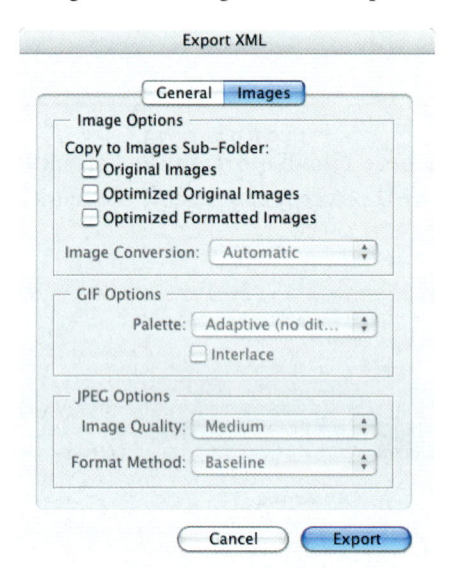

**FIGURE 8.30**

**9** Close the browser and return to InDesign. Save and close the file.

## LESSON 8  Importing XML

Earlier in this project, we said that InDesign not only can export (write) XML, but also import (interpret) it. This allows you to use generic encoding (applying styles independent from the publishing program into which you will place the file), create text and images for the document, then bring the pieces together just as if you were pre-tagging files for your style sheets in a word processor. As you work through this lesson, you will see just how fast and easy it can be to take XML's structure and create dynamic documents.

### Import XML

**1** Open the document ad_shell.indd and save it to the folder containing the exported XML file from the last exercise.

This file is based on the original ad file, but all the content is missing. All that remains are empty frames.

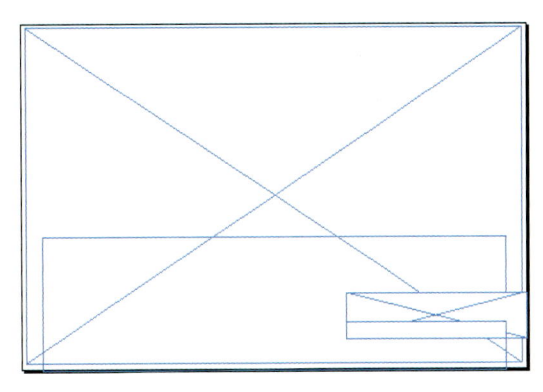

**FIGURE 8.31**

**2** **From the Tags palette Options menu, choose Load Tags and select the XML file that you exported in the last exercise.**

This doesn't import the entire XML file, it just loads the tag definitions from the file.

**3** **Choose Map Tags to Styles from the palette menu. Click the Map By Name button, then click OK.**

The tag and style names match, so this is an easy way to map these items. Note that not all the tags map to styles, nor should they.

**4** **Close the Tags palette. Choose File>Import XML, and select the bean_ad.xml (or bean_ad_xml.xml) file you exported earlier.**

**5** **Not much seems to happen, but choose View>Structure>Show Structure and look at the Structure view.**

All the elements from the exporting document are present.

**6** **Drag the Image element from the Structure window to the largest frame in the document.**

This simultaneously assigns the content to the frame and tags the frame.

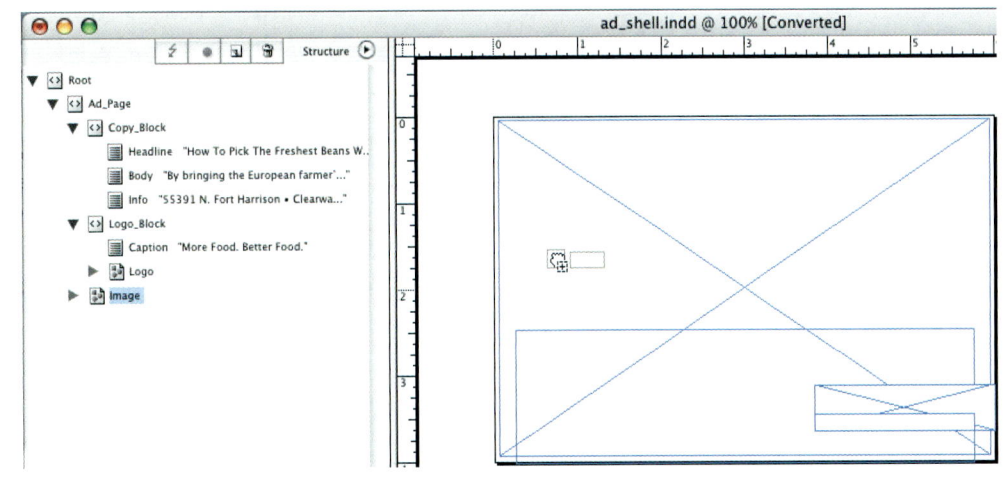

**FIGURE 8.32**

**Project 8** Creating HTML and XML Documents

**7** Drag the Copy_Block element to the empty text frame (the second-largest frame in the document).

Watch the text reformat itself, because you mapped tags to styles.

**8** Drag the Logo element to the logo frame then drag the Caption element to the caption frame below the logo frame.

The resulting layout may not match the original ad exactly. For example, InDesign can't tell if an image referenced in XML is centered or scaled; the default behavior is to place referenced images into the upper left of a frame at 100% scale. Documents with content from imported XML need some manual touch-up to achieve the desired outcome.

**9** Save and the file and leave it open for the final exercise.

## Modify Your Ad

**1** Open any text editor, such as Notepad, TextEdit, or Word.

**2** Open the XML file you just imported into the ad layout.

**3** In the headline, replace the word "Beans" with "Tomatoes".

**4** In the Logo_Block image, replace "greenbeans.psd" with "tomato.psd".

**5** Save the file.

**6** Copy the file tomato.psd from your Project_08 folder into your bean_ad_xml Folder.

**7** Re-import the XML file.

The text and the image are automatically updated.

FIGURE 8.33

**8** Close the file without saving.

## CAREERS IN DESIGN

**REPURPOSING DOCUMENTS**

Although InDesign is primarily intended for preparing print documents, today's communication professional is aware of, and able to produce documents for, a variety of document delivery methods.

You have prepared yourself to be a versatile player in the communications business. You are capable of converting InDesign documents to PDF with interactivity already embedded — they don't have to be further massaged after leaving your desk. You have also learned other export processes, which prepare InDesign documents for placement into other documents as EPS or PDF files, or for manipulation into effective Web pages with a minimum of intervention.

As the office and the creative environment become more intermingled, the ability to move documents in and out of generic text and database programs and into the publishing stream has become important — and will become more so. The standard that will be applied is XML, to which you have been introduced. You should be eager to expand your knowledge of Portable Document Format and XML to make yourself an even more valuable communication professional.

## SUMMARY

This chapter explained how InDesign works with XML and with Web-oriented formats. You prepared a document by adding hyperlinks, then packaged it for GoLive. You also exported files to SVG, a vector format, and JPEG, a raster format. The acronym "XML" encompasses a range of extremely complex technology — new formats and features are introduced constantly, creating an alphabet soup of acronyms, such as SOAP, DOM, XSLT, XHTML, and more. The information in this project barely scratched the surface of this technology; a full course in all the nuances and abilities of XML could easily fill more than a thousand pages. You learned about the InDesign tools used in the creation and use of XML. You exported XML and imported it back into an empty document, then edited it so the document automatically updated. With experience, you'll appreciate the ease of creating layouts from XML files compared to placing items one at a time. Future versions of InDesign should be able to generate complete, ready-to-print layouts from increasingly complex XML variants, but for now, a little grunt work is needed to use XML effectively with InDesign.

## KEY TERMS

| | | |
|---|---|---|
| absolute address | hyperlink | structure |
| Cascading Style Sheet | Internet Explorer | SVG |
| DTD | interpret | SVGZ |
| generate | JPEG | tag |
| GIF | package | URL |
| GoLive | PDF | XML |
| HTML | root | |

# CHECKING CONCEPTS AND TERMS

## MULTIPLE CHOICE

**Check the letter of the correct answer for each of the following:**

1. Which of the following is true with respect to creating hyperlinks?
   a. You must first define the point of origination.
   b. A hyperlink source can have many destinations.
   c. A destination point can have many sources.
   d. Hyperlinks must point only to destinations in the document.

2. When can you export directly to HTML?
   a. When you have defined all the hyperlinks
   b. When you have confirmed that all the links are correct
   c. When you use the Package feature
   d. Never

3. Which of the following is true of SVG files?
   a. SVG is an open-standard raster format.
   b. You will usually use low-resolution transparency flattening.
   c. You can export only whole pages.
   d. SVG files contain hyperlinks and are linked to other files.

4. Which of the following is true of JPEG files exported for the Web?
   a. You should always use high quality when exporting.
   b. The format is universally viewable.
   c. JPEG is a lossless compression method.
   d. JPEG images are vector images.

5. What do XML tags define?
   a. A document's structure
   b. A document's appearance
   c. Positioning of frames on pages
   d. Positioning of objects within frames

6. What is needed to properly interpret XML?
   a. Its tags must be mapped to styles.
   b. You must use a complex coding system.
   c. You must have a valid Document Type Descriptor.
   d. You need a PDF preview.

7. Which of the following is true about XML tags?
   a. They solely define content.
   b. They define content and appearance.
   c. They solely define appearance.
   d. They are proprietary.

8. What tags appear in an XML document by default?
   a. The Parent tag
   b. The Root tag
   c. The Story tag
   d. None of the above

9. How is XML structure assigned?
   a. It's picked up from the layout.
   b. It's assigned in the Tags palette.
   c. It's assigned in the Content menu.
   d. Elements are dragged into position.

10. How can you edit the content of an XML file?
    a. Redo it in InDesign, then re-export the file.
    b. Open it in a browser and modify it.
    c. Open it in a text editor and modify it.
    d. You can't edit the content of an XML file.

## DISCUSSION QUESTIONS

1. Discuss the advantages and disadvantages of repurposing InDesign documents as Web documents of all types.

2. Because it is so easy to format documents in InDesign, why would you choose to use XML as a publishing method?

# SKILL DRILL

Skill Drills reinforce project skills. Each skill reinforced is the same, or nearly the same, as a skill presented in the lessons. Detailed instructions are provided in a step-by-step format. The first two exercises and the last two exercises must be performed in the order in which they appear.

## 1. Create Hyperlinks for an Online Catalog

Back Country Outfitters is a large supplier of outdoor recreational equipment and clothing. They produce a quarterly catalog that is mailed to millions of customers. In a cost-cutting move, they are switching over, to a large extent, to an online catalog. Rather than linking to each product for navigation, they want to link from the cover of the catalog to each section. Their research has shown them that sales are greater by 33% when customers browse the catalog rather than having a direct link.

1. Open the document outfitters.indd. The document should open to Page 1. If it doesn't, access the page. You're going to create hyperlinks so Web viewers can more easily navigate the document. Save the document to your WIP_08 folder.

2. Open the Hyperlinks palette (Windows>Interactive>Hyperlinks).

3. Go to Page 5, then choose New Hyperlink Destination from the palette menu.

4. Type "Clothing" in the Name field and leave the Zoom Setting menu at Fixed. Do this for the remaining four sections (Tents, Packs, Fishing, and Cycling) and for the cover (refer to the page numbers on the cover).

5. Return to the cover and select the clothing icon. Choose New Hyperlink from the palette menu. Set the Type menu to Page, then type "Clothing Icon" in the Name field at the top, and choose Clothing from the Name menu in the Destination area. Choose Visible Rectangle in the Appearance Type menu. Click OK. Verify the link by selecting it in the palette, then clicking the right-arrow icon at the bottom of the palette. Click the left-arrow icon to return to the source.

6. Select the Clothing text with the Type tool and choose New Hyperlink from the palette menu. Type "Clothing Text" in the Name field and choose Clothing as the destination. Choose Invisible Rectangle in the Appearance Type menu and click OK.

**FIGURE 8.34**

7. Repeat Steps 5 and 6 for the remaining four links to section opening pages.

8. On each of the hyperlinked pages, use the Type tool to highlight the "Cover" text in the upper-right corner of the page. Link it back to the cover, accepting the default names.

9. Select the text "www.backcountry.com" on the cover and choose New Hyperlink from URL to add a hyperlink to a Web site.

10. Double-click the www.backcountry.com entry in the Hyperlinks palette; add "http://" to the beginning of the URL field, add a trailing "/" at the end, then click OK.

    If you were going to complete the links for the online catalog, you would link each page to the page before and after, and each page to the cover.

11. Save the document and leave it open for the next exercise.

## 2. Package for GoLive

After you have linked your catalog for online viewing you can package it for assembly into a Web page in Adobe GoLive. While InDesign does not support direct export to HTML, routing the data through a program such as GoLive ensures that the page will be properly constructed, instead of simply "repurposed" from a print document to a Web document.

1. Continue in the open document, outfitters.indd.

2. Choose File>Package For GoLive and save to your WIP_08 folder.

3. Choose to view the package when complete, with either GoLive or your Internet browser; leave the encoding at the default setting.

4. Click the Images tab and check only the Optimized Formatted Images box. Leave all other options at their defaults and click Package.

5. Review the file that is created, toc.html. Click several of the elements and note that the non-image files are viewable — though not necessarily understandable — XML. The image files are all viewable.

6. Close the HTML document without saving.

7. Save and close the InDesign document.

## 3. Tag an XML Document

Adventure Tours offers exciting travel opportunities for its clients. It produces flyers that contain "teasers" for four tours. Using XML will allow you to quickly create these documents.

1. Open adventuretours.indd and save the file to your WIP_08 folder.

2. Open the Tags palette from the Window menu.

3. Choose New Tag from the palette menu and create 7 new tags to match the names of the paragraph styles, plus two additional tags named "Image" and "Promo_Page".

4. Ensure that no paragraph styles are selected.

5. Choose Map Styles to Tags from the Tags palette menu. Map each paragraph style to the tag of the same name.

6. Select each of the color images and tag them with the Image tag.

7. Check the tagging by making tag frames and tag markers visible (View>Structure>Tag Frames/Tag Markers), then hide them.

8. Save the document and leave it open for the next exercise.

## 4. Structure Your XML Document

Once your document has its tags, you can apply structure to it. When you apply structure to a document, you truly begin to harness the power of XML.

1. Continue in the open document.

2. Show the Structure view.

3. Click the triangle next to each Story element to expand them and show the child elements.

4. Add five new tags to the Tags palette named "Head_Block", "UL_Block", "UR_Block", "LL_Block", and "LR_Block".

5. Click the first Story element, then click the Head_Block tag in the Tags palette to reassign it.

6. Click the four remaining stories, and assign the respective tags to the upper-left (UL), upper-right (UR), lower-left (LL) and lower-right (LR) stories. Drag the respective images into the appropriate story blocks.

7. Double-click the remaining Story tag and rename it "Ident_Block".

8. Click the Root element in the Structure view then add a new element. Assign the new element the Promo_Page tag.

9. Drag the Promo_Page element up to just below the Root element.

10. Select all elements below the Promo_Page element and drag them to the Promo_Page element.

11. Click the triangle next to the Promo_Page element to view your structured document.

12. Save the document and close it.

# CHALLENGE

Challenge exercises expand on, or are somewhat related to, skills presented in the lessons. Each exercise provides a brief introduction, followed by instructions presented in a numbered-step format that are not as detailed as those in the Skill Drill exercises. You should perform these exercises in the order in which they appear.

## 1. Export Files as Images

You will frequently find it useful to repurpose your documents by incorporating them into other documents. This might be the case with a poster or book cover — or even with an ad or catalog page. It certainly is not unheard of to advertise your free catalog in an ad that is also designed to sell a specific product. You will export both an entire document and selected images in SVG format for use in a Web page.

1. Open the document fi_promo.indd.

2. Export the document as SVG with the following specifications:

    Pages: All (do not check the Spreads box)
    Fonts Subsetting: All Glyphs
    Images Location: Embed
    Transparency Flattener Preset: Low Resolution

    Accept the default CSS Properties, Decimal Places, and Encoding settings.

3. Select the Heathergems image on Page 1.

4. Export this selection to your WIP_08 folder as "heathergems.svg", accepting the program's defaults.

5. View the pages and images in either GoLive or your Internet browser.

6. Close any open SVG files.

7. Go to Page 2 and select any single suncatcher.

8. Export it as a JPEG file to your WIP_08 folder with a Medium image quality and a Progressive format method.

9. Open the file in a browser to view it or place it in a Web-page layout program.

10. Close all files without saving.

## 2. Export to XML

Producing documents is more than simply creating them. It includes the somewhat demanding chore of exporting files to the formats in which they will be used. Your InDesign document is perfect for print, but a document with XML tags can be used in a number of other ways, as well. You're going to export a familiar XML file.

1. Open the document adventure_tag.indd and save it to your WIP_08 folder.

2. Use InDesign's Package function to move this file and its associated files to a new folder within your WIP_08 folder. Do not include fonts and ignore the warning during preflight about RGB images.

3. Open the folder and move all files to the same level. Remove the empty Links folder and the text file.

4. Open the InDesign file within the folder and display the Structure view.

5. Expand the elements until you are able to view the paths to the image files.

6. Remove path information between "file:///" and the beginning of the actual file name to change the addresses from absolute to relative addresses.

7. Save the document.

8. Export the document to XML. Ensure that no images are exported.

9. View the file in a browser or in GoLive.

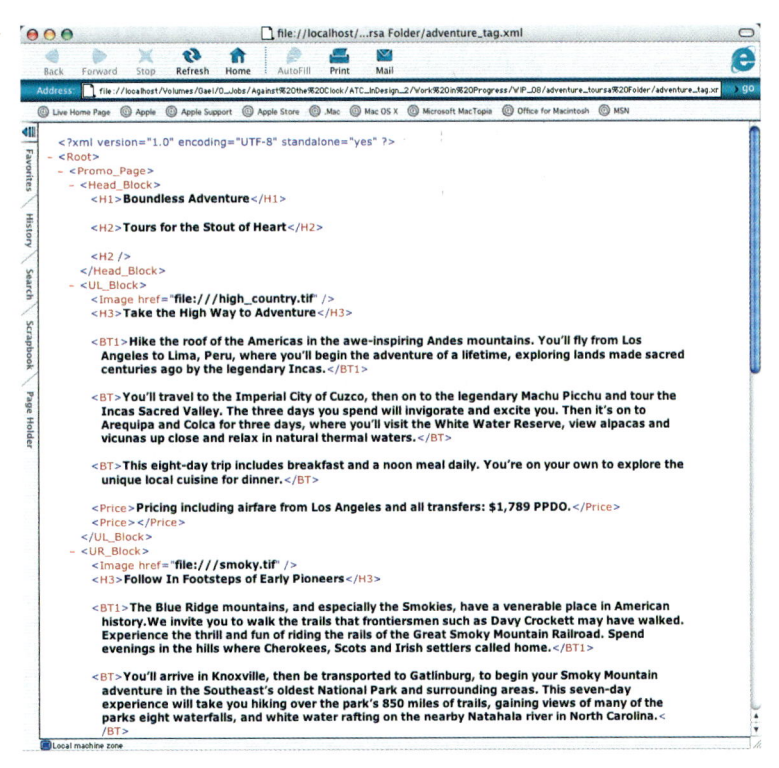

**FIGURE 8.35**

10. Save and close all open files.

## 3. Import an XML Document

XML documents can be imported into any programs that support this open format, including InDesign. In this Challenge, you will import the file you previously exported into a document that has been designed with pre-existing placeholder frames.

1. Open the document promo_shell.indd.

2. Load the tags from the document you just exported, adventure_tag.xml.

3. Map the tags to the styles of the same name.

4. Import the XML file adventure_tag.xml. The images again have an absolute reference.

5. Expand the Root, Promo_Page, and UL_Block elements.

6. Drag the UL image to the graphic frame in the upper-left block, then drag the UL_Block element to the upper-left block.

7. Fill the other blocks and images using the XML elements.

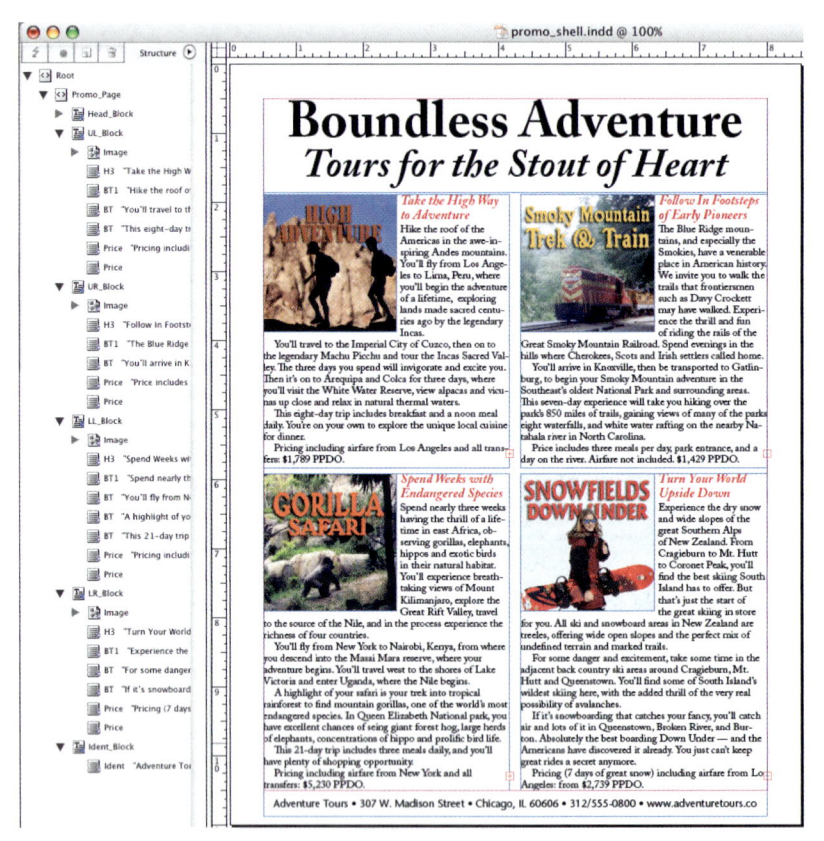

FIGURE 8.36

8. Save the document and leave it open for the next Challenge.

## 4. Edit Your XML Document

Rather than making simple changes in InDesign, then re-exporting and re-importing the XML file, it is easier and faster to simply make the changes in the XML file and re-import (assuming, of course, that you have other uses for the XML file). You want to change the "pitch" of the Smoky Mountain adventure to a different audience, and the travel planners have managed to negotiate a better price. You're going to change the picture and the price by typing in the XML file to change the image reference and the price; you will then import the file to InDesign.

1. Copy the file "mountaintop.tif" into your adventure_tag folder.
2. Open a text editor, and with it, open the document adventure_tag.xml.
3. If your text editor has a "Find" function, search for "smoky.tif" and replace this image with "mountaintop.tif".
4. Scroll down and change the price of this vacation to $1,379 PPDO.
5. Save the file as "adventure_tag_r1.xml". The "r1" designation tells you it is the first revision, so you can revert to the previous version if you wish.
6. Import adventure_tag_r1.xml, with the "Append Content" button selected.
7. Drag the UR_Block content you just imported (within the Root and Promo_Page at the bottom of the Structure list) into the upper Promo_Page list.
8. Delete the content of the old UR_Block and image, replacing it with the content you just imported.

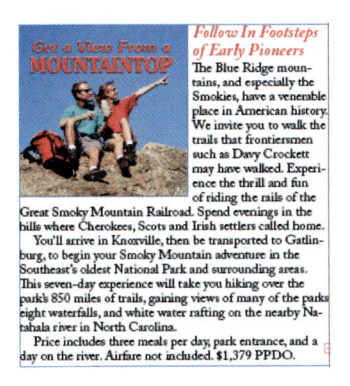

**FIGURE 8.37**

9. Save and close the document.

# PORTFOLIO BUILDER

## WORK WITH XML

True multipurpose documents must be device- and program-independent. You should be able to view the documents in a standard browser and edit them in any text editor. XML documents are such independent documents. XML data can be exported from programs such as Microsoft Word, Excel, and Access, then imported into InDesign. This allows you to combine the capabilities of databases with InDesign's publishing tools.

XML documents can be extremely powerful, or they can simply be generic style sheets. Design a document — or series of documents — that could effectively use XML as a means of information exchange.

To complete this project, use the following techniques:

- Determine the type of document or documents you wish to create.

- Determine the fields you will need and create a style sheet using sample information.

- Explain how the XML files can be effectively used with InDesign to accomplish your desired result.

# LEVEL 2

# INTEGRATING PROJECT

This Integrating Project is designed to reflect a real-world design job, drawing on the skills you learned throughout this book. The files you need to complete this project are located in the RF_InDesign_L2> IP folder.

## Design and Multipurpose a Newsletter

Almost every professional company produces a newsletter to help keep clients abreast of what is going on in the company, and to convey information that may simply be of value. Often, due to the nature of the information presented, clients get to see another side of the company, and increased sales result. Although most corporate newsletters usually don't accept advertising from outside sources, they frequently include ads for company events.

In this project, you will create a 2-color, 12-page newsletter that includes images and text, presented in a highly effective manner. You will then repurpose the newsletter for delivery to the GASP, and for electronic distribution. When you have finished, you will archive the year's newsletters into a book and create a table of contents.

Unless otherwise noted, all object coordinates included in this project assume that the upper-left proxy reference point is selected in the Control palette; be sure to check frequently, because the proxy reference point may default to the center. You will save the document to your WIP_IP folder several times throughout this project. At the end of each section, either leave it open for the next section, or close, if you are not going to immediately continue.

## Set Up the Newsletter Format

1. Create a new, 12-page, 3-column, letter-size document with facing pages, a master text frame, and gutters of 0.25 in. Set the top margin to 0.375 in., the bottom margin to 0.625 in., the inside margin to 0.5 in., and the outside margin to 0.375 in. Allow a 0.125-in. bleed on all sides.

2. Set your Units and Increments preferences to inches, with an origin of Page. Set your Composition preferences to Skip By Leading and Text Wrap Only Affects Text Beneath.

3. Remove all but the standard four colors (None, Paper, Black, and Registration) from your Swatches palette and add as a new spot-color swatch PANTONE Solid Coated 2985.

4. Change the name of the A-Master page to "A-3 Column".

5. Double-click the master page to access it.

6. Create a 0.25-in. diameter circle with a fill of None and a 1-pt. stroke of PANTONE 2985. Position it at X: 4.1875 in., Y: 10.5 in. on the left master, using the top-center proxy reference point.

7. In its own text frame, insert a page-number marker in 12-pt. Adobe Garamond Pro Semibold.

8. Center the page number within the text frame and position the frame so the number is centered over the circle. Group the frame and circle.

9. Draw a vertical 10-inch line beginning at X: 2.875 in., Y: 0.375 in. Change its weight to 4 pt., its type to one of the dashed styles and its color to PMS 2985. Step and repeat the line once with a horizontal offset of 2.625 in.

10. Select all elements and step and repeat with a horizontal offset of 8.625 in.

**FIGURE IP.1**

11. Save the document as "gasp_newsletter.indd".

## Add and Apply Additional Masters

**1** Duplicate the master spread and rename the duplicate "B-3 Column with Head". Change the top margin to 1 in. Shorten the intercolumnar rules to 9.375 in. using the bottom-center proxy reference point. Drag the top of the text frame to the new top margin.

**2** Create a text frame with a width of 7.625 in. and a height of 0.625 in. at X: 0.375 in., Y: 0.375 in. on the left page and X: 0.5 in., Y: 0.375 in. on the right page. Link this frame to the main text frame on the page.

**3** Create a new one-page master named "Nameplate". Set the top margin at 3 in., the bottom at 0.375 in., the left at 2.25 in., and the right at 0.375 in. Make the page two columns with 0.25-in. gutters. Create a text frame the width of the two-column area and make the frame two columns with a 0.25-in. gutter, to match the layout beneath it.

**4** Create six rectangular frames to the following specifications (all measurements are in inches):

| X | Y | Width | Height | Fill | Stroke |
|---|---|---|---|---|---|
| –0.125 | –0.125 | 8.75 | 2.375 | 100% Black | None |
| –0.125 | 2.25 | 2 | 8.875 | 10% Black | None |
| –0.125 | 2.25 | 8.75 | 0.125 | 50% Black | None |
| 1.875 | 2.25 | 0.125 | 8.875 | 70% Black | None |
| 0.25 | 9.875 | 1.5 | 0.875 | Paper | 1-pt. PMS 2985 |
| 2.25 | 2.5 | 5.875 | 0.5 | None | None |

**5** Click in the upper box (it's 100% black) with the Type tool. Type "GASP" in 150-pt. ATC Oak Bold, centered, 50% PMS 2985. Set the alignment of the text box to Centered and adjust the word's baseline up 5 pt. Kern and track to taste.

**6** Create a new text frame at X: 0.5 in., Y: 0.325 in., W: 7.625 in., H: 1.75 in. In Adobe Garamond Pro Regular, 72/66, type "THE" on one line, aligned left and "REPORT" on another line, aligned right. Assign a color of Paper.

**7** In the 10% Black box, type "In This Issue:" in 18/18 ATC Oak Bold, with small caps, centered. Set the First Baseline Offset Minimum for the frame to 0.375 in.

**8** In the white box with the PMS 2985 border, type the following in ATC Oak Normal, 10/11, horizontally scaled to 80%, tracked to –10, and centered horizontally and vertically (insert Return/Enter at ¶ notations):

> For subscription information ¶
> visit our Web site at ¶
> www.againsttheclock.com
> or call ¶
> 800/555-4282

Color the Web address and telephone number PMS 2985.

**Integrating Project**

9. Convert the remaining frame to a text frame and link it to the main text frame on the page.

**FIGURE IP.2**

10. Apply the Nameplate master to Page 1. Apply the left page only of the B-3 Column with Head master to Pages 6, 8, 10, and 12.

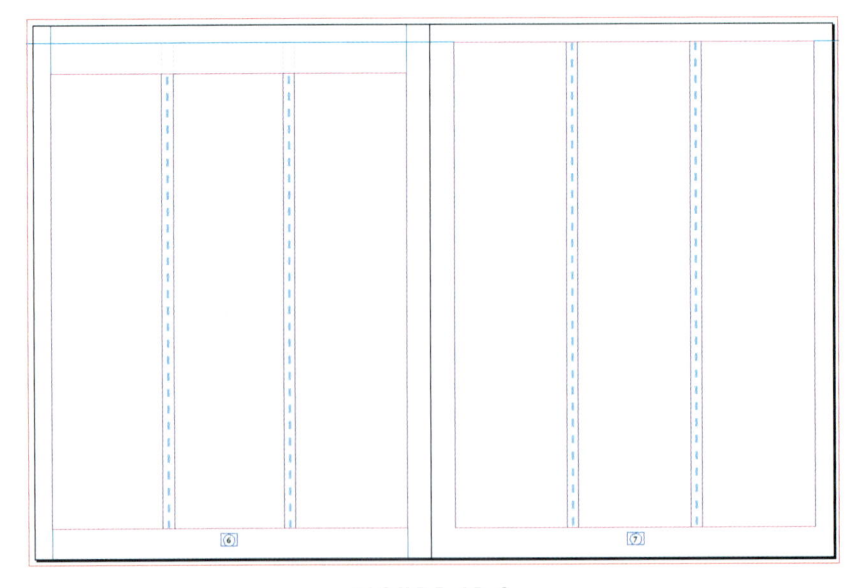

**FIGURE IP.3**

11. Save the document.

## Place Images

**1.** Place the following graphics. Note the upper-left X/Y position and scale.

| Page | Image | Scale | Instructions |
|---|---|---|---|
| 1 | row_master.tif | 100% | X: 3.25, Y: 6.125 |
| 2 | gasp_logo.eps | 67% | Place anywhere on the page. |
| 4 | figure_box.tif | 100% | Position so the image is against the top margin, centered across all columns; color it PMS 2985. |
| 5 | tall_box.tif | 100% | Position in two right-hand columns so it obscures the dotted rule; color it PMS 2985. |
| 11 | row_smarter.tif | 113% | Position centered at X: 0.375, Y: 4.0456; add a text wrap around the bounding box with all offset values set to 0. Be sure the text frame does not block the page number. |

**2.** Go to Page 8 and create a frame 1.25 in. high that spans all three columns; assign a fill of Paper. Position it at the 3.625-in. mark. Set text wrap outsets to 0 inches, and place the image airplane.tif. Fit the content to the frame.

**3.** Go to Page 3 and open the document gasp_sub_ad.indd.

This is supposed to be a prepared ad to fit an area at the bottom right of the page, 2 columns wide by 3 inches high. As you can see, they made the ad to inverted dimensions. Given the deadline, you're going to have to repair the ad as you go along.

**4.** Create a new layer named "Images". Select all four images and move them to the new Images layer.

**5.** Drag ruler guides to the left edge of the main frame of the ad and one to the top of the image that is highest on the page. Text and images share this common border.

**6.** Select Layer 1 and drag ruler guides to the top of the frame and the top of the text frame below the images.

**7.** From Layout>Layout Adjustment, enable Layout Adjustment, and check all boxes except Ignore Ruler Guide Alignments, then click OK.

**8.** From Document Setup, change the orientation from Portrait to Landscape.

The result looks like a mess, but you can fix it by reducing and moving some images and by working with the type.

**9** Do your creative best to make the resulting ad resemble the intent of the designers.

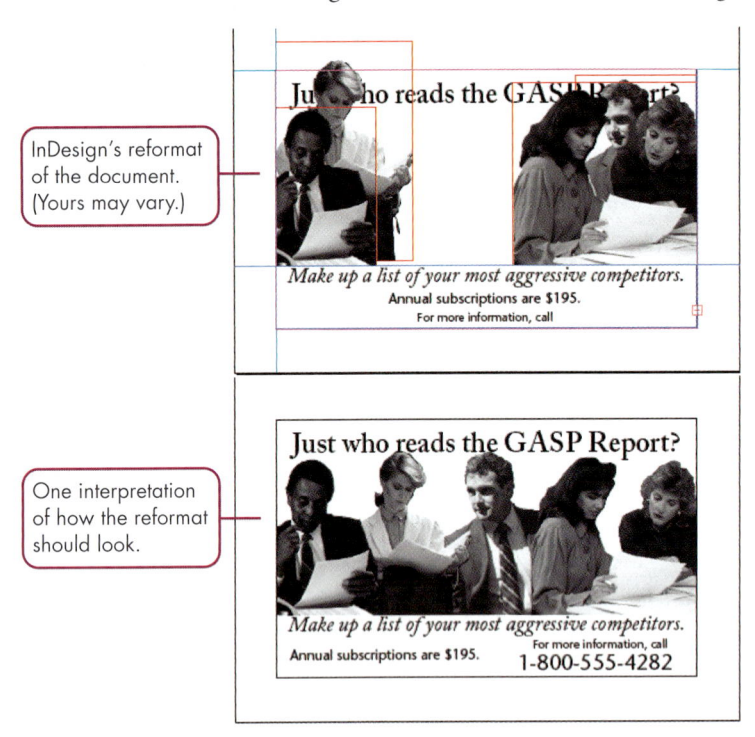

InDesign's reformat of the document. (Yours may vary.)

One interpretation of how the reformat should look.

**FIGURE IP.4**

**10** When you're finished, export the file to Grayscale EPS and place it in the lower-right corner of Page 3. Crop to the border of the ad and assign a top text offset of 0.25 in.

**11** Change the length of the rule between the second and third columns to 6.75 in.

**12** Save the new version of gasp_sub_ad.indd as "gasp_ad_reformat.indd" to your WIP_IP folder.

**13** Save the newsletter before you continue.

## Add Text Elements

**1** Go to Page 1 and load all styles from the document newsletter_styles.indd.

**2** Create a text frame with a width of 7.5 in. at X: 0.5 in., Y: 2.125 in. and type "[Tab]VOLUME 1[Tab]OCTOBER 2005". Apply the Dateline style and adjust the frame height so it fits the text tightly.

**3** Create a new text frame at X: 0.5 in., Y: 3 in., W: 1.25 in., H: 6.5 in. and place the file content.txt.

**4** Apply the Content Text style to all the text. Select the first paragraph, "GASP Management," and apply the Content Heads style; do the same with every other paragraph until the entire text block is formatted. You will need to break each head to two lines for formatting to work correctly.

**5** Create another text frame at X: 0 in., Y: 2.934 in., W: 0.5 in., H: 6.5 in. Type the numbers 1, 5, 6, 8, 9, 10, 12 in a column, with a Return/Enter after each number. Apply the Content Pages style.

**FIGURE IP.5**

**6** Go to Page 2. Create a rectangle 2.25 in. wide and 5.25 in. high, stroked with 1-pt. black and filled with Paper. Position it against the left margin at Y: 5 in. Apply a text wrap to the bounding box with no specified offset.

**7** Apply a drop shadow with an opacity of 75%, X and Y offsets of 0.15 in., a blur at 0.08 in., and a color of PMS 2985.

**8** Position the GASP logo in the first column at 4.5 in., centered horizontally in the column. Assign it a text wrap of 0.125-in. left and right, and 0.25-in. top and bottom. Bring it to the front.

**9** Place the file pub_info.doc in the rectangle you created; select all text and apply the Pub Info style.

**10** Modify the Pub Info style. Create a new nested style using the 12-pt. Oak Cond Blue character style that continues through one forced line break.

**11** Apply the Copyright paragraph style to the last four paragraphs. Adjust the text as necessary.

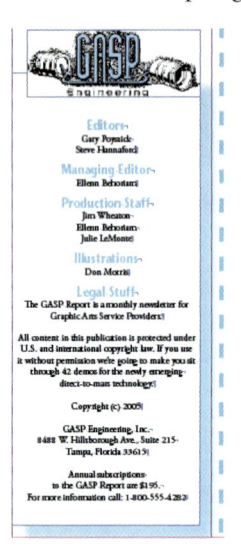

**FIGURE IP.6**

**12** Save the document.

## Create a Table

**1** Go to Page 4 and create a text frame 6 in. wide and 2.7 in. high. Position it at X: 1.2 in., Y: 0.85 in. and place the file table.xls as an unformatted table. Expand the table to fill the frame. If the table oversets, expand the frame to accommodate it.

**2** Set the table border to 2-pt. black.

**3** Set Alternating Column Strokes to Every Other Column. Make the first stroke 2 pt. and the second 1 pt.

**4** Set Alternating Row Fills to Every Other Row. Skip the first two rows and fill the first row with 20% PMS 2985.

**5** From Cell Options, center the text vertically in all cells.

**6** Assign the first row the Table Head style, the second row the Table Head 2 style, and the remaining rows the Table Text style.

**7** Above the table, create a text frame the width of all three columns. Type "Appropriate Scan Resolution" and assign it the Head 30 Blue paragraph style. Align the top of the text with the top margin of the page.

**8** Create another text frame the width of all three columns and a height of 0.25 in. Position it at Y: 3.6 in. Type "Supplying your customers with information such as this can save both of you time and money." Assign the Caption style.

**Appropriate Scan Resolution**

| Line Screen | GOOD QUALITY | | BEST QUALITY | |
|---|---|---|---|---|
| | Resolution | File Size per Sq. Inch | Resolution | File Size per Sq. Inch |
| 85lpi | 130ppi | 68k | 170ppi | 116k |
| 100lpi | 150ppi | 90k | 200ppi | 260k |
| 120lpi | 180ppi | 130k | 240ppi | 230k |
| 133lpi | 200ppi | 160k | 266ppi | 283k |
| 150lpi | 225ppi | 202k | 300ppi | 360k |
| 175lpi | 265ppi | 281k | 350ppi | 490k |
| 200lpi | 300ppi | 360k | 400ppi | 640k |

Supplying your customers with information such as this can save both of you time and money.

**FIGURE IP.7**

**9** Save your document.

## Flow the Main Text Article

When you flow text, it may flow over images. If so, you should send the text frame to the back. You may find in this project that articles seem to flow "backward," continuing from the previous article. If this is the case, find the beginning of the article and apply the Head 1 style to the first paragraph of the story. It has a built-in "Start Paragraph on Next Page" feature.

**1** Select the row_master image on Page 1. Establish a clipping path using the Photoshop Path method. Create a text wrap around the object shape that is Same As Clipping. Accept the default offset.

**2** Place the Microsoft Word document customers.doc in the small text frame on Page 1 above the main text frame, autoflowing the article.

3. Apply the Head 1 style to the first paragraph. Adjust the clipping path around the rowmaster image as necessary to achieve a good text wrap.

**FIGURE IP_08**

4. Flow the text to Page 2 and to succeeding pages until there is no more text to flow. On Page 4, drag the top of the text frame and the intercolumnar rules to Y: 4.125 in.

5. Apply the Body Text First style to the first paragraph in the article. Also apply this style to the first paragraph following all the Head 2 styles in the document. Fix any Head 2 text that looks awkward.

6. Select the last paragraph in the first column of Page 5 and italicize it. In this paragraph, select the "TM" after "Efforts" and after the two occurrences of "CARE" and replace it with the trademark symbol by typing Option/Alt-2.

7. In the next-to-last paragraph, apply the Body Text First style.

8. On Page 2, in the third column, locate the paragraph that begins with "A proactive…". Select it and the three following paragraphs (up to but not including "Finally, customers…"). Apply the Can Bullets paragraph style.

9. On the pasteboard, place ender.eps and scale to 25%. At the beginning of each of the paragraphs to which the Can Bullets style was applied, cut and place this graphic as an inline graphic, followed by a thin space.

10. Insert a line space before the "Finally, customers…" paragraph on the first column of Page 3.

11. Save the document.

## Flow Additional Articles

**1** Create a text frame on Page 5 the width of the two right columns. Place peas.doc into the frame and assign it the Boxed Text paragraph style. Format the headline, "PEAS" with the Head 30 Blue paragraph style.

**2** Place ender.eps, scaled to 25%, as an inline graphic at the end of the last paragraph. Insert a right-indent tab immediately before the graphic to push it to the right margin. Position the frame so the type fits the area appropriately and save the document.

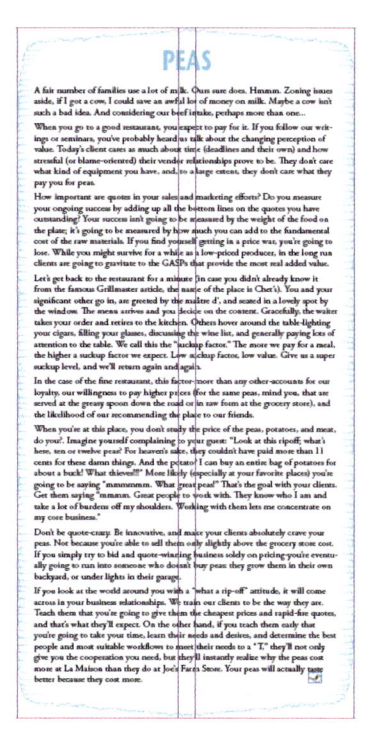

FIGURE IP.9

**3** On Page 6, place mission.doc in the small text frame above the main text frame. Flow the text through Page 7. Apply the Head 1 style to the first paragraph.

**4** Apply the Body Text First style to the first paragraph following the headline and to each paragraph immediately following subheads.

**5** Locate the paragraph beginning "Information…" in the first column of Page 6. Select it and the following paragraphs through the "Collaboration…" paragraph. Apply the Bullets style. In front of each paragraph, insert a bullet character (Command/Control-8) and a tab.

**6** Create a new paragraph style named "Bullets 2", based on the Bullets style. Create a nested style, including the Italic character style through the first sentence.

**7** Locate the paragraph "Were the flat…" in the first column of Page 7. Select it and all paragraphs through "They used three-color…". Apply the Bullets 2 style, and insert a bullet and tab in front of each paragraph. Add a line space before and after the series of bulleted paragraphs.

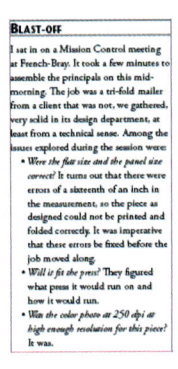

FIGURE IP.10

**8** Clean up any widows in the article and save the document.

**9** On Page 8, place paper_plastic.doc as you have the other articles. Flow the text through the first column of Page 9.

**10** Apply the Body Text First style to the first paragraph and to each paragraph following a Head 2.

**11** Create a text frame over the banner pulled by the airplane and type "For Consulting Information, call 800/555-4282". Apply the Banner style.

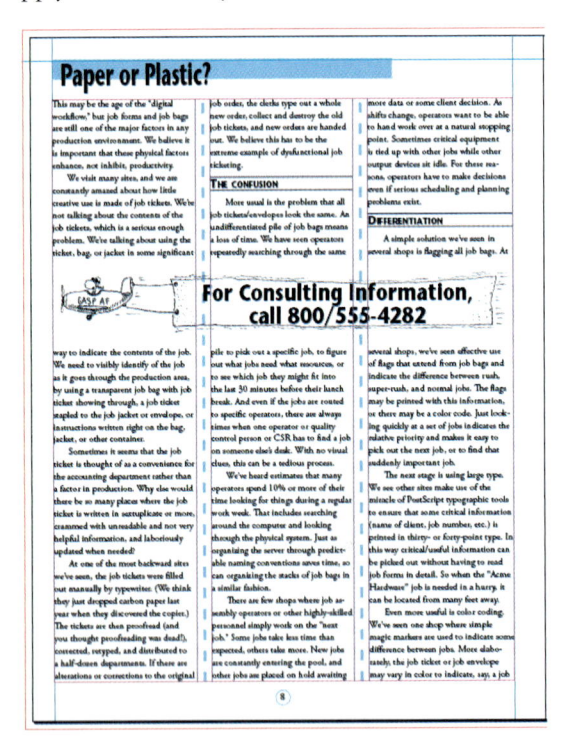

FIGURE IP.11

**12** Save the document.

## Add the Rest of the Text

**1** On Page 9, add a text frame 5 in. wide and 10 in. tall, and position it over the second and third columns. Fill the frame with Paper.

**2** Place drawing.doc in the frame. Select the first paragraph, "Drawing Attention," and format it as Head 30 Blue. Apply the Body Text First paragraph style to the next paragraph.

**3** Place bar.tif on Page 9 and resize to 5 inches in width, constraining proportions. Cut it and paste it as an inline graphic above and below the headline and after the last line of the article. Assign the Inline 2 style.

**4** Find "A Picture's Worth" in the fourth paragraph and italicize it; check the article for problems, then save the document.

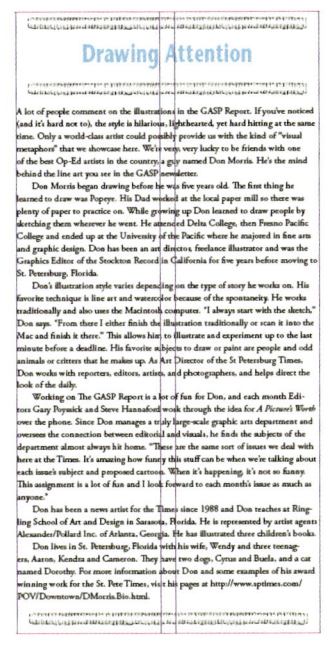

**FIGURE IP.12**

**5** Place rowing.doc on Pages 10 and 11 as you have the previous articles. Apply the Body Text First style to the first paragraph.

**6** Locate the memo that begins in the first column of Page 10. Select it (from "Memo" to "Supervisor") and italicize it. Add a line space before and after the memo and apply the Body Text First style to the first four lines. Add a tab to those four lines to align the words following the colon on each line.

**7** Apply a 3-line drop cap with the Blue Text character style to the first paragraph. Make the character Adobe Garamond Bold. Save the document.

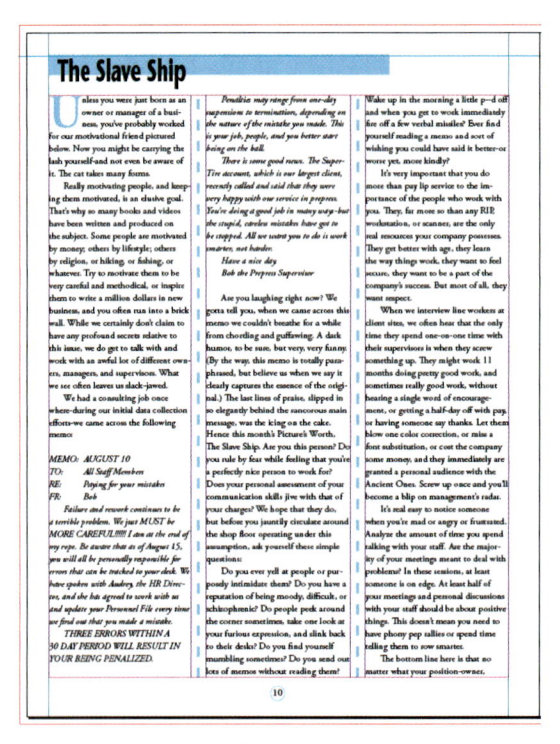

**FIGURE IP.13**

**8** On Page 12, place telecom.doc. Format it in the same manner in which the other articles have been formatted and save the document.

## Add Pull Quotes and Article Enders

**1** Go to Page 2 and create a text frame the width of a column with a vertical justification of Center. Type the following text in the frame: "Many customers sense that their salesperson is ill-informed about the new technology." Assign it the Pull Quote style and apply Balance Ragged Lines.

**2** Adjust the frame size so it just fits the text, then cut the frame and paste it as an inline graphic above the "Generally all customers…" paragraph in the third column. Apply the Inline paragraph style to the frame.

**3** Cut and paste this frame into the third column on Page 3 above the paragraph that begins "The first step…". Change the text to "With a sigh of relief, they began to understand why things were so confusing."

**4** Go through the article, adjust text wrap and column depths, and check for widows; ensure that the text fits.

**5** Create five more pull quotes, adjusting the frames so they just fit the text before cutting and pasting into the text stream. Insert them as follows:

Page 10, Column 1, above "We had a consulting…" paragraph:

"Do you ever yell at people or purposely intimidate them?"

Page 10, Column 3, approximately 2 in. from top of page:

"Do you have a reputation of being moody, difficult, or schizophrenic?"

Page 11, Column 2, centered vertically with a text wrap, not inserted as an inline graphic:

"Do you find yourself mumbling sometimes? Do you send out lots of memos without reading them?"

Page 12, Column 1, after first paragraph:

"There is a dizzying array of technologies out there."

Page 12, Column 3, before last paragraph:

"This is one area in which experts can be worth their weight in gold."

**6** Place ender.eps and scale to 25%. Add a right-indent tab and paste the graphic inline at the end of the third-to-last paragraph in the first column of Page 5. Paste at the end of each story in the newsletter.

**7** Go back and make final adjustments to each page to achieve the cleanest possible look.

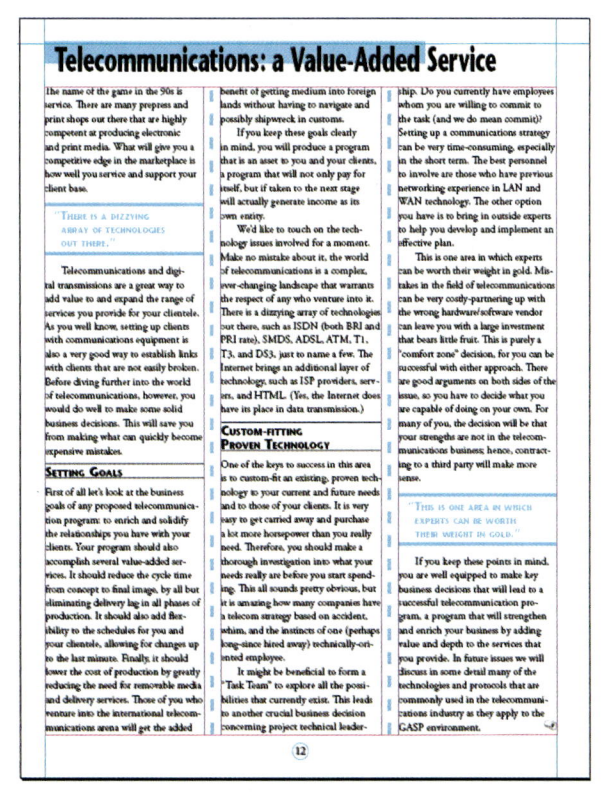

FIGURE IP.14

**8** Spell check the document. Make any necessary changes. This is a potentially painful step because of all the names and prepress terms. You can bypass it, for the sake of this project, but in real life it must be undertaken.

**9** Save the document.

**10** Package the document for the service provider.

## Prepare for Electronic Distribution

**1** Open the Hyperlinks palette from the Window>Interactive menu.

**2** Go to Page 5 and highlight the word "PEAS". Make it a text anchor hyperlink destination named "New Business".

**3** On Page 9, establish "Drawing Attention" as a text anchor named "Artist Profile".

**4** Establish page hyperlink destinations as follows:

> Page 6, named "Preflight"
> Page 8, named "Workflow"
> Page 10, named "Picture's Worth"
> Page 12, named "Technology"

**5** Return to Page 1 and highlight the corresponding text in the table of contents in the first column, establishing six hyperlinks. Highlight the text in the black boxes and use those words as the hyperlink names.

**6** In the subscription information box at the bottom of the column, highlight "www.againsttheclock.com" and set it as a Hyperlink from URL. Edit the URL to read "http://www.againsttheclock.com/".

**7** From the Edit menu, set the Transparency Flattener Preset to Low Resolution.

**8** Save the document.

**9** Export to PDF as "gasp_report_v1_n4.pdf" using the Screen preset.

**10** Close the document.

**11** View the PDF document and navigate to the articles using the hyperlinks you set up. Return to Page 1 using Acrobat's built-in navigation button. When you are finished, close the document and quit Acrobat.

## Archive the Year's Newsletters

1. From the File menu, choose New>Book and assign the name "gasp_v1_archive.indb".

2. From the Book palette Options menu, add the following as chapters: gasp_nl_01.indd, gasp_nl_02.indd, gasp_nl_03.indd, gasp_newsletter.indd.

3. Check the box in front of gasp_newsletter.indd to set it as the style source.

4. Ensure that no documents are selected in the Book palette and click the Synchronize button; dismiss the message that the documents may have changed.

5. From the Book palette Options menu, save the book.

## Create a Table of Contents

1. With the Book palette open, create a new two-page, letter-size document with facing pages and a master text frame. Set the top margin to 0.375 in., the bottom margin to 0.625 in., the inside margin to 2.5 in., and the outside margin to 0.375 in.

2. Select Page 1 in the Pages palette and,,,, choose Numbering & Section Options from the Options menu. Change the page-numbering style to lowercase Roman numerals (i, ii, iii).

3. Save the file as "gasp_report_2005_toc.indd".

4. Add gasp_report_2005_toc.indd to the book. Move it to the top, if necessary. Synchronize the book to add the styles to this document.

5. Create a new paragraph style, name it "TOC Text", and define it as 12/15 Adobe Garamond Pro Regular; set a right tab at 5.875 in. with a Period-Space leader.

6. Create a character style named "TOC Leader" defined as 10/15 Adobe Garamond Pro Regular.

7. Choose Layout>Table of Contents and click the More Options button. Add the Head 1 and Head 30 Blue styles from the Other Styles window.

8. Highlight the Head 1 style in the Include Paragraph Styles list. In the Style: Head 1 area, select TOC Text in the Entry Style menu. Select TOC Leader in the Between Entry and Number Style menu. Accept the default setting of 1 in the Level menu.

9. Highlight the Head 30 Blue style and give it the same specifications as you did for Head 1. Change the Level menu setting to 1.

10. Accept the default title of Contents, and assign it the Head 1 style.

11. Click the Save Style button, name the TOC style "TOC", then click OK.

12. Click the Type tool in Page 1. Save and leave the document open.

## Create the Contents for the Book

**1** Click gasp_nl_01.indd in the Book palette, then choose Document Page Numbering Options from the Options menu. This launches the document, which has only headlines placed.

**2** Start the page numbering at 1, then save and close the document.

**3** Choose Repaginate from the Book palette Options menu to make sure the page counts are all updated.

**4** Choose Layout>Table of Contents and check the Include Book Documents box.

**5** Click OK to create the table of contents.

### Contents

| | |
|---|---|
| Deliver What Customers Want, When They Want It | 1 |
| Identifying On-Demand Markets | 4 |
| Trending Toward Database Marketing | 6 |
| The Salesperson as Consultant | 8 |
| Digital Building Blocks | 10 |
| Troubleshooting Documents | 10 |
| A Gamut of Colors | 12 |
| A Portable Workflow | 13 |
| Preparing a 21st Century Workforce | 16 |
| Flexibility and CSRs | 18 |
| Business-to-Business e-Commerce Collaboration | 19 |
| Supply Side Collaboration | 21 |
| Managing Digital Assets | 22 |
| Getting the Most from a Diagnostic Audit | 24 |
| Teams, Empowerment and Self-direction | 25 |
| Implications of Good Communication | 29 |
| Results as a Measure of Productivity | 30 |
| TQM: Improving the Process | 32 |
| Robots or Decision Makers | 33 |
| Good Management Builds Bridges | 34 |
| Management by Memo | 36 |
| Customers As Allies Not Enemies | 37 |
| Appropriate Scan Resolution | 40 |
| PEAS | 41 |
| Mission Control at French-Bray | 42 |
| Paper or Plastic? | 44 |
| Drawing Attention | 45 |
| The Slave Ship | 46 |
| Telecommunications: a Value-Added Service | 48 |

**FIGURE IP.15**

**6** Save and close all documents.

# TASK GUIDE

| Task | Macintosh | Windows |
|---|---|---|

## Viewing Documents and Document Workspaces

### NAVIGATING DOCUMENTS AND PAGES

| Task | Macintosh | Windows |
|---|---|---|
| Open new default document | Command-Option-N | Control-Alt-N |
| Switch to next document window | Command-~ [tilde] | Control-~ [tilde] |
| Switch to previous document window | Command-Shift-~ [tilde] | Control-Shift-~ [tilde] |
| Scroll up one screen | Page Up | Page Up |
| Scroll down one screen | Page Down | Page Down |
| Go back to last-viewed page | Command-Page Up | Control-Page Up |
| Go forward to last-viewed page | Command-Page Down | Control-Page Down |
| Go to previous spread | Option-Page Up | Alt-Page Up |
| Go to next spread | Option-Page Down | Alt-Page Down |
| Select page number in page box | Command-J | Control-J |
| Go to master page (Pages palette closed) | Command-J, type prefix of master, Return | Control-J, type prefix of master, Enter |

### CONTROLLING THE DOCUMENT WINDOW

| Task | Macintosh | Windows |
|---|---|---|
| Toggle between Normal View and Preview Mode | W | W |
| Zoom to 50% | Command-5 | Control-5 |
| Zoom to 200% | Command-2 | Control-2 |
| Zoom to 400% | Command-4 | Control-4 |
| Access zoom percent field | Command-Option-5 | Control-Alt-5 |
| Switch between current and previous zoom levels | Command-Option-2 | Control-Alt-2 |
| Redraw screen | Shift-F5 | Shift-F5 |
| Optimize screen redraw | Command-. [period] | Control-. [period] |
| Fit selection in window | Command-Option- + [plus sign] | Control-Alt- + [plus sign] |
| Select magnification box in document window | Command-Option-5 (main keyboard) | Control-Alt-5 (main keyboard) |

### MANAGING GUIDES

| Task | Macintosh | Windows |
|---|---|---|
| Cycle through units of measurement | Command-Option-Shift-U | Control-Alt-Shift-U |
| Snap guide to ruler increments | Shift-drag guide | Shift-drag guide |
| Switch between page and spread guides (creation only) | Command-drag guide | Control-drag guide |
| Create vertical and horizontal ruler guides for the spread | Command-drag from zero point | Control-drag from zero point |
| Select all guides | Command-Option-G | Control-Alt-G |
| Lock or unlock zero point (contextual menu option) | Control-click zero point | Right-click zero point |
| Use current magnification for view threshold of new guide | Option-drag guide | Alt-drag guide |

| Task | Macintosh | Windows |
|---|---|---|

## Selecting Tools

| Task | Macintosh | Windows |
|---|---|---|
| Selection tool | V | V |
| Direct Selection tool | A | A |
| Toggle between Selection and Direct Selection tool | Command-Control-Tab | Control-Tab |
| Temporarily select Selection or Direct Selection tool (last used) | Command | Control |
| Temporarily select Group Selection tool (Direct Selection tool active) | Option | Alt |
| Temporarily select Group Selection tool (Pen, Add Anchor Point, or Delete Anchor Point tool active) | Command-Option | Control-Alt |
| Pen tool | P | P |
| Add Anchor Point tool | = | = |
| Delete Anchor Point tool | - [hyphen] | - [hyphen] |
| Convert Direction Point tool | Shift-C | Shift-C |
| Type tool | T | T |
| Type on a Path tool | Shift-T | Shift-T |
| Pencil tool | N | N |
| Line tool | \ | \ |
| Rectangle Frame tool | F | F |
| Rectangle tool | M | M |
| Ellipse tool | L | L |
| Rotate tool | R | R |
| Scale tool | S | S |
| Shear tool | O | O |
| Free Transform tool | E | E |
| Eyedropper tool | I | I |
| Measure tool | K | K |
| Gradient tool | G | G |
| Button tool | B | B |
| Scissors tool | C | C |
| Hand tool | H | H |
| Temporarily select Hand tool (Layout mode) | Spacebar | Spacebar |
| Temporarily select Hand tool (Text mode) | Option | Alt |
| Temporarily select Hand tool (Layout or Text mode) | Option-Spacebar | Alt-Spacebar |
| Zoom tool | Z | Z |
| Temporarily select Zoom In tool | Command-Spacebar | Control-Spacebar |
| Temporarily select Zoom Out tool | Command-Option-spacebar | Control-Alt-spacebar |

| Task | Macintosh | Windows |
|---|---|---|

## Using Palettes

| Task | Macintosh | Windows |
|---|---|---|
| Delete without confirmation | Option-click Trash icon | Alt-click Trash icon |
| Create item and set options | Option-click New icon | Alt-click New icon |
| Apply value and keep focus on option | Shift-Enter | Shift-Enter |
| Activate last-used option in last-used palette | Command-Option-~ [tilde] | Control-Alt-~ [tilde] |
| Select range of items* | Shift-click | Shift-click |
| Select nonadjacent items* | Command-click | Control-click |
| Apply value and select next value | Tab | Tab |
| Move focus to selected object, text, or window | Esc | Esc |

* Styles, Layer, Links, Swatches, or Library objects

### DISPLAYING PALETTES

| Task | Macintosh | Windows |
|---|---|---|
| Show/Hide Align palette | Shift-F7 | Shift-F7 |
| Show/Hide Character palette | Command-T | Control-T |
| Show/Hide Character Styles palette | Shift-F11 | Shift-F11 |
| Show/Hide Color palette | F6 | F6 |
| Show/Hide Control palette | Command-Option-6 | Control-Alt-6 |
| Show/Hide Index palette | Shift-F8 | Shift-F8 |
| Show/Hide Info palette | F8 | F8 |
| Show/Hide Layers palette | F7 | F7 |
| Show/Hide Links palette | Command-Shift-D | Control-Shift-D |
| Show/Hide Pages palette | F12 | F12 |
| Show/Hide Paragraph palette | Command-Option-T | Control-Alt-T |
| Show/Hide Paragraph Styles palette | F11 | F11 |
| Show/Hide Separations palette | Shift-F6 | Shift-F6 |
| Show/Hide Stroke palette | F10 | F10 |
| Show/Hide Swatches palette | F5 | F5 |
| Show/Hide Table palette | Shift-F9 | Shift-F9 |
| Show/Hide Tabs palette | Command-Shift-T | Control-Shift-T |
| Show/Hide Text Wrap palette | Command-Option-W | Control-Alt-W |
| Show/Hide Transform palette | F9 | F9 |
| Show/Hide Transparency palette | Shift-F10 | Shift-F10 |
| Show/Hide all palettes | Tab | Tab |
| Show/Hide all palettes except Toolbox and Control palette | Shift-Tab | Shift-Tab |
| Stash a palette group | Option-drag a palette tab to edge of window | Alt-drag a palette tab to edge of screen |
| Open or close all stashed palettes | Command-Option-Tab | Control-Alt-Tab |

| Task | Macintosh | Windows |
|---|---|---|

## Using Palettes (Cont'd)

### CHARACTER AND PARAGRAPH STYLES PALETTE

| Task | Macintosh | Windows |
|---|---|---|
| Make character style definition match selected text | Command-Option-Shift-C | Control-Alt-Shift-C |
| Make paragraph style definition match selected text | Command-Option-Shift-R | Contaol-Alt-Shift-R |
| Change options without applying style | Command-Option-Shift-double-click style | Control-Alt-Shift-double-click style |
| Remove style and local formatting | Option-click paragraph style name | Alt-click paragraph style name |
| Clear overrides from paragraph style | Option-Shift-click paragraph style name | Alt-Shift-click paragraph style name |

### COLOR PALETTE

| Task | Macintosh | Windows |
|---|---|---|
| Move color sliders in tandem | Shift-drag slider | Shift-drag slider |
| Select a color for the nonactive fill or stroke | Option-click color bar | Alt-click color bar |
| Switch between color modes (CMYK, RGB, LAB) | Shift-click color bar | Shift-click color bar |

### CONTROL PALETTE

| Task | Macintosh | Windows |
|---|---|---|
| Enable/Disable controls | Spacebar | Spacebar |
| Toggle Character/Paragraph text attributes mode | Command-Option-7 | Control-Alt-7 |
| Change reference point when proxy has focus | Any numeric-keypad key or keyboard numbers | Any numeric-keypad key or keyboard numbers |
| Open Character Style Options dialog box | Option-click Character Style icon | Alt-click Character Style icon |
| Open Drop Caps & Nested Styles dialog box | Option-click Drop Cap Number of Lines or Drop Cap One or More Characters icon | Alt-click Drop Cap Number of Lines or Drop Cap One or More Characters icon |
| Open Justification dialog box | Option-click Leading icon | Alt-click Leading icon |
| Open Move dialog box | Option-click X or Y icon | Alt-click X or Y icon |
| Open New Character Style Options dialog box | Double-click Character Style icon | Double-click Character Style icon |
| Open Paragraph Style Options dialog box | Option-click Paragraph Style icon | Alt-click Paragraph Style icon |
| Open Rotate dialog box | Option-click Angle icon | Alt-click Angle icon |
| Open Scale dialog box | Option-click X or Y Scale icon | Alt-click X or Y Scale icon |
| Open Shear dialog box | Option-click Shear icon | Alt-click Shear icon |
| Open Strikethrough Options dialog box | Option-click Strikethrough icon | Alt-click Strikethrough icon |
| Open Text Frame Options dialog box | Option-click Number of Columns icon | Alt-click Number of Columns icon |
| Open Underline Options dialog box | Option-click Underline icon | Alt-click Underline icon |
| Open Grids pane of the Preferences dialog box | Option-click Align to Baseline Grid or Do Not Align to Baseline Grid icon | Alt-click Align to Baseline Grid or Do Not Align to Baseline Grid icon |
| Open Text pane of the Preferences dialog box | Option-click Superscript, Subscript, or Small Caps icon | Alt-click Superscript, Subscript, or Small Caps icon |
| Open Units & Increments pane of Preferences dialog box | Option-click Kerning icon | Alt-click Kerning icon |

| Task | Macintosh | Windows |
|---|---|---|

## Using Palettes (Cont'd)

### LAYERS PALETTE

| | | |
|---|---|---|
| Select all objects on layer | Option-click layer | Alt-click layer |
| Copy selection to new layer | Option-drag small square to new layer | Alt-drag small square to new layer |

### LINKS PALETTE

| | | |
|---|---|---|
| Go to linked item | Option-double-click link file name | Alt-double-click link file name |
| Select all file names | Command-double-click link file name | Control-double-click link file name |

### PAGES PALETTE

| | | |
|---|---|---|
| Apply master to selected page | Option-click master | Alt-click master |
| Create master page | Command-click Create New Page icon | Control-click Create New Page icon |
| Open Insert Pages dialog box | Option-click New Page icon | Alt-click New Page icon |
| Override all master page items for current spread | Command-Option-Shift-L | Control-Alt-Shift-L |
| Add new page after last page | Command-Shift-P | Control-Shift-P |

### SEPARATIONS PREVIEW PALETTE

| | | |
|---|---|---|
| Turn on Overprint preview | Command-Option-Shift-Y | Control-Alt-Shift-Y |
| Show all plates | Command-Option-Shift-~ [tilde] | Control-Alt-Shift-~ [tilde] |
| Show Cyan plate | Command-Option-Shift-1 | Control-Alt-Shift-1 |
| Show Magenta plate | Command-Option-Shift-2 | Control-Alt-Shift-2 |
| Show Yellow plate | Command-Option-Shift-3 | Control-Alt-Shift-3 |
| Show Black plate | Command-Option-Shift-4 | Control-Alt-Shift-4 |
| Show 1st Spot plate | Command-Option-Shift-5 | Control-Alt-Shift-5 |
| Show 2nd Spot plate | Command-Option-Shift-6 | Control-Alt-Shift-6 |
| Show 3rd Spot plate | Command-Option-Shift-7 | Control-Alt-Shift-7 |
| Show 4th Spot plate | Command-Option-Shift-8 | Control-Alt-Shift-8 |
| Show 5th Spot plate | Command-Option-Shift-9 | Control-Alt-Shift-9 |

### SWATCHES PALETTE

| | | |
|---|---|---|
| Create new swatch based on current swatch | Option-click New Swatch icon | Alt-click New Swatch icon |
| Create spot color swatch based on current swatch | Command-Option-click New Swatch icon | Control-Alt-click New Swatch icon |
| Change options without applying swatch | Command-Option-Shift-double-click swatch | Control-Alt-Shift-double-click swatch |

### TABS PALETTE

| | | |
|---|---|---|
| Switch between alignment options | Option-click tab | Alt-click tab |

### TRANSFORM PALETTE

| | | |
|---|---|---|
| Apply value and copy object | Option-Return | Alt-Enter |
| Apply width, height, or scale value proportionally | Command-Return | Control-Enter |

# Task Guide

| Task | Macintosh | Windows |
|---|---|---|

## Selecting and Moving Objects

| Task | Macintosh | Windows |
|---|---|---|
| Add to or subtract from a selection of multiple objects (Selection, Direct Selection, or Group Selection tool active) | Shift-click | Shift-click |
| Select master page item from document page (Selection or Direct Selection tool active) | Command-Shift-click | Control-Shift-click |
| Select next object behind (Selection tool active) | Command-click | Control-click |
| Select next object in front (Selection tool active) | Command-Option-click | Control-Alt-click |
| Move selection* | Arrow keys | Arrow keys |
| Move selection by 10×* | Shift-Arrow keys | Shift-Arrow keys |
| Duplicate selection (Selection, Direct Selection, or Group Selection tool active) | Option-drag | Alt-drag |
| Duplicate and offset selection* | Option-Arrow keys | Alt-Arrow keys |
| Duplicate and offset selection by 10×* | Option-Shift-Arrow keys | Alt-Shift-Arrow keys |

*Amount is set in Units & Increments pane of the Preferences dialog box

## Transforming Objects

| Task | Macintosh | Windows |
|---|---|---|
| Duplicate and transform selection* | Transformation tool-Option-drag | Transformation tool-Alt-drag |
| Open Transform tool dialog box** | Double-click Scale, Rotate, or Shear tool in Toolbox | Double-click Scale, Rotate, or Shear tool in Toolbox |
| Decrease size by 1% | Command-< | Control-< |
| Decrease size by 5% | Command-Option-< | Control-Alt-< |
| Resize frame and content | Selection tool-Command-drag | Selection tool-Control-drag |
| Resize frame and content proportionately | Selection tool-Shift | Selection tool-Shift |

*After you select a transformation tool, hold down the mouse button, then hold down Option/Alt and drag.

**Transformation applies to selected object

## Editing Paths and Frames

| Task | Macintosh | Windows |
|---|---|---|
| Temporarily switch between Direct Seletion and Convert Direction Point tool | Command-Option | Control-Alt |
| Temporarily switch between Pen and Convert Direction Point tool | Option | Alt |
| Temporarily switch between Add Anchor Point and Delete Anchor Point tool | Option | Alt |
| Temporarily switch between Add Anchor Point and Scissors tool | Option | Alt |
| Keep Pen tool selected when pointer is over path/anchor point | Shift | Shift |
| Move anchor point and handles while drawing with Pen tool | Spacebar | Spacebar |

## Working with Color

| Task | Macintosh | Windows |
|---|---|---|
| Toggle Fill and Stroke | X | X |
| Swap Fill and Stroke | Shift-X | Shift-X |
| Apply color | , [comma] | , [comma] |
| Apply gradient | . [period] | . [period] |
| Apply No color | / | / |

## Working with Type

### NAVIGATING AND SELECTING TEXT

| Task | Macintosh | Windows |
|---|---|---|
| Move right one character* | Right Arrow | Right Arrow |
| Move left one character* | Left Arrow | Left Arrow |
| Move up one line* | Up Arrow | Up Arrow |
| Move down one line* | Down Arrow | Down Arrow |
| Move right one word | Command-Right Arrow | Control-Right Arrow |
| Move left one word | Command-Left Arrow | Control-Left Arrow |
| Move to start of line* | Home | Home |
| Move to end of line* | End | End |
| Move to beginning of current or to previous paragraph* | Command-Up Arrow | Control-Up Arrow |
| Move to beginning of next paragraph* | Command-Down Arrow | Control-Down Arrow |
| Move to start of story* | Command-Home | Control-Home |
| Move to end of story* | Command-End | Control-End |
| Select one word | Double-click word | Double-click word |
| Select one paragraph | Triple- or quadruple-click paragraph** | Triple- or quadruple-click paragraph** |
| Select current line | Command-Shift-\ | Control-Shift-\ |
| Select all in story | Command-A | Control-A |
| Select characters from insertion point | Shift-click | Shift-click |
| Select first frame | Command-Option-Shift-Page Up | Control-Alt-Shift-Page Up |
| Select last frame | Command-Option-Shift-Page Down | Control-Alt-Shift-Page Down |
| Select previous frame | Command-Option-Page Up | Control-Alt-Page Up |
| Select next frame | Command-Option-Page Down | Control-Alt-Page Down |
| Update missing font list | Command-Option-Shift-/ | Control-Alt-Shift-/ |

*Add the Shift key to select intervening text

**Depends on settings in the Text pane of the Preferences dialog box

## Working with Type (Cont'd)

| Task | Macintosh | Windows |
|---|---|---|
| **PLACING TEXT** | | |
| Automatically flow story | Shift-click loaded text icon | Shift-click loaded text icon |
| Semi-automatically flow story | Option-click loaded text icon | Alt-click loaded text icon |
| Recompose all stories | Command-Option-/ | Control-Alt-/ |
| Align to grid (on/off) | Command-Option-Shift-G | Control-Alt-Shift-G |
| **APPLYING CHARACTER FORMATTING** | | |
| Bold | Command-Shift-B | Control-Shift-B |
| Italic | Command-Shift-I | Control-Shift-I |
| Normal | Command-Shift-Y | Control-Shift-Y |
| Underline | Command-Shift-U | Control-Shift-U |
| Strikethrough | Command-Shift-/ | Control-Shift-/ |
| All caps (on/off) | Command-Shift-K | Control-Shift-K |
| Small caps (on/off) | Command-Shift-H | Control-Shift-H |
| Superscript | Command-Shift- + [plus sign] | Control-Shift- + [plus sign] |
| Subscript | Command-Option-Shift- + [plus sign] | Control-Alt-Shift- + [plus sign] |
| Reset horizontal scale to 100% | Command-Shift-X | Control-Shift-X |
| Reset vertical scale to 100% | Command-Option-Shift-X | Control-Alt-Shift-X |
| Increase point size* | Command-Shift-> | Control-Shift-> |
| Decrease point size* | Command-Shift-< | Control-Shift-< |
| Increase point size by 5×* | Command-Shift- Option-> | Control-Alt-Shift-> |
| Decrease point size by 5×* | Command-Shift- Option-< | Control-Alt-Shift-< |
| Increase kerning and tracking (horizontal text) | Option-Right Arrow | Alt-Right Arrow |
| Decrease kerning and tracking (horizontal text) | Option-Left Arrow | Alt-Left Arrow |
| Increase kerning and tracking (vertical text) | Option-Up Arrow | Alt-Up Arrow |
| Decrease kerning and tracking (vertical text) | Option-Down Arrow | Alt-Down Arrow |
| Increase kerning and tracking by 5× (horizontal text) | Command-Option-Right Arrow | Control-Alt-Right Arrow |
| Decrease kerning and tracking by 5× (horizontal text) | Command-Option-Left Arrow | Control-Alt-Left Arrow |
| Increase kerning and tracking by 5× (vertical text) | Command-Option-Up Arrow | Control-Alt-Up Arrow |
| Decrease kerning and tracking by 5× (vertical text) | Command-Option-Down Arrow | Control-Alt-Down Arrow |
| Increase kerning between words* | Command-Option-\ | Control-Alt-\ |
| Decrease kerning between words* | Command-Option-Delete | Control-Alt-Backspace |
| Clear manual kerning and reset tracking to 0 | Command-Option-Q | Control-Alt-Q |
| Select or deselect preferences setting for typographer's marks | Command-Option-Shift-" [quote] | Control-Alt-Shift-" [quote] |

| Task | Macintosh | Windows |
|---|---|---|

## Working with Type (Cont'd)

### APPLYING PARAGRAPH FORMATTING

| Task | Macintosh | Windows |
|---|---|---|
| Open Justification dialog box | Command-Option-Shift-J | Control-Alt-Shift-J |
| Open Paragraph Rules dialog box | Command-Option-J | Control-Alt-J |
| Open Keep Options dialog box | Command-Option-K | Control-Alt-K |
| Align left | Command-Shift-L | Control-Shift-L |
| Align right | Command-Shift-R | Control-Shift-R |
| Align center | Command-Shift-C | Control-Shift-C |
| Justify all lines (but last line) | Command-Shift-J | Control-Shift-J |
| Justify all lines (including last line) | Command-Shift-F | Control-Shift-F |
| Increase leading (horizontal text)* | Option-Up Arrow | Alt-Up Arrow |
| Decrease leading (horizontal text)* | Option-Down Arrow | Alt-Down Arrow |
| Increase leading (vertical text)* | Option-Right Arrow | Alt-Right Arrow |
| Decrease leading (vertical text)* | Option-Left Arrow | Alt-Left Arrow |
| Increase leading by 5× (horizontal text)* | Command-Option-Up Arrow | Control-Alt-Up Arrow |
| Decrease leading by 5× (horizontal text)* | Command-Option-Down Arrow | Control-Alt-Down Arrow |
| Increase leading by 5× (vertical text)* | Command-Option-Right Arrow | Control-Alt-Right Arrow |
| Decrease leading by 5× (vertical text)* | Command-Option-Left Arrow | Control-Alt-Left Arrow |
| Auto leading | Command-Option-Shift-A | Control-Alt-Shift-A |
| Auto-hyphenate (on/off) | Command-Option-Shift-H | Control-Alt-Shift-H |
| Increase baseline shift (horizontal text)** | Option-Shift-Up Arrow | Alt-Shift-Up Arrow |
| Decrease baseline shift (horizontal text)** | Option-Shift-Down Arrow | Alt-Shift-Down Arrow |
| Increase baseline shift (vertical text)** | Option-Shift-Right Arrow | Alt-Shift-Right Arrow |
| Decrease baseline shift (vertical text)** | Option-Shift-Left Arrow | Alt-Shift-Left Arrow |
| Increase baseline shift by 5× (horizontal text)** | Command-Option-Shift-Up Arrow | Control-Alt-Shift-Up Arrow |
| Decrease baseline shift by 5× (horizontal text)** | Command-Option-Shift-Down Arrow | Control-Alt-Shift-Down Arrow |
| Increase baseline shift by 5× (vertical text)** | Command-Option-Shift-Right Arrow | Control-Alt-Shift-Right Arrow |
| Decrease baseline shift by 5× (vertical text)** | Command-Option-Shift-Left Arrow | Control-Alt-Shift-Left Arrow |

*Press Shift to increase or decrease kerning between words by five times.

**Amount is set in Units & Increments pane of the Preferences dialog box

## Working with Type (Cont'd)

| Task | Macintosh | Windows |
|---|---|---|
| **USING SPECIAL CHARACTERS** | | |
| Column Break | Enter | Numeric Enter |
| Forced Line Break | Shift-Return | Shift-Enter |
| Frame Break | Shift-Enter | Shift-Numeric Enter |
| Page Break | Command-Enter | Control-Numeric Enter |
| Indent to Here | Command-\ | Control-\ |
| Right Indent Tab | Shift-Tab | Shift-Tab |
| Auto Page Number | Command-Option-Shift-N | Control-Alt-Shift-N |
| Previous Page Number | Command-Option-Shift-[ | Control-Alt-Shift-[ |
| Next Page Number | Command-Option-Shift-] | Control-Alt-Shift-] |
| Current Page Number | Command-Option-N | Control-Alt-N |
| Bullet Character (•) | Option-8 | Alt-8 |
| Copyright Symbol (©) | Option-G | Alt-G |
| Ellipsis (…) | Option-; | Alt-; |
| Paragraph Symbol (¶) | Option-7 | Alt-7 |
| Registered Trademark Symbol (®) | Option-R | Alt-R |
| Section Symbol (§) | Option-6 | Alt-6 |
| Single Left Quotation Mark (') | Option-] | Alt-] |
| Single Right Quotation Mark (') | Option-Shift-] | Alt-Shift-] |
| Double Left Quotation Mark (") | Option-[ | Alt-[ |
| Double Right Quotation Mark (") | Option-Shift-[ | Alt-Shift-[ |
| Discretionary Hyphen | Command-Shift- - [hyphen] | Control-Shift- - [hyphen] |
| Nonbreaking Hyphen | Command-Option- - [hyphen] | Control-Alt- - [hyphen] |
| Em Dash | Option-Shift- - [hyphen] | Alt-Shift- - [hyphen] |
| En Dash | Option- - [hyphen] | Alt- - [hyphen] |
| Em Space | Command-Shift-M | Control-Shift-M |
| En Space | Command-Shift-N | Control-Shift-N |
| Hair Space | Command-Option-Shift-I | Control-Alt-Shift-I |
| Nonbreaking Space | Command-Option-X | Control-Alt-X |
| Thin Space | Command-Option-Shift-M | Control-Alt-Shift-M |

| Task | Macintosh | Windows |
|---|---|---|

## Finding and Changing Text

| Task | Macintosh | Windows |
|---|---|---|
| Insert selected text into Find What box | Command-F1 | Control-F1 |
| Insert selected text into Find What box and finds next | Shift-F1 | Shift-F1 |
| Find next occurrence of Find What text | Shift-F2 or Command-Option-F | Shift-F2 or Control-Alt-F |
| Insert selected text into Change To box | Command-F2 | Control-F2 |
| Replace selection with Change To text | Command-F3 | Control-F3 |

## Working with Tables

| Task | Macintosh | Windows |
|---|---|---|
| Insert or delete rows or columns while dragging | Begin dragging row or column border, then hold down Option as you drag | Begin dragging row or column border, then hold down Alt as you drag |
| Resize rows or columns without changing table size | Shift-drag interior row/column border | Shift-drag interior row/column border |
| Resize rows or columns proportionally | Shift-drag right or bottom table border | Shift-drag right or bottom table border |
| Move to next cell | Tab | Tab |
| Move to previous cell | Shift-Tab | Shift-Tab |
| Move to first cell in column | Option-Page Up | Alt-Page Up |
| Move to last cell in column | Option-Page Down | Alt-Page Down |
| Move to first cell in row | Option-Home | Alt-Home |
| Move to last cell in row | Option-End | Alt-End |
| Move to first row in frame | Page Up | Page Up |
| Move to last row in frame | Page Down | Page Down |
| Move up, down, left, or right one cell | Arrow keys | Arrow keys |
| Select cell above the current cell | Shift-Up Arrow | Shift-Up Arrow |
| Select cell below the current cell | Shift-Down Arrow | Shift-Down Arrow |
| Select cell to the right of the current cell | Shift-Right Arrow | Shift-Right Arrow |
| Select cell to the left of the current cell | Shift-Left Arrow | Shift-Left Arrow |
| Start row on next column | Enter (numeric keypad) | Enter (numeric keypad) |
| Start row on next frame | Shift-Enter (numeric keypad) | Shift-Enter (numeric keypad) |
| Toggle between text selection and cell selection | Esc | Esc |

## Indexing

| Task | Macintosh | Windows |
|---|---|---|
| Create index entry without dialog box | Command-Option-U | Control-Alt-U |
| Open index entry dialog box | Command-U | Control-U |
| Create proper name index entry (last name, first name) | Command-Shift-F8 | Control-Shift-F8 |

| Task | Macintosh | Windows |
| --- | --- | --- |

## Navigating XML

| Task | Macintosh | Windows |
| --- | --- | --- |
| Expand/Collapse element | Right Arrow/Left Arrow key | Right Arrow/Left Arrow key |
| Expand/Collapse element and child elements | Option-Right Arrow/Left Arrow key | Alt-Right Arrow/Left Arrow key |
| Extend XML selection up/down | Shift-Up Arrow/Down Arrow key | Shift-Up Arrow/Down Arrow key |
| Move XML selection up/down | Up Arrow/Down Arrow key | Up Arrow/Down Arrow key |
| Scroll structure pane up/down one screen | Page Up/Page Down key | Page Up/Page Down key |
| Select first/last XML node | Home/End key | Home/End key |
| Extend selection to first/last XML node | Shift-Home/End key | Shift-Home/End key |
| Go to previous/next validation error | Command-Left Arrow/Right Arrow key | Control-Left Arrow/Right Arrow key |

# GLOSSARY

**A/As** Author's Alterations. Changes made to the copy by the author after typesetting, and thus chargeable to the author.

**absolute path** The location of a file or Web page beginning with the root. Includes all necessary information to find the file or page. In the case of a Web page, called "absolute URL." See *relative path*.

**additive color** The process of mixing red, green, and blue light to achieve a wide range of colors, as on a color television screen. See *subtractive color*.

**Adobe Paragraph Composer** The text composition engine present in Adobe InDesign. Loosely based on Donald Knuth's TeX composition algorithms, this is the only desktop product that can perform text composition on multiple lines of text at one time.

**Align palette** A palette that provides a number of options for aligning objects, relative to each other or to the document.

**alpha channel** An additional channel in an image that defines what parts of the image are transparent or semitransparent. Programs such as Adobe Illustrator, PhotoShop, Premiere, and After Effects use alpha channels to specify transparent regions in an image.

**anchor points** The individual points that define the shape of a vector-based graphic element. Anchor points are connected by line segments.

**ASCII** American Standard Code for Information Interchange. Worldwide, standard ASCII text does not include formatting, and can be exchanged and read by most computer systems.

**aspect ratio** The width-to-height proportions of an image.

**autoflow** The process of placing text in InDesign so it flows to all linked text frames.

**automatic text box** A text box that appears on the default master page; it snaps to the defined margin guides.

**balance ragged lines** In InDesign, a process that automatically adjusts all lines within a text frame to achieve a smooth appearance.

**banding** A visible stair-stepping of shades in a gradient.

**baseline** The implied reference line on which the bases of capital letters sit.

**baseline grid** In most page-layout programs, a series of equally spaced horizontal lines to which text may be aligned.

**baseline shift** A formatting option that moves selected characters above or below the baseline of normal text.

**Bézier curves** Vector curves that are defined mathematically. These curves can be scaled without the "jaggies" inherent in enlarging bitmapped fonts or graphics.

**binding** In general, the various methods used to secure signatures or leaves in a book. Examples include saddle-stitching (using staples in a folded spine), and perfect-bound (multiple sets of folded pages sewn or glued into a flat spine).

**binding edge** The page edge that is inserted into the binding of a publication.

**bitmap image** An image constructed from individual dots or pixels set to a grid-like mosaic. The file must contain information about the color and position of each pixel, so the disk space needed for bitmap images can be very large.

**bitmapped** Forming an image with a grid of pixels whose curved edges have discrete steps because of the approximation of the curve due to a finite number pixels.

**bitmapping** The stairstepped appearance of graphics, caused by enlarging raster images.

**bleed** Page data that extends beyond the trim marks on a page.

**bleed allowance** The extra portion of an element that extends beyond the page trim edge.

**bleed size** An element of page geometry; the trim size plus the bleed allowance.

**BMP** A Windows bitmap image format that features low-quality and large file sizes.

**book** Two or more InDesign documents that are combined and share styles, colors, and pagination criteria.

**bookmark** HTML feature that allows you to save a link to a Web page.

**border** A continual line that extends around an element.

**bounding box** An area that defines the outer border of an object.

**button** An element a user can click to cause an effect, such as the submission of a form.

**button state** A visual version of a button. For example, when clicked, the button is in its Down state; when dormant, it is in its Up state. When the mouse is hovered over the button, the button is in its Over state.

**calibration bars** A strip of color blocks or tonal values on film, proofs, and press sheets, used to check the accuracy of color registration, quality, density, and ink coverage during a print run.

**cap line** The theoretical line to which the tops of capital letters are aligned.

**carding** The process of inserting extra space only between paragraphs to achieve vertical justification.

**cell** A unit of information within a table.

**cell padding** The margin around the inside of a table cell.

**cell spacing** The margin between table cells.

**center marks** Press marks that appear on the center of all sides of a press sheet to aid in positioning the print area on the paper.

**character count** The number of characters (letters, figures, signs, or spaces) in a selected block of copy.

**character style sheet** A style sheet that defines only character formatting attributes, including font, type size, text color, and type style.

**clipboard** The portion of computer memory that holds data that has been cut or copied. The next item cut or copied replaces the data already in the clipboard.

**clipping path** A path that determines which parts of an image will show on the page. Anything inside the path will show and print; anything outside the path won't. The clipping path knocks out the unwanted part of the image

**CMYK** Cyan, Magenta, Yellow, Black. The subtractive primaries, or process colors, used in four-color printing.

**coated** Printing papers that have a surface coating (of clay or other material) to provide a smoother, more even finish with greater opacity.

**collate** To gather together separate sections or leaves of a publication in the correct order for binding.

**color chart** A printed chart of various combinations of CMYK colors used as an aid for the selection of colors during the design phase of a project.

**color composition** The ink components that are combined to make up a specific color.

**color management** The process of measuring and transferring color from one color space to another to ensure color consistency.

**color model** A system for describing color, such as RGB, CMYK or L*a*b*.

**color proof** A printed or simulated printed image of the color separations intended to produce a close representation of the final reproduction for approval and as a guide to the press operator.

**color separation** The process of transforming color artwork into components corresponding to the colors of ink being used, whether process or spot, or a combination of the two.

**color space** A three-dimensional coordinate system in which any color can be represented as a point.

**column** 1. A vertical area for type, used to constrain line length to enhance design and readability. 2. A series of cells arranged vertically.

**column guides** The guides that denote the location of gutters between columns.

**commercial printing** Typically, printing on high-capacity, high-resolution presses; processes include offset lithography, flexography, gravure, and screen printing. Offset printing is the most widely used commercial printing process.

**comp** Comprehensive artwork used to present the general color and layout of a page.

**composite proof** A version of an illustration or page in which the process colors appear together to represent full color. When produced on a monochrome output device, colors are represented as shades of gray.

**contextual menu** A menu containing options that are only relative to the object for which the menu is activated.

**control handle** Nonprinting lines that define the shape or segments that connect two anchor points.

**coordinates** Numbers signifying a place in a Cartesian plane, represented by (x,y).

**copyfitting** Making sure you don't write more text than you have room for.

**copyright** Ownership of a work. Permits the owner of material to prevent its use without express permission or acknowledgement of the originator. Copyright may be sold, transferred, or given up contractually.

**crop marks** Printed lines used as guides for final trimming of the pages within a press sheet. Also called "trim marks."

**cropping** The elimination of parts of a photograph or other original that are not required to be printed.

**cross-reference** An in-text notation that directs the reader's attention to an attached illustration or to another section of the publication.

**CSS** Cascading Style Sheets. Part of a Web-page file listing properties that affect the appearance of content, the content to which those properties apply, and their values.

**custom glyph set** A combination of characters that can be accessed from a custom glyph palette. The characters can come from different fonts.

**default** A specification for a mode of computer operation that occurs if no other is selected.

**device-independent color** Reproduction in which the output color is absolute, and is not determined by the output device characteristics.

**DICColor** A special-color library commonly used in Japan.

**dictionary**  A collection of words, used to determine appropriate spelling and hyphenation.

**dingbat**  1. A font character that displays a picture instead of a letter, number, or punctuation mark. 2. A printer's typographical ornament.

**discretionary hyphen**  A hyphen coded for display and printing only when formatting of the text puts the hyphenated word at the end of a line. Also called a "soft hyphen."

**display performance**  An InDesign option with three settings: Optimized Display, which grays out images so the pages paint up faster; Typical Display; and High-Quality Display, which enhances the display quality of images so the pages paint up slower.

**document grid**  A grid of horizontal and vertical lines at specified intervals used to align objects horizontally and vertically.

**double-page spread**  A design that spans the two pages visible to the reader at any open spot in a magazine, periodical, or book.

**drop cap**  Text formatting in which the first one or more characters in a paragraph is enlarged to occupy more than one line in the paragraph.

**editable text**  A text element that the user can modify by entering or deleting keystrokes.

**editorial priority**  The order of importance for text in a document.

**effective resolution**  The final resolution of an image, calculated by dividing the image resolution (pixels per inch) by the magnification percentage.

**element**  The smallest unit of a graphic, or a component of a page layout or design. Any object, text block, or graphic might be referred to as a design element.

**embedding**  Including a complete copy of a text file or image within a document, with or without a link.

**EPS**  Encapsulated PostScript. File format used to transfer PostScript data within compatible applications. EPS files can contain text, vector artwork, and images.

**expanded type**  A typeface in which the width of the letters is wider than that of the standard letters of the font. Expanded type can be a designed font, or the effect may be approximated using a horizontal scaling feature. Also called "extended."

**expert set**  A font that includes "cut" small caps, meaning that they were specially designed from the start to be used as small caps, and they maintain the same weight as the regular cap.

**export**  To save a file generated in one application into a format that is readable in another.

**extended characters**  Characters that cannot be accessed directly from the keyboard; for the most part, characters with an ASCII value higher than 128.

**facing pages**  A type of layout in which the pages of a design appear opposite each other, as in the pages of a book. See *nonfacing pages*.

**fair use**  Using copyrighted work without obtaining permission from the copyright holder for purposes such as critique, education, or research.

**feathering**  The process of achieving vertical justification by adding extra space between individual lines of text, may be combined with carding.

**fill**  To add a tone or color to the area inside a closed object in a graphic illustration program.

**fill character**  The character that appears between the text at each tab location.

**flatten**  The process of removing complexity from an object so it can be more easily printed.

**Focoltone**  A special-color library used in the United States.

**folder**  The digital equivalent of a paper file folder, used to organize files in the Macintosh and Windows operating systems. Double-clicking the icon opens it to reveal the files stored inside.

**folding dummy**  A template used for determining the page arrangement on a form to meet folding and binding requirements.

**fold-out**  An extra page that may be pasted or folded into a book or booklet.

**font**  The complete collection of all the characters (numbers, uppercase and lowercase letters, and in some cases, small caps and symbols) of a given typeface in a specific style; for example, Helvetica Bold.

**font embedding**  The technique of saving font data as a part of a file, which eliminates problems caused by missing font files.

**font license**  The legal right to use a font you have paid for; most licenses limit fonts to use on a single computer.

**font metrics**  The physical characteristics of a font, as defined in the font file.

**font subsetting**  Embedding only the used characters of a font into the final file. The advantage of font subsetting is that it decreases the overall size of your file. The disadvantage is that it limits the ability to make corrections at the printing service.

**font substitution**  A process in which your computer uses a font other than the one you used in your design to display or print your publication. Usually occurs when a used font is missing on the computer used to output the design.

**footer row**  A row at the bottom of a table that will repeat if the table is threaded across more than one frame.

**force justify** A type alignment command that causes the space between letters and words in a line of type to expand to fit within a line.

**FPO** For Position Only. A term applied to low-quality images or simple shapes used to indicate placement and scaling of an art element on mechanicals or camera-ready artwork.

**frame** The physical characteristics of a box edge.

**GASP** Graphic Arts Service Provider. A firm that provides a range of services somewhere on the continuum from design to fulfillment.

**GIF** Graphics Interchange Format. A popular graphics format for online clip art and drawn graphics. Graphics in this format are acceptable at low resolution. See *JPEG*.

**glyph** Any character of a font.

**gradient** A gradual transition from one color to another. The shape of the gradient and the proportion of the two colors can be varied. Also known as blends, gradations, graduated fills, and vignettes.

**grayed out** Any option (menu selection, button, etc.) that is not available.

**grayscale** 1. An image composed in grays ranging from black to white, usually using 256 different tones. 2. A tint ramp used to measure and control the accuracy of screen percentages. 3. An accessory used to define neutral density in a photographic image.

**greeking** 1. A software technique where areas of gray are used to simulate lines of text below a certain point size. 2. Nonsense text used to define a layout before copy is available.

**grid** A division of a page by horizontal and vertical guides into areas where text or graphics may be placed accurately.

**guide** A nonprinting line that can be pulled onto a page to aid in horizontal or vertical alignment of objects.

**gutter** Extra space between pages in a layout. Sometimes used interchangeably with "alley" to describe the space between columns on a page. Gutters can appear either between the top and bottom of two adjacent pages or between two sides of adjacent pages.

**gutter width** The space between columns on a layout page.

**H & J** Hyphenation and Justification. Parameters used by a page-layout program to determine how a line of text should be hyphenated, or how its inter-word and inter-character space should be adjusted.

**hairline rule** The thinnest rule that can be printed on a given device. A hairline rule on a 1200-dpi imagesetter is 1/1200 of an inch; on a 300-dpi laser printer, the same rule would print at 1/300 of an inch.

**halftone** An image generated for use in printing in which a range of continuous tones is simulated by an array of dots that create the illusion of continuous tone when seen at a distance.

**halftone tint** An area covered with a uniform halftone dot size to produce an even tone or color. Also called "flat tint" or "screen tint."

**hanging indent** Text in which the first line of a paragraph is placed farther left than the rest of the paragraph.

**header row** A row at the top of a page that will repeat if the table is threaded across more than one frame.

**horizontal scale** A technique used for creating artificially condensed type.

**HTML** Hypertext Mark-Up Language. A tagging language that allows content to be delivered over the World Wide Web and viewed by a browser.

**hyperlink** An HTML tag that directs the computer to a different anchor or URL. A hyperlink can be a word, phrase, sentence, graphic, or icon. A hyperlink can also cause an action, such as opening or downloading a file.

**hyphenation exception** A user-defined change to the way a specific word will be hyphenated in a layout.

**hyphenation zone** The space at the end of a line of text in which the hyphenation function will examine the word to determine whether it should be hyphenated and wrapped to the next line.

**imagesetter** A raster-based device used to output a digital file at high resolution (usually 1000–3000 dpi) onto photographic paper or film, from which printing plates are made, or directly to printing plates (called a "platesetter").

**imposition** The arrangement of pages on a printed sheet, which, when the sheet is finally printed, folded, and trimmed, will place the pages in their correct order.

**indexed-color image** An image that uses a limited, predetermined number of colors; often used in Web images. See *GIF*.

**indexing** Marking certain words within a document with hidden codes so an index can be automatically generated.

**inline graphic** A graphic that is inserted within a body of text, and may be formatted using normal text commands for justification and leading; inline graphics will move with the body of text in which they are placed.

**input** An element, such as a text box, that receives information from the user.

**insertion point** A flashing bar that indicates the location at which text will be placed.

**intellectual property** Any product of human intelligence that is unique, novel, unobvious, and valuable (such as a literary work, idea, or invention).

**international paper sizes** The International Standards Organization (ISO) system of paper sizes based on a series of three sizes — A, B, and C. Each size has the same proportion of length to width as the others.

**jaggies** Visible steps in the curved edge of a graphic or text character that result from enlarging a bitmapped image.

**job package** The collected group of all elements that must be sent to a service provide or printer, including a desktop proof, the project file, any images or graphics placed in the layout, and all fonts used in the design.

**job specifications** Detailed information about a particular job, required to complete the design and print the final product. Includes page geometry, number of ink colors, type of paper being used, finishing requirements, delivery instructions, and any other relevant information.

**JPEG** A compression algorithm that reduces the file size of bitmapped images, named for the Joint Photographic Experts Group, which created the standard. JPEG is "lossy" compression; image quality is reduced in direct proportion to the amount of compression.

**justification** The addition or subtraction of space from between words and/or letters to achieve the best possible appearance of the paragraph of text.

**keyboard equivalents** User-defined shortcuts to style sheets.

**L*a*b*** The lightness, red-green attribute, and yellow-blue attribute in the CIE L*a*b* color space, a three-dimensional color mapping system.

**laser printer** A printing system using a laser beam to produce an image on a photosensitive drum. The image is transferred to paper by a conventional xerographic printing process. Current laser printers used for desktop publishing have a resolution of 600 dpi.

**layer** A function of graphics applications in which elements may be isolated from each other, so a group of elements can be hidden from view, reordered, or otherwise manipulated as a unit, without affecting other elements in the design.

**layout** The arrangement of text and graphics on a page, usually produced in the preliminary design stage.

**layout space** Another term for layout.

**leading** Space added between lines of type. Named after the strips of lead that used to be inserted between lines of metal type. In specifying type, lines of 12-pt. type separated by a 14-pt. space is abbreviated "12/14," or "twelve over fourteen."

**letter spacing** The insertion or addition of white space between the letters of words.

**library** In the computer world, a collection of files having a similar purpose or function.

**ligature** Letters that are joined together as a single unit of type such as œ and fi.

**line art** A drawing or piece of black-and-white artwork with no screens. Line art can be represented by a graphic file having only 1-bit resolution.

**line coordinates** The location and length of a line; defined according to the position and type of anchor points that comprise the line.

**line segment** The part of a line between two anchor points.

**line style** The physical appearance of a line; can be plain (solid), dotted, dashed, thin-and-thick, etc.

**lithography** A mechanical printing process based on the principle of the natural aversion of water to grease. In modern offset lithography, the image on a photosensitive plate is first transferred to the blanket of a rotating drum, and then to the paper.

**live area** One of the elements of page geometry; the area of a page that can be safely printed without the possibility of being lost in the binding or cut off when the job is trimmed.

**LPI** Lines Per Inch. The number of lines per inch used when converting a photograph to a halftone. Typical values range from 85 for newspaper work to 150 or higher for high-quality reproduction on smooth or coated paper. Also called "line screen."

**margin guides** Guides that denote the live area of a layout page.

**margins** The non-printing areas of a page, or the line at which text starts or stops.

**master document** In an InDesign book, the document upon which style sheet and color definitions are based.

**master font** The primary font in a family, from which variations are derived.

**master pages** Page-layout templates containing repeating elements that will appear on all pages to which the master is applied.

**mechanical** A pasted-up page of camera-ready art that is photographed to produce a plate for the press.

**menu styling** Artificial type styling, typically applied by choosing shortcuts from a menu or palette, or by using a keyboard shortcut.

**merge** The process of combining two or more cells into one cell.

**misregister** The unwanted result of incorrectly aligned process inks and spot colors on a finished printed piece. Misregistration can be caused by many factors, including paper stretch and improper plate alignment. Trapping can compensate for misregistration.

**mixed ink** A combination of process and spot inks.

**nested style** In InDesign, a paragraph option that allows the user to embed a character style within the paragraph, based on specific variables.

**nested tag** A tag contained within another tag.

**neutral density** A measurement of the lightness or darkness of a color. A neutral density of zero (0.00) is the lightest value possible, and is equivalent to pure white; 3.294 is roughly equivalent to 100% of each of the CMYK components.

**nonbreaking space** 1. A typographic command that connects two words with a space, but prevents the words from being broken apart if the space occurs within the hyphenation zone. 2. A space added to an HTML page (using " ") which will not be eliminated by the browser.

**nonfacing pages** A type of layout in which the pages of a design do not appear opposite each other. See *facing pages*.

**nonprinting characters** Formatting characters (such as paragraph returns and tabs) that do not appear in the final printed piece.

**nudge** To move a graphic or text element in small, preset increments, usually with the Arrow keys.

**object-oriented art** Vector-based artwork composed of separate elements or shapes described mathematically rather than by specifying the color and position of every point. This is in contrast to bitmap images, which are composed of individual pixels.

**oblique** A slanted character; often used when referring to italic versions of sans-serif typefaces.

**offset** The distance at which rules are placed above or below paragraphs of text; can be defined as a specific measurement or as a percentage of the paragraph spacing.

**offset lithography** A printing method whereby the image is transferred from a plate onto a rubber-covered cylinder, from which printing takes place. See *lithography*.

**opacity** The degree to which an element obscures underlying elements.

**OpenType** A font format developed by Adobe and Microsoft that can be used on both the Windows and Macintosh platforms; can contain over 65,000 distinct glyphs, and offers advanced typographic features.

**optical margin alignment** An InDesign utility that allows certain characters to be placed to the left or right of the escapement of a text frame, "hanging" into the margin.

**output device** Any hardware equipment, such as a monitor, laser printer, or imagesetter, that depicts text or graphics created on a computer.

**outset** The distance at which text will flow around the edge of a picture or box.

**overprint color** A color made by overprinting any two or more of the primary yellow, magenta, and cyan process colors.

**package** The process of gathering all elements of a project for delivery to another entity, such as a GASP.

**page geometry** The physical attributes of a layout page. See *trim size, live area, bleed size*.

**palette** 1. As derived from the term in the traditional art world, a collection of selectable colors. 2. A collection of related tools and options.

**PANTONE Matching System** PMS. A system for specifying colors by number for both coated and uncoated paper; used by printers and in color desktop publishing to assure uniform color matching.

**paragraph style sheet** A style sheet that defines the appearance of the paragraph, combining the character style that is to be used in the paragraph with the line spacing, indents, tabs, rules, and other paragraph attributes.

**parent style sheet** The style sheet on which other styles are based; changing the definition of the parent affects any style sheet that is based on the parent.

**pasteboard** In a page-layout program, the desktop area outside the printing-page area.

**PDF** Portable Document Format. Developed by Adobe Systems, Inc. (read by Acrobat Reader), this format has become a de facto standard for document transfer across platforms.

**PDF workflow** A workflow in which PDF files are used to transmit designs to a service provider for output.

**Photoshop path** A mask prepared in Photoshop that delineates the portion of the image that will print.

**pica** A traditional typographic measurement of 12 points, or approximately 1/6 of an inch. Most applications specify a pica as exactly 1/6 of an inch.

**PICT/PICT2** A common format for defining bitmapped images on the Macintosh. The more recent PICT2 format supports 24-bit color.

**placeholder text** An InDesign utility for placing nonsense text into a text box. Used to experiment with formatting and layout before the actual job text is ready. See *greeking*.

**portrait** Printing from left to right across the narrow dimension of the page. Portrait orientation on a letter-size page uses a standard 8.5-in. width and 11-in. length.

**poster** In InDesign, a visual representation of an embedded movie or sound file in an interactive document.

**PostScript** 1. A page-description language, developed by Adobe Systems, Inc., that describes elements and their positional relationships on the page. 2. A computer-programming language.

**PPD** PostScript Printer Description file. A file format developed by Adobe Systems, Inc., that contains device-specific information that enables software to produce the best results possible for each type of designated printer.

**preflight check** A final check of a page layout that verifies all fonts and linked graphics are available, that colors are properly defined, and that any necessary traps have been applied.

**prepress** All work done between writing and printing, such as typesetting, scanning, layout, and imposition.

**preproduction** Preparation of all production details.

**preset** Predefined specifications for printing, trapping, and other document elements or functions.

**printer driver** The device that communicates between the software program and the printer. When using an application, the printer driver tells the application what the printer can do, and also tells the printer how to print the publication.

**printer fonts** The image outlines for type in PostScript that are sent to the printer.

**printer's marks** See *trim marks, registration marks*.

**printer's spread** The two pages that abut on press in a multi-page document.

**process colors** The four inks (cyan, magenta, yellow, and black) used in four-color process printing. A printing method in which a full range of colors is reproduced by combining four semi-transparent inks. See *color separation, CMYK*.

**profile** A file containing data representing the color reproduction characteristics of a device determined by a calibration of some sort.

**proof** A representation of the printed job that is made from plates (press proof), film, or electronic data (prepress proofs); generally used for customer inspection and approval before mass production.

**pull quote** An excerpt from the body of a story used to emphasize an idea, draw readers' attention, or generate interest.

**range kerning** Another term for tracking.

**raster** A bitmapped representation of graphic data.

**raster image** A type of picture created and organized in a rectangular array of bitmaps. Often created by paint software, scanners, or digital cameras.

**reader's spread** The two (or more) pages a reader will view when the document is open.

**recto** A right-hand page.

**registration** Aligning plates on a multicolor printing press so the images will superimpose properly to produce the required composite output.

**registration color** A default color selection that can be applied to design elements so they will print on every separation from a PostScript printer. "Registration" is often used to print identification text that will appear outside the page area on a set of separations.

**registration marks** Figures (often crossed lines and a circle) placed outside the trim page boundaries on all color separation overlays to provide a common element for proper alignment.

**relative path** The location of a file or Web page that uses the location of the current file or page as a reference. In the case of a Web page, called "relative URL." See *absolute path*.

**repurposing** Converting an existing document for another different use; usually refers to creating an electronic version of existing print publications.

**resolution** The density of graphic information expressed in dots per inch (dpi) or pixels per inch (ppi).

**resolution dependent** A characteristic of raster images, in which the file's resolution is determined when the file is created, scanned, or photographed.

**resolution independent** A characteristic of vector graphics, in which the file adopt its resolution at the time of output based on the capabilities of the device being used.

**RGB** 1. The colors of projected light from a computer monitor that, when combined, simulate a subset of the visual spectrum. 2. The color model of most digital artwork. See also *CMYK, additive color*.

**RIP** Raster Image Processor. That part of a PostScript printer or imagesetting device that converts the page information from the PostScript Page Description Language into the bitmap pattern that is applied to the film or paper output.

**robust kerning** A feature of professionally designed fonts, in which kerning values for specific letter pairs are built into the font metrics.

**rosette** The pattern created when color halftone screens are printed at traditional screen angles.

**row** A series of cells arranged horizontally.

**ruler** Like a physical ruler, a feature of graphics software used for precise measurement and alignment of objects. Rulers appear in the top and left edges of the project window. See *grid*.

**ruler guides** Horizontal and vertical guides that can be placed anywhere on the page by dragging from the rulers at the edge of the project window.

**rules** 1. Straight lines. 2. Lines that are placed above or below paragraphs of text.

**runaround** A technique used to flow text around the outside of another shape; text can be wrapped around the edges of a box, or contoured to the shape of a placed image.

**running head** Text at the top of the page that provides information about the publication. Chapter names and book titles are often included in the running head. Also called a "header."

**saturation** The intensity or purity of a color; a color with no saturation is gray.

**scaling** The means within a program to reduce or enlarge the amount of space an image occupies by multiplying the data by a factor. Scaling can be proportional, or in one dimension only.

**screen angle** The angle at which the rulings of a halftone screen are set when making halftones for commercial printing.

**screen frequency** The number of lines per inch in a halftone screen, which may vary from 85 to 300.

**screen ruling** See *LPI*.

**section** Part of a document. Page numbering may be changed on a section-by-section basis.

**select** Place the cursor on an object and click the mouse button to make the object active.

**selection** The currently active object(s) in a window. Often made by clicking with the mouse or by dragging a marquee around the desired object(s).

**service bureau** An organization that provides services, such as scanning and prepress checks, that prepare your publication to be printed on a commercial printing press. Service bureaus do not, however, print your publication.

**service mark** A legal designation that identifies and protects the ownership of a specific term or phrase.

**service provider** Any organization, including a commercial printer, that processes design files for output.

**shading** Color added to table cells.

**shortcut** 1. A quick method for accessing a menu item or command, usually through a series of keystrokes. 2. The icon that can be created in Windows to open an application without having to penetrate layers of various folders.

**silhouette** To remove part of the background of a photograph or illustration, leaving only the desired portion.

**smart quotes** The curly quotation marks used by typographers, as opposed to the straight marks on the typewriter. Use of smart quotes is usually a setup option in a word-processing or page-layout application.

**snap-to** An optional feature in graphics applications that drives objects to line up with guides, margins, or other objects if they are within a preset pixel range. This eliminates the need for very precise manual placement of an object with the mouse.

**soft proof** An on-screen representation of the document used to check for errors.

**soft return** A return command that ends a line but does not apply a paragraph mark that would end the continuity of the style for that paragraph.

**special color** Colors that are reproduced using premixed inks, often used to print colors that are outside the CMYK gamut.

**spine** The binding edge at the back of a book that contains title information and joins the front and back covers.

**split** The process of dividing one cell into two cells of equal height (if split horizontally) or width (if split vertically).

**spot color** Any pre-mixed ink that is not one of the four process-color inks.

**spot-color printing** The printing method in which special ink colors are used independently or in conjunction with process colors to create a specific color that is outside the gamut of process-color printing.

**spread** 1. Two abutting pages; in InDesign, a single page is also called a spread. 2. A trapping process that slightly enlarges a lighter foreground object to prevent white paper gaps caused by misregistration.

**stacking order** 1. The order of elements on a PostScript page, where the topmost item can obscure underlying items. 2. The order in which elements are placed on a page; the first is at the bottom and the last is at the top. 3. The order of layers, from top to bottom.

**stripping** The act of manually assembling individual film negatives into flats for printing. Also referred to as "film assembly."

**stroke** The width and color attributes of a line.

**structural tags** Tags that provide information about content.

**style** A defined set of formatting instructions for font and paragraph attributes, tabs, and other properties of text.

**subhead** A second-level heading used to organize body text by topic.

**subscript** Small-size characters set below the normal letters or figures, usually to convey technical information.

**subtractive color** Color observed when light strikes pigments or dyes, which absorb certain wavelengths of light; the light that is reflected back is perceived as a color. See *CMYK, process colors*.

**superior** Small characters set above the normal letters or figures; set as a percentage of the defined type size and aligned to the top edge of ascenders in that type size/font combination.

**superscript** Small characters set above the normal letters or figures, such as numbers referring to footnotes; similar to superior characters, but raised in percentages from the baseline instead of aligned to the ascender height.

**SVG** Scalable Vector Graphics. A language for the creation of graphics using only tags.

**synchronize** In InDesign, the process of ensuring that all book chapters share the styles and colors defined in the master document.

**tab-delimited** A block of data that can be converted to a table; tabs are used to separate columns of information and paragraph returns to separate rows.

**table** A grid used for displaying data or organizing information in columns and rows. It is also used to control placement of text and graphics.

**table of contents (TOC)** A chart that lists the illustrations, credits, and page numbers that appear in a published work, usually in order of appearance.

**tabloid** 11 × 17-in. paper.

**tags** The various formats in a style sheet that indicate paragraph settings, margins and columns, page layouts, hyphenation and justification, widow and orphan control, and other parameters. An indication of the start and end of an element.

**template** A document file containing layout, styles, and repeating elements (such as logos) by which a series of documents can maintain the same look and feel. A model publication you can use as the basis for creating a new publication.

**text attribute** A characteristic applied directly to a letter or letters in text, such as bold, italic, or underline.

**text box** A box into which users can type.

**text editor** An application used to create or make changes to text files.

**text effects** Means by which the appearance of text can be modified, such as bolding, underlining, and italicizing.

**text inset** The distance from the edge of a box to the position of the placed text.

**text-overflow icon** An icon at the end of a text box that indicates more text exists at the end of the story, but does not fit into the box (or chain of boxes).

**thin space** A fixed space, equal to half an en space or the width of a period in most fonts.

**thread** The process of linking text from frame to frame.

**TIFF** Tagged Image File Format. A common format used for scanned or computer-generated bitmapped images.

**tint** 1. A halftone area that contains dots of uniform size; that is, no modeling or texture. 2. A percentage of a color; a 10% tint is one part of the original color and nine parts substrate color.

**tool tip** Small text explaining the item to which the mouse is pointing.

**tracking** Adjusting the spacing of letters in a line of text to achieve proper justification or general appearance.

**trademark** A legal designation that identifies and protects the ownership of a specific device (such as a name, symbol, or mark).

**transformation** A change in the shape, color, position, or opacity of an object.

**transparency** 1. A full-color photographically-produced image on transparent film. 2. The quality of an image element that allows background elements to partially or entirely show through.

**trapping** The process of creating an overlap between abutting inks to compensate for imprecise registration in the printing process. Extending the lighter colors of one object into the darker colors of an adjoining object.

**trim marks** Printer's marks that denote the edge of the layout before it is printed and cut to final size.

**trim size** Area of the finished page after the job is printed, folded, bound, and cut.

**Trumatch** A special-color library used in the United States.

**type family** A set of typefaces created from the same basic design but in different variations, such as bold, light, italic, book, and heavy.

**type on a path** Text that follows a non-linear path; useful for creating special effects with type.

**type size** Typeface as measured (in points) from the bottom of descenders to the body clearance line, which is slightly higher than the top of ascenders.

**typesetting** The arrangement of individual characters of text into words, sentences, and paragraphs.

**typo** Abbreviation for typographical error. A keystroke error in the typeset copy.

**typographer's quotes**   See *smart quotes*.

**typography**   The art and process of placing, arranging, and formatting type in a design.

**vector graphics**   Graphics defined using coordinate points and mathematically drawn lines and curves, which may be freely scaled and rotated without image degradation in the final output.

**verso**   A left-hand page.

**vertical justification**   The ability to automatically adjust the interline spacing (leading) to make columns and pages end at the same point on a page.

**weight**   1. The thickness of the strokes of a typeface. The weight of a typeface is usually denoted in the name of the font; for example, light, book, or ultra (thin, medium, and thick strokes, respectively). 2. The thickness of a line or rule.

**white space**   Areas on the page that contain no images or type.

**word break**   The division of a word at the end of a line in accordance with hyphenation principles.

**word space**   The space inserted between words in a desktop publishing application. The optimal value is built into the typeface, and may usually be modified within an application.

**wrap**   Type set on the page so it wraps around the shape of another element.

**x-height**   The height of the lowercase letter "x" in a given typeface, which represents the basic size of the bodies of all of the lowercase letters (excluding ascenders and descenders).

**XML**   An acronym for eXtensible Markup Language.

**zero point**   The mathematical origin of the coordinates of the two-dimensional page. The zero point may be moved to any location on the page, and the ruler dimensions change accordingly.

**zooming**   The process of electronically enlarging or reducing an image on a monitor to facilitate detailed design or editing and navigation.

# INDEX

3D ribbon effect   122

## A

absolute addresses   307
absolute colorimetric intent   195
add all   73, 74
additive color   176, 177, 180
Adobe GoLive   292, 293, 297-299, 300, 316-317
Adobe Illustrator   216, 246
Adobe Paragraph Composer   105, 106, 132
Adobe Photoshop   223, 246
Adobe Single-Line Composer   105, 112, 130
Align palette   211, 219-220
aligning objects   219-220, 236-237, 237-238
allow pages to shuffle   11, 14
alpha channels   212, 223, 227, 228, 229
alternating fills   156
assigning structure   305-307, 317-318
automatic page number   18, 44, 45
automatic pagination   84
automatic text flow   3-4, 15-17

## B

background colors   251
balance lines   116
baseline   105, 109
baseline display   301
baseline grid   4, 23, 24-26
behaviors   278
bleed allowance   2
bleed and slug options   254
bleeds   246, 247-248, 253-255, 284
blend space   193, 194
blending   264
blur value   190, 191

body   143
Book palette   84, 85, 86
bookmarks   247, 272
books   2, 3, 5, 15, 54, 58, 83-89, 89-90, 96
bounding box   227, 228
break character   22
Button tool   277
buttons   250, 277, 286, 289

## C

carding   109
cascading style sheets (CSS)   292
cell contents   157-159
cell formatting   156-157, 166
cell inset   160
chapters   83
choke   251
clipping paths   212, 213, 223-227, 228, 239-241
CMYK   176, 177, 180, 182-184, 193, 195, 198, 200, 262
color   175-208
color management   180, 195-200, 233, 256, 260, 268
color separation   182, 246, 248, 259, 264-267
color settings   196, 197
column formatting   151, 152-153
columns   2, 4
compound paths   210, 211, 215-216, 223, 236
contour options   228, 229
convert text to table   142, 148-149, 167
copyright law   270
covert table to text   149
create outlines   210, 211, 213, 214, 235, 239
creating tables   143-145
cross-references   57, 73, 78-79
custom glyphs   104, 107, 119-120, 134, 135

## D

databases   57
delete column   142
delete row   142
delimiters   145
destination color space   195
destinations   293, 295, 296
detect edges   212, 225, 228
DICColor   184
diffused corners   191
distributing objects   219-220, 236-237
document presets   39-41, 47-48
document type descriptor (DTD)   302, 307
drop caps   231-232
drop shadows   190-191, 193

## E

eBook tags   272
embedded fonts   267
endnotes   61
EPS   89, 298
escapement   115
exclude overlap   216
exporting   89-90
exporting EPS   246, 249, 261-264, 287
Eyedropper tool   107, 117-118, 133

## F

facing pages   14
feathering   109, 191-193
field delimiter   145
FileMaker   141, 145
fills   156-157, 166
finishing   5
first baseline   109, 110, 130
fit guides to margin   28
fit guides to page   28
flattening   179, 193-194

# Index

Focoltone 184
folding 2, 5, 35-38, 49-50
foldout pages 3, 11-13, 36-38
folios 18
fonts 247, 267
footer 143
footnotes 61
for next # of pages 76, 77
for next # of paragraphs 77
foreground colors 251
formatting affects text 158
formatting tables 149-151

## G

gamut 180
gamut alarm 200
generate index 74
GIF 298
Glyphs palette 119
gradient and mesh resolutions 179
gradient fill 213
graphic frame 228
graphics in tables 159-161
gravity effect 122
grids 4, 23-26, 49
grouping objects 210, 211, 217-219
guides 2, 4, 27-28

## H

H&J routines 82, 106
hanging punctuation 105, 107, 115
header 143
HKS 184
HTML 89, 292, 293, 299
hyperlinks 247, 250, 272, 273-274, 288-289, 295-297, 315-316
Hyperlinks palette 273, 274, 293, 295, 297, 315, 316
hyphen limit 132
hyphenation 105, 106, 112-113, 130, 132
hyphenation zone 112

## I

ICC profiles 247, 267, 268
ignore text wrap 228
image color settings 197, 198
image links 85
import options 146, 148, 197
importing tables 145-147, 169
imposition 35
in-RIP trapping 246, 248
include inside edges 223, 228
Index palette 57
indexed color 180
indexes 54, 57, 73-79, 83, 98-99, 100
ink coverage 246, 250, 264
ink density 249, 250
ink limit 266
ink manager 259, 268
ink order 249
inkjet printers 176
inline objects 210, 220-222, 237-238
insert column 142, 152, 153
insert row 142, 152
insert table 144
inset frame 223
inset spacing 110
intersect 216
invert 223

## J

JPEG 292, 294, 298, 301
jump object 227
jump to next column 227
jumps 54, 62-64
justification 105, 106, 114-115, 130, 132

## K

keep spread together 13
keywords 56
knockout group 189

## L

L*a*b* 177, 182, 195, 200
layer options 29, 30, 32
layers 2, 4, 29-32, 48
layout adjustment 2, 5, 32-35, 51
libraries 54, 56, 64-68, 93-94
library options 67-68
Library palette 65, 67
line art and text resolution 179
linking pages 9
Links palette 85
lists 54, 56, 69-72
load paragraph styles 80
load swatches 82
load tags 311
long documents 53-102

## M

map styles to tags 303
map tags to styles 311
margins 2, 44
Markzware FlightCheck 247
masks 212
master documents 58, 79-82, 83
master options 17-18, 20, 37
master pages 2, 3, 4, 6-8, 9-10, 35, 43-44
maximum word spacing 115
merge cells 143, 154-155
metadata 56, 64, 65
Microsoft Excel 140-148, 163, 164, 172, 173, 219
Microsoft PowerPoint 272
Microsoft Word 141, 145, 148
minimum word spacing 115
minus back 216
mixed inks 176, 178, 186-187
modifying tables 148-149
movie options 277
movies 250, 272, 277-279, 289

## N

nested groups   217
nested styles   108, 121-122, 131
nested tables   159-173
nesting objects   210, 212, 220-222
next page number   62, 63
notes   54, 61-62, 94-95
numbering & section options   21, 55, 59, 87

## O

object shape   227
offset   190, 191
opacity   188, 189
open original   17, 19
open prepress interface (OPI)   256
optical margin alignment   105, 106-107, 115-117, 132
optimized formatted images   293, 298
overprinting   176, 246, 251, 264

## P

packaging   83, 270-272, 288
packaging for GoLive   297-299
page geometry   2, 35, 58
page numbering   6, 13-14, 21, 36, 44, 45, 56, 59-60, 72, 83, 84
page reference options   75
Pages palette   3, 6, 9, 11, 21
PANTONE Matching System   176, 184
paper   2, 35
paragraph spacing limit   110, 111
Paragraph Styles palette   8
parsing   302
paste into   212, 224
paste remembers layers   29, 32
path options   125
pathfinder   216-217
PDF   89-90, 193, 247, 249, 250, 261, 267, 268, 272-279, 289, 292, 299

Pen tool   122, 224, 230
Pencil tool   122
perceptual intent   195
Photoshop paths   212, 223, 226, 228, 229
play options   278, 279, 286, 289
poster   275, 277
PostScript   248, 256, 261, 267, 268
PostScript Printer Description (PPD)   256, 257, 268
preferences   23
   composition   43
   general   59
   grids   23, 25, 26
   guides & pasteboard   23
   units and increments   36
preflighting   83, 247, 267-270, 285, 287
previous page number   62, 64
printer's marks   248, 253-255, 258
printing   31-32, 83, 89-90, 193-194, 256-261, 285
printing instructions   270
process color   176, 177, 182
profiles   196, 197, 198
progressive display   301
proof setup   199

## R

rainbow effect   122
record delimiter   145
reference order   77
references   73
registration   2
relative colorimetric intent   195
rendering intent   195
resolution   179, 194
restrict to frame   223
reverse path   216
RGB   176, 177, 180-182, 193, 195, 200, 262
rich black   246, 264
rosette   182
rounded corners   191
row formatting   150, 152-153

## S

same as clipping   228, 229
saturation intent   195
screen angles   249, 283
screen printing   282-283
section markers   60
sections   59-60, 83, 94
Separations Preview palette   246, 250, 264-267
sharp corners   191
signatures   5
silhouettes   223
single word justification   132
skew effect   122
slugs   246, 248, 253-255, 284
soft proofing   199
sort order   77
sound options   275
sounds   247, 250, 272, 275-276, 289
source color space   195
sources   295
split cells   143, 154-155
spot colors   176-178, 184-185, 249
spread   251
spread guides   27
spreads   3
stacking order   7, 29, 251
stairstep effect   122
step-and-repeat   38
strokes   156-157, 166
structure view   305, 306, 308, 311
styles   4, 69, 80, 83, 104, 108
subtractive color   176, 177, 180
suppress page range   77
SVG   89, 292, 294, 299-300, 301, 318
swatch options   181, 183
swatches   81-82, 83
Swatches palette   177, 181, 183
synchronizing files   83, 86-87, 96-97

# Index

## T

Table menu   141
Table palette   141, 142, 149, 154
tables   139-174
   creating   143-145
   formatting   149-151
   importing   145-147
   modifying   148-149
tables of contents   54, 56, 69-72, 83, 87-89, 97
tag markers   304
tagging content   302-304, 317
Tags palette   302, 303, 305, 311
templates   2, 4, 17-22, 46-47, 58
text anchors   274, 295
text frame options   45, 105, 109-112, 130, 132, 228
text frames   16-17
text resolution   179
text wrap   19, 20, 25-26, 43, 95-96, 210, 213, 227-232, 241-242
text wrap palette   227, 228
threading text   15, 16, 168
threshold   223, 225
TIF   298
TIFF preview   262
to end of document   77
to end of section   77
to end of story   77
to next style change   77
to next use of style   77
tolerance   223, 225
topics   73
Toyo Color Finder   184
Transform palette   219
transparency   176, 178, 179, 188-189, 193-194, 264
transparency flattener   299
Transparency palette   188
Trap Presets palette   252
trapping   176, 246, 247, 248, 249, 251-253, 259, 282-283
trim marks   2
trimming   5
TruMatch   184
type on a path   108, 122-127, 136, 137
type outlines   210, 211, 213-215, 235, 239
Type on a Path tool   123-124, 127
Type tool   8

## U

use high resolution image   223
use spacing   219, 220

## V

vertical justification   26, 109, 111

## W

word spacing   115
working space   195
wrap around bounding box   20, 25-26

## X

XML   57, 89, 292, 294, 302-304, 305-307, 307-310, 310-312
   editing   312, 321
   exporting   307-310, 319
   importing   310-312, 320
XML export options   309